American Folklore: A Bibliography, 1950-1974

by

Cathleen C. Flanagan

and

John T. Flanagan

The Scarecrow Press, Inc.
Metuchen, N.J. & London
1977

Library of Congress Cataloging in Publication Data

Flanagan, Cathleen C
   American folklore.

   Includes index.
   1. Folk-lore—United States—Bibliography.
I. Flanagan, John Theodore, 1906–   joint author.
II. Title.
Z5984.U6F55 [GR105]   016.398'0973   77–23381
ISBN 0–8108–1073–5

TABLE OF CONTENTS

iii

PREFACE

No bibliography is ever complete and every bibliography is to some extent selective. Thus certain guidelines need to be defined for a bibliography of American folklore which covers twenty-five years. Chronologically, the period includes the years 1950 to 1974. Geographically, the material relates to the fifty states of the United States but occasionally it spills over into Canada, Mexico, or the Caribbean area. There is also a third basic limitation. Historically, American scholars have been somewhat slow to develop an interest in material folklore or what European scholars call folk life --for example, folk architecture, folk art, folk toys, festivals, carving, weaving, quilting, costumes, cookery, the dance. In recent years, however, considerable attention has been paid to such fields, scholars have published monographs on individual folk occupations, and museums have appeared throughout the country. Because of the current flood of publications relating to material life it has seemed desirable to exclude this area of folklore scholarship in the present bibliography. Consequently, we are concerned here only with verbal folklore: more specifically ballads, folk songs, myths, legends, tales, superstitions, beliefs, cures, proverbs, riddles, and the like.

The enormous interest in folklore in the United States in the last quarter of a century, confirmed most of all perhaps by the surprising proliferation of folklore courses in our colleges and universities, has been visible in the willingness of periodicals of all kinds, newspapers and popular magazines and academic journals, to print folklore items. Many of these are brief, trivial, and certainly ephemeral. In order to confine this bibliography to a reasonable bulk without omitting significant or serious material regardless of length, it has seemed advisable to exclude mere notes or extremely short items, reviews unless they are review articles dealing with a number of publications, reprints of material published prior to 1950 unless they contain significant revision or new introductions, newspaper articles, and letters to the editors.

The annotation may justly be called spotty but is intended to be helpful. In many cases when the title of the article or even book is self-explanatory no annotation seems called for. Elsewhere, brief informative comments on the contents seem desirable. Evaluative judgments have occasionally been made and it can only be hoped that readers will find them reasonably objective. In general, evaluations derive from personal examination of the items concerned, although they may also depend on the published reviews of qualified scholars. Extensive annotation would add immensely to the bulk of this bibliography and this we have tried to avoid. Our guide here is the old maxim, multum in parvo, and we hope that we have kept this goal in view.

On the whole it has seemed best to cite each entry only once, despite the fact that an article or book might conceivably appear in more than one place. Exceptions occur only when a secondary interest (the appearance of proverbs, for example, in an article about literature) seems to warrant a second listing.

It might perhaps go without saying, but we should like to indicate here our great indebtedness to previous bibliographers, to various regional and state compilations, and especially to those bibliographies which have appeared for many years in three major journals: Journal of American Folklore, Southern Folklore Quarterly, and Publications of the Modern Language Association.

Cathleen C. Flanagan
University of Utah

John T. Flanagan
University of Illinois

1. LIST OF MAGAZINES AND ABBREVIATIONS

AA	American Anthropologist
ABC	American Book Collector
AE	Acta Ethnographica: Academiae Scientiarium Hungaricae (Budapest)
AF	Arkansas Folklore
AFFword	Arizona Friends of Folklore
AFN	American Folklore Newsletter
AFS	Abstracts of Folklore Studies
AH	Arizona Highways
AHQ	Arkansas Historical Quarterly
AI	American Imago
AJ	Appalachian Journal
AJS	American Journal of Sociology
AL	American Literature
AlaR	Alabama Review
AM	American Mercury
AmQ	American Quarterly
AN	American Neptune
AnI	Annals of Iowa
AnthQ	Anthropological Quarterly
Anthropos	
APS	American Philosophical Society
AQ	American Quarterly
AQ	Arizona Quarterly
AR	Antioch Review
ARV	Arv (Journal of Scandinavian Folklore)
AS	American Speech

ASch	American Scholar
AtL	Atlantic Monthly
AW	American West
Black Scholar	
BMHS	Bulletin Missouri Historical Society
BRMMLA	Bulletin of Rocky Mountain Modern Language Assoc.
BYUStudies	Brigham Young University Studies
CA	Current Anthropology
Caravan	
CE	College English
CentR	Centennial Review
CF	Colorado Folklore
CLQ	Colby Library Quarterly
CM	Colorado Magazine
CO	Chronicles of Oklahoma
Cosmopolitan	
CWH	Civil War History
Daedalus	
DFB	Delaware Folklore Bulletin
EAL	Early American Literature
EE	Elementary English
EJ	English Journal
ER	Evergreen Review
ETC	ETC: a Review of General Semantics
Ethnohistory	
Ethnology	
Ethnomusicology	
FA	Folklore Americas
Fabula	
FF	Folklore Forum
FFC	Folklore Fellows Communications
FFemC	Folklore Feminists Communications

FFMA	Folklore and Folkmusic Archivist
FH	Forest History
Folklore	
Folkways	
Foxfire	
Genre	
GHQ	Georgia Historical Quarterly
GR	Georgia Review
HF	Hoosier Folklore
HLB	Harvard Library Bulletin
Horn Book	
Idaho Yesterdays	
IEJ	Indiana English Journal
IF	Indiana Folklore
IN	Indiana Names
IR	Industrial Relations
JA	Jahrbuch für Amerikastudien
JAF	Journal of American Folklore
JCM	Journal of Country Music
JEFDSS	Journal of the English Folk Dance and Song Society
JEMFQ	John Edwards Memorial Foundation Quarterly
JFI	Journal of the Folklore Institute
JISHS	Journal of the Illinois State Historical Society
JOFS	Journal of the Ohio Folklore Society
JPC	Journal of Popular Culture
JQ	Journalism Quarterly
JSA	Journal de la Société des Américanistes
JSR	Journal of Sex Research
KASP	Kroeber Anthropological Society Papers
KF	Keystone Folklore (formerly KFQ, Keystone Folklore Quarterly)
KFR	Kentucky Folklore Record

KM	Kansas Magazine
Lang&S	Language and Style
LARR	Latin American Research Review
LFM	Louisiana Folklore Miscellany
LH	Labor History
LHQ	Louisiana Historical Quarterly
Life	
LJ	Library Journal
Man	
MD	Modern Drama
MEJ	Michigan Education Journal
MF	Midwest Folklore
MFR	Mississippi Folklore Register
MHR	Missouri Historical Review
MichA	Michigan Academician
MichH	Michigan History
Midstream	
MinnH	Minnesota History
MissQ	Mississippi Quarterly
MJ	Midwest Journal
MLJ	Modern Language Journal
MLW	Mountain Life and Work
Montana	Montana, the Magazine of Western History
MQ	Midwest Quarterly
MR	Massachusetts Review
MSF	Mid-South Folklore
Names	
NCarFJ	North Carolina Folklore Journal (formerly NCarF--North Carolina Folklore)
NEF	Northeast Folklore
NegroALF	Negro American Literature Forum
NEQ	New England Quarterly

Neurotica

NH	Nebraska History
NLB	Newberry Library Bulletin
NM	Neuphilologische Mitteilungen
NMFR	New Mexico Folklore Record
NMHR	New Mexico Historical Review
NR	Northwest Review
NWF	Northwest Folklore
NYFQ	New York Folklore Quarterly
NYH	New York History
NYHSQ	New York Historical Society Quarterly
NYTMag	New York Times Magazine
OF	Oregon Folklore
OhF	Ohio Folklore
OHQ	Oregon Historical Quarterly

Onoma

PADS	Publications of the American Dialect Society
PD	Pennsylvania Dutchman
PF	Pennsylvania Folklife
PM	Primitive Man
PMASAL	Papers of the Michigan Academy of Science, Arts, and Letters
PMHB	Pennsylvania Magazine of History and Biography
PMLA	Publications of the Modern Language Association
PPGFS	Publications of the Pennsylvania German Folklore Society

Proverbium

PS	Prairie Schooner
PTFS	Publications of the Texas Folklore Society
PUASAL	Proceedings of the Utah Academy of Sciences, Arts & Letters
PULC	Princeton University Library Chronicle
QJLC	Quarterly Journal of the Library of Congress

Rendezvous	Rendezvous, Journal of Arts and Letters
Reporter	
RLLR	Revue de Louisiane/Louisiana Review
SAF	Studies in American Fiction
SAQ	South Atlantic Quarterly
SAR	St. Andrews Review
SAV	Schweizerisches Archiv für Volkskunde
SBL	Studies in Black Literature
Semiotica	
SFQ	Southern Folklore Quarterly
SHQ	Southwestern Historical Quarterly
SHR	Southern Humanities Review
Sing Out!	
SJA	Southwestern Journal of Anthropology
SLI	Studies in the Literary Imagination
SPHQ	Swedish Pioneer Historical Quarterly
SR	Southern Review
SRL	Saturday Review of Literature
SS	Science and Society
StQ	Steinbeck Quarterly
StudiaS	Studia Septentrionalia
SWR	Southwest Review
TFSB	Tennessee Folklore Society Bulletin
THQ	Tennessee Historical Quarterly
Time	
TQ	Texas Quarterly
UA	Urban Anthropology
UHQ	Utah Historical Quarterly
UVaNewsletter	University of Virginia Newsletter
VH	Vermont History
WA	Wisconsin Archaeologist
WAL	Western American Literature

WF	Western Folklore (formerly California Folklore)
WHR	Western Humanities Review
WVF	West Virginia Folklore
Yachting	
YR	Yale Review
ZfürV	Zeitschrift für Volkskunde

2. FESTSCHRIFTEN, SYMPOSIA, COLLECTIONS

1. Bauman, Richard, ed. "Toward New Perspectives in Folklore," JAF (Jan-Mr, 1971), 84: ix, 171. Thirteen essays on theoretical aspects of folklore.

2. Beck, Horace P., ed. Folklore in Action, Essays for Discussion in Honor of MacEdward Leach (Philadelphia: Am. Folklore Soc., 1962), xii, 210pp.

3. Browne, Ray B., Donald M. Winkelman, and Allen Hayman, eds. New Voices in American Studies (Indianapolis: C. E. Pauley & Co., 1966), 164pp. Anthology with a section on popular culture and folklore which includes six essays.

4. Byington, Robert H. and Kenneth S. Goldstein, eds. Two Penny Ballads and Four Dollar Whiskey: a Pennsylvania Folklore Miscellany (Hatboro, Penn.: Folklore Associates, 1966), xi, 176pp. Most articles deal with folk song and folk singing.

5. Cheney, Thomas E., Austin E. Fife, and Juanita Brooks, eds. Lore of Faith and Folly (Salt Lake City: U. of Utah P., 1971), ix, 247pp. Some 25 studies of Utah lore and history; only a few are immediately concerned with folklore

6. Coffin, Tristram P., ed. Our Living Traditions: an Introduction to American Folklore (New York and London: Basic Books, 1968), xviii, 310pp. Some 25 brief articles on various aspects of folklore by different authors, indexed separately.

7. _____, and Hennig Cohen, eds. Folklore in America: Tales, Songs, Superstitions, Proverbs, Riddles, Games, Folk Drama, and Folk Festivals (Garden City: Doubleday, 1966), xxiii, 256pp. Ethnic, regional, and occupational lore.

8. Diamond, Stanley, ed. Culture in History, Essays in
   Honor of Paul Radin (New York: Columbia U. P.,
   1960), xviii, 1014pp. Includes four papers on myth
   by Claude Lévi-Strauss, Ake Hultkranz, Earl W.
   Count, and Melville Jacobs.

9. Dorson, Richard M., ed. Folklore and Folklife: an
   Introduction (Chicago and London: U. of Chicago P.,
   1972), x, 561pp. Some 26 essays by a variety of
   specialists, most of which are indexed separately in
   this bibliography.

10. Dundes, Alan, ed. The Study of Folklore (Englewood
    Cliffs, N. J.: Prentice-Hall, 1965), xi, 481pp. A
    controversial anthology of reprinted material from
    books, monographs, and journals (many quite eso-
    teric); 34 essays by 33 different authors. For criti-
    cal reviews see KFQ (S, 1966), 11: 127-143; and
    KFR (Jan-Mr, 1966), 12: 26-34.

11. Fife, Austin, Alta Fife, and Henry H. Glassie, eds.
    Forms Upon the Frontier: Folklore and Folk Art in
    the United States (Logan, Utah: Utah State U. P.,
    1969), vii, 189pp.

12. _____ and J. Golden Taylor, eds. The West-
    ern Folklore Conference: Selected Papers (Logan,
    Utah: Utah State U. P., 1964), 84pp.

13. Foltin, Hans Friedrich, ed. Kontakte und Grenzen,
    Probleme d. Volks-, Kultur, und Sozialforschung.
    Festschrift für Gerhard Heilfurth zum 60 Geburtstag
    (Göttingen: Schwartz, 1969), xviii, 556pp.

14. Hand, Wayland D. and Gustave O. Arlt, eds. Hu-
    maniora: Essays in Literature, Folklore, Bibliogra-
    phy Honoring Archer Taylor on His Seventieth Birth-
    day (Locust Valley, N. Y.: J. J. Augustin, 1960),
    374pp. Some 35 articles.

15. Harkort, Fritz, Karel C. Peeters, and Robert Wild-
    haber, eds. Volksüberlieferung (Göttingen: Verlag
    Otto Schwartz, 1968), 607pp.

16. Jackson, Bruce, ed. Folklore & Society: Essays in
    Honor of Benj. A. Botkin (Hatboro, Penn.: Folk-
    lore Associates, 1966). xii, 192pp. Biographical

introduction by Jackson, 11 essays, and a bibliography of Botkin's work (pp. 169-192).

17. Mandel, Jerome and Bruce A. Rosenberg, eds. Medi-
     eval Literature and Folklore Studies: Essays in
     Honor of Francis Lee Utley (New Brunswick, N. J. :
     Rutgers U. P. , 1970), viii, 408pp. Some 25 essays
     of which 10 deal with folklore.

18. Murray, Henry A. , ed. Myth and Myth Making (New
     York: George Braziller, 1960), 381pp. Essays
     originally published in Daedalus (Spr, 1959), 88:
     211-380.

19. Olch, Peter D. and Forrest C. Pogue, eds. Selections
     from the Fifth and Sixth National Colloquia on Oral
     History (New York: Oral History Assn. , 1972), vi,
     110pp. Includes papers by R. M. Dorson, W. L.
     Montell, Henry Glassie, and William Ivey.

20. Paredes, Américo and Richard Bauman, eds. Toward
     New Perspectives in Folklore (Austin and London:
     U. of Texas P. , 1972), 181pp. Theoretical articles
     dealing with myth, identity, translation, riddles,
     games.

21. Patai, Raphael, Francis Lee Utley, and Dov Noy, eds.
     Studies in Biblical and Jewish Folklore (Blooming-
     ton: Indiana U. P. , 1960), vii, 374pp.

22. [Patterson, Daniel W. , ed.] Folklore Studies in Honor
     of Arthur Palmer Hudson (Chapel Hill: No. Carolina
     Folklore Soc. , 1965), 157pp. Eleven essays.

Publications of the Texas Folklore Society (arranged chronologically):

23. Hudson, Wilson M. , ed. The Healer of Los Olmos and
     Other Mexican Lore (Dallas: So. Methodist U. P. ,
     1951), ix, 139pp. No. XXIV.

24. Boatright, Mody C. , Wilson M. Hudson, and Allen
     Maxwell, eds. Folk Travelers, Ballads, Tales, and
     Talk (Dallas: So. Methodist U. P. , 1953), 261pp.
     No. XXV.

25. _____, _____, _____, eds. Texas Folk and
    Folklore (Dallas: So. Methodist U. P. , 1955), xv,
    356pp. No. XXVI.

26. _____, _____, _____, eds. Mesquite and Wil-
    low (Dallas: So. Methodist U. P. , 1957), viii,
    203pp. No. XXVII.

27. _____, _____, _____, eds. Madstones and
    Twisters (Dallas: So. Methodist U. P. , 1958), x,
    169pp. No. XXVIII.

28. _____, _____, _____, eds. And Horns on the
    Toads (Dallas: So. Methodist U. P. , 1959), x,
    237pp. No. XXIX.

29. _____, _____, _____, eds. Singers and Story-
    tellers (Dallas: So. Methodist U. P. , 1961), 298pp.
    No. XXX.

30. _____, _____, _____, eds. The Golden Log
    (Dallas: So. Methodist U. P. , 1962), 168pp. No.
    XXXI.

31. _____, _____, _____, eds. A Good Tale and
    A Bonnie Tune (Dallas: So. Methodist U. P. , 1964),
    274pp. No. XXXII.

32. Hudson, Wilson M. and Allen Maxwell, eds. The Sun-
    ny Slopes of Long Ago (Dallas: So. Methodist U. P. ,
    1966), 204pp. No. XXXIII.

33. Hudson, Wilson M. , ed. Tire Shrinker to Dragster
    (Austin: Encino P. , 1968), 248pp. No. XXXIV.

34. _____, ed. Hunters & Healers: Folklore Types &
    Topics (Austin: Encino P. , 1971), 171pp. No.
    XXXV.

35. _____, ed. Diamond Bessie & the Shepherds (Aus-
    tin: Encino P. , 1972), 158pp. No. XXXVI.

36. Abernethy, Francis Edward, ed. Observations & Re-
    flections on Texas Folklore (Austin: 1972), 151pp.
    No. XXXVII.

37. _____, ed. The Folklore of Texas Cultures (Austin:
    Encino P. , 1974), 366pp. No. XXXVIII.

38. _____, ed. Some Still Do: Essays on Texas Customs (Austin: Encino P., 1975), 153pp. No. XXXIX.

39. Richmond, W. Edson, ed. Studies in Folklore. In Honor of Distinguished Service Professor Stith Thompson (Bloomington: Indiana U. P., 1958), xv, 270pp. Some 17 articles. Reprinted by Greenwood P., 1972.

40. Sebeok, Thomas A., ed. Myth, a Symposium (Bloomington and London: Indiana U. P., 1958), 180pp. Originally published in JAF (Oct-Dec, 1955), 68: 379-481. Nine essays.

41. _____, ed. Style in Language (New York: Wiley, 1960), xvii, 470pp. Some 20 papers given originally at Bloomington, Indiana, 1958. Few relate specifically to folklore but see R. M. Dorson.

42. Thompson, Stith, ed. Four Symposia on Folklore (Bloomington: Indiana U. P., 1953), xi, 340pp.

43. Walker, Warren S., ed. What Makes Papa Laugh, a Folklore Sheaf Honoring Harold W. Thompson (Cooperstown, N.Y.: New York Folklore Soc., 1958), iii, 105pp. Four reminiscent and biographical articles plus five on aspects of N.Y. state folklore.

44. Wilgus, D. K., ed. Folklore International: Essays in Traditional Literature, Belief, and Custom in Honor of Wayland Debs Hand (Hatboro, Penn.: Folklore Associates, 1967), xiv, 259pp. Some 26 essays illustrating a wide variety of folklore interests.

3. BIBLIOGRAPHY, DICTIONARIES, ARCHIVES

45. Abstracts of Folklore Studies, ed. Donald M. Winkelman et al., Vols. I-V, iii (Jan, 1963-F, 1967); Herbert Halpert et al., Vols. V, iv, to Vol. VII (W, 1967-W, 1969); Richard E. Buehler et al., Vols. VIII-XIII (1970-1975). Described in initial issue as "brief, factual summaries of articles relevant to the folklore discipline." International in coverage and catholic in scope, AFS provides useful synopses of familiar and recondite items. Individual issues seldom cover a large field and the corps of reviewers tends to run two or three years behind the publication dates of the articles.

46. Adams, Ramon F. The Rampaging Herd: A Bibliography of Books and Pamphlets on Men and Events in the Cattle Industry (Norman: U. of Oklahoma P., 1959), xix, 463pp. Chiefly historical material but the lore of the cattlemen is not neglected.

47. _____. Six-guns and Saddle Leather. A Bibliography of Books and Pamphlets on Western Outlaws and Gunmen (Norman: U. of Oklahoma P., 1954), xiii, 426pp.

48. "Annual Folklore Bibliography for 1954," ed. Paul A. Brown and W. Edson Richmond, JAF Supplement (Apr, 1955), 68: 26-46. Items not numbered.

49. "Annual Folklore Bibliography for 1955," ed. Paul A. Brown and W. Edson Richmond, JAF Supplement (Apr, 1956), 69: 18-45.

50. "Annual Folklore Bibliography for 1956," ed. W. Edson Richmond, JAF Supplement (Apr, 1957), 70: 19-43.

51. "Annual Bibliography of Folklore," ed. W. Edson Richmond, JAF Supplement (Apr, 1958), 71: 19-59. 1147 numbered items.

52. "Annual Bibliography of Folklore," ed. W. Edson Rich-
     mond, JAF Supplement (Apr, 1959), 72: 27-64.
     1224 items.

53. "Annual Bibliography of Folklore," ed. W. Edson Rich-
     mond, JAF Supplement (Apr, 1960), 73: 21-41.   395
     items.

54. "Annual Bibliography of Folklore," ed. W. Edson Rich-
     mond, JAF Supplement (Apr, 1961), 74: 28a-99.
     1328 items.

55. "Annual Bibliography of Folklore," ed. W. Edson Rich-
     mond, JAF Supplement (Apr, 1962), 75: 24-114.
     1335 items.

56. "Annual Bibliography of Folklore," ed. W. Edson Rich-
     mond, JAF Supplement (Apr, 1963), 76: 45-105.
     891 items.

57. Baker, Ronald L. "Folklore Courses and Programs in
     American Colleges and Universities," JAF (Apr-Je,
     1971), 84: 221-229. Material elicited by question-
     naire.

58. Barrick, Mac E. The Complete and Official Index of
     the First Fifteen Volumes, KFQ (1970), Supplement,
     15: ii, 55pp.

59. Baughman, Ernest W. Type and Motif-Index of the
     Folktales of England and North America (The Hague:
     Mouton, 1966), lxxvii, 606pp. Limited to English
     language folktales. Data on frequency and distribu-
     tion of tales with relationships between the two areas
     concerned.

60. Ben-Amos, Dan. "University of Pennsylvania Folklore
     Archives: a Progress Report," KFQ (F, 1970), 15:
     148-157.

61. Bethke, Robert D. "A Compilation by Department of
     University of Pennsylvania Theses and Dissertations
     of Relevance for Interdisciplinary Research in Folk-
     lore and Folklife," FF (Mr, 1970), 3: 59-64.

62. "Bibliography of New England--Maritimes Folklore, 1950-
     1957," NEF (S, 1958), 1: 18-31.

62a. "Bibliography of New England--Maritimes Folklore,"
NEF (S, 1959; S, 1960), 2: 19-24; 3: 20-24. The
first item includes some material prior to 1950.

63. Boger, Loris C. The Southern Mountaineer in Literature: an Annotated Bibliography (Morgantown, W.
Virginia Lib., 1964), 105pp. Some 496 titles,
mostly novels.

64. Boswell, George W. "Kentucky Folksongs in the Tennessee Archives," KFR (Jl-Sept, 1958), 4: 115-121.

65. _____. "Progress Report: Collection of Tennessee
Folksongs in Recent Years," TFSB (Je, 1959), 25:
31-79. Boswell's own collection of 770 variants of
446 folksongs from Tenn. and southern Kentucky.

66. _____. "The Several Folklore Archives at Oxford,"
MFR (Spr, 1972), 6: 9-17. Material at Univ. of
Mississippi.

67. Bratcher, James C. Analytical Index to the Publications of the Texas Folklore Society: Volumes 1-36
(Dallas: So. Methodist U. P., 1973), 322pp. Foreword by Wilson M. Hudson.

68. Brewton, John E. "Scholarship in Tennessee Folklore,"
TFSB (Dec, 1954), 20: 91-97. Useful list of
courses offered and of M. A. and Ph. D. theses com-
pleted.

69. Briggs, Katharine M. A Dictionary of British Folk-
Tales in the English Language, Incorporating the
F. J. Norton Collection (Bloomington: Indiana U.
P., 1970-1971), four volumes, 580pp., 580pp.,
623pp., and 761pp. respectively. A massive compilation of British folktales, many of which are
familiar in the U. S. Divided generally into folk
narratives and folk legends with many subheadings,
plus bibliography and tale type index. Short tales
given in full, longer tales often summarized.

70. Brunvand, Jan Harold. "A Classification for Shaggy
Dog Stories," JAF (Jan.-Mr., 1963), 76: 42-68.
Definition and discussion; type index modelled on
Thompson proposal.

71. _____. "Norwegian-American Folklore in the Indi-
    ana University Archives," MF (Winter, 1957), 7:
    221-228.

72. _____. "Preface to the Idaho Number," WF (Oct,
    1965), 24: 228-230. Short bibliography of Idaho
    folklore, 22 items.

73. Buermann, Theodore Barry. "An Analytical Index to
    North Carolina Folklore, Vols. 1-8," NCarF (Dec,
    1961), 9: 1-59. Indexes of contributors, titles,
    subjects.

74. Burrison, John A. "Pennsylvania German Folktales:
    An Annotated Bibliography," PF (Autumn, 1965),
    15: i, 30-38. Two parts: general reference, 55
    items; actual tales and anecdotes, 284 items. Fic-
    tion generally excluded.

75. Cantrell, Clyde H. and Walton R. Patrick. Southern
    Literary Culture: a Bibliography of Masters' and
    Doctors' Theses (n. p.: Alabama P., 1955), xiv,
    124pp. Some 201 of 2,529 entries deal with folklore
    but are not easily located.

76. Casterline, Gail Farr. "Sources and Literature for
    Western American History; a List of Dissertations,"
    WHQ (Jl, 1973), 4: 307-326. A few specific folk-
    lore items and folklore material in dissertations on
    Indians and ethnic groups.

77. Clarke, Kenneth W. "From Drouth to Deluge: Publica-
    tions in Folklore," KFR (Oct-Dec, 1968), 14: 81-
    87. Emphasis on reprints and new editions.

78. _____, and Mary W. Clarke. A Concise Dic-
    tionary of Folklore (Bowling Green, Ky.: West-
    ern Kentucky U. P., 1971), 46pp. Reprint of the
    1965 edition.

79. _____. _____. Kentucky Folklore Record Ten-
    Year Index, 1955-1964; Bibliography of Kentucky
    Folklore for 1964, 1965 (Bowling Green, Ky.: Ken-
    tucky Folklore Soc., 1966), 45pp.

80. Clarke, Mary W. "Bibliography of Kentucky Folklore
    for 1966," KFR (Jan-Mr, 1967), 13: 1-10.

81. _____. "Bibliography of Kentucky Folklore for 1967,"
    KFR (Apr-Je, 1968), 14: 51-57.

82. _____. "Bibliography of Kentucky Folklore for 1968,"
    KFR (Apr-Je, 1969), 15: 46-54.

83. Clements, William M. The Types of the Polack Joke
    (Bloomington: Folklore Forum, 1969), 45pp. Index
    of some 500 jokes in Indiana U. Folklore Archives.

84. Coffin, Tristram P. An Analytical Index to the Journal
    of American Folklore (Philadelphia: Am. Folklore
    Soc., 1958), xvi, 384pp. Despite imperfections a
    valuable index to 70 volumes of JAF and its articles,
    notes, texts, reviews.

85. Colby, B. N., George A. Collier, and Susan K. Postal.
    "Comparison of Themes in Folktales by the General
    Inquirer System," JAF (Oct-Dec, 1963), 76: 318-
    323. A system of content analysis applied tentative-
    ly to folktales.

86. Conklin, Harold C. Folk Classification: a Topically
    Arranged Bibliography of Contemporary and Back-
    ground References Through 1971 (New Haven: Dept.
    of Anthropology, Yale U., 1972), 501pp. Some
    5,000 entries.

87. Cooley, Marguerite and Vernon Parks (revised by
    Juanita C. Jackson). American Folklore: a Bibli-
    ography (Nashville: George Peabody Col., 1954),
    51pp. Pamphlet serving as guide to Nashville li-
    brary holdings.

88. Daiken, Leslie H. "Children's Games; a Bibliography,"
    Folklore (Dec, 1950), 61: 218-222. List of ancient
    and modern, European and oriental material. Some
    American items. Not annotated.

89. De Caro, F. A. and W. K. McNeil. American Prov-
    erb Literature: a Bibliography (Bloomington:
    Folklore Forum Series, 1970), 81pp. Incomplete
    but valuable compilation of 374 items. Introduction
    by De Caro, pp. i, ix. Annotation.

90. De Lys, Claudia. A Treasury of Superstitions (New
    York: Philosophical Lib., 1957), 317pp. Popular

beliefs about birds, foods, illnesses, numbers,
human beings. No sources given, extremely superficial.

91. Diehl, Katherine Smith. Religions, Mythologies,
Folklores: an Annotated Bibliography (New York:
Scarecrow P., 1956), 315pp.; second ed., 1962,
573pp. Books only and heavily weighted toward
religion and theology. Chap. 3 deals with folklore.

92. Dobie, J. Frank. Life and Literature of the Southwest (Dallas: So. Methodist U. P., 1952), viii,
222pp. Dobie's famous reading list expanded from
1943 ed.

93. Dorson, Richard M. "Folklore in Periodical Literature," JAF (Jan-Mr, Apr-Je, Jl-Sept, Oct-Dec,
1951), 64: 135-138, 227-231, 322-324, 425-427;
(Jan-Mr, Apr-Je, 1952), 65: 91-94, 191-194.

94. _____. "The Growth of Folklore Courses," JAF
(Jl-Sept, 1950), 63: 345-359. Description of
courses offered at 37 Am. universities and colleges.

95. _____. "The Identification of Folklore in American
Literature," JAF (Jan-Mr, 1957), 70: 1-8. Footnote 13 contains a valuable list of works.

96. _____. "The Michigan State College Folklore Archives," MF (Spr, 1955), 5: 51-59. Account of
the genesis of an important collection.

97. Earle, Eugene W. "Collectors and Collections," WF
(Apr, 1964), 23: 111-113. Useful description of
John Edwards Memorial Foundation collection of
folk music.

98. _____. "The John Edwards Memorial Foundation,"
WF (Jl, 1971), 30: 177-181. Brief account of a
collection of country and/or hillbilly music.

99. Emrich, Duncan. "Children's Folklore in the Archive
of Folk Song," QJLC (Apr, 1973), 30: 140-151.
General description of holdings with stress on
games, rhymes, songs.

100. Feather, Rebecca. "Indiana University Theses and Dissertations in Folklore," FF (Sept, 1969), 2: 119-123. 83 items listed. An incomplete list.

101. Ferris, William R., Jr. Mississippi Black Folklore: a Research Bibliography and Discography (Hattiesburg, Miss.: Univ. and College Press of Miss., 1971), vi, 61pp.

102. Fife, Austin E. and Alta S. Fife. "The Fife Collection of Western American Folksongs and Folklore," FFMA (Spr, 1964), 7: ii, 41-44. Description of a collection of folksongs and ballads.

103. Flanagan, John T. "The Meine Library of Folklore and Humor," NYFQ (S, 1957), 13: 114-126. Description of a collection acquired by Univ. of Illinois Lib. in 1955.

104. "Folklore" in American Bibliography, 1950, ed. Millett Henshaw et al., PMLA (Apr, 1951), 66: 41-43.

105. "Folklore" in American Bibliography, 1951, ed. Paul A. Brown et al., PMLA (Apr, 1952), 67: 7-10.

106. "Folklore" in American Bibliography, 1952, ed. Paul A. Brown et al., PMLA (Apr, 1953), 68: 87-92.

107. "Folklore" in American Bibliography, 1953, ed. Paul A. Brown et al., PMLA (Apr, 1954), 69: 74-78.

108. "Folklore" in American Bibliography, 1954, ed. Paul A. Brown et al., PMLA (Apr, 1955), 70: 109-113.

109. "Folklore" in American Bibliography, 1955, ed. Paul A. Brown et al., PMLA (Apr, 1956), 71: 109-113. The final compilation limited to American writers.

110. "Folklore" in American Bibliography, 1956, ed. Paul A. Brown et al., PMLA (Apr, 1957), 72: 174-178; items 1082-1234. The first list with numbered items.

111. "Folklore" in Annual Bibliography, 1957, ed. Paul A. Brown et al., PMLA (Apr, 1958), 73: 137-140; items 1152-1333.

112. "Folklore" in Annual Bibliography, 1958, ed. Paul A.
     Brown et al., PMLA (May, 1959), 74: 106-110;
     items 1186-1356.

113. "Folklore" in Annual Bibliography, 1959, ed. Paul A.
     Brown et al., PMLA (May, 1960), 75: 180-184;
     items 1360-1592.

114. "Folklore" in Annual Bibliography, 1960, ed. Paul A.
     Brown et al., PMLA (May, 1961), 76: 140-143,
     197; items 1389-1550, 4384-4397.

115. "Folklore" in Annual Bibliography, 1961, ed. Paul A.
     Brown et al., PMLA (May, 1962), 77: 156-159,
     215; items 1720-1908, 4727-4744.

116. "Folklore" in Annual Bibliography, 1962, ed. Paul A.
     Brown et al., PMLA (May, 1963), 78: 123-126,
     177; items 1778-1967, 5010-5036.

117. "Folklore" in MLA International Bibliography, 1963,
     ed. Paul A. Brown et al., PMLA (May, 1964),
     79: 139-142, 189; items 2090-2268, 5057-5078.

118. "Folklore" in MLA International Bibliography, 1964,
     ed. Paul A. Brown and Harrison T. Messerole
     et al., PMLA (May, 1965), 80: 93-97, 157; items
     2069-2286, 5890-5913.

119. "Folklore" in MLA International Bibliography, 1965,
     ed. Paul A. Brown and Harrison T. Messerole
     et al., PMLA (May, 1966), 81: 110-113, 173;
     items 2805-2980, 6555-6566.

120. "Folklore" in MLA International Bibliography, 1966,
     ed. Harrison T. Messerole et al., PMLA (June
     1967), 82: 112-116, 187; items 3140-3362, 7582-
     7624.

121. "Folklore" in MLA International Bibliography, 1967,
     ed. Harrison T. Messerole et al., PMLA (June,
     1968), 83: 655-658, 719; items 4946-5165, 8888-
     8933.

122. "Folklore" in MLA International Bibliography, 1968,
     ed. Harrison T. Messerole et al., PMLA (June,
     1969), 84: 809-811, 879-880; items 5492-5598,
     9781-9805.

123. "Folklore" in MLA International Bibliography, 1969, ed. Harrison T. Messerole et al., (1970), 1: 43-46, 119-120; items 1246-1398, 5832-5860.

124. "Folklore" in MLA International Bibliography, 1970, ed. Harrison T. Messerole et al., (1972), 1: 159-187; items 9475-11143. North American items are now segregated and folklore material is divided into 9 principal categories with subdivisions.

125. "Folklore" in MLA International Bibliography, 1971, ed. Harrison T. Messerole et al., (1973), 1: 178-211; items 10605-12545.

126. "Folklore" in MLA International Bibliography, 1972, ed. Harrison T. Messerole et al., (1974), 1: 187-227; items 11349-13753.

127. "Folklore" in MLA International Bibliography, 1973, ed. Harrison T. Messerole et al., (1975), 1: 197-245; items 12111-14783.

128. "Folklore Bibliography for 1949," ed. Ralph S. Boggs, SFQ (March, 1950), 14: 1-77.

129. "Folklore Bibliography for 1950," ed. Ralph S. Boggs, SFQ (March 1951), 15: 1-107.

130. "Folklore Bibliography for 1951," ed. Ralph S. Boggs, SFQ (March, 1952), 16: 1-78.

131. "Folklore Bibliography for 1952," ed. Ralph S. Boggs, SFQ (March, 1953), 17: 1-88.

132. "Folklore Bibliography for 1953," ed. Ralph S. Boggs, SFQ (March, 1954), 18: 1-84.

133. "Folklore Bibliography for 1954," ed. Ralph S. Boggs, SFQ (March, 1955), 19: 1-75.

134. "Folklore Bibliography for 1955," ed. Ralph S. Boggs, SFQ (March, 1956), 20: 1-88.

135. "Folklore Bibliography for 1956," ed. Ralph S. Boggs, SFQ (March, 1957), 21: 1-77.

136. "Folklore Bibliography for 1957," ed. Ralph S. Boggs, SFQ (March, 1958), 22: 1-68.

137. "Folklore Bibliography for 1958," ed. Ralph S. Boggs, SFQ (March, 1959), 23: 1-77.

138. "Folklore Bibliography for 1959," ed. Ralph S. Boggs and Sarah Elizabeth Roberts, SFQ (March, 1960), 24: 1-75.

139. "Folklore Bibliography for 1960," ed. Américo Paredes, SFQ (March, 1961), 25: 1-89.

140. "Folklore Bibliography for 1961," ed. Américo Paredes, SFQ (March, 1962), 26: 1-96.

141. "Folklore Bibliography for 1962," ed. Américo Paredes, SFQ (March, 1963), 27: 1-111.

142. "Folklore Bibliography for 1963," ed. Américo Paredes, SFQ (March, 1964), 28: 1-94.

143. "Folklore Bibliography for 1964," ed. Merle E. Simmons, SFQ (March, 1965), 29: 1-125.

144. "Folklore Bibliography for 1965," ed. Merle E. Simmons, SFQ (March, 1966), 30: 1-148.

145. "Folklore Bibliography for 1966," ed. Merle E. Simmons, SFQ (June, 1967), 31: 79-213.

146. "Folklore Bibliography for 1967," ed. Merle E. Simmons, SFQ (June, 1968), 32: 73-208.

147. "Folklore Bibliography for 1968," ed. Merle E. Simmons, SFQ (Sept, 1969), 33: 135-295.

148. "Folklore Bibliography for 1969," ed. Merle E. Simmons, SFQ (Sept, 1970), 34: 149-313.

149. "Folklore Bibliography for 1970," ed. Merle E. Simmons, SFQ (Sept, 1971), 35: 173-323.

150. "Folklore Bibliography for 1971," ed. Merle E. Simmons, SFQ (Sept, 1972), 36: 177-367.

151. "Folklore Bibliography for 1972," ed. Merle E. Simmons, SFQ (Sept, 1973), 37: 153-313.

152. Folklore Bibliography for 1973, ed. Merle E. Sim-

mons (Bloomington: Folklore Institute, Indiana
Univ., 1975), xiv, 175pp.

153. FF Communications: an Index to Volumes I-LXXXI,
Nos. 1-195, 1910-1964 (Helsinki: Suomalainen
Tiedeakatemia, 1963), 19pp.   Useful index to an
important series.

154. Gallacher, Stuart A., "Folklore in Periodical Literature," JAF (Jan-Mr, Apr-Je, Jl-Sept, Oct-Dec
1950), 63: 101-104, 245-249, 368-373, 472-476.

155. Georges, Robert A., Beth Blumenreich, and Kathie
O'Reilly. "Two Mechanical Indexing Systems for
Folklore Archives: a Preliminary Report," JAF
(Jan-Mr, 1974), 87: 39-52.

156. Goldin, Hyman et al. Dictionary of American Underworld Lingo (New York: Twayne, 1950), 327pp.
Reprinted (New York: Citadel, 1962).   Unscholarly
list of unusual items with some helpful folk etymologies.

157. Goldstein, Kenneth S. A Guide for Field Workers in
Folklore (Hatboro, Penn.: Folklore Associates,
1964), xi, 199pp.   Practical advice in conducting
field work based on personal experience.   Some of
it is very elementary but there are useful hints.

158. Green, Archie. "A Discography (LP) of American
Labor Union Songs," NYFQ (A, 1961), 17: 187-
193.   Prefatory discussion of history of labor
songs; some 100 listed.

159. Griffin, William J. "Indexes to the First Thirty
Volumes of the Tennessee Folklore Society Bulletin," TFSB (Sept, 1965), 31: 68-97.   Valuable
tripartite index: author list, title list, topic list.

160. [_____.] "A Survey of U.S. and Canadian Folklore
Serials," TFSB (Mr, 1964; Dec, 1964; Mr, 1966;
Dec, 1967; Je, 1968), 30: 26-32, 129-139; 32:
13-17; 33: 121-124; 34: 50-53.

161. _____. "The TFS Bulletin and Other Folklore
Serials in the United States: a Preliminary Survey," TFSB (Sept, 1959), 25: 91-96.   List of folklore journals with first date of issue.

162.   _____ and Richard L. Castner. "A Survey of U.S.
        Folklore Serials," TFSB (Je, 1963), 29: 42-46.
        First instalment of a survey intended to deal with
        serials published through Dec. 31, 1962. Publish-
        ing data and contents considered.

163.   Hand, Wayland D. "Folklore and Mythology at UCLA;
        Folklore, Mythology, Folk Music, and Ethnomusi-
        cology," WF (Jan, 1964), 23: 35-38. Brief ac-
        count of the university program in these fields.

164.   _____. "North American Folklore Societies, Sup-
        plement II," JAF (Jan, 1969), 82: 3-33. Vital sta-
        tistics about 15 regional or state societies.

165.   Haque, Abu Saeed Zahurul. "A Bibliography of Mis-
        sissippi Folklore," MFR (S, 1968), 2: 43-50. Cf.
        "A Bibliography of Mississippi Folklore--1968,
        MFR (Spr, 1970), 4: 28-36; and "A Bibliography
        of Mississippi Folklore--1969 and 1970," MFR
        (Spr, 1972), 6: 20-33. All three list newspaper
        articles and much ephemeral material.

166.   Haywood, Charles. A Bibliography of North American
        Folklore and Folksong (New York: Dover, 1961),
        two volumes, I, xxx, 748pp.; II, ix, 749-1301pp.
        Rev. second ed. of work originally published in
        1951. Miscellaneous and inaccurate but still use-
        ful; revision casually done with many omissions.

167.   Heilbron, Bertha. "North Star Folklore in Minnesota
        History: a Bibliography," WF (Oct, 1950), 9: 366-
        371. Some 75 items from 30 volumes of Minn.
        Hist., 1915-1949.

168.   Hendricks, King et al., "Utah State University Folklore
        Collection," WF (Apr, 1959), 18: 107-120.

169.   Hickerson, Joseph C. "Hoosier Materials in the Indi-
        ana University Folklore Archive," MF (S, 1961),
        11: 75-83.

170.   _____. "A Tentative Beginning Toward a Bibli-
        ography on the History of American Folkloristics
        and the American Folklore Society," JFI (Je-Aug,
        1973), 10: 109-111.

171. Hoffmann, Frank A. Analytical Survey of Anglo-
     American Traditional Erotica (Bowling Green:
     Bowling Green State U. P., 1973), x, 309pp.
     Analytical survey of materials of erotic folklore
     plus six appendices of annotated bibliographies.

172. Hunter, Don L. "Sound Recording of History," WF
     (Jl, 1952), 11: 208-211. U. of Oregon Library
     records speech mannerisms, songs, and oral cul-
     ture on magnetic tapes.

173. Hurley, Gerard T. "Buried Treasure Tales in Ameri-
     ca," WF (Jl, 1951), 10: 197-216. A discussion of
     the genre plus a list of 102 representative titles
     and bibliography.

174. Hyde, Ralph W. "A Review and Preview of Folklore
     in Literature Studies Suitable for Publication in
     Regional Journals," MFR (F, 1968), 2: 79-88.
     Editorial advice.

175. Ireland, Florence. "The Northeast Archives of Folk-
     lore and Oral History, a Brief Description and a
     Catalogue of Its Holdings 1958-1972," NEF (1972).
     Inventory of folklore and folksong materials at U.
     of Maine, collected mostly by Edward D. Ives.

176. Ireland, Norma O. Index to Fairy Tales, 1949-1972,
     Including Folklore, Legends & Myths, in Collec-
     tions (Westwood, Mass.: Faxon, 1973), xxxviii,
     741pp. Continuation of Mary Huse Eastman's Index
     to Fairy Tales.

177. Jaffe, Harry J. "American Negro Folklore: a Check
     List of Scarce Items," SFQ (Mr, 1972), 36: 68-
     70. List of rare items given without annotation.

178. Jobes, Gertrude. Dictionary of Mythology, Folklore
     and Symbols (New York: Scarecrow, 1961), two
     volumes, 1759pp. The folklore section is erratic
     and unsatisfactory.

179. Landy, Eugene E. The Underground Dictionary (New
     York: Simon and Schuster, 1971), 206pp.

180. Lawless, Ray M. Folksingers and Folksongs in
     America (New York: Duell, Sloan and Pearce,

1960), xviii, 662pp. Correctly subtitled "A hand-
book of biography, bibliography, and discography."
An invaluable compilation.

181. Leach, MacEdward. "Folklore in American Regional
Literature," JFI (Dec, 1966), 3: 376-397. Writers
in eight different regions of the U.S. have used
folklore in different but overlapping ways. Selected
bibliography appended.

182. _____ and Henry Glassie. A Guide for Collectors
of Oral Traditions and Folk Cultural Material in
Pennsylvania (Harrisburg, Penn.: Historical and
Museum Commission, 1968), vii, 70pp. Suggestions for collecting all kinds of folk data.

183. Leach, Maria. A Dictionary of Folklore, Mythology,
and Legend (New York: Funk and Wagnalls, 1949-
1950), two volumes, I: x, 531pp; II, 532-1196pp.
One volume reissue, 1972, 1236pp. Impressive
collection of long and short articles on many subjects by a variety of scholars. Cf. review by W.
D. Hand, MF (W, 1951), 1: 267-272.

184. Legman, Gershon. The Horn Book: Studies in Erotic
Folklore and Bibliography (London: Jonathan Cape,
1970), 565pp. Twelve essays, most previously
published, on erotic bibliography, limericks, obscene material, a proposed motif-index by the
acknowledged specialist in the field. Book appeared
earlier, in briefer form, in 1964.

185. _____. "Toward a Motif-Index of Erotic Humor,"
JAF (Jl-Sept, 1962), 75: 227-248. Most type indexes omit obscene and scatological humor; Legman describes his work in this field.

186. Lehner, Ernst. A Fantastic Bestiary (New York:
Tudor, 1969), 192pp. With 300 illus.

187. List, George. "An Approach to the Indexing of Ballad
Tunes," FFMA (1963), 6: 7-16.

188. _____. "Archiving," in Folklore and Folklife, ed.
Richard M. Dorson, pp. 455-463. Explanation of
the functions of a folklore archive, etc.

189. _____. "Toward the Indexing of Ballad Texts,"
JAF (Jan-Mr, 1968), 81: 44-61. Ballad classification might be aided by reducing ballads to plot
gists.

190. Loranth, Alice N. "The European Ethnic Folklore
Resources of the White Collection," JOFS (Dec,
1972), n.s., 1: 25-37. Summary of folklore holdings in the John G. White collection, Cleveland
Public Library.

191. Lumpkin, Ben Gray et al. Folksongs on Records,
3rd ed. and cumulative (Denver: Alan Swallow,
1950), viii, 98pp. Listing of almost 4,000 commercial phonograph recordings of ballads, songs,
dance music, etc. from U.S. and elsewhere.

192. McDade, Thomas M. The Annals of Murder. A
Bibliography of Books and Pamphlets on American
Murders from Colonial Times to 1900 (Norman:
U. of Oklahoma P., 1961), xii, 360pp. Helpful
especially to the study of broadsides and ballads.

193. Maciuszko, George J. "Folklore Holdings in the John
G. White Collection of the Cleveland Public Library," JOFS (A, 1967), 2: 97-108. Description
of the collection.

194. McMillan, Douglas J. "ECU Folklore Archive,"
NCarF (May, 1971), 19: 131-134. Description of
folklore archive at E. Carolina U. begun 1969-
1970.

195. McNeil, William K. "An Annotated Bibliography of
Indiana Folklore," IF (1973), 6: i, 100-134.
Supplement to Donald M. Winkelman's earlier
compilation.

196. McVicker, Mary Louise. The Writings of J. Frank
Dobie: a Bibliography (Lawton, Okla.: Museum
of the Great Plains, 1968), xv, 258pp. Introduction by Harry H. Ransom.

197. Major, Mabel and T. M. Pearce. Southwest Heritage: a Literary History with Bibliographies (Albuquerque: U. of New Mexico P., 1972), 378pp.
3rd. ed. revised and expanded; folklore material
added.

198.   Mencken, H. L. The American Language, 4th ed. and
        2 supplements, abridged by Raven I. McDavid, Jr.
        with aid of David Maurer (New York: Knopf, 1963),
        xxv, 777, cxxiv pp. Not a revision but a consoli-
        dation with considerable new material. Mencken's
        landmark volume first appeared in 1919.

199.   Nugent, Donald. "Witchcraft Studies, 1959-1971: a
        Bibliographical Survey," JPC (W, 1971), 5: 710-
        725.

200.   Patterson, Daniel W. "Folklore" in A Bibliographical
        Guide to the Study of Southern Literature, ed.
        Louis D. Ruben, Jr. (Baton Rouge: Louisiana
        State U. P., 1969), pp. 102-119. Folklore is
        limited here to traditional beliefs and oral artistic
        expression.

201.   Perkal, Joan Ruman. Western Folklore. Twenty-
        Five Year Index (Berkeley: U. of California P.,
        1969), 180pp. Index to California Folklore Quar-
        terly, Vols. 1-4, and WF, Vols. 6-25.

202.   Perkins, David and Norman Tanis. Native Americans
        of North America (Northridge, Cal.: California
        State U., 1974), 558pp. (Reprinted, Metuchen,
        N.J.: Scarecrow Press, 1975). Some 3,400
        items relating to the ethnology, tribal history,
        culture, religion, etc. of the No. Am. Indians.
        There is no section for folklore but folklore ma-
        terial is abundant throughout. Helpful indexes.

203.   Peuckert, Will-Erich and Otto Laufer. Volkskunde,
        Quellen und Forschungen seit 1930 (Bern: A.
        Francke, 1951), 343pp. Twenty years of folklore
        scholarship chiefly from Europe but with some
        American material cited.

204.   Posen, I. Sheldon, Michael Taft, and Richard Tall-
        man. Index to Hoosier Folklore Bulletin (1942-
        1945) and Hoosier Folklore (1946-1950), Blooming-
        ton: Folklore Forum Soc., 1973), ix, 83pp. In-
        troduction by Herbert Halpert.

205.   Pownall, David E. Articles on Twentieth Century
        Literature: an Annotated Bibliography 1954 to
        1970 (New York: Kraus-Thomson, 1963), three

volumes covering authors A to I. Scattered folklore items appear under names of authors.

206. Ramsey, Eloise. Folklore for Children and Young
People (Philadelphia: Am. Folklore Soc., 1952),
xii, 110pp. Descriptive bibliography done with
Dorothy Mills Howard for elementary and inter-
mediate schools.

207. Randolph, Vance. Ozark Folklore: a Bibliography
(Bloomington: Indiana U. P., 1972), 572pp. Some
2,489 entries by the outstanding specialist in the
field. Lively personal annotations.

208. Reaver, J. Russell and George W. Boswell. Funda-
mentals of Folk Literature (Oosterhout: Anthropological Publications, 1962), 221pp. Includes
scattered bibliographical data.

209. Reuss, Richard. A Woody Guthrie Bibliography, 1912-
1967 (New York: Guthrie Children's Trust Fund,
1968), 94pp. Annotated list of 501 items.

210. _____ and Ellen J. Stekert. "A Preliminary Bibliography of Urban Folklore Materials," in The Urban Experience and Folk Tradition, ed. Américo
Paredes and Ellen Stekert (Austin and London: U.
of Texas P., 1971), 181-200.

211. Richmond, W. Edson. "Folklore in Periodical Literature," JAF (Jl-Sept, Oct-Dec, 1952; Jan-Mr, Apr-
Je, Jl-Sept, Oct-Dec, 1953), 65: 312-317, 425-
430; 66: 79-86, 165-172, 269-274, 344-353.

212. Robbins, Rossell Hope. The Encyclopedia of Witchcraft and Demonology (New York: Crown, 1959),
571pp. Readable and accurate. Long account of
Salem witches.

213. Robe, Stanley L. Index of Mexican Folktales (Berkeley: U. of California P., 1973), xxiii, 276pp.
Classified texts from Mexico, Central America,
the Hispanic U. S.

214. _____. "The Ralph Steele Boggs Folklore Collection," WF (Jan, 1961), 20: 38-40. Summary account of collection bought by UCLA library.

215. Roberts, Warren E. "Stith Thompson: His Major
      Works and a Bibliography," ARV (1965), 21: 5-20.

216. Rosenberg, Bruce A. The Folksongs of Virginia
      (Charlottesville: U. Press of Virginia, 1969), xx,
      145pp. Checklist of WPA holdings in Alderman
      Library, U. of Va.

217. Rosenberg, Neil V. "The Indiana University Folklore
      Archives," IF (1968), 1: 110-112.

218. Schmitt, Martin. "Folklore Sources in the University
      of Oregon Library," WF (Oct, 1951), 10: 325-328.
      An inventory.

219. Sealock, Richard B. and Pauline A. Seely. Bibli-
      ography of Place-Name Literature, United States
      and Canada (Chicago: Am. Lib. Assn, 1967),
      second ed., x, 352pp. Some 3,599 entries with
      annotation. Original ed. 1948.

220. _____ and _____. "Place Name Literature,
      United States and Canada, 1952-1954," Names (Je,
      1955), 3: 102-116. Supplement to 1948 book.

221. _____ and Margaret S. Powell. "Place-Name Lit-
      erature, United States and Canada 1971-1974,"
      Names (Dec, 1974), 22: 150-164. Supplements
      earlier lists.

222. Seely, Pauline A. and Richard B. Sealock. "Place-
      Name Literature, United States 1955-1959," Names
      (Dec, 1959), 7: 203-232.

223. Smith, Elsdon C. Personal Names: a Bibliography
      (New York: N.Y. Public Lib., 1952), 226pp.
      Reprinted 1965 (Detroit: Gale).

224. Stekert, Ellen J. "The Wayne State University Folk-
      lore Archive: In Process," FFMA (Spr, 1967),
      9: 61-78. An account of its origin, financing, and
      classification.

225. Tallman, Marjorie. Dictionary of American Folklore
      (New York: Philosophical Lib., 1959), 324pp.
      Brief lexicon of limited utility; no references given.

226. Thigpen, Kenneth A., Jr. "An Index to the Known
      Oral Sources of the Child Collection," FF (Apr,
      1972), 5: 55-69. Variants of Child ballads listed
      by informants only.

227. Thompson, Lawrence S. "Some Sources for Folklore
      Studies in the University of Kentucky Libraries,"
      MF (W, 1955), 5: 237-241.

228. Thompson, Stith. "Fifty Years of Folktale Indexing,"
      in Humaniora, ed. W. D. Hand and G. O. Arlt,
      pp. 49-57.

229. _____. Motif-Index of Folk Literature (Bloomington
      Indiana U. P., 1955-1958, six volumes. Revision,
      much amplified, of the 1938 ed., with new classifi-
      cations added and new motif numbers assigned.
      One of the indispensable tools of the folklore schol-
      ar.

230. _____. The Types of the Folktale (Helsinki: Suo-
      malainen Tiedeakatemia, 1961), 588pp. Second
      revision of the indispensable Verzeichnis der
      Märchentypen originally published by Antti Aarne
      in 1910. Immensely expanded.

231. Tierney, Judith. "The George Korson Folklore Ar-
      chive," KFQ (S, 1971), 16: 108-111. Material
      collected by the chief student of Penn. coal mining
      lore.

232. Toelken, J. Barre. "The Randall V. Mills Memorial
      Archive of Northwest Folklore," FFMA (F, 1962),
      5: iii, 3. Description of Univ. of Oregon archive
      which includes Robert W. Gordon collection of
      American folksong.

233. "Treasury of Song," Time (July 18, 1956), 66: iii,
      44-46. Brief biographical sketch of Duncan Em-
      rich and an account of Lib. of Congress archives.

234. Tully, Marjorie and Juan B. Rael. An Annotated
      Bibliography of Spanish Folklore in New Mexico
      and Southern Colorado (Albuquerque: U. of New
      Mexico P., 1950), 124pp. Coverage up to 1948.
      Brief and accurate data.

235. Ullom, Judith C. Folklore of the North American
     Indians, an Annotated Bibliography (Washington:
     Lib. of Congress, 1969), x, 126pp. Attractive
     selective bibliography, arranged by regions and
     separated into source books and children's eds.

236. Waldhorn, Arthur. A Concise Dictionary of the Ameri-
     can Language (New York: Philosophical Lib.,
     1956), vi, 186pp. Derivative from Mencken and
     Matthews and better in definitions than in etymolo-
     gies but useful.

237. Wentworth, Harold and Stuart Berg Flexner. Diction-
     ary of American Slang (New York: Crowell, 1960),
     xviii, 669pp. A landmark in American lexicography.

238. Wildhaber, Robert. "A Bibliographical Introduction to
     American Folklife," NYFQ (Dec, 1965), 21: 259-
     302. Much of this invaluable bibliography relates
     to material life but tales, songs, ballads, anec-
     dotes, proverbs are included.

239. Wilgus, D. K. "The Josiah H. Combs Collection of
     Songs and Rhymes," KFR (Oct-Dec, 1960; Apr-Je,
     1961), 6: 125-126; 7: 63-76. 162 items in W.
     Kentucky folklore archive.

240. _____. "A Type-Index of Anglo-American Tradi-
     tional Narrative Songs," JFI (Aug-Dec, 1970), 7:
     161-177.

241. Winkelman, Donald M. "Bibliography of Indiana Folk-
     lore," MF (S, 1961; W, 1963-4), 11: 115-124; 13:
     237-244.

242. Woodbridge, Hensley C. "A Tentative Bibliography of
     Kentucky Speech," PADS (Nov, 1958), No. 30, 17-
     37. Books, articles, masters' theses.

243. _____ and Wilgus, D. K. "Bibliography of Kentucky
     Folklore for 1956," KFR (Jan-Mr, 1957), 3: 17-28.
     First of series of annual compilations including
     newspaper stories, reviews, discography.

244. _____ and _____. "Bibliography of Kentucky
     Folklore for 1957," KFR (Jan-Mr, 1958), 4: 15-28.

245. _____ and _____. "Bibliography of Kentucky
Folklore for 1958," KFR (Jan-Mr, 1959), 5: 15-31.

246. _____ and _____. "Bibliography of Kentucky
Folklore for 1959," KFR (Jan-Mr, 1960), 6: 21-30.

247. _____ and _____. "Bibliography of Kentucky
Folklore for 1960," KFR (Jan-Mr, 1961), 7: 23-33.

248. _____ and _____. "Bibliography of Kentucky
Folklore for 1961," KFR (Jan-Mr, 1962), 8: 21-28.

249. _____ and _____. "Bibliography of Kentucky
Folklore for 1962," KFR (Apr-Je, 1963), 9: 29-36.

250. _____. "Bibliography of Kentucky Folklore for
1963," KFR (Jl-Sept, 1964), 10: 47-50.

251. Woods, Barbara Allen. The Devil in Dog-Form--a
Partial Type-Index of Devil Legends (Berkeley: U.
of California P., 1959), x, 168pp. Some 200
legend-types of author's own devising chiefly from
German language area. Rich bibliography.

252. Yoder, Don. "Introductory Bibliography on Folk Religion," WF (Jan, 1974), 33: 16-34. Excellent
compilation, much of it European in emphasis.

253. _____. "The Pennsylvania Germans; A Preliminary
Reading List," PF (W, 1971), 21: ii, 2-17.

254. _____. "What to Read on the Amish," PF (S,
1969), 18: iv, 14-19.

254a. Ziegler, Elsie B. Folklore: an Annotated Bibliography and Index to Single Editions (Westwood, Mass.:
Faxon, 1973), x, 203pp. Folklore is indexed by
title, subject, country of origin, and motif (only
16 are used). Limited utility.

4. FOLKLORE: STUDY AND TEACHING

255. Abrahams, Roger D. "Folklore and Literature as Performance," JFI (Aug-Dec, 1972), 9: 75-94. A plea for studying traditions and practices in evaluating literature with Robert Herrick's verse used as an example.

256. _____. "Folklore in Culture: Notes Toward an Analytic Method," TSLL (Spr, 1963), 5: 98-110. Analysis of folklore texts should combine the disciplines of literature, psychology, and anthropology for greater success.

257. _____. "Introductory Remarks to a Rhetorical Theory of Folklore," JAF (Apr-Je, 1968), 81: 143-158.

258. _____. "Personal Power and Social Restraint in the Definition of Folklore," JAF (Jan-Mr, 1971), 84: 16-30. Folklorists should study both tradition and performance.

259. Adams, Robert G. Introduction to Folklore (Columbus: Collegiate Pub. Co., 1973), iii, 186pp. Serviceable college text.

260. Alford, Violet. "Why Do We Study Folklore?" Folklore (Dec, 1953), 64: 473-83. Folklore is studied for continuity, curiosity, necessity, and seasonal observances. Mostly British and Continental examples but some charivari items from Oklahoma and Louisiana.

261. Almeida, Renato. "Folklore and Education," FA (Jan, 1967), 27: 1-8. A plea for wider use of folklore in the classroom.

262. Ames, Karl. "Teaching Folklore in an Urban High
      School, " NYFQ (Sept, 1965), 21: 206-12. Experi-
      ences in a New York City high school.

263. Ballard, Lou Ellen. "Collecting Folk Materials, "
      MFR (1967), 1: 71-79.

264. Bascom, William R. "Folklore and Anthropology, "
      JAF (Oct-Dec, 1953), 66: 283-90. Definition of
      the anthropological approach to folklore.

265. _____. "Folklore, Verbal Art, and Culture, " JAF
      (Oct-Dec, 1973), 86: 374-81. A kind of debate
      with Richard M. Dorson about definitions of terms.

266. _____. "Four Functions of Folklore, " JAF (Oct-
      Dec, 1954), 67: 333-49. Folklore can provide
      amusement, validate culture, be educational (es-
      pecially in nonliterate societies), and maintain
      conformity to accepted behavior patterns.

267. _____. "Verbal Art, " JAF (Jl-Sept, 1955), 68:
      245-252. Bascom defends his use of the term
      for tales, myths, legends, etc., but not for all
      folklore.

268. Bauman, Richard. "Differential Identity and the So-
      cial Base of Folklore, " JAF (Jan-Mr, 1971), 84:
      31-41. "The most fundamental prerequisite for
      artistic verbal communication remains a shared
      esthetic of spoken language.... "

269. _____. "Towards a Behavioral Theory of Folk-
      lore, " JAF (Apr-Je, 1969), 82: 167-170.

270. _____. "Y. L. Cahan's Instructions on Collecting
      Folklore, " NYFQ (W, 1962), 18: 284-289. Prac-
      tical advice by the great collector of Yiddish lore.

271. Bayard, Samuel P. "The Materials of Folklore, "
      JAF (Jan-Mr, 1953), 66: 1-17. Folklore is con-
      cerned with "the religious, philosophical, ethical,
      and esthetic aspects of the entire human tradition-
      al being.... "

272. Bell, Michael J. "William Wells Newell and the
      Foundation of American Folklore Scholarship, "

JFI (Je-Aug, 1973), 10: 7-21. Newell's early
interests in collecting are stressed as well as his
editorship of the fledgling JAF.

273. Ben-Amos, Dan. "A History of Folklore Studies--Why
      Do We Need It?" JFI (Je-Aug, 1973), 10: 113-
      124.

274. _____. "Toward a Definition of Folklore in Con-
      text," JAF (Jan-Mr, 1971), 84: 3-15. After a
      diffuse rejection of other definitions Ben-Amos
      suggests one of his own: "folklore is artistic
      communication in small groups."

275. Birdsall, Esther K. "Folklore Problems and Folklore
      Samplings of the American Guide Series," JOFS
      (F, 1968), 3: 169-185. Discussion of collecting
      and writing problems of WPA material from Ohio,
      So. Carolina, N. J., and Miss.

276. Boggs, Ralph Steele. El Folklore en Los Estados
      Unidos de Norteamerica (Buenos Aires: Editorial
      Raigal, 1954), 268pp. Survey of American folk-
      lore for Spanish readers. Mixed with useful but
      rather irrelevant comments on American life.

277. Botkin, B. A. "Applied Folklore: Creating Under-
      standing Through Folklore," SFQ (Sept, 1953), 17:
      199-206. Applied folklore means folklore used for
      something beyond itself, as in folk festival, folk
      culture seminar, group conversation.

278. _____. "The Folkness of the Folk," in Folklore
      in Action, ed. H. P. Beck, pp. 44-57. Reprint
      of an EJ essay (Je, 1933), 6: 461-469. Folklore
      as experience and understanding.

279. Boyd, Joe Dan. "Collecting Folklore on the Job,"
      NCarF (May, 1969), 17: 21-26.

280. Bradley, Francis Wright. "The Press as an Ally in
      Collecting Folk Speech," PADS (Apr, 1952), No.
      17: 29-39. Newspapers can help academic col-
      lectors.

281. Brunvand, Jan Harold. A Guide for Collectors of
      Folklore in Utah (Salt Lake City: U. of Utah P.,

1971), xiii, 124pp. A manual designed for one
state with special conditions but with wider application.

282. _____. "New Directions for the Study of American
Folklore," Folklore (Spr, 1971), 80: 25-35. A
survey of developments in U.S. since 1950; academic study of folklore has become respectable.

283. _____. The Study of American Folklore: an Introduction (New York: Norton, 1968), xii, 383pp.
A careful classification and description of the various folklore genres with numerous and well chosen
examples. Designed as a text but with wide utility.

284. Burress, Lee A., Jr. "Folklore Collecting in Wisconsin," JOFS (A, 1967), 2: 125-133.

285. Burrison, John A. "What to Collect and How to Ask
for It," Folkways (Jan, 1963), 1: iii, 25-29. A
discussion of collecting techniques.

286. Cabaniss, Allen. "The Folklore of Bus Travel,"
NCarF (Jl, 1962), 10: 1-5. Signs, place names,
speech, as observed from Mississippi buses.

287. Carlson, Signe M. "An Interdisciplinary Approach to
Folklore Study," JOFS (W, 1967), 2: 149-165. A
plea for greater breadth in folklore research.

288. Carvalho-Neto, Paolo de. The Concept of Folklore,
trans. Jacques M. P. Wilson (Coral Gables: U.
of Miami P., 1971), 152pp. Essays on the theory
of folklore by a distinguished Brazilian folklorist,
whose views differ somewhat from those of North
American scholars.

289. Cashion, Gerald, ed. "Conceptual Problems in Contemporary Folklore Study," FF (Bibliographical
and Special Series, no. 12, 1974), iii, 118pp.
Fourteen papers concerned with a variety of theoretical matters; oral history, ethics, aesthetic
concepts, the history of folkloristics, improved
terms for "folklore."

290. Cassidy, Frederic G. "A Method for Collecting
Dialect," PADS (Nov, 1953), No. 20: 5-96.
Methodology plus a specimen questionnaire.

291. Chavez, Fray Angelica. "The Inter-Relation of His-
        tory and Folklore," NMFR (1950-51), 5: 1-3.
        Pure history and pure folklore are separate but
        may combine with good results.

292. Christiansen, Reidar Th. "A European Folklorist
        Looks at American Folklore," in Madstones and
        Twisters, ed. Mody C. Boatright et al., pp. 18-
        44. Perceptive article by a distinguished Norwegian
        scholar on differences between European and Amer-
        ican folklore (fairies, witchcraft, the supernatural,
        etc.).

293. Clark, Joseph D. "Fifty Years of Meetings and Pro-
        grams of the North Carolina Folklore Society,"
        NCarF (Jl, 1964), 12: 27-32. Inventory of meet-
        ings since 1912.

294. Clarke, Kenneth W. "From Drouth to Deluge: Publi-
        cations in Folklore," KFR (Oct-Dec, 1968), 14:
        81-87. Survey of recently published books and re-
        prints.

295. _____ and Mary Clarke. Introducing Folklore
        (New York: Holt, Rinehart, and Winston, 1963),
        154pp. An elementary text with rather obvious
        limitations.

296. Coffin, Tristram Potter. "Another Sunset, Another
        Kiss," SFQ (Je, 1964), 28: 95-102. Twentieth
        century folklorists are more professional and sci-
        entific than their predecessors but they have lost
        aesthetic feelings for their material.

297. _____. "Image of the Folklorist," NYFQ (Spr,
        1962), 18: 39-43. Folklore studies lack breadth
        and vitality; folklore ought to attract more psychol-
        ogists and anthropologists.

298. _____, ed. Our Living Traditions (New York and
        London: Basic Books, 1968), xviii, 301pp. Twen-
        ty-four brief essays by specialists grouped under
        Folklore as a Field for Study, Areas of Focus,
        and Folklore and Modern Times. Sponsored by
        the Voice of America.

299. _____. "The State of Folklore and the State of

Ohio," MF (Spr, 1953), 3: 19-27. Coffin laments general lack of interest in the subject.

300. Cohen, Anne and Norm Cohen. "A Word on Hypotheses," JAF (Apr-Je, 1974), 87: 156-160. Proposed modifications or corrections of Kenneth Ketner's discussion.

301. Crocker, W. Jack. "Collecting Folklore, a Brief Guide," MFR (1967), 1: 5-14. Instructions and bibliography.

302. Custred, Glynn and Robert Blankmann. "Folklore in Anthropological Research," FF (Jan, Mr, 1969), 2: 2-18, 32-53. Lengthy discussion of methodology for analyzing folklore and the suggestion that this might aid anthropological research.

303. Darnell, Regna. "American Anthropology and the Development of Folklore Scholarship, 1890-1920," JFI (Je-Aug, 1973), 10: 23-39. The role of Franz Boas is emphasized.

304. Davidson, H. R. Ellis. "Folklore and History," Folklore (S, 1974), 85: 73-92. Presidential address to the English Folklore Society (1974).

305. Davidson, Levette J. "The Teaching of Folklore," WF (Jl, 1955), 14: 188-195.

306. Dégh, Linda. "Approaches to Folklore Research among Immigrant Groups," JAF (Oct-Dec, 1966), 79: 551-556. Experiences in collecting among Hungarians in northern Indiana.

307. _____ and Andrew Vázsonyi. "The Memorate and the Proto-Memorate," JAF (Jl-Sept, 1974), 87: 225-239. Close analysis of terms suggested originally by Carl Von Sydow. The suggestion of the "proto-memorate" doesn't seem very helpful.

308. Dorson, Richard M. American Folklore and the Historian (Chicago and London: U. of Chicago P., 1971), xii, 239pp. Twelve reprinted essays. Dorson contends broadly that the folklorist must know folklore, American civilization, and anthropology.

309. _____. "The American Folklore Scene, 1963,"
Folklore (A, 1963), 74: 433-39. Address to English Folklore Society surveying American folklore
and concentrating on popular interest, history of
American Folklore Society, and university support
of folklore activities and courses (Indiana U. given
as example).

310. _____. "Current Folklore Theories," CA (Febru-
ary, 1963), 4: 93-112. Excellent article sum-
marizing folklore research in various national
areas including U. S. Lists scholars, evaluates
methods and approaches.

311. _____. "The Debate Over the Trustworthiness of
Oral Traditional History," in Volksüberlieferung,
eds. Fritz Harkort et al., pp. 19-35. Careful account of opponents and supporters of validity of
oral history for establishing factual past. Dorson
takes no clear position but finds merit in both ar-
guments.

312. _____. "Five Directions in American Folklore,"
MF (F, 1951), 1: 149-65. Folklore in relation to
literature, history, folk music, and education.

313. _____. "Folklore and Cultural History," in Research Opportunities in American Cultural History,
ed. J. F. McDermott (Lexington: U. of Kentucky
P., 1961), pp. 124-39. A plea for a more serious
study of American folklore, field collections, the
folk museum, and printed and manuscript sources.

314. _____. "Folklore and Fake Lore," AM (Mr, 1950),
70: 335-43. Dorson's famous attack on spurious
folklore which shows no signs of oral vitality.
Chief villains are B. A. Botkin and James Stevens.

315. _____. "Folklore in Higher Education," NYFQ
(Spr, 1962), 18: 44-57. The need to make folk-
lore into a respected academic discipline. Indiana
U. becomes the paradigm.

316. _____. "Folklore in Relation to American Studies,"
in Frontiers of American Culture, ed. Ray B.
Brown et al, (Lafayette: Purdue U. Studies, 1968),
pp. 180-193. Comments on folk, popular, mass,
and elite culture.

317. _____. "Folklore Studies in the United States To-
      day," Folklore (Sept, 1951), 62: 353-66. History
      of folklore studies reviewed, with comments on
      JAF, scholars, meetings, methods, and populariza-
      tion (Botkin.). Scholars must be aware of role of
      frontier, immigration, the press, and regionalism.

318. _____. "Is Folklore a Discipline?" Folklore (A,
      1973), 84: 177-205. Plausible and convincing at-
      tempt to defend folklore as a genuine discipline on
      practical and intellectual lines. Evidence from
      history and the author's personal experiences.

319. _____. "The Oral Historian and the Folklorist,"
      in Selections from the Fifth and Sixth National Col-
      loquia on Oral History, ed. Peter D. Olch and
      Forrest C. Pogue, pp. 40-49. Oral history should
      not be confined to elitist history.

320. _____. "Oral Tradition and Written History: the
      Case for the United States," JFI (1964), 1: 220-
      238.

321. _____. "A Southern Indiana Field Station," MF (F,
      1961), 11: 133-138. Suggestions about collecting
      technique.

322. _____. "Techniques of the Folklorist," LFM (Aug,
      1968), 2: 1-23. Discussion of the methods avail-
      able (fieldwork, print, archives) and the utility of
      other disciplines.

323. _____. "A Theory for American Folklore," JAF
      (Jl-Sept, 1959), 72: 197-215. Controversial paper
      delivered at 1957 meeting of American Folklore
      Society and followed by prepared discussion and
      comments from the floor (pp. 216-42).

324. _____. "A Theory for American Folklore Re-
      viewed," JAF (Jl-Sept, 1969), 82: 226-44. Refu-
      tation of some criticism and some revision sug-
      gested.

325. Drake, Carlos C. "Jungian Psychology and Its Uses
      in Folklore," JAF (Apr.Je, 1969), 82: 122-31.
      Analytical psychology can be of great value to
      folklorists. The Grimms' "Valiant Little Tailor"
      used as a cardinal example.

326. Driver, Harold E. "A Method of Investigating Individu-
      al Differences in Folklorist Beliefs and Practices,"
      MF (S, 1951), 1: 99-105. Tabulation of responses
      to a questionnaire on superstitions.

327. Dundes, Alan. "The Devolutionary Premise in Folk-
      lore Theory," JFI (Je, 1969), 6: 5-19.

328. _____. "Folk Ideas as Units of World View," JAF
      (Jan-Mr, 1971), 84: 93-103. Dundes suggests
      still another term--folk ideas--for the concept of
      traditional notions.

329. _____. "Folklore as a Mirror of Culture," EE
      (Apr, 1969), 46: 471-482. Folklore defined as
      "autobiographical ethnography" and topics such as
      symbolism, sibling rivalry, and three as a ritual
      number discussed.

330. _____. "North American Indian Folklore Studies,"
      JSA (1967), 56: 53-79. Survey of North American
      Indian folklore plus an extensive bibliography.

331. _____. "On Computers and Folk Tales," WF (Jl,
      1965), 24: 185-189. Computers could help folk-
      tale research but a rigorous methodology will be
      needed.

332. _____. "On the Psychology of Collecting Folklore,"
      TFSB (Sept, 1962), 28: 65-74. Collectors, clas-
      sifiers, archivists, and publishers of folklore
      classified in Freudian terms.

333. _____. "The Study of Folklore in Literature and
      Culture: Identification and Interpretation," JAF
      (Apr-Je, 1965), 78: 136-142. Same methodology
      can be used to study Joyce's Ulysses and a Pota-
      wotomi folk tale.

334. _____. "Texture, Text, and Context," SFQ (Dec,
      1964), 28: 251-265. The genres of folklore need
      closer definition to be valid but definition must
      include texture (rhyme, stress, pitch, etc.), text,
      and context.

335. _____. "Thinking Ahead: a Folkloristic Reflection
      of the Future Orientation in American Worldview,"

AnthQ (Apr, 1969), 2: 53-72. The tendency of
Americans to think or plan ahead appears in
proverbs, folk speech, advertising, rituals.

336. _____. "Ways of Studying Folklore," in Our Living
Traditions, ed. T. P. Coffin, pp. 37-46. Various
methods briefly defined and illustrated.

337. Fenton, Alexander. "An Approach to Folklife Studies,"
KFQ (Spr, 1967), 12: 5-21.

338. Filler, Louis. "Why Historians Neglect Folklore,"
MF (S, 1954), 4: 5-12.

339. Fishwick, Marshall. "Folklore, Fakelore, and Pop-
lore," SRL (Aug. 26, 1967), 50: 20-31, 43-44.
Lively discussion of three levels of material with
many examples.

340. Foster, George M. "What is Folk Culture?" AA
(Apr-Je, 1953), 55: 159-173.

341. Foster, John Wilson. "A Descriptive Nomenclature
for the Study of Folklore, Part II: the Evolution-
ary Model," WF (Apr, 1969), 28: 101-111. Bi-
ology can provide vocabulary and methodology for
folklorists.

342. _____. "The Plight of Current Folklore Theory,"
SFQ (Sept, 1968), 32: 237-248. Discussion of the
difficulty of defining theoretical concepts in folklore; the biological sciences might suggest parallels.

343. Freeman, Douglas Southall. "The Tonic of Southern
Folklore," ASch (Spr, 1950), 19: 187-193. Brief
account of influence of folklore on southern cultures and oratory. Elemental human qualities defined by folklore are strength and cunning.

344. Gilbert, Helen. "Folklore Studies, a Curriculum Proposal," FF (Jl, 1973), 6: 165-167. An under-
graduate program submitted to College of St. Bene-
dict, St. Joseph, Minn.

345. Gillespie, Angus K. "Teaching Folklore in the Secondary School: the Institutional Setting," JOFS

(Aug, 1973), 2: 17-25. Experiences in a private
school.

346. Glassie, Henry. "A Folkloristic Thought on the
Promise of Oral History," in Selections from the
Fifth and Sixth National Colloquia on Oral History,
ed. P. D. Olch and F. C. Pogue, pp. 54-57.
Oral traditions and history of common people need
attention.

347. _____. "Structure and Function, Folklore and the
Artifact," Semiotica (1973), 4: 313-351.

348. Goldstein, Kenneth S. "Bowdlerization and Expurga-
tion: Academic and Folk," JAF (Oct-Dec, 1967),
80: 374-386. Practice of singers in performance
where sexual folklore is involved.

349. _____. "The Collecting of Superstitious Beliefs,"
KFQ (Spr, 1964), 9: 13-22. Technical suggestions
about the collecting of such material.

350. _____. "Experimental Folklore: Laboratory vs.
Field," in Folklore International, ed. D. K. Wilgus, pp. 71-82.

351. _____. "On the Application of the Concepts of
Active and Inactive Traditions to the Study of Repertory," JAF (Jan-Mr, 1971), 84: 62-67. An extension of Carl Von Sydow's distinction between active
and passive bearers of tradition.

352. González, Rosalinda. "Work and Play on a Border
Ranch," in The Golden Log, ed. Mody C. Boatright et al., pp. 141-155. Miscellaneous collection of beliefs, customs, games, riddles from
Texas-Mexican populace.

353. Goodwyn, Frank. "A Proposed Terminology for
Clarifying the Relationship Between Folklore and
Literature," SFQ (Sept, 1950), 14: 143-149.
Chiefly concerned with useful definitions. Folk
literature is distinguished from folkloristic litera-
ture. Not too viable a distinction.

354. Gray, Bennison. "Repetition in Oral Literature,"
JAF (Jl-Sept, 1971), 84: 289-303. Perceptive

discussion of repetition in balladry, tales, and Am.
Negro sermons.

355. Halpert, Herbert. "Folklore and Obscenity: Definitions and Prejudices, " JAF (Jl-Sept, 1962), 75:
190-194. A plea for frankness in publishing.

356. _____. "Folklore: Breadth versus Depth, " JAF
(Apr-Je, 1958), 71: 96-103. Suggestions from
personal experience about collecting and archival
technique.

357. _____. "Some Undeveloped Areas in American
Folklore, " JAF (Oct-Dec, 1957), 70: 299-305. A
plea to go beyond tales, ballads, and superstitions.

357. Hand, Wayland D. "American Folklore After Seventy
Years: Survey and Prospect, " JAF (Jan-Mr, 1960),
73: 1-11. Hand's presidential address to the Am.
Folklore Soc. in 1958.

359. _____. "Folklore Societies and the Research Effort, " KFQ (F, 1969), 14: 97-104.

360. Hardman, Kay. "An Experiential Approach to Folklore Studies for Teachers, " FF (Jl, 1974), 7: 192-
197. Practical teaching methods used in a California classroom.

361. _____. "They Taught Folklore, " NYFQ (Dec, 1974),
30: 295-298.

362. Haring, Lee. "Folklore in Colleges: a College
Course in the Ballad, or What to Do with 'Little
Matty Groves,'" NYFQ (Dec, 1967), 23: 298-304.
Suggestions about making ballad study more attrac-
tive to the student.

363. Harris, Jesse W. "Illinois Folklore, Past and
Present, " MF (F, 1954), 4: 134-138. Brief survey of professional activities, collecting and teaching.

364. Hatcher, Mildred. "The Influences of Geography on
North American Folklore, " TFSB (Je, 1953), 19:
40-42. Trivial treatment of a big subject.

46 American Folklore

365. Henderson, Lois Taylor and Lew Girdler. "Folklore in the Junior High School," JOFS (W, 1967), 2: 180-190. Enthusiastic support for teaching folklore at this level.

366. Honko, Lauri. "Memorates and the Study of Folk Beliefs," JFI (1964), 1: 5-19. Discussion of a traditional genre, the memorate.

367. Hudson, Charles. "Folk History and Ethnohistory," Ethnohistory (W-Spr, 1966), 13: 52-70. Discussion of both terms; comments on methods employed and future research.

368. Hufford, David J. "Psychology, Psychoanalysis, and Folklore," SFQ (Sept, 1974), 38: 187-197. A plea for increasing interdisciplinary work by the folklorist, particularly in developing his reliance on psychology and psychological laboratories.

369. Hymes, Dell. "The Contribution of Folklore to Sociolinguistic Research," JAF (Jan-Mr, 1971), 84: 42-50. Folklore has value for those who work in linguistics.

370. Ives, Edward D. "A Manual for Field Workers," NEF (1974), 15: 1-76. Instructions for collecting folklore.

371. Ivey, William. "The Folklorist as Oral Historian," in Selections from the Fifth and Sixth National Colloquia on Oral History, ed. P. D. Olch and F. C. Pogue, pp. 50-53. Oral history in folk communities should complement written historical literature.

372. Jacobs, Melville. "A Look Ahead in Oral Literature Research," JAF (Jl-Sept, 1966), 79: 413-427. Jacobs contends that scholars must go beyond collecting and archiving.

373. _____. "Our Knowledge of Pacific Northwest Indian Folklore," NWF (Nov, 1967), 2: ii, 14-21. Survey of work done by Boas, Skeels, Jacobs, etc., with suggestions of what should still be done.

374. Jansen, William Hugh. "The Esoteric-Exoteric Factor

in Folklore," Fabula (1959), 2: iii, 205-211.
Isolation, special knowledge or training, and the
admirable or awesome nature of the group produce
esoteric or exoteric qualities.

375. _____. "From Field to Library," Folklore (Sept,
1952), 63: 152-157. Misconceptions of folklore:
the folk artist, folk aesthetics, lack of frame of
reference. Jansen urges collecting of local legends,
anecdotes, Jack tales, Schwänke.

376. Jones, Louis C. "Folk Culture and the Historical
Society," MinnH (Mr, 1950), 31: 11-17.

377. _____. "Three Eyes on the Past," NYFQ (Spr/S,
1956), 12: 3-13, 143-149. Suggested methodology
for collecting local history and folklore.

378. Jones, Michael Owen. "The Concept of 'Aesthetic' in
the Traditional Arts," WF (Apr, 1971), 30: 77-104.
Pretentious and prolix discussion of folk aesthetics.

379. Jordan, Philip D. "The Folklorist as Social Historian," WF (Jl, 1953), 12: 194-201. An argument
for interrelationship of folklorist and historian;
many examples.

380. _____. "History and Folklore," MHR (Jan, 1950),
44: 119-129. Folklore enriches history, makes
the past immediate and personal, and adds color
and life to chronicles.

381. _____. "Research Possibilities in Folklore," SFQ
(Sept, 1954), 18: 157-164. Folklorists must collect, preserve, and interpret. But why can't they
also popularize? Historians do.

382. Ketner, Kenneth L. "The Role of Hypotheses in Folkloristics," JAF (Apr-Je, 1973), 86: 114-30. A
laborious discussion stimulated by Goldstein's A
Guide for Field Workers in Folklore.

383. Köngäs, Elli Kaija and Pierre Maranda. "Structural
Models in Folklore," MF (F, 1962), 12: 133-92.
An elaborate theoretical article which reviews
previous definitions and formulas, suggests differences, and becomes virtually unreadable.

384. Larson, Mildred H. "The Fascination of Folklore, "
      NYFQ (F, 1956), 12: 177-81. Folklore in the
      classroom.

385. Leach, MacEdward. "Folk Lore Collection, " KFQ
      (Spr, 1962), 7, i: 3-6. Succinct account for the
      neophyte of how and what to collect. Books cited.

386. _____. "Problems of Collecting Oral Literature, "
      PMLA (Je, 1962), 77: 335-40. Collectors of oral
      literature must provide material about cultural
      background and life of informants; they must also
      know something about folk aesthetics.

387. _____. "What Shall We Do With 'Little Matty
      Groves', " JAF (Jl-Sept, 1963), 76: 189-94. A
      plea for folklorists to aim at a larger audience
      than their technical studies would attract.

388. Legman, Gershon. "Misconceptions in Erotic Folk-
      lore, " JAF (Jl-Sept, 1962), 75: 200-208. Erotic
      folklore is not always humorous, nor does it differ
      substantially from other kinds of folklore. Diffi-
      culty of publishing erotic folklore discussed.

389. _____. "Who Owns Folklore?" WF (Jan, 1962),
      21: 1-12. Folklore collectors do not always have
      the right to publish their materials. Copyrighting
      of folklore materials should be carefully consid-
      ered.

390. Lopatin, Ivan A. "The Role of Folklore in Teaching
      Language and Literature, " MLJ (Nov, 1951), 35:
      543-548. A plea for the use of folklore, especial-
      ly Slavic folklore, in the teaching of Russian.

391. McDavid, Raven I., Jr. "Linguistic Geography and
      the Study of Folklore, " NYFQ (F, 1968), 14: 242-
      262. Stresses links between linguistics, dialects,
      and folklore.

392. Manning, Ambrose. "Collecting Folklore: One Pro-
      cedure, " TFSB (Dec, 1969), 4: 117-123.

393. Maranda, Elli Kaija Köngäs. "The Concept of Folk-
      lore, " MF (S, 1963), 13: 69-88. Survey of defini-
      tions of folklore, which as a concept preceded 1846.

394. Maranda, Pierre and Elli Köngäs Maranda. Structural
Analysis of Oral Tradition (Philadelphia: U. of
Pennsylvania P., 1971), xxxiv, 324pp. Eleven papers dealing with structural analysis and various
kinds of folklore (ritual, myth, riddle, etc.); the
editors provide a lengthy introduction.

395. Miller, E. Joan Wilson. "The Ozark Culture Region
as Revealed by Traditional Materials," Annals of
Association of American Geographers (Mr, 1968),
58: 51-77. Regional study based on analysis of
four books of folktales collected by Vance Randolph.

396. Montell, William Lynwood. "The Oral Historian as
Folklorist," in Selections from the Fifth and Sixth
National Colloquia on Oral History, ed. P. D.
Olch and F. C. Pogue, pp. 40-49. Oral history
should not be confined to elitist history.

397. Nicolaisen, W. F. H. "Folklore and Geography:
Towards an Atlas of American Folk Culture,"
NYFQ (Mr, 1973), 29: 3-20. Geographers and
folklorists are equally concerned about place, time,
and causative factors; a folklore atlas is desirable.

398. Oring, Elliott and James Durham. Perspectives on
Folklore and Education (Bloomington: FF Pubs.,
1969), 53pp. Essays on the teaching of folklore.

399. Paredes, Américo. "Concepts about Folklore in Latin
America and the United States," JFI (Je, 1969), 6:
20-38. Folklore theories differ between the two
areas, especially in the use of terms like "peasant"
and "primitive."

400. _____. "El folklore en los Estados Unidos durante
la última década (1953-1962)," Folklore americano
órgano del Comité interamericano de folklore
(Lima, 1962), 10: 256-262. Review of a decade of
folklore work in the U. S.

401. Pendleton, Charles S. "Folklore as a Foundation in
Public School Education," TFSB (Mr, 1950), 16:
1-6.

402. Pilant, Elizabeth. "American Folklore for Remedial
Reading," EJ (Apr, 1951), 40: 227-228.

403.   Pound, Louise. "The Scholarly Study of Folklore,"
       WF (Apr, 1952), 11: 100-108. Brief factual sur-
       vey of folklore scholarship with some attention to
       the U. S. and especially Nebraska.

404.   Reaver, J. Russell. "Teaching Folklore to College
       Students," SFQ (Dec, 1960), 24: 242-47. Com-
       ments on folklore courses and publications avail-
       able. An open future predicted.

405.   Redfield, Margaret. "The Expressive Utterance, Folk
       and Popular," JAF (Oct-Dec, 1956), 69: 357-62.
       Folklore can be distinguished from modern popular
       expressive utterances because it has a quality of
       genuine art.

406.   Reusch, Kathy. "Folklore for Children: Study Units
       for Fifth and Sixth Grades," JOFS (Aug, 1973), 2:
       32-42. Experiences in teaching in an elementary
       school.

407.   Reuss, Richard A. "On Folklore and Women Folk-
       lorists," FFemC (Spr, 1974), no. 3, 29-37. In-
       teresting statistical account of contributions of
       women to professional folklore study. Special at-
       tention paid Fletcher, Pound, and Benedict.

408.   Riedl, Norbert F. "Folklore and the Study of Ma-
       terial Aspects of Folk Culture," JAF (Oct-Dec,
       1966), 79: 557-63. Comparison of American folk-
       lorists and European students of Volkskunde with
       the suggestion that more attention be given in the
       U. S. to material culture.

409.   _____. "Folklore vs. 'Volkskunde'," TFSB (Je,
       1965), 31: 47-53. A plea for anthropologists to
       pay more attention to American folk culture.

410.   Roach, Bruce B. "Abuse and Disabuse: Structural
       Folklore and the College Classroom," JOFS (Aug,
       1973), 2: 4-15. Personal experiences in teaching
       college students.

411.   Robe, Stanley R. "Contemporary Trends in Folklore
       Research," LARR (1967), 2: 26-54. Emphasis on
       Latin American folklore.

412. Rysan, Josef. "Is Our Civilization Creating a New
      Folklore?" SFQ (Je, 1952), 16: 79-91. Ancient
      folklore was natural and religious (superstitions,
      beliefs, demonism, witchcraft); modern folklore is
      social and political (totalitarian nations, the Nazi
      Volk, the Aryan super-race, munition magnates,
      the capitalists).

413. _____. "The Science of Folklore and Modern So-
      ciety," TFSB (Dec, 1955), 21: 93-98. The study
      of folklore should not be limited to primitive soci-
      eties but should relate to modern myths.

414. Sackett, S. J. "Poetry and Folklore: Some Points of
      Affinity," JAF (Apr-Je, 1964), 77: 143-153.

415. _____. "Using a Computer on a Belief Collection,"
      WF (Apr, 1970), 29: 105-110. Suggested use of
      computer with a Kansas collection of beliefs and
      superstitions.

416. Schwarz, Jeanne M. "Folklore in the Schools,"
      NYFQ (S, 1956), 12: 83-86. Use of folklore in
      elementary schools discussed.

417. Scott, John Anthony. "Folklore and Folksong in Edu-
      cation," NYFQ (W, 1962), 18: 294-302. A plea
      for the use of folksongs in elementary education.

418. Seager, Robert II. "American Folklore and History:
      Observations on Potential Integration," MF (W,
      1951), 1: 213-222.

419. Seeger, Charles. "Who Owns Folklore?--a Rejoind-
      er," WF (Apr, 1962), 21: 93-101. Reply to arti-
      cle by G. Legman. Seeger contends folksong is
      impossible to copyright.

420. Smith, Robert Jerome. "The Concept of Equivalence:
      a Polemical Analysis," JAF (Oct-Dec, 1969), 82:
      329-341. Analysis of methodology in folklore and
      anthropology.

421. _____. "The Structure of Esthetic Response,"
      JAF (Jan-Mr, 1971), 84: 68-79. Discussion of
      distinctions and interrelationships between folklore
      genres. Illustrations taken mostly from folk tales.

422. Snortum, Niel K. "Ballads and the Teacher," SFQ
      (Sept, 1959), 23: 184-189.

423. Strong, Leah A. "American Folklore for the Under-
      graduate," NCarF (Nov, 1971), 19: 194-200.
      American folklore can easily fit into an American
      Studies course.

424. Studer, Norman. "The Place of Folklore in Educa-
      tion," NYFQ (Spr, 1962), 18: 3-12. Folklore can
      assist children in appreciating cultural awareness
      and other peoples.

425. Sutton-Smith, Brian. "The Expressive Profile," JAF
      (Jan-Mr, 1971), 84: 80-92. A folklorist-psycholo-
      gist should deal with games, rhymes, dreams, and
      tales.

426. _____. "Psychology of Childlore: the Triviality
      Barrier," WF (Jan, 1970), 29: 1-8. Childlore
      should not be neglected because it is deemed trivi-
      al.

427. Tallman, Richard S. "Folklore in the Schools: Teach-
      ing, Collecting, and Publishing," NYFQ (Sept,
      1972), 28: 163-86. Experiences in teaching folk-
      lore to high school classes in Nova Scotia.

428. Taylor, Archer. "The Place of Folklore," PMLA
      (Feb, 1952), 67: i, 59-66. Presidential address.

429. _____ and Wayland D. Hand. "Twenty-five Years
      of Folklore Study in the West," WF (Oct, 1966),
      25: 229-45. Survey of regional folklore societies.

430. Thill, Richard S. "'A Rose by any Other Name':
      Computers, Traditions, and the Folklorist," TFSB
      (Mr, 1974), 40: 1-8. There are computer jokes
      but computers can also aid the folklore researcher.

431. Thompson, Stith. "Advances in Folklore Studies," in
      Anthropology Today, ed. A. L. Kroeber (Chicago:
      U. of Chicago P., 1953), pp. 587-96. Survey of
      current folklore research.

432. _____. "The Challenge of Folklore," PMLA (Sept,
      1964), 79: 357-65. Survey of trends in folklore

scholarship with a plea for better trained folklore
scholars to do comparative analysis.

433.   _____. "Folklore at Midcentury," MF (Apr, 1951),
        1: 5-12. A survey.

434.   _____, ed. Four Symposia on Folklore (Blooming-
        ton, Folklore Series, no. 8; Bloomington: Indiana
        U. P., 1953), xi, 340pp. Concerned with the
        collecting, archiving, studying, and making avail-
        able of folklore material.

435.   Thoresen, Timothy H. H. "Folkloristics in A. L.
        Kroeber's Early Theory of Culture," JFI (Je-Aug,
        1973), 10: 41-55. An exposition of the California
        anthropologist's early theories about folklore.

436.   Toelken, J. Barre. "A Descriptive Nomenclature for
        the Study of Folklore: Part I: the Process of
        Tradition," WF (Apr, 1969), 28: 91-100. More
        technical and descriptive terminology is needed.
        See article by J. W. Foster above.

437.   _____. "A Prospectus for Folklore Research in
        the Northwest," NWF (1967), 2: 28-32. Peculiari-
        ties of and opportunities for research in the region.

438.   Trindell, Roger T. "American Folklore Studies and
        Geography," SFQ (Mr, 1970), 34: 1-11. A close
        relationship exists between folklore and aspects of
        geography.

439.   Utley, Francis Lee. "The Academic Status of Folk-
        lore in the United States," JFI (Aug-Dec, 1970),
        7: 110-115.

440.   _____. "Anthropology and Folklore's Second Cen-
        tury," HF (1950), 9: 69-78.

441.   _____. "Conflict and Promise in Folklore," JAF
        (Apr-Je, 1952), 65: 111-119. Survey of four con-
        flicting factors in the study of folklore.

442.   _____. "The Study of Folk Literature: Its Scope
        and Use," JAF (Apr-Je, 1958), 71: 139-148.
        Helpful survey, stressing definition, scope, col-
        lecting, classification, and history.

443. _____ . "Three Kinds of Honesty," JAF (Jl-Sept, 1953), 66: 189-199. Discussion of artistic, scholarly, and intellectual honesty.

444. Voegelin, C. F. "A Modern Method for Field Work Treatment of Previously Collected Texts," JAF (Jan-Mr, 1954), 67: 15-20. Injecting junctures into old texts produces different results.

445. Walter, Marie. "The Fable of the Folklorist," MF (Spr, 1960), 10: 33-39. The image of the folklorist in the popular press is changing.

446. Webb, James. "Collecting Regional Materials in Mississippi," MFR (1967), 1: 63-70. Mostly personal experience.

447. Wilson, William A. "Folklore and History: Fact Amid the Legends," UHQ (W, 1973), 41: 40-58.

448. Winkelman, Donald M. "Folklore in a Small College," KFR (Jan-Mr, 1961), 7: 17-22. Teaching folklore at Cottey College, Missouri.

449. _____ and Ray B. Browne. "Folklore Studies in Universities," Sing Out! (Sept, 1964), 14, iv, 47-49. Tabulation of folklore courses.

450. Zemljanova, L. "The Struggle Between the Reactionary and the Progressive Forces in Contemporary American Folkloristics," JFI (1964), 1-2: 13-144. Translation of a Russian essay dividing American folklorists into bourgeois reactionaries and progressives. A partisan account.

5. GENERAL FOLKLORE

451. Abernethy, Francis Edward. J. Frank Dobie (Austin: Steck-Vaughn Co., 1967), 47pp. Short biographical sketch and selected bibliography. Stress on Dobie as a folklorist.

452. Abrahams, Roger D. "The Negro Stereotype: Negro Folklore and the Riots," JAF (Apr-Je, 1970), 83: 229-49.

453. _____. "On Meaning and Gaming," JAF (Jl-Sept, 1969), 82: 268-272. A note.

454. _____. "A Performance-Centred Approach to Gossip," Man (Je, 1970), 5: 290-301. The role of gossip as communication, entertainment, and irony, with evidence from the island of St. Vincent, British West Indies.

455. _____. "Personal Power and Social Restraint in the Definition of Folklore," JAF (Jan-Mr, 1971), 84: 16-30. Folklore can effect both continuity and change.

456. _____. Positively Black (Englewood Cliffs, N.J.: Prentice-Hall, 1970), xi, 177pp. More concerned with black culture than with black folklore though interesting in its discussion of two types: the preacher and the street-man.

457. Ainsworth, Catherine Harris. "Hallowe'en," NYFQ (Sept, 1973), 29: 163-93. Trivial survey of Hallowe'en practices and beliefs with some 24 statements from teenagers.

458. Allen, John W. Legends and Lore of Southern Illinois (Carbondale: Southern Illinois U.P., 1963), 404pp.

Miscellaneous history and anecdotes (Chapter 3
concerns folklore).

459. Anderson, Henry E. "The Folklore of Draft Re-
      sistance," NYFQ (Je, 1972), 28: 135-50. Mem-
      orates collected in California from young men de-
      termined to evade the draft.

460. Anderson, John Q. "And Horns on the Toads," in
      And Horns on the Toads, ed. Mody C. Boatright
      et al., pp. 69-87. Facts and delusions about the
      Texas horned toad, which is actually a kind of
      lizard.

461. Astrov, Margot. "The Concept of Motion as the Psy-
      chological Leitmotif of Navaho Life and Litera-
      ture," JAF (Jan-Mr, 1950), 63: 45-56. Motion is
      the keynote in Navaho linguistics, literature, cere-
      monialism, and social behavior.

462. _____. "The Indian and the Word," NMFR (1951-
      52), 6: 7-10. Indian chants, poetry, words are
      equal to the Kalevala, Gilgamesh, or Mabinogion.
      Indians do not use rhyme but make much use of
      repetition, parallelism, balance, and rhythm.

463. Auser, Cortland P. "The Viable Community: Re-
      directions Through Applied Folklore," NYFQ (Mr,
      1970), 26: 3-13. Personal experiences in a small
      township suggest ways in which folk life and folk
      materials can be used.

464. Bachrach, Arthur J. "An Experimental Approach to
      Superstitious Behavior," JAF (Jan-Mr, 1962), 75:
      1-9.

465. Badger, Andrew. "Rural Salesmanship: Some Glean-
      ings from Thigpen's Store News," MSF (Spr, 1974),
      2: 19-26. Ads and announcements from a promo-
      tional flier.

466. Bailey, Wilfrid C. "Folklore Aspects in Mormon Cul-
      ture," WF (Jl, 1951), 10: 217-25. Brief survey
      of books, songs, and tales prominent in Mormon
      folklore.

467. Bancroft, Caroline. "Folklore versus History," CF
      (1954), 2: 7-12.

468. Bartlett, Steve. "Social Interaction Patterns of
       Adolescents in a Folklore Performance," FF (May-
       Jl, 1971), 4: 39-67. Songs, jokes, and stories of
       five adolescent boys from Austin, Texas.

469. Bascom, William. "Folklore," in International Ency-
       clopedia of Social Sciences, ed. David L. Sills
       (New York: Macmillan and the Free Press, 1968),
       V, pp. 496-500.

470. _____. "Folklore and the Africanist," JAF (Jl-
       Sept, 1973), 86: 253-259.

471. Bayard, Samuel P. "The Materials of Folklore,"
       JAF (Jan-Mr, 1953), 66: 1-17.

472. Beck, Horace P. Folklore and the Sea (Middletown,
       Conn.: Wesleyan U.P., 1973), xvii, 463pp. Ex-
       tensive collection of marine folklore including su-
       perstitions, songs, names, legends, language.
       Much of the material is coastal, and the texts are
       sometimes edited or paraphrased.

473. _____. "Folklore in Rhode Island," NEF (F, 1959),
       2: 33-40. Rhode Island folklore seems sparse and
       has been neglected.

474. _____. "Say Something Dirty!" JAF (Jl-Sept, 1962),
       75: 195-99. Obscene and erotic material should
       be collected although it may not be the folklorist's
       immediate goal.

475. _____. "Sea Lore," NWF (Nov, 1967), 2: ii, 1-
       13. General sampling of East Coast lore.

476. _____. "Where the Workers of the World Unite:
       the American Occupations," in Our Living Tradi-
       tions, ed. T. P. Coffin, pp. 58-69. Brief com-
       ments on occupational categories: lumbering, sea-
       faring, farming, mining, etc.

477. Bedichek, Roy. "Animal Tails: Function and Folk-
       lore," in Mesquite and Willow, ed. Mody C. Boat-
       right et al., pp. 105-12. Folklore about rats,
       civet cats, foxes, etc.

478. _____. "Folklore in Natural History," in Folk

Travelers, ed. Mody C. Boatright et al., pp. 18-
39. Truth and lore about such natural creatures
as bat and opossum.

479. Benner, Dorothea O. "Neighbors: The D. and H.
Canal, Pennsylvania and New York," NYFQ (W,
1950), 6: 260-67. Canaler anecdotes and songs.

480. Boatright, Mody C. "Folklore in a Literate Society,"
in Madstones and Twisters, ed. Mody C. Boatright et al., pp. 45-51. Oral and written traditions crossfertilize each other to their mutual benefit.

481. _____. Folklore of the Oil Industry (Dallas:
Southern Methodist U.P., 1963), xii, 220pp.
Tales and balladry of the oil workers.

482. _____, Wilson M. Hudson, and Allen Maxwell, eds.
Texas Folk and Folklore (Dallas: Southern Methodist U.P., 1954), xv, 356pp. Anthology of reprinted items by J. F. Dobie, John Lomax, M. C.
Boatright, William Owens, and others. Chief cri-
terion for selection is readability.

483. Bode, J. Winston. J. Frank Dobie: a Portrait of
Pancho (Austin: Steck-Vaughn, 1968), xi, 156pp.
Biography of Texas professor and folklorist; good
photographs.

484. Bond, Charles. "Unpublished Folklore in the Brown
Collection," NCarF (Feb, 1972), 20: 11-20. In-
ventory of material still unpublished in the unique
Frank C. Brown Collection of North Carolina Folklore: proverbs, rhymes, folk speech, etc.

485. Boswell, George W. "Humor from the Kentucky Hills,"
NCarF (Nov, 1969), 17: 71-76. A miscellany.

486. Botkin, Benjamin A. A Civil War Treasury of Tales,
Legends, and Folklore (New York: Random House,
1960), xx, 625pp. Chronological gathering of Civil
War anecdotes, letters, diaries, memories, and
songs. Mostly historical; little folklore presented
orally.

487. _____. New York City Folklore (New York: Ran-

dom House, 1956), xix, 492pp. Miscellaneous
collection of <u>Manhattan</u> material, mostly from
secondary sources.

488.   _____. <u>A Pocket Treasury of American Folklore</u>
(New York: Pocket Books, 1950), 407pp. Reduced
and rev. ed. with new introduction.

489.   _____. "A Sampler of Western Folklore and
Songs," in <u>The Book of the American West</u>, ed.
Jay Monaghan (New York: Julian Messner, 1963),
pp. 503-560.

490.   _____. <u>Sidewalks of America</u> (Indianapolis: Bobbs-
Merrill, 1954), xxii, 605pp.

491.   _____. <u>A Treasury of American Anecdotes</u> (New
York: Random House, 1957), 321pp. A collection
gleaned from printed sources.

492.   _____. <u>A Treasury of Mississippi River Folklore</u>
(New York: Crown, 1955), xx, 620pp.

493.   _____. <u>A Treasury of Western Folklore</u> (New
York: Crown, 1951), xxvi, 806pp. The usual
voluminous Botkin collection, with journalistic humor, historical and literary material, and occasional bits of true folklore.

494.   _____. "We Called it 'Living Lore'," <u>NYFQ</u> (F,
1958), 14: 189-201. Experiences and conclusions
from work with New York City Writers' Project,
1938.

495.   Botkin, B(enjamin) A. and Alvin Harlow. <u>A Treasury
of Railroad Folklore</u> (New York: Crown, 1953),
xiv, 530pp. More railroad history than folklore
but readable and useful.

496.   _____ and Carl Withers. <u>The Illustrated Book of
American Folklore</u> (New York: Grosset and Dunlap, 1958), 101pp. Popularized collection for
younger readers.

497.   Braddy, Haldeen. <u>Mexico and the Old Southwest</u>
(Port Washington, N.Y. and London: Kennikat
P., 1971), xi, 229pp. Reprinted essays dealing

with people, palaver, and places. Legends included and the lingo of cowboys and smugglers.

498.   Bradley, Jean Ann. "Whistles, Throttles, and
       Trestles: Lore of the D. L. & W. R. R.," NYFQ
       (5, 1955), 11: 97-105. Anecdotes and pranks as-
       sociated with the railroad.

499.   Brewster, Paul G. "Folklore Invades the Comic
       Strips," SFQ (Sept, 1950), 14: 97-102. Schmoo,
       Superman, Tiny Tim, Tillie the Toiler, Katzen-
       jammer Kids, Li'l Abner--all use folklore themes
       and incidents at least occasionally.

500.   Briggs, Harold E. "Folklore of Southern Illinois,"
       SFQ (Dec, 1952), 16: 207-12.

501.   Bright, Verne. "Black Harris, Mountain Man, Teller
       of Tales," OHQ (Mr, 1951), 52: 3-20.

502.   _____. "The Folklore and History of the 'Oregon
       Fever'," OHQ (Dec, 1951), 52: 241-53.

503.   Brooks, Juanita. "Memories of a Mormon Girlhood,"
       JAF (Jl-Sept, 1964), 77: 195-219. Melange of
       personal and anecdotal material with descriptive
       details.

504.   Brown, Marice C. "Notes on Classical and Renais-
       sance Analogues of Mississippi Negro Folklore,"
       MFR (S, 1968), 2: 27-41.

505.   Brunvand, Jan Harold. "Folklore of the Great Basin,"
       NWF (S, 1968), 3: 17-32. Mormon folklore, pri-
       marily from Utah. Customs, anecdotes, songs,
       and legends.

506.   Bunch, John B. "The Legal Considerations of Pri-
       vacy, Property, Copyright, and Unfair Practices
       in the Publication of Folklore Material," FF (Oct,
       1973), 6: 211-216. A legalistic interpretation of
       folklore ownership.

507.   Burns, Thomas A. "Aesthetic Judgment: the Inter-
       pretive Side of the Structure of Performance,"
       KF (S-F, 1974), 19: 61-94. Stress on the per-
       former rather than the performance; example se-
       lected, the professional football game.

508. _____. "Folklore in the Mass Media: Television,"
     FF (Jl, 1969), 2: 90-106.

509. Burrison, John A., ed. "Creativity in Southern Folk-
     lore," SLI (Atlanta: Georgia State U. P., Apr,
     1970), iii, 107pp. Brief articles on a folk sculptor,
     folk singers, and folk storytellers.

510. Burton, Glynn. "Some Folkways of a Lincoln County
     Community," TFSB (Mr, 1955), 21: 3-8. Beliefs,
     signs, and speech from the Camargo community in
     So. Tenn.

511. Burton, Thomas G. and Ambrose N. Manning. A
     Collection of Folklore by Undergraduate Students
     of East Tennessee State University (Johnson
     City, Tenn.: East Tenn. State U. P., 1970),
     v, 129pp. Miscellaneous data without annota-
     tion.

512. Butterfield, Roger. "The Folklore of Politics,"
     PMHB (Apr, 1950), 74: 164-177.

513. Byrd, James W. J. Mason Brewer, Negro Folklorist
     (Austin: Steck-Vaughn Co., 1967), 44pp. Brief
     biographical sketch with samples of his work in
     Negro folklore.

514. Campa, Arthur L. "Folklore and History," WF (Jan,
     1965), 24: 1-5.

515. Carey, George G. "Folklore of the Chesapeake Bay
     Watermen: A Preview," KFQ (F, 1968), 13: 185-
     92.

516. _____. Maryland Folklore and Folklife (Cambridge,
     Md.: Tidewater Pubs., 1970), xii, 98pp. Mis-
     cellaneous collection of ballads, speech, beliefs,
     etc.

517. Charles, Lucille Hoerr. "Drama in War," JAF (Jl-
     Sept, 1955), 68: 253-81. Extensive examination
     of dramatic elements in war between primitive
     peoples. Material includes data from 20 North
     American Indian tribes.

518. Cheney, Thomas E. The Golden Legacy: A Folk

History of J. Golden Kimball (Santa Barbara and
Salt Lake City: Peregrine-Smith, 1974), xii,
155pp. Reprint of a 1973 book now withdrawn.
Mostly anecdotes about a salty Mormon leader.

519. _____. Lore of Faith & Folly (Salt Lake City: U.
of Utah P., 1971), ix, 274pp. Medley of Mormon
folklore and local history.

520. Clark, LaVerne Harrell. They Sang for Horses: the
Impact of the Horse on Navajo and Apache Folklore
(Tucson: U. of Arizona P., 1966), xx, 225pp.

521. Clarke, Kenneth. "The Folk Wisdom of Appalachia,"
TFSB (Mr, 1968), 34: 1-5. An explanation of why
the Appalachian area is so rich in many areas of
folklore.

522. _____. "Folklore of Negro Children in Greater
Louisville Reflecting Attitudes Toward Race," KFR
(Jan-Mr, 1964), 10: 1-11. Collection of rhymes
and sayings confirms value of racial lore in understanding racial attitudes.

523. Coffin, Tristram P. The Book of Christmas Folklore
(New York: Seabury P., 1973), ix, 192pp. A
collection of Yuletide traditions and customs designed for the Christmas trade.

524. _____. "Folklore in the American Twentieth Century," AmQ (W, 1961), 13: 526-33. Most American
folk legends are really propaganda; there is not
much American national folklore. The tall tale is
indigenous but pulp writers have expanded the
Crockett and Fink sagas.

525. _____. The Old Ball Game: Baseball in Folklore
and Fiction (New York: Herder and Herder, 1971),
197pp. Baseball superstitions, anecdotes, and
speech. Good example of collecting the folklore
attached to a sport.

526. _____. Uncertain Glory. Folklore and the American Revolution (Detroit: Folklore Assoc., 1971),
270pp. Uncertain terminology and mixed examples
confuse the story.

527. _____ and Hennig Cohen. Folklore from the Work-
     ing Folk of America (Garden City, N. Y.: Anchor
     Press/Doubleday, 1973), xxxviii, 464pp. Anthology
     of miscellaneous folklore derived from journals and
     archives. In three parts: folk literature, folk life
     and speech, a dozen legendary heroes.

528. Conners, Mary Alice. "The Hook and Eye People of
     Northern New York," NYFQ (Spr, 1961), 17: 63-69.
     Details about the New York Mennonites, whose aver-
     sion to buttons brought them an unusual sobriquet.

529. Cooper, Horton. North Carolina Mountain Folklore
     and Miscellany (Murfreesboro, N.C.: Johnson Pub-
     lishing Co., 1972), 168pp. A potpourri of speech,
     songs, rhymes, riddles, folk medicine, and customs
     collected by a native.

530. Cothran, Kay L. "Magazine Travel Accounts of Piney
     Woods Folklife," TFSB (Sept, 1973), 39: 80-86.
     Accounts of southern crackers in magazines such
     as Harper's, Lippincott's, etc., are useful but
     often present inaccurate pictures of folklife.

531. Curtis, Martha E. "Folklore of Feast and Famine
     Among the Menomini," PMASAL (1954), 39: 407-
     19.

532. Cutting, Edith E. Whistling Girls and Jumping Sheep
     (Cooperstown, N.Y.: Farmers Museum, 1951),
     85pp. Booklet containing miscellaneous farm lore.

533. _____. "York State Farm Lore," NYFQ (Spr,
     1951), 7: 4-77. Extensive survey of New York
     rural lore, both material and verbal. Considerable
     weather and planting lore. Informants named.

534. Davidson, T. W. Stealing Sticks: the Folklore of
     Pioneer East Texas (Marshall, Texas: Port Caddo
     P., 1969), 99pp.

535. Davis, Arthur Kyle, Jr. "Folklore in Virginia: Its
     Collection and Study," UVaNewsletter (Mr 15,
     1963), 39: vii, 25-28. Chiefly a resumé of the
     history of the Virginia Folklore Society, founded
     1913.

536. De Caro, Rosann Jordan. "Language Loyalty and
      Folklore Studies: The Mexican-American," WF
      (Apr, 1972), 31: 77-86. Discussion of bilingualism
      in Fort Worth and its reflection of cultural alliances.

537. Denby, Priscilla. "Folklore in the Mass Media," FF
      (Sept, 1971), 4: 113-25. Discussion of the influ-
      ence of various media on folklore. Bibliography
      provided.

538. Denisoff, R. Serge. "The Proletarian Renascence:
      The Folkness of the Ideological Folk," JAF (Jan-
      Mr, 1969), 82: 51-65. Cluttered discussion of the
      relationship of folk song to leftist workers and ur-
      ban singers.

539. DeTurk, David A. and A. Poulin, Jr., eds. The
      American Folk Scene: Dimensions of the Folksong
      Revival (New York: Dell, 1967), 334pp. Anthology
      of widely uneven pieces touching on music, ideology,
      and singing groups.

540. Dorson, Richard M. American Folklore (Chicago: U.
      of Chicago P., 1959), ix, 328pp. Folk cultures
      of special groups (Pennsylvania Dutch, Ozarks,
      New Mexico Spanish-Americans, Mormons, Maine
      Yankees, Negroes). Stress on tales and beliefs,
      immigrants, urban folklore; Indians and balladry
      excluded.

541. _____. "American Folklorists in Britain," JFI
      (Aug-Dec, 1970), 7: 187-219. Emphasis on the
      work of Jeremiah Curtin and Charles G. Leland.

542. _____. Buying the Wind (Chicago: U. of Chicago
      P., 1964), xvii, 574pp. Extensive collection of
      oral texts divided regionally. Includes tales, songs,
      ballads, proverbs, riddles, folk speech, with a
      pertinent introduction dealing with field collecting.

543. _____. "The Ethnic Research Survey of Northwest
      Indiana," in Kontakte und Grenzen, ed. Hans
      Friedrich Foltin, pp. 65-69. Report of field work
      in Gary, Ind., in 1968.

544. _____. "Ethnohistory and Ethnic Folklore,"
      Ethnohistory (W, 1961), 8: 12-30. Folklore could

help to understand such minorities as Negroes,
Puerto Ricans, Poles, and Italians as well as the
American Indian.

545. _____. "Fakelore," Z für V (1969), 1: 56-64.
Explanation of Dorson's coinage of the term and an
account of the subsequent controversy.

546. _____. "Folklore in Michigan," MJE (Apr 1, 1956),
32: xv, 343, 374-76.

547. _____. "Is There a Folk in the City?" JAF (Apr-
Je, 1970), 83: 185-216. Material collected from
immigrant groups in Gary and East Chicago.

548. _____. "Oral Styles of American Folk Narrators,"
in Style in Language (New York: Wiley, 1960).
Comments on two Negro storytellers, a Maine
lobsterman, and Lincoln. Reprinted in Folklore
in Action, ed. H. P. Beck, pp. 77-100.

549. _____. "Oral Tradition and Written History: the
Case for the United States," JFI (Dec, 1964), 1:
220-34. Oral history can aid the historian.

550. _____. "The Question of Folklore in a New Na-
tion," in Folklore & Society, ed. Bruce Jackson,
pp. 21-33. Folklore is important in emerging na-
tionalism.

551. _____. "Southern Negro Storytellers in Michigan,"
MichH (Je, 1953), 37: 197-204. Description of
field trips in 1952.

552. Dresser, Norine. "'The Boys in the Band is Not
Another Musical': Male Homosexuals and Their
Folklore," WF (Jl, 1974), 33: 205-18. Evidence
from Los Angeles gay bars to prove the existence
of much homosexual folklore.

553. _____. "I Tot Phoclor," NYFQ (Dec, 1974), 30:
299-308. Grade school pupils.

554. Dundes, Alan. "The American Concept of Folklore,"
JFI (Dec, 1966), 3: 226-49. Useful survey of
trends, research, etc., in U.S. with differences
between American and European scholarship clari-
fied.

555.   . Mother Wit from the Laughing Barrel:
              Readings in the Interpretation of Afro-American
              Folklore (Englewood Cliffs: Prentice-Hall, 1973),
              xiv, 673pp. Useful anthology of essays and de-
              scriptions of Negro folklore in the U.S. Extra-
              ordinarily wide range. Bibliography.

556.   . "Robert Lee J. Vance: American Folklore
              Surveyor of the 1890's," WF (Jan, 1964), 23: 27-
              34. Discussion of a virtually forgotten folklorist
              who contributed to magazines like The Open Court.
              Bibliography of his work.

557.   Edmunds, James M. "Our Vanishing Folklore,"
              NYFQ (A, 1957), 13: 224-31. Miscellaneous nine-
              teenth-century lore.

558.   Emrich, Duncan. "America's Folkways," Holiday
              (Jl, 1956), 18: i, 60-61, 63, 112-13, 115. Folk-
              lore defined by examples and tradition emphasized.

559.   . The Folklore of Love and Courtship (New
              York: Am. Heritage P., 1970), 52pp. Designed
              for the gift book market.

560.   . The Folklore of Weddings and Marriage
              (New York: Am. Heritage P., 1970), 51p. Ditto.

561.   . Folklore on the American Land (Boston
              and Toronto: Little, Brown, 1972), xxviii, 707pp.
              Huge potpourri of names, songs, beliefs, tales,
              and rhymes. Designed for the popular market.
              No comparative notes.

562.   Evers, Alf. "Bluestone Lore and Bluestone Men,"
              NYFQ (5, 1962), 18: 86-107. Miscellaneous lore
              about Woodstock, New York.

563.   . "Rattlesnake Lore of the Catskills,"
              NYFQ (S, 1951), 7: 108-15. Tall tales about
              snakes.

564.   Ferris, William R., Jr. "Black and White Folklore
              in Mississippi: A Resumé," MFR (W, 1972), 6:
              121-37. Rapid survey of folklore genres. Photo-
              graphs.

565. _____. "Black Delta Religion," MSF (Spr, 1974),
     2: 27-33. Negro hymns, preaching, and baptismal
     practices.

566. _____. "The Collection of Racial Lore: Ap-
     proaches and Problems," NYFQ (Sept, 1971), 27:
     261-79. A white collector of Negro lore in Mis-
     sissippi.

567. _____. "Prison Lore: A Neglected Tradition,"
     MFR (W, 1961), 5: 114-20. Discussion of poems,
     letters, novels written in penitentiaries.

568. _____. "Railroad Folklore: An Overview,"
     NCarFJ (Nov, 1974), 22: 169-76. "The railroad
     has been probably the single greatest catalyst for
     folklore in American life."

569. _____. "The Rose Hill Service," MFR (S, 1972),
     6: 37-56. A black service in Warren Co., Miss.
     Transcripts of singing, photographs.

570. Fife, Austin E. "Folk Elements in the Formation of
     the Mormon Personality," BYU Studies (A, 1959-
     W, 1960), 1: 1-17. Largely autobiographical.

571. _____. "Folklore and Local History," UHQ (F,
     1963), 31: 315-323.

572. _____. "Folkways of a Mormon Missionary in
     Virginia," SFQ (Je, 1952), 16: 92-123.

573. _____. "Folkways of the Mormons from the
     Journals of John D. Lee," WF (Oct, 1962), 21:
     229-46. Folk medicine, religious folklore, weather
     lore, etc.

574. _____. "The Prayer Book in Cards," WF (Jl,
     1968), 27: 208-12.

575. _____. "Virginia Folkways from a Mormon Jour-
     nal," WF (Oct, 1950), 9: 348-58. Material deals
     with household life, folk medicine, tall tales.
     Three spirituals given.

576. _____ and J. Golden Taylor, eds. The Western
     Folklore Conference: Selected Papers (Monograph

Series, Vol. IX; Logan: Utah State U. P., 1964),
84pp. Papers on mythical horses in Indian culture, cowboy music, a bear story, and folklore in
Twain's Roughing It.

577. Flanagan, John T. "Chisago Reminiscences," SPHQ
(Jan, 1963), 14: 6-18. Personal memories of
fifty years summering in Chisago Co., Minn.,
with data on traditions, names, cookery, and language.

578. "The Folklore of America," Life (Aug 31, Nov 2,
1959; Jan 25, Apr 11, Aug 22, 1960), 47: ix, 55-
67; 47: xviii, 66-79; 48: iii, 50-61; 48: xiv, 86-
97; 49: viii, 45-63. Romanticized and sentimentalized paintings in high color by artist James Le-
wicki. Subjects include scenes and figures supposedly representing American folklore. Article
appeared later as The Life Treasury of American
Folklore (New York: Time, Inc., 1961), 348pp.

579. Foster, James R. "Brooklyn Folklore," NYFQ (S,
1957), 13: 83-91.

580. Franklin, Colin. "Publishing Folklore," Folklore (A,
1966), 77: 184-204. An English publisher speaks
interestingly about professional folklore publishing.

581. Ganim, Mary. "A Study of Children's Folklore,"
NYFQ (Mr, 1970), 16: 50-63. Children's folk-
lore--especially games--is the acting out of life
situations.

582. Gard, Robert E. and L. G. Sorden. Wisconsin Lore,
Antics and Anecdotes of Wisconsin People and
Places (New York: Duell, Sloan, and Pearce,
1962), xii, 368pp. Miscellaneous superstitions,
tales, lumberjack lore, curses, and proverbs
lumped loosely together in eleven chapters.

583. Gayton, A. H. "Perspectives in Folklore," JAF
(Apr-Je, 1951), 64: 147-50. Presidential address
to the Am. Folklore Society.

584. Georges, Robert A. "The Greeks of Tarpon Springs:
An American Folk Group," SFQ (Je, 1965), 29:
129-41. Account of the sponge fishermen on the

west coast of Florida--their superstitions, customs, and folk religion.

585. Geurin, Wayne. "Some Folkways of a Stewart County Community," ed. Herbert Halpert, TFSB (Sept, 1953), 19: 49-58. Weather signs, folk medicine, death signs.

5i6. Gibbon, William B. "Asiatic Parallels in North American Star Lore: Milky Way, Pleiades, Orion," JAF (Jl-Sept, 1972), 85: 236-47. American aboriginal star lore has parallels on other continents.

587. _____. "Asiatic Parallels in North American Star Lore: Ursa Major," JAF (Jl-Sept, 1964), 77: 236-50. Striking parallels in regard to one constellation.

588. Gilbert, Helen. "Pregnancy Cravings as a Motif in Folktales," FF (Oct, 1972), 5: 129-42.

589. Glanz, Rudolph. The Jew in the Old American Folklore (New York: Waldo P., 1961), 234pp. Seventeen chapters include discussions of the Jew as peddler and as businessman, physical appearances, nicknames, and Jewish stereotypes.

590. Goldstein, Kenneth S. "Harvesting Folklore," in Our Living Traditions, ed. T. P. Coffin, pp. 24-36. Practical advice on how and what to collect.

591. Goodwin, Thelma. "The Devil in American Folklore," TFSB (Je, 1960), 26: 36-45. Miscellaneous devil lore supported by quotations from printed tales and writers' programs from southern states.

592. Gordon, Dudley C. "Charles L. Lummis: Pioneer American Folklorist," WF (Jl, 1969), 28: 175-81. Brief biographical sketch.

593. Granger, Byrd Howell. "Of the Teeth," JAF (Jan-Mr, 1961), 74: 47-56.

594. Green, Archie. "American Labor Lore: Its Meaning and Uses," IR (Feb, 1965), 4: 50-68.

595. _____. "Ben Robertson Meets Aunt Molly," KFR
(Oct-Dec, 1961), 7: 133-39. Reprint of a 1931
interview with editorial comment.

596. _____. "John Neuhaus: Wobbly Folklorist," JAF
(Jl-Sept, 1960), 73: 189-217. Biographical data
about a collector of IWW songs and lore.

597. _____. "The Workers in the Dawn: Labor Lore,"
in Our Living Traditions, ed. T. P. Coffin, pp.
251-62. Miscellaneous labor lore with a number
of short quotations.

598. Greene, Sarah. "From Amnesia to Illegitimacy: the
Soap Opera as Contemporary Folklore," in Obser-
vations & Reflections on Texas Folklore, ed. F.
E. Abernethy, pp. 79-90.

599. Greenway, John. "Aunt Molly Jackson as an Informant," KFR (Oct-Dec, 1961), 7: 141-46. A
memorial tribute.

600. _____. Folklore of the Great West (Palo Alto:
American West, 1972), 453pp. An anthology of
material selected from the Journal of American
Folklore by a former JAF editor.

601. _____. Literature Among the Primitives (Hatboro,
Penn.: Folklore Assoc., 1964), xviii, 346pp.
Examination of Eskimo, Indian, African, Polynesian, and Australian oral literature (tales and
songs) with extensive examples. Specific accounts
of folklore themes and forms plus survey of chief
scholarly approaches.

602. _____. "Woody Guthrie: the Man, the Land, the
Understanding," AW (F, 1968), 3: iv, 24-30, 74-
78. A valuable appreciation of Guthrie's work
and career despite the author's exuberant enthusi-
asm.

603. Gridley, Lou Ella E. Folklore of Chenango County
(Chenango, N.Y.: Chenango Union Print., 1970),
2 vols., 1: 55pp; 2: 64pp. Folklore of a New
York county.

604. Hall, Clifton L. "The Folklore of Education," TFSB

(Sept, 1952), 18: 59-64. Miscellaneous items
from the red color of school buildings to textbook
inscriptions.

605. Hall, Joseph S. Smoky Mountain Folks and Their
Lore (Asheville: Norman Printing Co., 1960),
71pp. Anecdotes, sketches of mountain people,
and miscellaneous lore.

606. Hallowell, A. Irving. "The Impact of the American
Indian on American Culture," AA (Apr, 1957), 59:
201-17. Reprinted in Folklore in Action, ed. H.
P. Beck, pp. 120-38.

607. Hand, Wayland D. "American Occupational and Industrial Folklore; the Miner," in Kontakte und
Grenzen, ed. Hans Friedrich Foltin, pp. 453-60.
Stress on failure to collect and discuss industrial
folklore; evidence given from Butte, Mont.

608. _____. "California Folklore Quarterly and Western
Folklore: An Editorial Survey, 1942-1966," WF
(Oct, 1966), 25: 247-53. The editor of WF sur-
veys his magazine.

609. Harrison, Lowell H. "The Folklore of Some Kentucky
Slaves," KFR (Apr-Je, Jl-Sept, 1971), 17: 25-30,
53-60. Narratives from Library of Congress data.

610. Hatfield, Dorothy Blackmon and Eugene Current-Garcia.
"William Orrie Tuggle and the Creek Indian Folk
Tales," SFQ (Dec, 1961), 25: 238-55. Account of
Tuggle, an Indian agent (1879-81), and his manu-
script of tales, songs, and customs.

611. Haun, Mildred. "The Traditions of Cocke County,"
TFSB (Sept, 1967), 33: 72-79. Recollections of a
girlhood in Cocke Co., Tenn.

612. Hawkins, Beverly. "Folklore of a Black Family,"
JOFS (Apr, 1973), n.s., 2: 2-19. Tales, proverbs, and rhymes from a Dayton, Ohio, black
family.

613. Hawthorne, Ruth. "The Folklore Repertory of a
Third-Grade Class," PF (A, 1967), 17: i, 18-25.
Texts from a Delaware field collection made in
1966.

614. Hendricks, George D. "Southpaws, Psychology, and
        Social Science," in And Horns on the Toads, ed.
        Mody C. Boatright et al., pp. 69-87. A study of
        lefthandedness with a Texas superstition, "All left-
        handed people owe the Devil a day's work," as an
        epigraph.

615. Hendricks, King, ed. "Utah State University Folklore
        Collection," WF (Apr, 1959), 18: 107-20. Miscel-
        laneous student-collected material.

616. Hernandez, Juan. "Cactus Whips and Wooden Crosses,"
        JAF (Jl-Sept, 1963), 76: 216-24. Practices and
        beliefs of the Penitentes in New Mexico.

617. Holmes, John Clellon. "The Lost Cause: Gershon
        Legman," ER (Dec, 1966), 10: 28-32, 93-101.
        Biographical data and a discussion of the work of
        the most famous student of sexual folklore.

618. Houston, Maude. "The Education of John A. Lomax,"
        SHQ (Oct, 1956), 60: 201-218.

619. [Hudowalski, Grace L.] "The Schroon Lake Area,"
        NYFQ (Je, 1966), 22: 122-31. Material collected
        by high school students.

620. Hudson, Arthur Palmer. Folklore Keeps the Past
        Alive (Athens: U. of Georgia P., 1962), viii,
        63pp. Three lectures (on folksongs, history, and
        literature).

621. _____. "La Poésia Folklórica," FA (1950), 10:
        1-14. General treatise on folk poetry (song and
        ballad), including definitions, types, contents,
        metrics, and a bibliography.

622. Hudson, Wilson M. "The Twelve Truths in the
        Spanish Southwest," in Mesquite and Willow, ed.
        Mody C. Boatright et al., pp. 138-50. A tradi-
        tional prayer or numbered doctrinal examination
        retains currency in Texas and New Mexico.

623. Hughes, Langston and Arna Bontemps, eds. The
        Book of Negro Folklore (New York: Dodd, Mead,
        1958), xv, 624pp. A real miscellany, which con-
        tains among other things 108 tales, 86 songs, and
        64 rhymes.

624. Hunter, Barbara Way. "The Counties: Judge Brew-
      ster's Tales of Essex County," NYFQ (W, 1954),
      10: 298-307. Anecdotes of local figures and celeb-
      rities.

625. Hurdle, Virginia Jo. "Folklore of a Negro Couple in
      Henry County," ed. Herbert Halpert, TFSB (Sept,
      1953), 19: 71-78. Folk medicine, song fragments,
      and brief supernatural tales.

626. Hurst, Richard M. "History and Folklore," NYFQ
      (Dec, 1969), 25: 243-60.

627. Jablow, Alta and Carl Withers. "Social Sense and
      Verbal Nonsense in Urban Children's Folklore,"
      NYFQ (Dec, 1965), 21: 243-57. Miscellaneous
      material.

628. Jackson, Bruce. "Prison Folklore," JAF (Oct-Dec,
      1965), 78: 317-29. Miscellaneous data collected
      from various prisons.

629. Jackson, Ewing. "God's Country," ed. Herbert Hal-
      pert, TFSB (Sept, 1953), 19: 58-64. Henry County
      beliefs and customs.

630. Jackson, George Pullen. "Suffering Mores," SFQ
      (Sept, 1950), 14: 155-157. We must learn to be
      ourselves and know ourselves. Goethe: "Im
      Anfang war die Tat."

631. Jackson, Margaret Y. "Folklore in Slave Narratives
      Before the Civil War," NYFQ (Spr, 1955), 11:
      5-19. Miscellaneous folklore from slave stories,
      1840-1860.

632. Jagendorf, Moritz A. "Apples in Life and Lore,"
      NYFQ (W, 1962), 18: 273-283. Miscellaneous
      myths and recipes.

633. Jansen, William Hugh. "A Culture's Stereotypes and
      Their Expression in Folk Cliches," SJA (S, 1957),
      13: 184-200. The article suggests that Morris
      Opler's "theme" and "expression" be replaced by
      "stereotype" and "cliche." Turkish märchen and
      minstrel tales used as examples.

634. Johnson, Robbie Davis. "Folklore and Women: A
      Social Interactional Analysis of the Folklore of a
      Texas Madam," JAF (Jl-Sept, 1973), 86: 211-24.
      Interviews with the proprietor of a Texas brothel
      confirm the value of folklore or folk knowledge in
      manipulating both the girls and the customers.
      Basically a sociological study.

635. Jones, Louis C. "The Little People," NYFQ (W,
      1962), 18: 243-64. Miscellaneous Irish folklore
      collected by students in upstate New York.

636. _____. Things That Go Bump in the Night (New
      York: Hill and Wang, 1959), xii, 208pp. Ghost
      lore without substantial comparative analysis.

637. Jones, Michael Owen. "Folk Beliefs: Knowledge
      and Action," SFQ (Dec, 1967), 31: 304-309.

638. _____. "'For Myself I Like a Decent, Plain-Made
      Chair'; the Concept of Taste and the Traditional
      Arts in America," WF (Jan, 1972), 31: 27-52.
      A discussion of Appalachian chair-making leads to
      aesthetic interpretation.

639. _____. "'There's Gotta Be New Designs Once in
      Awhile': Culture Change and the 'Folk' Arts,"
      SFQ (Mr, 1972), 36: 43-60.

640. _____. "Two Directions for Folkloristics in the
      Study of American Art," SFQ (Sept, 1968), 32:
      249-259.

641. _____. "The Useful and the Useless in Folk Art,"
      JPC (Spr, 1973), 6: 794-819.

642. _____. "Violations of Standards of Excellence and
      Preference in Utilitarian Art," WF (Jan, 1973),
      32: 19-32.

643. Joyner, Charles W. "Southern Folklore as a Key to
      Southern Identity," SHR (F, 1967), 1: 211-222.
      Folk music shows mixture of slave and master
      heritage.

644. Kahn, Ed. "Will Roy Hearn: Peripheral Folk Song
      Scholar," WF (Jl, 1964), 23: 173-79. A Louisi-

ana collector of Negro songs and records until
handicapped by blindness.

645. Karpeles, Maud. Cecil Sharp (London: Routledge and
Kegan Paul, 1967), 228pp. Revision of 1933 biography by Fox-Strangways and Karpeles, with
much data about Sharp's work in the U. S.

646. Keach, Everett T., Jr. "Occupational Folklore," EE
(Dec, 1959), 36: 573-76. Children should be
taught folklore of occupations such as mining,
railroads, and firefighting.

647. Keith, Sam. "The Flying Nightmares," NYFQ (A,
1950), 6: 154-60. Marine bomber lore.

648. Kell, Katherine T. "The Folklore of the Daisy,"
JAF (Jan-Mr, Oct-Dec, 1956), 69: 13-21, 369-76.
Extensive venture into folk botany with attention
to superstitions, associations, legends, and literary use of one common flower.

649. Killion, Ronald G. and Charles T. Waller. A Treasury of Georgia Folklore (Atlanta: Cherokee Pub.
Co., 1972), 267pp.

650. Kilpatrick, Jack Frederick. "Folk Formulas of the
Oklahoma Cherokees," JFI (1964), 1: 214-219.

651. Kirtley, Bacil F. "Folklore from Aroostook County,
Maine, and Neighboring Canada," NEF (F, W,
1958; Spr, S, F, W, 1959), 1: 33-47, 65-73; 2:
12-17, 26-29, 46-50, 55-58. Miscellaneous folklore from a variety of collectors.

652. Klees, Fredric. The Pennsylvania Dutch (New York:
Macmillan, 1950), 451pp. Folk culture in general
with an excellent chapter on food. Place names,
customs, and folk medicine are also treated.

653. Köngäs, Elli Kaija. "Immigrant Folklore: Survival
or Living Tradition," MF (F, 1960), 10: 117-23.
Account of a Finnish-born woman living in St.
Albans, Vermont.

654. Korson, George. Black Rock: Mining Folklore of the
Pennsylvania Dutch (Baltimore: Johns Hopkins P.,

1960), xi, 453pp. Careful review of mining
speech, songs, folk medicine, religious lore, etc.

655. Kramer, Frank H. Voices in the Valley, Mythmaking
and Folk Belief in the Making of the Middle West
(Madison: U. of Wisconsin P. , 1964), xvii, 300pp.
Despite the title considerably more history than
folklore.

656. Lacy, James M. "Folklore of the South and Racial
Discrimination, " in A Good Tale and a Bonnie Tune,
ed. Mody C. Boatright et al. , pp. 101-11. Folklore of and about the Negro, the basis of racial
prejudice, is slowly altering.

657. Lame Deer, John (Fire) and Richard Erdoes. Lame
Deer, Seeker of Visions: the Life of a Sioux
Medicine Man (New York: Simon and Schuster,
1972), 288pp.

658. Larson, Mildred R. "Lore from Snow Country, "
NYFQ (W, 1955), 11: 262-74. Tales and anecdotes of winter experiences from pioneers in Camden, New York.

659. Law, Harry. "Some Folklore of Macon County, Tennessee, " TFSB (Dec, 1952), 18: 97-100.

660. Lawrence, Ellen S. "The Lore of the Building Trade, "
NYFQ (A, 1950), 6: 143-54. Composite account
of construction in New York City with terms and
customs.

661. Lea, Aurora Lucero-White. "Our Treasury of Spanish
Folklore, " NMFR (1954-55), 9: 15-19. Attention
directed to fiestas, baptisms, ballads, folk plays,
cuentos. A rich legacy.

662. Leach, MacEdward. "The Men Who Made Folklore a
Scholarly Discipline, " in Our Living Traditions,
ed. T. P. Coffin, pp. 15-24. Rapid survey of the
great names from Bishop Percy and the Grimms to
Frazer and Child.

663. Leach, Maria. God Had A Dog: Folklore of the Dog
(New Brunswick, N. J. : Rutgers U. P. , 1961),
544pp.

664. _____. The Rainbow Book of American Folk Tales
      and Legends (Cleveland and New York: World,
      1958), 318pp. A popularized collection for children.

665. _____. The Soup Stone: The Magic of Familiar
      Things (New York: Funk and Wagnalls, 1954),
      160pp. Folklore associated with objects but includ-
      ing some oral traditions.

666. Lee, Hector H. and Donald Robertson. Lore of Our
      Land: A Book of American Folklore (Evanston:
      Harper and Row, 1963), xxiv, 328pp. An informal
      potpourri probably designed for a youthful audience.

667. Loomis, Ormand. "The Ford-McCoy Killing," FF
      (Oct, 1974), 7: 244-59. Proof that the formal his-
      torical account of an Indiana murder in 1907 varies
      considerably from oral history versions of the
      event.

668. Louisiana Folklore Miscellany (n. p., Louisiana Folk-
      lore Society, no. 3, 1958), 43pp. Brief articles
      by John Q. Anderson, William S. Wirdorn, Jr.,
      and Harry Oster. Carelessly edited.

669. Lowe, Maggie L. "An Old Ballad Composer of the
      Nineties," TFSB (Dec, 1953), 19: 85-94. Account
      of a college graduate and lawyer named Sol Ewell.

670. Lowie, Robert H. "The Oral Literature of the Crow
      Indians," JAF (Apr-Je, 1959), 72: 97-104.

671. _____. Robert H. Lowie, Ethnologist: A Personal
      Record (Berkeley and Los Angeles: U. of Cali-
      fornia P., 1959), x, 198pp. Miscellaneous details
      about his professional career. Chapter V deals
      with the land of the Hopi.

672. Lum, Peter. Fabulous Beasts (New York: Pantheon
      Books, 1951), 256pp. Account of a wide variety
      of mythical monsters. Designed primarily for a
      juvenile audience.

673. McAtee, W. L. "Odds and Ends of North American
      Folklore on Birds," MF (F, 1955), 5: 169-83.
      Medicinal uses, omens, and weather lore; useful
      bibliography.

674. MacDonald, Marilyn. "Lore from the Military Tract:
      Camillus, Onondaga County," NYFQ (A, 1951), 7:
      193-204. Chiefly historical data.

675. McEwen, George M. "Ivan H. Walton, a Pioneer
      Michigan Folklorist," MichA (1970), 1: iii, 73-77.

676. McNeil, W. K. "The Eastern Kentucky Mountaineer:
      An External and Internal View of History," MSF
      (S, 1973), 1: 35-53. Since historians and novelists
      have misrepresented the eastern Kentucky moun-
      taineer it is essential that folk material (ballads,
      beliefs, traditions, customs) be tapped to redress
      the balance.

677. Mead, Margaret, ed. An Anthropologist at Work:
      Writings of Ruth Benedict (Boston: Houghton Mif-
      flin, 1959), xxiv, 583pp. Journals, letters, pa-
      pers, and poetry by a distinguished folklorist and
      anthropologist.

678. Meeker, Doret. "Back to the Blanket: Lore of Steu-
      ben County," NYFQ (A, 1952), 8: 165-90. Miscel-
      laneous tales, anecdotes, and sayings.

679. Miller, Carolyn. "Neighbors: Lore of Lake County,
      Ohio," NYFQ (A, 1950), 6: 168-94. Mostly his-
      torical data.

680. Miller, Mary E. "A Folklore Survey of Dickson Coun-
      ty, Tennessee," TFSB (Je, 1958), 24: 57-71.
      Miscellaneous superstitions, proverbs, remedies,
      etc.

681. Mills, Randall V. "Oregon's Pigger: A College Tra-
      dition," WF (Oct, 1951), 10: 298-309. At the U.
      of Oregon a pigger is a boy who escorts a coed to
      an athletic contest, a custom once frowned on.

682. Mook, Maurice A. "Quaker Knowledge of Quaker
      Folklore," KFQ (Spr-S, 1959), 4: 101-105.

683. Murphy, Robert F. Robert H. Lowie (New York &
      London: Columbia U. P., 1972), 179pp. Rem-
      iniscences of the distinguished anthropologist plus
      selections from his writings.

684. Nathan, Hans. "The First Negro Minstrel Band and
      Its Origins," SFQ (Je, 1952), 16: 132-44. The
      Virginia Minstrels (four blackface musicians per-
      forming on violin, banjo, bones, and tambourine)
      first performed about 1843.

685. Neal, Janice C. "Grandad--Pioneer Medicine Man,"
      NYFQ (W, 1955), 11: 277-91. Composite picture
      of folk medicine from printed sources and oral re-
      ports.

686. Newton, Hilah Foote. "Schoolcraft on the Iroquois,"
      NYFQ (S, A, 1954), 10: 127-32, 176-88. Some
      folklore material scattered among historical data.

687. Nickerson, Bruce E. "Is There a Folk in the Fac-
      tory?" JAF (Apr-Je, 1974), 87: 133-39. Factory
      evidence (ritual and customs) answers affirmatively.

688. Nielson, George R. "Folklore of the German-Wends
      in Texas," in Singers and Story-Tellers, ed. Mody
      C. Boatright et al., pp. 244-59. In 1840 a
      Wendish immigrant group settled in Texas; they
      generally practiced folk medicine.

689. Nothdurft, Lillian. Folklore and Early Customs of
      Southeast Missouri (New York: Exposition P.,
      1972), 77pp. Reminiscences about folk characters
      (like the circuit rider, water witch, fortune teller)
      and samples of folklore.

690. Ortiz, Alfonso. "A Uniquely American Heritage,"
      PULC (1969), 30: 147-157. Report of the author's
      collecting of myths, songs, tales, etc., from
      Pueblo Indians.

691. Paredes, Américo. "The Anglo-American in Mexican
      Folklore," in New Voices in American Studies, ed.
      Ray B. Browne et al., pp. 113-28.

692. _____. "Tributaries to the Mainstream: The
      Ethnic Groups," in Our Living Traditions, ed.
      Tristram P. Coffin, pp. 70-80. Principally about
      Mexican-Americans.

693. Parmly, Eleazar, III. "West Point Folklore," NYH
      (Jl, 1952), 33: 294-302. Brief and poorly or-
      ganized account of traditions at West Point.

694. Parsons, Mildred. "Negro Folklore from Fayette
      County," ed. Herbert Halpert, TFSB (Sept, 1953),
      19: 67-70.

695. Payne, Mildred. "Night Rider Lore and Legend,"
      KFR (Apr-Je, 1966), 12: 59-66.

696. Pearce, T. M. "The Rainbow in Southwestern Folk-
      lore," NMFR (1969-70), 12: 29-34. Account of
      symbolic use of the rainbow in petroglyphs, sand-
      paintings, pottery and blanket designs, and in ritu-
      als of blessing or healing. Tales from Franc
      Johnson Newcomb.

697. _____. "What Is a Folk Poet?" WF (Oct, 1953),
      12: 242-248. Account of work of Prospero S. Baca.

698. Perez, Soledad. "Mexican Folklore from Austin,
      Texas," in The Healer of Los Olmos and Other
      Mexican Lore, ed. W. M. Hudson, pp. 1-139.

699. Perrow, Eber C. "Background," KFR (Jan-Mr, 1957),
      3: 31-37. Autobiographical sketch by an early col-
      lector of southern folksongs.

700. Pietripaoli, Lydia Q. "The Italians Came Up Water-
      town Way," NYFQ (Mr, 1973), 29: 58-79. A
      mishmash of folklore about New York State Italians
      (history, speech, cuisine, social and religious cus-
      toms, festivals, and superstitions such as the evil
      eye).

701. Poggie, John J., Jr. and Carl Gersuny. "Risk and
      Ritual: An Interpretation of Fisherman's Folklore
      in a New England Community," JAF (Jan-Mr,
      1972), 85: 66-72. Fishermen pay more attention
      to ritual and tales than do low-risk textile workers.

702. Porter, Daniel R. "Folk Humor in Ohio," JOFS
      (Spr, 1968), 3: 3-18. Miscellaneous material
      gleaned from Ohio histories and newspapers.

703. Porter, Marjorie Lansing. "Collecting Adirondack
      Folklore," NYFQ (Je, 1966), 22: 113-21. Rem-
      iniscences and experiences. Words of three folk-
      songs.

704.   Pound, Louise. "The American Dialect Society--A
       Historical Sketch," PADS (Apr, 1952), no. 17, 3-
       28. The Am. Dialect. Soc. was founded in 1889;
       Miss Pound, a member from 1901, writes from
       sources and memories.

705.   _____. Nebraska Folklore (Lincoln: U. of Nebras-
       ka P., 1959), xii, 243pp. Reprinted essays by a
       distinguished regionalist and student of the ballad.
       Miss Pound was not a field collector but commented
       intelligently on the work of others.

706.   Rayburn, Otto E. "Arkansas Folklore: Its Preserva-
       tion," AHQ (S, 1951), 10: 210-20.

707.   Resseguie, Harry E. "The Folklore of A. T. Stewart,"
       NYFQ (S, 1962), 18: 125-41. Anecdotes and bibli-
       ographical data about a famous New York merchant.

708.   Reuss, Richard A. "'That Can't Be Alan Dundes!
       Alan Dundes is Taller Than That!' The Folklore
       of Folklorists," JAF (Oct-Dec, 1974), 87: 303-17.
       Despite the cute title the article suggests that much
       folklore circulates about people prominent in the
       field: Kittredge, Dorson, Thompson, Taylor, etc.

709.   Ringe, Donald A. "Two Items of Midwest Folklore
       Noted by William Cullen Bryant," MF (F, 1956),
       6: 141-46. Bryant in his travels heard the Capt.
       Martin Scott coon story and a version of "Michi-
       gania."

710.   Rioux, Marcel. "Folk and Folklore," JAF (Apr-Je,
       1950), 63: 192-198.

711.   Robacker, Earl F. "The Fraktur of Monroe County,"
       PF (A, 1971), 21: i, 2-15. Account of Penn.
       German folk art (birth and baptismal certificates,
       copybooks, house blessings, flyleaves) more
       graphic than verbal.

712.   Roberts, Leonard W. "Floyd County Folklore," KFR
       (Apr-Je, 1956), 2: 33-66. Miscellaneous collec-
       tion of tales, songs, and superstitions, all student-
       collected.

713.   Roberts, Roderick J. "Legend and Local History,"

NYFQ (Je, 1970), 26: 83-90. Legendary material can be profitably utilized by the local historian.

714. Roberts, Warren E. "Stith Thompson: His Major Works and a Bibliography," ARV (1965), 21: 5-20.

715. Rollins, Alfred B. , Jr. "College Folklore," NYFQ (A, 1961), 17: 163-73. Survey of the kinds of college folklore: examinations, grading, professional behavior.

716. Rosenberg, Neil V. "The Communication of Attitudes: White Folklore about Negroes," NegroALF (F, 1969), 3: 88-90.

717. Rowles, Catherine Bryant. "Lore and Legends from Johnstown," NYFQ (Je, 1965), 21: 109-18.

718. Rysan, Josef. "Defamation in Folklore," SFQ (Sept, 1955), 19: 143-49. Defamation is a branch of folklore and should be so considered.

719. _____. "The Solution by Scapegoat," TFSB (Mr, 1956), 22: 10-20. Crises of a mythical or stereotyped nature are solved provisionally by scapegoats.

720. Sackett, S. J. and William E. Koch. Kansas Folklore (Lincoln: U. of Nebraska P., 1961), xi, 251pp. Most folklore genres are represented here but not all the material is peculiar to Kansas.

721. Seeger, Charles. "The Folkness of the Non-Folk and the Non-Folkness of the Folk," in Folklore & Society, ed. Bruce Jackson, pp. 1-9. Seeger terms this paper a "rather jaunty little piece of home-learning."

722. Shay, Frank. A Sailor's Treasury (New York: Norton, 1951), 196pp. Popular compendium of lore, superstitions, yarns, cries, epithets, and speech. Sources inaccurately cited.

723. Shelby, Carolyn. "Folklore of Jordan Springs, Tennessee," TFSB (Mr, 1959), 25: 6-17. Miscellaneous material from the area now part of Ft. Campbell, Ky.

724. Sherman, Constance D. "Some Fabulous Birds,"
NYFQ (Spr, 1960), 16: 37-47. Folklore about
nightingales, peacocks, owls, robins, and the
swallows of San Juan Capistrano.

725. Shoemaker, Alfred L. "Belsnickel Lore," PD (W,
1954-55), 6, iii: 34-38.

726. Sjoberg, Gideon. "Folk and 'Feudal' Societies," AJS
(Nov, 1952), 58: 231-39.

727. Snorf, Annie Laurie and Hazel Vineyard. Yucca Land:
A Collection of Folklore of New Mexico (Dallas:
American Guild P., 1958), 224pp.

728. Sonnichsen, C. L. "The Folklore of Texas Feuds,"
in Observations & Reflections on Texas Folklore,
ed. F. E. Abernethy, pp. 35-47. Mostly historical.

729. Speck, Ernest B., ed. Mody Boatright, Folklorist
(Austin and London: U. of Texas P., 1973), 198pp.
Anthology of Boatright's published essays (1927-
70) divided into four areas: the cowboy, the frontier, the oil industry, and folklore and the folklorist in contemporary society.

730. _____. Mody C. Boatright (Austin: Steck-Vaughan,
1971), 44pp. Brief biography with an account of
Boatright's work as a folklorist.

731. Spratte, Carol Lynn. "Wyoming County Folklore,"
AFFword (Apr, 1973), 3: 16-39. Miscellany from
Wyoming County, West Virginia: tales, cures, be-
liefs, place names.

732. Stansberry, Freddye Belle. "Folklore and Its Effects
on Black History," MFR (W, 1973), 7: 115-22.
Survey of Negro contributions to American culture.

733. Steiner, Franz. Taboo (New York: Philosophical Lib.,
1956), 154pp. Originally lectures at Oxford University. Three chapters on definitions, eight on
relevant theories, and one summary.

734. Stekert, Ellen J. "The Hidden Informant," MF (Spr,
1963), 13: 21-28. Account of a farmer-carpenter

in northern Ohio, source of anecdotes and recollections.

735. _____. Introduction to "Folklore Archives: Ethics
and the Law," FF (Oct, 1973), 6: 197-210. Panel
discussion held at Washington, Nov. 11, 1971, with
various participants.

736. _____. "The Urban Experience and Folk Tradition," JAF (Apr-Je, 1970), 83: 115-270. Papers
by Ellen Stekert, R. M. Dorson, D. K. Wilgus,
and R. D. Abrahams.

737. Stoudt, John Joseph. "Pennsylvania German Folklore:
an Interpretation," PPGFS (Allentown, Penn.:
Schlacter's, 1951), 16: 159-170.

738. Stuckey, Sterling. "Through the Prism of Folklore:
the Black Ethos in Slavery," MR (S, 1968), 9:
417-437. Negro slaves expressed their emotions
in chants and songs.

739. Studer, Norman. "City Slickers in the Catskill
Woods," NYFQ (Je, 1964), 20: 110-114. Folklore
from the Catskill region reflects rural and urban
folk differences.

740. Sturges, Philip C. "Utah Mining Folklore," WF (Apr,
1959), 18: 137-139.

741. Sullivan, Jeremiah J. and James F. McCloy. "The
Jersey Devil's Finest Hour," NYFQ (Sept, 1974),
30: 233-39. A diabolical figure appeared in
eighteenth century N.J. and supposedly again in
1909.

742. Sweeney, Margaret. Fact, Fiction and Folklore of
Southern Indiana (New York: Vantage, 1967), 369pp.
A melange from Clark County and adjacent areas.

743. Taylor, Archer. "The Classics of Folklore," ARV
(1964), 20: 113-24. References to past studies of
folklore which might be called classics and a call
to produce more.

744. Thompson, Stith. "Folklore and Folk Festivals,"
MF (Spr, 1954), 4: 5-12.

745. _____. "Problems in Folklore," in An Introduction
     to Research in English Literary History, ed.
     Chauncey Sanders (New York: Macmillan, 1952),
     pp. 253-276.

746. _____. "Recollections of an Itinerant Folklorist,"
     in Mesquite and Willow, ed. Mody C. Boatright
     et al., pp. 118-28. Distinguished American folk-
     lorist summarizes his career.

747. Thorpe, Peter. "Buying the Farm: Notes on the
     Folklore of the Modern Military Aviator," NWF
     (1967), 2, i: 11-17. Notes on taboo, language,
     and myth.

748. Toelken, J. Barre. "The Folklore of Academe," in
     Jan H. Brunvand, The Study of American Folklore:
     An Introduction (New York: Norton, 1968), pp.
     317-37.

749. Truzzi, Marcello. "The American Circus as a Source
     of Folklore: an Introduction," SFQ (Dec, 1966),
     30: 289-300.

750. Tyler, Robert L. "The I.W.W. and the West," AmQ
     (S, 1960), 12: 175-87. Factual article on the
     I.W.W. plus suggestion that writers and novelists
     have made the I.W.W.'s into a myth comparable
     to cowboys, sodbusters, and mountain men.

751. Utley, Francis Lee. "A Definition of Folklore," in
     Our Living Traditions, ed. T. P. Coffin, pp. 3-14.
     Variations of the theme that folklore is oral tradi-
     tion.

752. Valentine, Andrus T. "Lore of Mills and Millers,"
     NYFQ (W, 1959), 15: 255-63. Rhymes, beliefs,
     and recipes associated with early flour milling.

753. Veysey, Laurence R. "Myth and Reality in Approach-
     ing American Regionalism," AmQ (Spr, 1960), 12:
     31-43. Two kinds of regionalism: continuity (New
     England or Creole New Orleans), and shifting or
     frontier traits (California).

754. Wahlgren, Erik. "Scandinavian Folklore and Folk
     Culture in the Trans-Mississippi West," NWF (S,

1968), 3: 1-16. Miscellaneous Pacific Coast lore
from memorates and ghost tales to smörgasbords
and saunas.

755.   Wax, Murray. "The Notions of Nature, Man, and
Time of a Hunting People," SFQ (Sept, 1962), 26:
175-86. Notions of western civilization compared
with those of the Pawnees as reflected in their
tales.

756.   Welsch, Roger L. A Treasury of Nebraska Pioneer
Folklore (Lincoln: U. of Nebraska P., 1966),
xviii, 391pp. Songs and dances, tales, customs.

757.   Weston, George F., Jr. Boston Ways: High, By,
and Folk (Boston: Beacon, 1957), xvi, 261pp.
Personalities, customs, and places of Boston.

758.   White, Alison. "Mother Goose Reread," SFQ (Sept,
1955), 19: 156-63. A brief essay stressing the
real meaning, satire, metrical form, and possible
ritual survivals in Mother Goose rhymes.

759.   White, Newman Ivey, general ed. The Frank C.
Brown Collection of North Carolina Folklore (Durham, No. Car.: Duke U. P., 1952-1964), Vol. I,
xiv, 712pp. For subsequent volumes dealing with
ballads, folk song, folk music, and superstitions
see Henry M. Belden, Arthur Palmer Hudson, Jan
Philip Schinhan, and Wayland D. Hand. The most
extensive collection of folklore published for any
single American state up to the present day.

760.   Whiting, B. J. "William Johnson of Natchez: Free
Negro," SFQ (Je, 1952), 16: 145-153. Proverbs
and folkways quoted from Johnson's diary, published in 1951.

761.   Wigginton, Eliot ed. The Foxfire Book (Garden City:
Doubleday, 1972), pp. 384. Foxfire 2 (Garden
City: Anchor Press/Doubleday, 1973), 410pp.
Both books derive from the magazine Foxfire and
are miscellanies of customs, craftsmanship, beliefs, tales, etc.--mostly folk life. Material collected originally by students from a North Georgia
high school.

762. [Wilgus, D. K. ?] "The Kentucky Folklore Society,
       1912-1962," KFR (Jan-Mr, 1962), 8: 1-6. A
       resume.

763. Wilson, Eddie W. "The Gourd in Folk Music," SFQ
       (Sept, 1951), 15: 188-195. The gourd has been
       used as a percussion, wind, and string instrument
       in folk music.

764. _____. "The Gourd in Folk Symbolism," WF (Apr,
       1951), 10: 162-164. The gourd is used as a sym-
       bol in literature, art, and folklor.

765. _____. "The Moon and the American Indian," WF
       (Apr, 1965), 24: 87-100.

766. _____. "The Owl and the American Indian," JAF
       (Jl-Sept, 1950), 63: 336-44. Aboriginal concepts
       of the owl, unaffected by foreign influences, show
       the bird to be both beneficent and pernicious, often
       portentously sacred.

767. _____. "The Shell and the American Indian," SFQ
       (Sept, 1952), 16: 192-200. Indians normally used
       shells for practical purposes (jewelry, scrapers,
       knives, containers) but also for wampum, as war
       tokens, and in medicine, religious ceremonials,
       and symbolism.

768. _____. "The Spider and the American Indian,"
       WF (Oct, 1951), 10: 290-97. Proof from various
       texts that the spider was important to the Indian
       in creation stories, myths, magic, medicine, and
       such arts as weaving and basketry.

769. Wilson, George P. "Shakespeare and Southern Folk-
       lore," GR (W, 1967), 21: 508-20. Folklore from
       the plays which is preserved or confirmed in the
       South.

770. Wilson, Gordon. Folklore of the Mammoth Cave Re-
       gion, ed. Lawrence S. Thompson (Bowling Green,
       Ky: Kentucky Folklore Soc., 1968), 112pp. Re-
       printing of previously published essays on diction,
       place names, remedies, beliefs, etc.

771. _____. "Studying Folklore in a Small Region,"

TFSB (1963), 29: 1-4, 34-39, 53-60, 79-86. Long
article running through four issues on various kinds
of folklore in central Kentucky.

772. _____. "Studying Folklore in a Small Region--V:
Pronunciation," TFSB (Dec, 1964), 30: 119-26.

773. _____. "Studying Folklore in a Small Region,"
TFSB (1965), 31: 33-41, 57-67, 99-104.

774. _____. "Studying Folklore in a Small Region,"
TFSB (1966), 32: 31-40, 106-11.

775. _____. "Studying Folklore in a Small Region,"
TFSB (1967), 33: 1-6, 27-35.

776. Winslow, David J. "Children's Picture Books and
the Popularization of Folklore," KFQ (W, 1969),
14: 142-57. Folkloristic themes appear in illustrations.

777. _____. "An Introduction to Oral Tradition Among
Children," KFQ (Spr, 1966), 11: 43-58. Part II
appeared in KFQ (S, 1966), 11: 89-98; Part III in
KFQ (F, 1966), 11: 151-202. Rhymes, jokes,
riddles, taunts, epithets, etc. Extensive bibliography.

778. Wolkstein, Diane. "An Interview with Harold Courlander," LJ (May 15, 1974), 99: 1437-1440.

779. Woods, Barbara Allen. "The Devil in Dog Form,"
WF (Oct, 1954), 13: 229-235.

780. Wright, Barbara. "Lore of Montgomery County,"
NYFQ (S, 1951), 7: 131-140.

781. Wyman, Walker D. "Folklore on the Middlewestern
Frontier," in Studies in History and the Social
Sciences: Essays in Honor of John A. Kinneman
(Normal, Ill.: Illinois State U.P., 1965), pp. 87-
96. Miscellaneous beliefs about health, soil and
water, food, and animals, as well as superstitions
and speech localisms.

782. Yetman, Norman R. Life Under the 'Peculiar Insti-
tution': Selections from the Slave Narrative Col-

lection (New York: Holt, Rinehart, Winston, 1970),
xi, 368pp. Miscellaneous selection from the WPA
compilation of Library of Congress, rich in both
material and verbal folklore.

783.   Yoder, Don. "The Folklife Studies Movement," PF
(Jl, 1963), 13, iii: 43-56. Good account of the
activities of the Pennsylvania Folklife Society.

784.   _____. "Pennsylvania Broadsides," PF (W, 1966-
67; Spr, 1967), 16, ii: 14-21; iii, 28-33. Discussion with ample illustration of broadsides published
by a Philadelphia press in the nineteenth century.

785.   _____, ed. "Symposium on Folk Religion," WF
(Jan, 1974), 33: 1-87. Articles by Yoder (includ-
ing a bibliography), E. Mathias, Y. Lange, G.
Gizelis, R. Hulan.

786.   Young, Aurelia. "Black Folk Music," MFR (Spr,
1972), 6: 1-4. Brief plea for more study of Negro
religious music.

787.   Zanger, Jules. "The Eleventh Newberry Library Conference on American Studies," NLB (Apr, 1961),
5: 227-39. Discussion by panel of scholars of
R. M. Dorson's paper "Bogies of American Folklore."

6. BALLADS AND SONGS

A. Collections

788. Amburgey, Don Carlos. "Folk Songs," KFR (Jan-Mr, 1963), 9: 11-19. Song texts without annotation or music.

789. Anderson, David D. "Songs and Sayings of the Lakes," MF (Spr, 1962), 12: 5-16. Texts of ballads, shanties, and rhymes from Great Lakes sailors; no music given.

790. Arnold, Byron. Folksongs of Alabama (University, Ala.: U. of Alabama P., 1950), xiv, 193pp. Texts of 153 songs collected in 1945; interesting notes on the singers.

791. Asch, Moses. American Folksong: Woody Guthrie (New York: Oak Publications, 1961), 54pp.

792. _____ and Alan Lomax. The Leadbelly Songbook (New York: Oak Publications, 1962), 96pp. Ballads, blues, and folksongs of the famed Negro singer plus biographical materials by various contributors.

793. Badeaux, Ed. "Please Don't Tell What Train I'm On," Sing Out! (Sept, 1964), 14: iv, 6-13. Article about ethnic singer Elizabeth Cotton and her song "Freight Train."

794. Belden, Henry M. and Arthur Palmer Hudson. Folk Ballads from North Carolina, Vol. II of Frank C. Brown Collection of North Carolina Folklore (Durham: Duke U. P., 1952), xxiii, 747pp. Some 314 titles with many variant texts, valuable head

notes, and information about the singers. A monumental collection.

795. _____ and _____. Folk Songs from North Carolina, Vol. III of Frank C. Brown Collection of
North Carolina Folklore (Durham: Duke U. P.,
1952), xxx, 709pp. Some 658 songs printed with
the same scholarly care given ballads in the com-
panion volume. No music.

796. Bennett, Gertrude R. Ballads of Colonial Days
(Francestown, N.H.: Golden Quill, 1972), 160pp.
Texts with historical background.

797. Berry, Cecilia Ray. Folk Songs of Old Vincennes
(Chicago: H. T. Fitzsimons, 1950), 95pp. English
and French texts with annotations by J. M. Car-
riere.

798. Bierhorst, John. Songs of the Chippewa (New York:
Farrar, Straus, 1974), 47pp.

799. Boggs, Doc. "I Always Loved the Lonesome Songs,"
Sing Out! (Jl, 1964), 14: iii, 32-39. Reminiscences
of a Virginia folk singer with words and music for
three songs.

800. Borcherdt, Donn. "Armenian Folk Songs and Dances
in the Fresno and Los Angeles Areas," WF (Jan,
1959), 18: 1-12. Original texts, translations, and
music.

801. Boswell, George W. "Five Choice Tennessee Folk
Songs," TFSB (Je, 1950), 16: 25-30. Songs with
music, including "The Death of Floyd Collins."

802. _____. "Five More Choice Tennessee Folksongs,"
TFSB (Sept, 1950), 16: 46-53. Text of "The
State of Arkansas" with music.

803. _____. "Seven Comic Tennessee Folksongs,"
TFSB (Je, 1958), 24: 72-83. Amusing texts from
Tennessee singers, including a variant of Child
#278.

804. _____. "Third Edition: Five Tennessee Folksongs," TFSB (Dec, 1951), 17: 85-92b. Three
ballads, a play-party song, and a cumulative song.

805.   Boyer, Walter E., Albert F. Buffington, and Don
       Yoder. Songs Along the Mahantongo (Lancaster:
       Franklin and Marshall College, 1951), 231pp.

806.   Braddy, Haldeen. "The Anonymous Verses of a Nar-
       cotics Addict," SFQ (Sept, 1958), 22: 129-38.
       Six poems collected by a narcotics agent from a
       Creole octoroon woman. Careful definitions of
       terms in texts.

807.   Bradley, F. W. "Old Joe Clarke," SFQ (Sept, 1959),
       23: 172-74. Text of the familiar ballad reported
       by Dr. John Bennett, undated. No comments.

808.   Brand, Oscar. Songs of '76: a Folksinger's History
       of the American Revolution (New York: M. Evans,
       1973), xiv, 178pp.

809.   Burrison, John A. "Cap'n George Wheatley, Oldest
       Tangier Man," KFQ (Spr, 1966), 11: 27-42. Folk-
       singer of Tangier Island, Va., with four of his
       songs and music.

810.   Burt, Olive Woolley. American Murder Ballads and
       Their Stories (New York: Oxford, 1958), 272pp.
       Indigenous American songs, often of poor quality,
       dealing with the folklore of murder. Elaborate
       comment, some musical accompaniments, the bal-
       lads often fragmentary.

811.   _____. "The Minstrelsy of Murder," WF (Oct,
       1958), 17: 263-72. Preview of American Murder
       Ballads and Their Stories.

812.   _____. "Murder Ballads of Mormondom," WF
       (Apr, 1959), 18: 141-56. Material from American
       Murder Ballads and Their Stories.

813.   Burton, Thomas G. and Ambrose N. Manning. The
       East Tennessee State University Collection of Folk-
       lore: Folksongs I and II (Johnson City, Tenn.:
       East Tenn. State U., 1967, 1969), vi, 114pp.;
       viii, 119pp. Transcriptions of recordings from
       Beech Mt., No. Car. Little documentation.

814.   Bush, Michael. Folk Songs of Central West Virginia
       (Ripley, W. Va.: M. Bush, 1969), 96pp. Folk

Songs of Central West Virginia (Ravenswood, W.
Va.: Custom Printing Co., 1970), 104pp. Volume
two contains 44 songs.

815. Campbell, Marie. "Answering-Back Song-Ballads,"
TFSB (Mr, 1958), 24: 3-10. Songs from oral tradition in eastern Kentucky. Answers to "Lorena"
and "I Wish I Was Single."

816. Carawan, Guy and Candie Carawan. We Shall Over-
come!: Songs of the Southern Freedom Movement
(New York: Oak Publications, 1963), 112pp. Popular collection, including spirituals, hymns, gospel songs, and contemporary material.

817. Cardozo-Freeman, Inez. "Arnulfo Castillo: Mexican
Folk Poet in Ohio," JOFS (Aug, 1972), n.s., 1:
2-28. Account of Mexican-born worker poet who
wrote his own corridos, one about J. F. Kennedy.

818. Carey, George G. "A Collection of Airborne Cadence
Chants," JAF (Jan-Mr, 1965), 78: 52-61. Material collected at Fort Campbell, Kentucky, in April,
1961.

819. _____. "Songs of Jack Tar in the Darbies," JAF
(Apr-Je, 1972), 85: 167-180. Songs, often fragmentary, written down by a Yankee privateersman
incarcerated in Forton Prison, England, during the
Revolution.

820. Cazden, Norman. The Abelard Folk Song Book (New
York: Abelard-Schuman, 1958), iv, 127pp. Mostly songs from the Catskills.

821. _____. A Book of Nonsense Songs: Over 100
Songs, Words and Music (New York: Crown, 1961),
106pp.

822. _____. "Catskill Lockup Songs," NYFQ (S, 1960),
16: 90-103. Music and texts of six jail songs,
five of which originated in the Catskills.

823. _____. "Songs: 'The Foggy Dew' (Irish)," NYFQ
(A, 1954), 10: 213-17. Text and music of an
Irish song collected in the Catskills, unrelated to
"The Foggy, Foggy Dew."

824.   Chambers, Henry Alban. The Treasury of Negro
       Spirituals (New York: Emerson Books, 1963),
       125pp.

825.   Charters, Samuel B. The Poetry of the Blues (New
       York: Oak Publications, 1963), 111pp. Discus-
       sion of character and poetic effects of the blues;
       many texts without music.

826.   Cheney, Thomas E. Mormon Songs from the Rocky
       Mountains: A Compilation of Mormon Folksong
       (Austin and London: U. of Texas P., 1968), xix,
       221pp. An excellent collection although not all the
       songs were sung traditionally.

827.   Coffin, Tristram P. "Six Unusual Texts from Mildred
       Haun's 'Cocke County Ballads and Songs'," SFQ
       (Je, 1965), 29: 179-87. East Tennessee texts of
       five Child ballads and "The Wagoner's Lad."

828.   Cohen, Norman. "Railroad Folk Songs on Record--A
       Survey," NYFQ (Je, 1970), 26: 91-113. Brief
       study of railroad folksongs, their authorship, his-
       torical relevance, and popularity. Discographies
       of five examples.

829.   Colorado Folksong Bulletin (Jan, Apr, Nov, 1962), 1:
       Nos. 1-3, pp. 23, 27, 33, respectively. Altogether
       some 75 songs, many with music.

830.   Cone, James H. The Spirituals and the Blues (New
       York: Seabury P., 1972), viii, 152pp.

831.   Cothran, Kay L. "Songs, Games, and Memories of
       Mr. George W. Mitchell," TFSB (Sept, 1968), 34:
       63-84. Transcriptions of three songs collected in
       1968.

832.   Courlander, Harold. Negro Folk Music, U.S.A. (New
       York: Columbia U.P., 1963), x, 324pp. Re-
       printed in 1970.

833.   _____. Negro Songs from Alabama (New York:
       Wenner-Green Foundation, 1960), 76pp. Seventy-
       four songs with music derived from Alabama and
       Mississippi Negroes in 1950. Reprinted by Oak
       Publications in 1963.

834. Cox, John Harrington. Folk-Songs of the South (Hat-
      boro, Penn.: Folklore Assoc., 1963), xxxi, 545pp.
      Some 185 songs, with variants and a few tunes,
      mostly collected in West Va., originally published
      in 1925.

835. Cranmer, H. M. "Two Early Pennsylvania Ballads,"
      KFQ (W, 1960), 5: iv, 13-18. Texts of local bal-
      lads, "Saga of Billy French" and "Amanda."

836. Cray, Ed. The Erotic Muse (New York: Oak Publi-
      cations, 1969), xxxv, 272pp. Texts and music of
      150 unexpurgated obscene songs, with an erudite
      introduction and commentary, and both bibliography
      and index.

837. _____. "Some Rarities from Arkansas," MF (Spr,
      1959), 9: 21-30. Eight songs by Emma Dusenberry
      of Mena, Ark. from the Library of Congress col-
      lection.

838. Creighton, Helen. Maritime Folk Songs (East Lansing,
      Mich.: Mich. State U. P., 1962), xvi, 214pp.

839. _____ and Doreen Senior. Traditional Songs from
      Nova Scotia (Toronto: Ryerson P., 1950), 284pp.
      Some 36 Child ballads and about 100 more items.
      Some ballads here are relatively rare in the U.S.
      (as Child 3, 17, 46, 106, 112, 114, 132, etc.).

840. Cromwell, Ida M. "Songs I Sang on an Iowa Farm,"
      WF (Oct, 1958), 17: 229-47. A mixture of popu-
      lar songs and true ballads as sung sixty years ago.
      With notes by T. P. Coffin and S. P. Bayard.

841. Curtis, Otis F., Jr. "The Curtis Collection of
      Songs," NYFQ (S, W, 1953), 9: 94-103, 273-281.
      Texts and discussion (no music) of 18 temperance,
      sentimental, military, and patriotic songs found in
      a scrapbook owned by a New York family.

842. Davis, Arthur Kyle, Jr. More Traditional Ballads
      of Virginia: Collected with the Cooperation of
      Members of the Virginia Folklore Society (Chapel
      Hill: U. of No. Car. P., 1960), xxvii, 371pp.
      148 texts of 46 Child ballads with 101 tunes. Ex-
      cellent comparative headnotes.

843. Day, A. Grove. The Sky Clears (New York: Mac-
     millan, 1951), xv, 204pp. Excellent anthology of
     American Indian poetry (chants, ritualistic songs,
     prayers) arranged geographically by tribal groups.
     Reprinted 1964 by University of Nebraska Press.

844. Doerflinger, William H. Shantymen and Shantyboys:
     the Songs of the Sailor and Lumberman (New York:
     Macmillan, 1951), xxiii, 374pp. Probably the best
     single collection of American occupational songs.
     Reprinted in 1972 as Songs of the Sailor and Lum-
     berman.

845. Dorson, Richard M. "Folksongs of the Maine Woods,"
     FFMA (F, 1965), 8: 1-33. Nine songs with texts
     and music collected by Dorson; transcriptions by
     George List and headnotes by Neil Rosenberg.

846. _____, George List, and Neil Rosenberg. "Negro
     Folksongs from Michigan, from the Repertoire of
     J. D. Suggs; Annotated Transcriptions," FFMA
     (F, 1966-1967), 9: 5-41.

847. Dwyer, Richard A. and Richard E. Lingenfelter. The
     Songs of the Gold Rush (Berkeley and Los Angeles:
     U. of California P., 1964), xi, 200pp.

848. Eddy, Mary O. Ballads and Songs from Ohio (Hat-
     boro, Penn.: Folklore Assoc., 1964), xi, 330pp.
     Facsimile reprint of 1939 ed., with a foreword by
     D. K. Wilgus.

849. _____. "Twenty Folk Hymns," MF (Spr, 1953),
     3: 35-45. Examples of religious words fitted to
     secular songs.

850. _____. "William Reilly's Courtship," MF (S,
     1952), 2: 113-18. A nineteenth century broadside.
     No annotation.

851. Emrich, Duncan. American Folk Poetry, An Anthology
     (Boston and Toronto: Little, Brown, 1974), 831pp.
     With an important bibliography by Joseph Hickerson,
     pp. 774-816.

852. Felton, Harold W. Cowboy Jamboree: Western Songs
     and Lore (New York: Knopf, 1951), 107pp.

853. Fernández, Madeleine. "Romances from the Mexican Tradition of Southern California," FA (Dec, 1966), 26: 35-45. Six ballads in Spanish published with music. Collected in Los Angeles.

854. Fife, Austin E. and Alta S. Fife. Ballads of the Great West (Palo Alto: American West. Pub. Co., 1970), 272pp. Mostly popular verse but without tunes.

855. _____ and _____. "Ballads of the Little Big Horn," AW (Feb, 1967), 4: i, 46-49, 86-89. Words and music of a number of ballads commemorating General Custer and his last stand.

856. _____ and _____. Cowboy and Western Songs: A Comprehensive Anthology (New York: Clarkson N. Potter, 1969), xii, 372pp. Some 128 different songs, often familiar, but many with variant texts from different archives.

857. _____ and _____. Heaven on Horseback: Revivalist Songs and Verse in the Cowboy Idiom (Logan, Ut.: Utah State U. P., 1970), 114pp. Songs from oral tradition and from printed texts. The cowboy milieu is well presented.

858. _____ and _____. Saints of Sage & Saddle (Bloomington: Indiana U. P., 1956), xiv, 367pp. Excellent survey of Mormon folklore with copious anecdotes and sketches of personalities. Many Mormon songs included, some fragmentary.

859. Fisher, Miles Mark. Negro Slave Songs in the United States (Ithaca: Cornell U. P., 1953), xv, 223pp. Reprinted 1963 by Citadel Press.

860. Flanders, Helen Hartness. Ancient Ballads Traditionally Sung in New England (Philadelphia: U. of Penn. P., 1960-65), 4 vols. Vol. I, ballads 1-51, 343pp.; Vol. II, ballads 53-93, 320pp.; Vol. III, ballads 95-243, 326pp.; Vol. IV, ballads 250-295, 297pp. Invaluable collection of New England versions of Child ballads, many with variant texts. Critical analyses by T. P. Coffin, musical annotation by Bruno Nettl.

861.   _____ and Marguerite Olney. Ballads Migrant in
            New England (New York: Farrar, Straus and
            Young, 1953), xiv, 248pp. Words and music of
            97 ballads with running commentary. Introduction
            by Robert Frost.

862.   Foster, John Wilson. "Some Irish Songs in the Gordon
            Collection," NWF (W, 1968), 3: 16-29. Texts of
            six songs and titles of 79 others from the U. of
            Oregon collection.

863.   Fowke, Edith. "American Cowboy and Western Pioneer
            Songs in Canada," WF (Oct, 1962), 21: 247-56.
            Texts of songs collected in Canada; some may have
            originated there.

864.   _____, ed. Lumbering Songs from the North Woods
            (Austin: U. of Texas P., 1970), ix, 232pp. Sixty-
            five lumbering songs with musical annotation by
            Norman Cazden.

865.   _____ and Joe Glazer. Songs of Work and Freedom
            (Chicago: Roosevelt U., 1960), 203pp. Proletari-
            an and unionist songs for a popular audience.

866.   _____ and Richard Johnston. Folk Songs of Canada
            (Waterloo, Ont.: Waterloo Music Co., 1954),
            198pp. Seventy-seven songs, many of which are
            known south of the border.

867.   No entry.

868.   Friedman, Albert B. The Viking Book of Folk Bal-
            lads of the English-Speaking World (New York:
            Viking, 1956), xxxv, 473pp. Excellent selection
            of Child ballads with American occupational bal-
            lads: succinct introduction and headnotes.

869.   Gardner, Emelyn Elizabeth and Geraldine Jencks
            Chickering. Ballads and Songs of Southern Michi-
            gan (Hatboro, Penn.: Folklore Associates, 1967),
            501pp., with a new Foreword by Albert B. Fried-
            man, pp. i-viii. Originally published 1939.

870.   Glassie, Henry. "Blue Ridge Song Sampler," MLW
            (F, 1964; W, 1964), 40: 53-60, 19-28. Folksongs

and traditional ballads from North Carolina; texts
and music given.

871. Gravelle, Jean F. "The Civil War Songster of a Monroe County Farmer," NYFQ (Je, 1971), 27: 163-
230. Thirty-four ballads and songs printed from a
New York farmer's manuscript with useful headnotes. No music.

872. Graves, Robert. English and Scottish Ballads (New
York: Macmillan, 1957), xxvi, 163pp. Representative selection but much tampering with the
texts.

873. Greenway, John. American Folksongs of Protest
(Philadelphia: U. of Penn. P., 1953), x, 348pp.
A sampling of songs of economic and social
protest, most of them poor, both musically
and as songs. Best selections are by Guthrie,
Aunt Molly Jackson, Joe Glazer, and Ella May
Wiggins.

874. Grossman, Stefan. The Country Blues Songbook (New
York: Oak Publications, 1973), 208pp. Songs by
Mississippi John Hurt, Robert Johnson, Charlie
Patton, etc.

875. Gunn, Larry. "Three Negro Folk Songs from the
Northern Mississippi Delta," MFR (F, 1969), 3:
89-94. Transcriptions of three songs collected in
1968.

876. Hagerty, Gilbert. "Crime and Catastrophe in New
York State in 1841 as Reported in Two Broadside
Accounts," NYFQ (Mr, 1963), 19: 37-47.

877. Hand, Wayland D., Charles Cutts, Robert C. Wylder,
and Betty Wylder. "Songs of the Butte Miners,"
WF (Jan, 1950), 9: 1-49. Some 30 songs, some
with music; British Isles ballads, fragments, and
parodies. Extensive discussion and annotation.

878. Hansen, Terence L. "Corridos in Southern California,"
WF (Jl, Oct, 1959), 18: 203-32, 295-315. Some
33 corridos (Spanish folk ballads), collected in
Southern California, with informants, original texts,
and translations.

879. Harlow, Frederick Pease. Chanteying Aboard Ameri-
      can Ships (Barre, Mass.: Barre Pub. Co., 1962),
      xii, 250pp. Chanteys recorded by an actual sailor
      on a square-rigger.

880. Harrison, Russell M. "Folk Songs from Oregon,"
      WF (Jl, 1952), 11: 174-84. Repertoire of Mrs.
      Clarice Judkins. Over 100 songs, including 8
      Child ballads; six given with music; for the rest,
      titles only.

881. Haviland, Virginia. "Who Killed Cock Robin?" QJLC
      (Apr, 1973), 30: 95-139. Mostly facsimiles of
      Lib. of Congress editions of the famous rhyme.

882. Haywood, Charles. Folk Songs of the World (New
      York: John Day, 1966), 320pp. Songs in original
      texts with translations and tunes, 4 from Canada,
      8 from the U.S.

883. Heaps, Willard A. and Porter W. Heaps. The Sing-
      ing Sixties (Norman: U. of Oklahoma P., 1960),
      xiv, 423pp. Popular Civil War songs; only a few
      accompanied by tunes.

884. Horn, Dorothy D. "English Sources of American Folk
      Hymns: Additions to the Jackson Lists," SFQ
      (Sept, 1964), 28: 222-27. Fragments of 7 hymns
      from English archives which were once current in
      the U.S.

885. _____. "Folk-Hymn Texts in Three Old Harp
      Books," TFSB (Dec, 1956), 22: 91-97. Quota-
      tions from hymnals still in use.

886. _____. Sing to Me of Heaven: A Study of Folk and
      Early American Materials in Three Old Harp Books
      (Gainesville: U. of Florida P., 1970), xi, 212pp.

887. Hubbard, Lester A. Ballads and Songs from Utah
      (Salt Lake City: U. of Utah P., 1961), 463pp.
      Some 204 general songs and 46 Mormon songs,
      some without tunes.

888. _____. "Militant Songs of the Mormons," WF (Apr,
      1959), 18: 121-30. Songs with sociological and
      historical values but little artistry.

889. Hubbard, Lester A. and LeRoy J. Robertson. "Tra-
      ditional Ballads from Utah," JAF (Jan-Mr, 1951),
      64: 37-53. Music and texts of nine Child ballads
      from Utah.

890. Hugill, Stan. Shanties and Sailors' Songs (New York:
      F. A. Praeger, 1969), x, 243pp. Discussion of
      history and types of shanties. Music and text of
      songs.

891. _____. Shanties from the Seven Seas (London:
      Routledge and Kegan Paul; New York; Dutton, 1961),
      xix, 604pp. About 450 worksongs, collected and
      analyzed by a deep water seaman.

892. Huntington, Gale. "Folksongs from Martha's Vine-
      yard," NEF (1966), 8: 1-87. Twenty-nine songs
      from the Tilton family of Chilmark.

893. _____. Songs the Whaleman Sang (Barre, Mass.:
      Barre Publishing Co., 1964), xix, 328pp. Some
      174 songs with music, grouped according to themes.

894. Ives, Burl. The Burl Ives Song Book: American
      Song in Historical Perspective (New York: Bal-
      lantine Books, 1963), 303pp. 115 pieces including
      many folk songs.

895. _____. Sea Songs of Sailing, Whaling, and Fishing
      (New York: Ballantine Books, 1956), 134pp.
      Popular collection of 68 songs with melodies and
      guitar chords.

896. _____. Songs in America: Our Musical Heritage
      (New York: Duell, Sloan, and Pearce, 1962),
      312pp. With arrangements by Albert Hague.

897. [Ives, Edward D.] "Folksongs from Maine," NEF
      (1965), 7: 1-89. Twenty songs (local, native
      American, and British traditional). With care-
      ful annotations.

898. _____. "The Life and Work of Larry Gorman: A
      Preliminary Report," WF (Jan, 1960), 19: 17-23.
      Preview of Ives' monograph on Gorman.

899. _____. "Satirical Songs in Maine and the Mari-

time Provinces of Canada," JIFMC (1962), 14:
65-69. Material concerning Larry Gorman and his
satirical songs.

900. Jackson, Bruce. Get Your Ass in the Water and
Swim Like Me (Cambridge: Harvard U.P., 1974),
244pp. Narrative poetry from the black oral tradition.

901. _____. "Prison Worksongs: The Composer in
Negatives," WF (Oct, 1967), 26: 245-68. Songs
from J. B. Smith, a Texas Prison System inmate.

902. _____. Wake Up Dead Man: Afro-American Worksongs from Texas Prisons (Cambridge: Harvard
U.P., 1972), xxii, 326pp.

903. _____. "What Happened to Jody," JAF (Oct-Dec,
1967), 80: 387-96. Comments on Jody the Grind-
er, an important figure in Negro songs and toasts.
Four texts included.

904. Jackson, George Pullen. Another Sheaf of White
Spirituals (Gainesville: U. of Florida P., 1952),
xviii, 233pp.

905. Jameson, Gladys. Sweet Rivers of Song: Authentic
Ballads, Hymns, Folksongs from the Appalachian
Region (Berea, Ky.: Berea College, 1967), 81pp.

906. Johnson, Charlotte I. "Navaho Corn Grinding Songs,"
Ethnomusicology (1964), 8: 101-120. Texts without
music. Analysis of structure, content, and metrical pattern.

907. Johnson, James Weldon. The Books of American
Negro Spirituals (New York: Viking, 1969). Two
volumes in one. Reissue of two collections first
published 1925-1926.

908. Joyner, Charles W. Folk Song in South Carolina
(Columbia, S.C.: U. of So. Carolina P., 1971),
112pp. Brief introduction to S. Carolina folk
songs with 45 examples. Most texts are reprinted
but a few are newly transcribed by Joyner.

909. Kaufman, Charles H. "An Ethnomusicological Survey

Among the People of the Ramapo Mountains,"
NYFQ (Mr, Je, 1967), 23: 3-43, 109-31. Soci-
ological study of an isolated group of New Yorkers
with ballads sung by the Conklin family.

910. Kennedy, Charles O'Brien. A Treasury of American
      Ballads: Gay, Naughty, and Classic (New York:
      McBride, 1954), xviii, 398pp. Actually a collec-
      tion of popular songs.

911. Krelove, Harold. "New Year's Verses of the Print-
      er's Boy," KFQ (S, 1964), 9: 68-73. Year-end
      verses in newspapers represent a type of surviving
      broadside.

912. Landeck, Beatrice. Echoes of Africa in Folk Songs
      of the Americas (New York: McKay, 1961), viii,
      184pp. Music and texts but little annotation. Part
      four deals with the roots of jazz. Second rev. ed.,
      1969.

913. Larkin, Margaret. Singing Cowboy (New York: Oak
      Publications, 1963), 176pp. A collection of western
      songs with music; original ed. published in 1931.

914. Leach, MacEdward. The Ballad Book (New York:
      Harper, 1955), xiv, 842pp. Excellent anthology of
      British and American ballads, including 185 Child
      items. With headnotes, glossary, bibliography,
      and ballad discography. Reissued 1963.

915. _____. The Book of Ballads (New York: Heritage
      Press, 1967), xxiv. 215pp. Sixty-nine ballads.

916. _____ and Horace P. Beck. "Songs from Rappa-
      hannock County, Virginia," JAF (Jl-Sept, 1950),
      63: 257-284. Child ballads, American ballads,
      and songs from eight different informants.

917. Lee, Katie. "Folk Songs of the Colorado," AH (May,
      1954), 30: v, 2, 14-18, 23.

918. Lingenfelter, Richard E., Richard A. Dwyer, and
      David Cohen. Songs of the American West (Berke-
      ley and Los Angeles: U. of California P., 1968),
      xii, 595pp. Some 283 representative songs of
      railroaders, Mormons, cowboys, Wobblies, etc.

919.   Linscott, Eloise Hubbard.   Folk Songs of Old New
       England (Hamden, Conn.:   Archon Books, 1962),
       xxiii, 344pp.   Sec. ed. of a collection of folk
       songs, children's songs, and singing games.   First
       published 1939.

920.   Lloyd, Timothy.   "Sam Bowles; the Traditional Coun-
       try Musician in Rural and Urban Contexts," JOFS
       (Spr, 1972), n. s., 1: 37-49.   Account of a Negro
       farmer and musician from Kentucky and Ohio.

921.   Logan, William A.   Road to Heaven (University, Ala.:
       U. of Alabama P., 1955), 37pp.   28 Negro spirit-
       uals collected by the compiler around Murfrees-
       boro, Ark.

922.   Lomax, Alan.   The Folk Songs of North America, in
       the English Language (Garden City, N. Y.:   Double-
       day, 1960), xxx, 623pp.   317 songs, some with
       fragmentary texts, plus melodies, guitar chords,
       piano arrangements.   Brief bibliography.   Reviewed
       by G. Legman and D. K. Wilgus in JAF (1961),
       74: 265-269.

923.   Lomax, John A. and Alan Lomax.   Cowboy Songs and
       Other Frontier Ballads (New York: Macmillan,
       1966), xxxviii, 431pp.   Rearrangement of and ad-
       ditions to the famous 1910 volume.

924.   _____ and _____.   Leadbelly: a Collection of
       World-Famous Songs by Huddie Ledbetter (New
       York: Folkways Music Publishers, 1959), 80pp.
       Seventy songs with music from the repertoire of
       the famous Negro ex-convict and folk singer.

925.   Lumpkin, Ben Gray.   "Colorado Folk Songs," WF
       (Apr, 1960), 19: 77-97.   Miscellaneous songs and
       song fragments collected by the author.

926.   _____.   "Folksongs from a Nebraska Family,"
       SFQ (Mr, 1972), 36: 14-35.   Members of the
       Cummings family of Beatrice, Neb., cultured and
       educated, sang ballads for fun.

927.   _____.   "Four Folksongs from Kemper County,"
       MFR (1967), 1: 20-24.   Texts of "The Lazy Man,"
       "Old Dan Tucker," "Little Omie," and "Hole in
       the Bottom of the Sea."

928. McAllester, David P. "A Review Essay: Alan Lomax and American Folk Song," Ethnomusicology (Sept, 1962), 6: 233-38. Discussion of Alan Lomax's Folk Songs of North America and of four folksong publications by John Lomax as well.

929. McCurry, John Gordon. The Social Harp, ed. Daniel W. Patterson and John E. Garst (Athens: U. of Georgia P., 1973), xxv, 268pp. New edition of book on sacred harp music first published in 1855. Patterson's introduction is readable and informative.

930. McIntosh, David Seneff. Folk Songs and Singing Games of the Illinois Ozarks, ed. Dale Whiteside (Carbondale: Southern Illinois U.P., 1974), 119pp. Local songs, traditional ballads, play-party songs, and children's songs from southern Illinois.

931. McNeil, William K. "A Schoharie County Songster," NYFQ (Mr, 1969), 25: 3-58. Texts of 28 songs (Civil War, temperance, and sentimental songs, and murder and tragedy tales) from a notebook kept by Ida Finkell in 1879-1883.

932. Manning, Ambrose. "Railroad Work Songs," TFSB (Je, 1966), 32: 41-47. Chants collected from Southern Railroad gandy dancers.

933. Moore, Ethel and Chauncey Moore. Ballads and Folk Songs of the Southwest (Norman: U. of Oklahoma P., 1964), xv, 414pp.

934. Morris, Alton C. Folksongs of Florida (Gainesville: U. of Florida P., 1950), xvi, 464pp. Informative and documented footnotes. Two divisions: Songs of the New World (West, History, Outlawry, Disaster, Domestic Relations, etc.) and Songs of the Old World (ballads, Anglo-Irish songs).

935. Morse, Jim. The Dell Book of Great American Folk Songs (New York: Dell, 1963), 255pp. With a foreword by Carl Sandburg.

936. Muir, Willa. Living with Ballads (New York: Oxford, 1965), 260pp.

937. Mullen, Patrick B. "Folk Songs & Family Tradition,"

in Observations & Reflections on Texas Folklore,
ed. F. E. Abernethy, pp. 49-63. Songs of the
author's grandfather, an Arkansas ballad singer.

938. _____. "A Negro Street Performer: Tradition and
Innovation," WF (Apr, 1970), 29: 91-103. Account
of a Galveston performer.

939. Musick, Ruth Ann. "Ballads and Folksongs Collected
from Mrs. Howard Glasscock of Wetzel County,
W. Va.," WVF (W, 1956), 5: ii, 22-40. Six
Child ballads plus others.

940. _____. "Ballads and Folksongs from West Virginia," JAF (Jl-Sept, Oct-Dec, 1957), 70: 247-61,
336-57. Twenty-six examples from West Virginia.
Local and Child ballads given without substantial
comment.

941. Neuffer, Claude Henry. "The Bottle Alley Song,"
SFQ (Sept, 1965), 29: 234-38. A Gullah-flavored
ditty about a second-hand clothing store in Charleston.

942. Niles, John Jacob. The Ballad Book of John Jacob
Niles (Boston: Houghton Mifflin, 1961), xxii, 369pp.
Contains 110 ballads. Reprinted 1973.

943. Ohrlin, Glenn. The Hell-Bound Train, a Cowboy Songbook (Urbana: U. of Illinois P., 1973), xix, 290pp.
Foreword by Archie Green, Biblio-Discography by
Harlan Daniel. Texts of 100 songs (most with music) as sung by a cowboy-rancher from the Ozarks.

944. _____. "Selections from The Hell-Bound Train,"
MSF (S, 1972), 1: 55-68. Excerpts including four
songs from Ohrlin's 1973 book.

945. Older, Lawrence. "Once More A-Lumbering Go,"
NYFQ (Je, 1966), 22: 96-103.

946. Oster, Harry. "A Delanson Manuscript of Songs,"
NYFQ (W, 1952), 8: 267-282. Text and discussion
(no music) of 40 temperance, sentimental, military,
and patriotic songs found in a ms. owned by a
Schenectady Co. family.

947.   _____. Living Country Blues (Detroit: Folklore
        Assoc., 1969), xv, 464pp. Some 221 blues col-
        lected in Louisiana, chiefly in Angola Prison. Cf.
        critical review by B. Jackson in JAF (1971), 84:
        253-255.

948.   Owens, William A. Texas Folk Songs (Austin and
        Dallas: U. P. in Dallas, 1950), 302pp. A medi-
        ocre collection including sentimental popular songs,
        a few genuine ballads, and folksy comment about
        the songs.

949.   Page, Marian Taylor. "Child Ballads from Mont-
        gomery County," TFSB (Mr, 1971), 37: 9-14.
        Three Child ballads (Nos. 18, 75, 277), from St.
        Bethlehem, Tenn.

950.   Parler, Mary Celestia. "Two Yarrow Ballads from
        the Ozarks," SFQ (Dec, 1958), 22: 195-200.
        Two rare ballads from Missouri and Arkansas.

951.   Patterson, Daniel W. "Turtle Creek to Busro: Notes
        on Shaker Ballads," NCarF (Dec, 1955), 3: 31-37.

952.   _____. "A Sheaf of North Carolina Folksongs,"
        NCarF (Jl, 1956), 4: 23-31.

953.   Pawlowska, Harriet M. Merrily We Sing. 105 Polish
        Folksongs (Detroit: Wayne State U. P., 1961),
        xx, 263pp. Material collected in Detroit, presented
        with music and English translations.

954.   Porter, Marjorie Lansing. "Collecting Adirondack
        Folklore," NYFQ (Je, 1966), 22: 113-21. Details
        about traditional singers and three ballads.

955.   Purcell, Joanne B. "Traditional Ballads among the
        Portuguese in California," WF (Jan, Apr, 1969),
        28: 1-19, 77-90. Original texts, translations, and
        tunes.

956.   Rael, Juan B. The New Mexican Alabado (Stanford:
        Stanford U. P., 1951), 154pp. Spanish texts of
        some 89 religious hymns of the flagellant brothers,
        as sung at Christmas, wakes, burials, and saints'
        days. Only four in English translation.

957. Randolph, Vance. Ozark Folksongs (Columbia: State
      Hist. Soc. of Missouri, 1946-1950), four volumes,
      883 songs with tunes. An invaluable work. Vol.
      IV, 455pp., Religious Songs and Other Items (1950),
      contains indexes for all volumes.

958. Rathvon, Simon Snyder. "English Folksong Tradition,"
      PD (Feb 15, 1953), 4: xii, 6-13. Fourteen songs
      without music, part of a diary kept in Lancaster
      Co., Penn., in 1854-58.

959. Richardson, Ethel Park. American Mountain Songs,
      ed. Sigmund Spaeth (New York: Greenberg, 1956).
      120pp. Ballads, lovesongs, spirituals, and non-
      sense songs.

960. Ring, Constance Varney, Samuel P. Bayard, and
      Tristram P. Coffin, eds. "Mid-Hudson Song and
      Verse," JAF (Jan-Mr, 1953), 66: 43-68. Twenty-
      eight items collected by folklore classes from 1920
      to 1930.

961. Rinzler, Ralph. "Doc Watson: Folksinging is a Way
      of Life," Sing Out! (Feb-Mr, 1964), 14: i, 8-12.
      Data about a North Carolina folk singer with texts
      and music of two songs.

962. Ritchie, Jean. The Dulcimer Book (New York: Oak
      Publications, 1963), 45pp. History of and instruc-
      tions for playing the 3-string Appalachian dulcimer,
      plus words and music for 16 songs performed by
      the Ritchie family of Kentucky.

963. _____. Folk Songs of the Southern Appalachians
      as Sung by Jean Ritchie (New York: Oak Publica-
      tions, 1965), 96pp. Seventy-seven songs, tunes,
      and ballads. Foreword by Alan Lomax.

964. [_____.] "Jean Ritchie's Songs," Folkways (Jan,
      1963), 1: 4-10. Ten ballads and songs.

965. _____. Singing Family of the Cumberlands (New
      York: Oak Publications, 1963), vi, 282pp. Re-
      print of a book first issued in 1955. Biography of
      a Kentucky mountain family devoted to song; 42
      songs with music are interwoven with text.

966. Robb, John Donald. Hispanic Folk Songs of New Mexico (Albuquerque: U. of New Mexico P., 1954), 83pp. A discussion of literary and musical characteristics of both religious and secular songs of New Mexico. Reprinted in 1962.

967. _____. "The J. D. Robb Collection of Folk Music Recordings," NMFR (1952-1953), 7: 6-20. List of recordings made by Robb and now on deposit at UNM Library.

968. Roberts, Leonard W. Sang Branch Settlers, Folksongs and Tales of a Kentucky Mountain Family (Austin and London: U. of Texas P., 1974), xxi, 401pp. One hundred folksongs and hymns and 61 folktales, most of them previously published, from the Couch family of eastern Kentucky.

969. Rothenberg, Jerome. Shaking the Pumpkin: Traditional Poetry of the Indian North Americas (New York: Doubleday, 1972), xxvi, 475pp. Myths, songs, poetry, etc. Extensive annotation by the compiler (sources, background, translators).

970. Rybak, Shulamith. "Puerto Rican Children's Songs in New York," MF (Spr, 1958), 8: 5-20. Spanish texts, translations, and music.

971. Sackheim, Eric. The Blues Line; A Collection of Blues Lyrics (New York: Grossman Pubs., 1969), 500pp. Large collection of Negro blues texts. No music. Illustrated by Jonathan Shahn.

972. Schrader, Arthur F. "Arcade Revisited: Some Additional Notes for A Pioneer Songster," NYFQ (Mr, 1968), 24: 16-26. Addenda for Harold Thompson's 1958 volume.

973. Seeger, Peggy. Folk Songs of Peggy Seeger (New York: Oak Publications, 1964), 96pp. Eighty-eight items.

974. Seeger, Pete. American Favorite Ballads (New York: Oak Publications, 1961), 96pp. From the repertoire of a capable and admired performer.

975. _____. "Woody Guthrie--Some Reminiscences,"

Sing Out! (Jl, 1964), 14: iii, 25-29. Transcription
of a radio interview.

976. Seeger, Ruth Crawford. American Folk Songs for
Christmas (Garden City; Doubleday, 1953), 80pp.
Some 55 songs with words and music. Designed
for children.

977. _____. Animal Folksongs for Children (New York:
Doubleday, 1950), 80pp. Some 43 songs, chiefly
from the southern U.S. Words and music with attractive illustrations.

978. Sharp, Cecil. English Folk Songs from the Southern
Appalachians, ed. Maud Karpeles (London: Oxford,
1952), Vol. I, xxxviii, 436pp.; Vol. II, xi, 411pp.
Enlarged second ed. of a book first published in
1917. A landmark in American song collecting
with 273 songs and ballads and 968 tunes.

979. Shellans, Herbert. Folk Songs of the Blue Ridge
Mountains (New York: Oak Publications, 1968),
96pp. Fifty songs from southwestern Virginia.

980. Silber, Irwin. 900 Miles; the Ballads, Blues, and
Folksongs of Cisco Houston (New York: Oak Publications, 1965), 96pp.

981. _____. Songs America Voted By (Harrisburg:
Stackpole Books, 1971), 320pp.

982. _____. Songs of the Civil War (New York: Columbia U. P., 1960), xii, 385pp. 124 complete
songs, some from folk sources, others quoted.

983. _____. "You're Hedy West," Sing Out! (Sept,
1964), 14: iv, 29-33. A Georgia folksinger and
some of her songs.

984. _____ and Earl Robinson. Songs of the Great
American West (New York: Macmillan, 1967),
xvi, 334pp. Ninety-two songs, more popular than
folk.

985. _____ with Fred Silber. Folksinger's Wordbook
(New York: Oak Publications, 1973), 430pp.

986. Silverman, Jerry. Folk Blues: 110 American Folk
     Blues (New York: Macmillan, 1958), 297pp. Re-
     vised edition published by Oak Publications in 1968.

987. Stegner, S. Page. "Protest Songs from the Butte
     Mines," WF (Jl, 1967), 26: 157-67. Songs by
     "Scottie," an IWW hard rock miner from the Butte
     area.

988. Studer, Norman. "'Whirling' and Applejack in the
     Catskills," NYFQ (W, 1952), 8: 301-6. Rhymed
     insults.

989. Sturges, Philip C. "Utah Mining Folklore," WF (Apr,
     1959), 18: 137-39. Three ballads.

990. Sturgill, Virgil L. "The Murder of Lottie Yates,"
     KFR (Apr-Je, 1959), 5: 61-64. A Kentucky ballad
     based on an event of 1895.

991. Swetnam, George. "Some Very Old Ballad and Hymn
     Texts," KFQ (W, 1961), 6, iv: 21-29. Old texts
     of "Paul Jones," "Sinclair's Defeat," and several
     hymns from a Lancaster County, Penn., tavern
     ledger.

992. [Thompson, Harold W.] "Irish Lore from New York
     State's Capital District," NYFQ (Spr, 1954), 10:
     35-39. Five songs recorded from Irish immigrants
     to New York.

993. Thompson, Harold W., ed. A Pioneer Songster:
     Texts from the Stevens-Douglas Manuscript of
     Western New York, 1841-1856 (Ithaca: Cornell
     U. P., 1958), xxii, 203pp. Child ballads, Ameri-
     can songs and ballads, and sentimental ditties as
     sung by Artemus Stevens, a New York and Kansas
     resident. Ably edited by Thompson and Edith E.
     Cutting.

994. Thorp, N. Howard (Jack). Songs of the Cowboys
     (New York: Clarkson N. Potter, 1966), 346pp.
     New edition of Thorp's famous 1908 work with ex-
     tensive comment by Austin E. Fife and Alta S.
     Fife.

995. Thurman, Howard. The Negro Spiritual Speaks of

Life and Death (New York: Harper, 1947), 55pp.
Reprinted in 1969.

996.   Tinker, Edward L.   Corridos & Calaveras (Austin:
       U. of Texas P. , 1961), 58pp.   Mexican ballads
       and broadsides with notes and translations by
       Américo Paredes.

997.   Toelken, J. Barre.   "Northwest Traditional Ballads:
       A Collector's Dilemma, " NR (W, 1962), 5: 9-18.
       Ten ballad texts with notes.   Comments on the
       rarity of indigenous folklore in the Pacific North-
       west.

998.   Truzzi, Marcello.   "Folksongs of the American Cir-
       cus, " NYFQ (Sept, 1968), 24: 163-75.   Discus-
       sion of an interesting body of circus songs often
       sung by the clowns.

998a.   _____.   "The 100% American Songbag: Conserva-
       tive Folksongs in America, " WF (Jan, 1969), 28:
       27-40.   Songs of the American right, some of
       them parodies.

999.   Wallrich, William Jones.   Air Force Airs (New York:
       Duell, Sloan & Pearce, 1957), xxii, 232pp.
       Songs and ballads from World War I through the
       Korean conflict.

1000.   _____.   "U. S. Air Force Parodies Based upon
       'The Dying Hobo,' " WF (Oct, 1954), 13: 236-
       244.   Parodies from air force personnel in the
       two world wars and Korean war.

1001.   _____.   "U. S. Air Force Parodies: World War
       II and Korean War, " WF (Oct, 1953), 12: 270-
       282.   A dozen parodies sung to familiar tunes;
       no music given.

1002.   Walton, Ivan H.   "Folk Singing on Beaver Island, "
       MF (W, 1952), 2: 243-50.   Song titles from Irish
       fishermen and farmers on a Lake Michigan island.
       No texts.

1003.   Warner, Frank M.   "A Salute and a Sampling of
       Songs, " NYFQ (F, 1958), 14: 202-23.   Titles of
       many songs sung by John Galusha and Mrs. Lena

Fish; music and texts of four songs by each singer.

1004. _____. "Three Civil War Songs," NYFQ (S, 1961),
17: 90-95. "The Red, White and Red," "The
Twenty-Third," and "Virginia's Bloody Soil."
Sung by John Galusha.

1005. _____ and Anne Warner. "'That's the Way They
Lived,'" NYFQ (Je, 1966), 22: 104-13. More
details about and songs by Yankee John Galusha
of Minerva, N.Y.

1006. Wheeler, Ann King. "Ballads and Tales of Blue Mt.
Lake, Adirondacks," NYFQ (S, 1954), 10: 115-22.
Text of the lumbering ballad "Blue Mountain
Lake" without music.

1007. Whiting, Bartlett Jere. Traditional British Ballads
(New York: Appleton, Century, Crofts, 1955),
xii, 148pp. Forty Child ballads and representative texts.

1008. Wilgus, D. K. "Arch and Gordon," KFR (Apr-Je,
1960), 6: 51-56. Two variants of a Kentucky
murder ballad relating to an event of 1895.

1009. _____. "Down Our Way, Sing Us a Kentucky
Song," KFR (Apr-Je, 1959), 5: 45-59. Local
ballads, some fragmentary.

1010. _____. "Folksongs of Kentucky, East and West,"
KFR (Jl-Sept, 1957), 3: 89-119. Whole issue
devoted to songs from unpublished collections of
Kentucky material. Brief headnotes and music
given.

1011. _____. "Local Ballads," KFR (Oct-Dec, 1959),
5: 131-35. Two variants of the murder ballad
"Stella Kenney."

1012. Williams, Cratis D. "John Ferguson," KFR (Jan-
Mr, 1960), 6: 15-17. A local ballad.

1012a. _____. "Lottie Yates," KFR (Apr-Je, 1959), 5:
65-69.

1013.   Wright, Robert L.   Swedish Emigrant Ballads (Lincoln: U. of Nebraska P., 1965), xii, 209pp.
Forty songs from printed Swedish sources with
English translations.   Music for 19 but little annotation.

1014.   Yates, Thelma R.   "Unwritten Negro Folk Songs,"
MichH (Je, 1953), 37: 183-196.   Twenty-four
songs recorded from Negroes residing in Michigan.   Music and texts given and informants identified.

1015.   Yoder, Don.   "Pennsylvania Broadsides: I," PF (W,
1966-1967), 16: ii, 14-21.   Political broadsides
printed in Philadelphia.   "Pennsylvania Broadsides: II," PF (Spr, 1967), 16: iii, 28-33.
Mostly spirituals in both German and English.

1016.   _____. Pennsylvania Spirituals (Lancaster, Penn.:
Penn. Folklife Soc., 1961), xi, 528pp.   Study of
folk hymns in Penn. with 150 song texts, translations, music, and thematic discussion.   A scholarly labor of love.

1017.   _____. "Spirituals from the Pennsylvania Dutch
Country," PD (F-W, 1956-1957), 8: ii, 22-33.
The impact of Methodism on Penn. Dutch country
produced many spirituals; these are transcribed
without music.

B.   Criticism

1018.   Abrahams, Roger D.   A Singer and Her Songs:
Almeda Riddle's Ballad Book (Baton Rouge:
Louisiana State U. P., 1970), xi, 191pp.   Bi-
ographical data about the Ozark singer Almeda
Riddle plus words and music of some 50 songs
and commentary.

1019.   Abrams, W. Amos.   "Horton Barker: Folk Singer
Supreme," NCarF (Nov, 1974), 22: 141-153.
Brief biography and appraisal of Barker plus
texts of some of his songs.

1020. _____. "Uncle Pat Fry: Yadkin County Minstrel or the Blind Balladeer of East Bend," NCarF (Nov, 1968), 16: 153-160. Biographical notes plus three song texts.

1021. Albright, R. L. H. "The Fate of Sir Patrick Spens: the Ballad as a Strategy for Living," KFQ (Spr, 1972), 17: 19-26. Analysis of several versions of a famous ballad.

1022. _____. "The Problem of Ballad Story-Variation and Eugene Haun's 'The Drowsy Sleeper,'" SFQ (Je, 1950), 14: 87-96.

1023. Anderson, John Q. "Another Texas Variant of 'Cole Younger,' Ballad of a Badman," WF (Apr, 1972), 31: 103-15.

1024. _____. "The Ballad of Graham Barnett," WF (Apr, 1965), 24: 77-85. Ballad about bad man Grim Barnett from Texas's West Bend country.

1025. _____. "'The Waco Girl'--Another Variant of a British Broadside Ballad," WF (Apr, 1960), 19: 107-18. An old English murder ballad lives in an American variant.

1026. Barsness, John. "The Dying Cowboy," WAL (Spr, 1967), 2: 50-57. To the writer most cowboy songs are sentimentalized.

1027. Bayard, Samuel P. "American Folksongs and Their Music," SFQ (Je, 1953), 17: 122-39. A study of American musical repertoires from British, Scotch, and Irish sources. Seven tune families listed with examples of each. Names are his or Phillips Barry's.

1028. Beard, Anne. "'Lord Thomas' in America," SFQ (Dec, 1955), 19: 257-261. American variants probably spring from a lost broadside but no proof given.

1029. Beck, Horace P. "The Riddle of 'The Flying Cloud,'" JAF (Apr-Je, 1953), 66: 123-133.

1030. Bluestein, Gene. "The Lomaxes' New Canon of

American Folksong," TQ (Spr, 1962), 5: 49-59.
New evaluation of John A. Lomax as a critic of
folksong.

1031. Blum, Margaret Morton. "'Edward' and the Folk
      Tradition," SFQ (Sept, 1957), 21: 131-142.
      Child #13b is a literary rather than a folk ballad.
      Am. variants considered.

1032. Boswell, George. "An Analysis of Text-Controlled
      Tune Variations in 'The Boston Burglar,'" TFSB
      (Mr, 1953), 19: 5-10. A variant of the old
      English ballad "Botany Bay."

1033. _____. "Progress Report: Collection of Tennes-
      see Folksongs in Recent Years," TFSB (Je,
      1959), 25: 31-79.

1034. Bradley, F. W. "Charles Guiteau," SFQ (Dec, 1960),
      24: 282-83. Two South Carolina texts of Ameri-
      can ballad about Garfield's assassination.

1035. _____. "Little Mary Fagan," SFQ (Je, 1960), 24:
      144-46. Two South Carolina versions of a native
      ballad about the death of a young factory girl in
      1913.

1036. Brewster, Paul G. "The Two Sisters," FFC (Hel-
      sinki: Suomalainen Tiedeakatemia, 1953), No.
      147, pp. 3-101. Exhaustive study of Child ballad
      No. 10, based on study of 254 texts and about
      100 tunes.

1037. Buchanan, Annabel Morris. "Creation and Fall of
      Man, A Kentucky Ballad-Carol," KFR (Oct-Dec,
      1955), 1: 91-99. An old Scriptural narrative
      carol in oral tradition.

1038. Buckley, Bruce R. "'Uncle' Ira Cephas--a Negro
      Folk Singer in Ohio," MF (Spr, 1953), 3: 5-18.
      Account of a versatile Negro bard.

1039. Buehler, Richard E. "Stacker Lee: a Partial In-
      vestigation into the Historicity of a Negro Murder
      Ballad," KFQ (F, 1967), 12: 187-191. Data
      about one Stacker Lee, presumably the model for
      the hero of "Stackerlee."

1040.   Burress, Lee A., Jr.   "The Miller and His Three
        Sons," WF (Jl, 1962), 21: 183-85.   Text and
        music of the ballad with some account of the role
        of the miller in rural U. S.

1041.   Burrison, John.   "'James Harris' in Britain Since
        Child," JAF (Jl-Sept, 1967), 80: 271-84.   Later
        history of a ballad (Child #243) well-known in the
        U. S.

1042.   Burton, Thomas G.   "The Anglo-American Ballad
        'By Indirections Find Directions Out,'" NCarF
        (Nov, 1971), 19: 185-190.   Ballads may prove
        to be valid means of analyzing people and more
        reliable than the fine arts.

1043.   _____.   "Kinnie Wagner on the Banks of the Hol-
        ston River," KFR (Jan-Mr, 1968), 14: 2-7.
        Background material for a Tennessee murder
        ballad.

1044.   _____.   "'Sir Hugh' in Sullivan County," TFSB
        (Je, 1965), 31: 42-47.   A Tennessee variant of
        Child #155.

1045.   Callcott, George H.   "The Good Old Rebel," SFQ
        (Sept, 1954), 18: 175-176.   Data on and text of
        Innes Randolph's famous ballad.

1046.   Campa, Arthur L.   "Spanish Folksongs in Metro-
        politan Denver," SFQ (Sept, 1960), 24: 179-92.
        Spanish-speaking residents of Denver have kept
        ballads, corridos, canciones, and inditas alive.
        Spanish texts given without music or translations.

1047.   Campbell, Marie.   "A Study of Twenty-Five Variants
        of 'Little Musgrave and Lady Barnard' in Ballad
        Collections of North America," TFSB (Mr, 1955),
        21: 14-19.

1048.   Cansler, Loman D.   "Boyhood Songs of My Grand-
        father," SFQ (Sept, 1954), 18: 177-89.   Songs
        of James R. Broyles of Laclede Co., Missouri;
        7 songs, among them 3 Child ballads.

1049.   _____.   "What Folksongs Reveal about Our Cul-
        tural Heritage," SFQ (Je, 1956), 20: 126-29.
        Brief exposition of what folksongs do.

1050.   Carpenter, Ann Miller. "The Railroad in American
        Folk Song, 1876-1902," in Diamond Bessie & the
        Shepherds, ed. Wilson M. Hudson, pp. 103-119.
        The occurrence of trains, wrecks, and railroad
        laborers in folk songs.

1051.   Cazden, Norman. "The Bold Soldier of Yarrow,"
        JAF (Apr.Je, 1955), 68: 201-9. Study of a Cat-
        skill Mountain variant of "The Bold Soldier."

1052.   _____. "The Story of a Catskill Ballad," NYFQ
        (W, 1952), 8: 245-66. Careful study of a New
        York variant of Child #214, "The Braes of Yar-
        row."

1053.   Chatman, Vernon W., III. "The Three Ravens Ex-
        plicated," MF (F, 1963), 13: 177-86. Close tex-
        tual reading of Child ballad #26.

1054.   Cheney, Thomas E. "Mormon Folk Song and the Fife
        Collection," BYUStudies (A, 1960), 3: 57-63.
        Rather astringent commentary on collection ac-
        quired by Brigham Young Univ.

1055.   Clayton, Lawrence. "'The Last Longhorn': a Poetic
        Denouement of an Era," SFQ (Je, 1973), 37: 115-
        122. Song published by John A. Lomax in 1916
        reveals historical and geographical background of
        the cattle country.

1056.   Cobos, Rubén. "The New Mexican Memoria, or In
        Memoriam Poem," WF (Jan, 1959), 18: 25-30.
        Comments and examples. Spanish texts and
        translations.

1057.   Coffin, Tristram P. "The 'Braes of Yarrow' Tradi-
        tion in America," JAF (Jl-Sept, 1950), 63: 328-
        335. Chiefly a comparison of five American
        variants.

1058.   _____. "The Golden Ball and the Hangman's
        Tree," in Folklore International, ed. D. K. Wil-
        gus, pp. 23-28.

1059.   _____. "'Mary Hamilton' and the Anglo-American
        Ballad as an Art Form," JAF (Jl-Sept, 1957),
        70: 208-14. The emotional core of the ballad is
        more important than details and clichés.

1060. _____. "The Problem of Ballad-Story Variation
and Eugene Haun's 'The Drowsy Sleeper'," SFQ
(Je, 1950), 14: 87-96. American version of "The
Drowsy Sleeper" learned from Eugene Haun who
got it from a hill woman. Ballad ends in double
suicide.

1061. _____. "A Tentative Study of a Typical Folk
Lyric: 'Green Grows the Laurel'," JAF (Oct-
Dec, 1952), 65: 341-51.

1062. Cohen, Anne B. Poor Pearl, Poor Girl: The Murdered Girl Stereotype in Ballad and Newspaper
(Austin and London: U. of Texas P., 1973),
131pp. Pearl Bryan's headless corpse was dis-
covered Feb. 1, 1896, near Ft. Thomas, Kentucky. This is a study of the factual evidence,
basic types, and variants of the ballad.

1063. Cohen, Norm. "'Casey Jones': At The Crossroads
of Two Ballad Traditions," WF (Apr, 1973), 32:
77-103. Genesis of the famous railroad ballad.
John Luther Jones, the ill-fated engineer, was
born in 1863; first published version of the ballad dated 1908.

1064. _____. "'The Persian's Crew'--the Ballad, its
Author, and the Incident," NYFQ (Dec, 1969),
25: 289-96. Data about an American ballad stem-
ming from a poem by Patrick Fennell; Cohen also
prints text of another shipwreck poem by Fennell.

1065. _____. "Robert W. Gordon and the Second Wreck
of the 'Old 97,'" JAF (Jan-Mr, 1974), 87: 12-38.
Comments on Gordon's collection and a history
of the composition and recording of the famous
railroad ballad. Excellent study.

1066. Cray, Ed. "'Barbara Allen': Cheap Print and Reprint," in Folklore International, ed. D. K. Wilgus, pp. 41-50.

1067. Cuccinello, Louis S. "The Frog Went a-Courting,"
SFQ (Je, 1962), 26: 97-106. Brief account of an
old song with some American variants added.

1068. Danker, Frederick E. "Towards an Intrinsic Study
of the Blues Ballad: 'Casey Jones' and 'Louis

Collins,'" SFQ (Je, 1970), 34: 90-103.

1069. Davis, Arthur Kyle, Jr. "'Far Fannil Town': a Ballad of Mystery Examined," SFQ (Mr, 1972), 36: 1-13. Suggestion that a recently collected ballad should be added to the Child collection.

1070. _____. "'The Unquiet Grave': a New-Old Ballad from Virginia," in English Studies in Honor of James Southall Wilson, ed. Fredson Bowers (Charlottesville: U. of Virginia P., 1951), Univ. of Va. Studies, 4: 99-110. A six-quatrain text, Child #78. No music.

1071. _____ and Paul C. Worthington. "Another New Traditional Ballad from Virginia: 'Jellom Grame' (Child, No. 90)," SFQ (Dec, 1958), 22: 163-172. A 20-stanza text recovered in 1932.

1072. _____ and _____. "A New Traditional Ballad from Virginia: 'The Whummill Bore' (Child, No. 27)," SFQ (Dec, 1957), 21: 187-193. American text of a ballad seldom found in tradition.

1073. Dippie, Brian W. "Bards of the Little Big Horn," WAL (F, 1966), 1: 175-95. Study of literary ballads stimulated by General Custer's last stand; poets cited include Longfellow, Neihardt, Whittier, and others.

1074. Dober, Virginia. "The Marital Status of Child Ballad Heroines," SFQ (Je, 1957), 21: 93-99. Misconceptions about the women of the ballads, seen against the mores of their times.

1075. Dongan, Michael B. "Two Manuscript Folksongs from Civil War Arkansas and Their Background," MSF (W, 1974), 2: 83-88.

1076. Drake, Carlos C. "'Mary Hamilton' in Tradition," SFQ (Mr, 1969), 33: 39-47. Problems of dating the ballad discussed as well as its place in oral tradition.

1077. Drake, Robert Y., Jr. "Casey Jones: the Man and the Song," TFSB (Dec, 1953), 19: 95-101. Review of the events and the variants.

1078. Dunn, James Taylor. "'Dunbar, the Murderer',"
       NYFQ (Spr, 1958), 14: 28-33. An account of a
       doggerel ballad by Henry S. Backus.

1079. _____. "'The Murdered Peddlar' and the Sau-
       gerties Bard," NYFQ (S, 1955), 11: 116-22.
       Ballad about a murderer composed by Henry S.
       Backus.

1080. Eddy, Mary O. "Alexander Auld and The Ohio
       Harmonist," MF (Apr, 1951), 1: 19-21. Brief
       account of Auld's 1847 hymnbook with shape notes.

1081. Evanson, Jacob A. "Pittsburgh-Region Folksongs for
       Pittsburgh Children," KFQ (Spr and S, 1960),
       5, i, ii: 30-40. Since American folk songs are
       the first real music American children have, they
       should be taught and sung. Curiously no songs
       are mentioned.

1082. Ewing, George W. "The Well-Tempered Lyre:
       Songs of the Temperance Movement," SWR (Spr,
       1971), 46: 139-55. Discussion of the temperance
       movement and its songs, but with spare documen-
       tation.

1083. Fife, Austin E. "A Ballad of the Mountain Meadows
       Massacre," WF (Oct, 1953), 12: 229-41. Data
       about a famous event in Mormon history and five
       variants of a ballad commemorating it.

1084. _____. "The Strawberry Roan and His Progeny,"
       JEMFQ (1972), 8: 149-165. Variants and paro-
       dies.

1085. _____. "'The Trail to Mexico,'" MSF (W, 1973),
       1: 85-102. Study of a familiar cowboy ballad
       based on 118 texts from mss., printed sources,
       and recordings. No single text can be deemed
       basic.

1086. Flanagan, John T. "An Early American Printing of
       'Barbara Allen,'" NYFQ (Mr, 1964), 20: 47-54.

1087. Flattio, E. "'Lord Randal,'" SFQ (Dec, 1970), 34:
       331-336. Analysis of style and narrative to ex-
       plain the ballad's emotional impact.

1088. Fletcher, John Gould. "Some Folk-Ballads and the
       Background of History," AHQ (S, 1950), 9: 87-
       98. Analysis of Vance Randolph's Ozark Folk-
       songs (1946-1949) with special reference to Civil
       War ballads and songs of murderers and desper-
       adoes.

1089. Foss, George. "More on a Unique and Anomalous
       Version of 'The Two Sisters'," SFQ (Je, 1964),
       28: 119-33. Careful study of versions of "The
       Two Sisters" (Child #10) from W. Virginia (1931)
       and N. Carolina (1962).

1090. _____ and Roger D. Abrahams. "Fa'r Nottalin
       Town," KFR (Oct-Dec, 1968), 14: 88-91. Com-
       ments on a widely known nonsense song.

1091. Foster, John Wilson. "Some Irish Songs in the Gor-
       don Collection," NWF (Nov, 1969), 3, ii: 16-29.
       Anonymous collection in the U. of Oregon Li-
       brary; texts of six songs given plus 79 titles.

1092. Fowke, Edith. "Canadian Variations of a Civil War
       Song," MF (S, 1963), 13: 101-4. Variants of
       George T. Root's "Tramp! Tramp! Tramp!,"
       1863.

1093. _____. "'The Red River Valley' Re-Examined,"
       WF (Jl, 1964), 23: 163-71. Evidence of Canadi-
       an popularity of a well known North American
       folk song.

1094. Fowler, David C. "'The Hunting of the Cheviot' and
       'The Battle of Otterburn'," WF (Jl, 1966), 25:
       165-71. Child ballads 161 and 162 considered to-
       gether.

1095. Freedman, Morris. "Natural Jazz Rhythms in Folk
       Songs," SFQ (Dec, 1957), 21: 194-205. Natural
       jazz rhythms appear in folk songs and children's
       songs. Examples cited: "Edward," "Sir Patrick
       Spens," "Swannanoa Town," and children's non-
       sense rhymes.

1096. Freeman, Linton C. "The Changing Functions of a
       Folksong," JAF (Jl-Sept, 1957), 70: 215-20.
       Verses sung in Hawaii about the time of World
       War II.

1097. Friedman, Albert B. The Ballad Revival (Chicago:
       U. of Chicago P., 1961), vii, 376pp. Survey of
       the history of ballad publication and criticism by
       a recognized scholar with an interesting chapter
       on literary limitations of the ballad.

1098. Gardner-Medwin, Alisoun. "The Ancestry of 'The
       House Carpenter'," JAF (Oct-Dec, 1971), 84:
       414-27. Child ballad #243 came to America in
       the mid-18th century and has survived in altered
       form.

1099. Glassie, Henry H. "The Gypsy Laddie (Child 200)--
       Two New Texts with Tunes and Some Observa-
       tions," TFSB (Mr, 1964), 30: 1-6. North Caro-
       lina variants.

1100. _____. "'Take That Night Train to Selma': An
       Excursion to the Outskirts of Scholarship," in
       Folksongs and Their Makers, ed. Ray B. Browne
       (Bowling Green, Ohio: Bowling Green U. Popu-
       lar P., 1971), pp. 1-68. An account of the New
       York farmer-laborer and folk composer, Dorrance
       Weir.

1101. Gold, Charles H. "Once There was a Town: the
       Birth of a Folksong," MF (S, 1962), 12: 87-92.
       "The Ballad of Bagnell Dam" commemorates the
       rise and disappearance of an Ozark town named
       Zebra.

1102. Goldstein, Kenneth S. "'The Texas Rangers' in
       Aberdeenshire," in A Good Tale and A Bonnie
       Tune, ed. Mody C. Boatright et al., pp. 188-98.
       Discussion of "The Gallant Ranger," a variant of
       "The Texas Rangers," as heard in Scotland.

1103. Gower, Herschel. "The Great West as Seen in the
       Ballads of Cocke County," TFSB (Mr, 1954), 20:
       14-20. Comments on Mildred Haun's manuscript
       collection.

1104. Green, Archie. "The Carter Family's 'Coal Miner's
       Blues'," SFQ (Dec, 1961), 25: 226-37. Study of
       the Carter family and one of their famous songs.

1105. _____. "The Death of Mother Jones," LH (W,

1960), 1: no pagination. Study of song commemorating Mother Jones (1830-1930); author remains unknown.

1106. _____. "A Discographical Appraisal of American Balladry from British Broadsides," Caravan (Feb-Mr, 1959), no. 15: 7-13. Review of the book by Laws (1957) with special emphasis on his inadequate discography. Informative comments on singers and records.

1107. _____. "'Will the Weaver's' Hillbilly Kinfolk," Caravan (Aug-Sept, 1959), no. 18: 14-23. Printed variants of ballad with Parker-Woolbright version of 1931.

1108. Greene, David Mason. "'The Lady and the Dragoon': A Broadside Ballad in Oral Tradition," JAF (Jl-Sept, 1957), 70: 221-30. Some 40 American versions found.

1109. Greenway, John. "Aunt Molly Jackson and Robin Hood: A Study in Folk Re-Creation," JAF (Jan-Mr, 1956), 69: 23-38. Aunt Molly Jackson's version of Robin Hood ballads.

1110. _____. "The Flight of the Gray Goose: Literary Symbolism in the Traditional Ballad," SFQ (Sept, 1954), 18: 165-74. Studies of "The Hunting of the Wren" and "The Gray Goose" suggest remarkable polygenesis and an undistinguished bird as a vehicle for social symbolism. Clever parallel.

1111. _____. "Folksongs as Socio-Historical Documents," WF (Jan, 1960), 19: 1-9. Folksongs should be used as a means of understanding the people who made them, as is now done in Australian scholarship. Reprinted in Folklore in Action, ed. H. P. Beck, pp. 112-19.

1112. _____. "Jimmie Rodgers--a Folksong Catalyst," JAF (Jl-Sept, 1957), 70: 231-234.

1113. _____. "Songs of the Ludlow Massacre," Sing Out! (W, 1959), 8: iii, 17-22. Material about the Colorado coal strike of 1914 with relevant songs, including Woody Guthrie's "Ludlow Massacre."

1114. Griffith, Benjamin W. "A Longer Version of 'Guinea Negro Song': From a Georgia Frontier Songster," SFQ (Je, 1964), 28: 116-18. Text of "The Negro and the Buckra Man," from an early manuscript collection by Thomas Hurry Morgan.

1115. Gyemant, Robert E. "'Jack Haggerty' and a California Legend," WF (Apr, 1965), 24: 105-8. Interesting relationship between a Michigan ballad and a California tale.

1116. Halpert, Herbert. "The Cante Fable in Decay," SFQ (Sept, 1941), 5: 191-200. Reprinted with additions in Folklore in Action, ed. H. P. Beck, pp. 139-50.

1117. _____. "Shakespeare, Abelard, and 'The Unquiet Grave'," JAF (Jan-Mr, 1956), 69: 74-5, 98. An American variant of Child #78.

1118. Halpert, Violetta Maloney. "Collectors and Students of Folksong, U.S.A.," SFQ (Je, 1953), 17: 167-188. Useful even if outdated list of interested persons, with addresses and special interests.

1119. Hand, Wayland D. "'Springfield Mountain' and the Mexican War," WF (Apr, 1970), 29: 113-116. The familiar ballad was used in a juvenile novel about the Mexican War.

1120. _____. "Two Child Ballads in the West," WF (Jan, 1959), 18: 42-45. Variants of "The House Carpenter" and "Little Musgrave and Lady Barnard."

1121. _____. "Wo sind 'die Strassen von Laredo'? Die Entwicklungsgeschichte einer amerikanischen Cowboy-Ballade," in Festschrift für Will-Erich Peuckert zum 60. Geburtstag, ed. Helmut Dölker (Berlin: Erich Schmidt, 1955), pp. 144-161. Text of main ballad (no music) with variants from several American states.

1122. Harris, Richard. "'Lord Thomas and Fair Ellinor': A Preliminary Study of the Ballad," MF (S, 1955), 5: 79-94. A study of Child #73 based on 36 variants, mostly American.

1123.   Hawes, Bess Lomax.   "El Corrido de la Inundacion
        de la Presa de San Francisquito: the Story of a
        Local Ballad," WF (Jl, 1974), 33: 219-30.   Ac-
        count of a Spanish language ballad about a Cali-
        fornia dam break that took place in 1928.

1124.   Hayakawa, S. I.   "Popular Songs vs. the Facts of
        Life," ETC (1955), 12: 83-95.

1125.   Hendren, Joseph W.   "Bonny Barbara Allen," in
        Folk Travelers, ed. Mody B. Boatright et al.,
        pp. 47-74.   History and diffusion of a well-known
        ballad.   Ballad has not degenerated but kept its
        story line in many states.   Erudite and extensive
        notes.

1126.   _____.   "The Scholar and the Ballad Singer," SFQ
        (Je, 1954), 18: 139-46.   Ballad scholars were
        concerned with poems.   Today people sing folk
        songs.   America is rich and diverse in its folk-
        songs.

1127.   Hippensteel, Faith.   "'Sir Hugh': the Hoosier Con-
        tribution to the Ballad," IF (1969), 2: 75-140.

1128.   Hoeptner, Fred G.   "Folk and Hillbilly Music, the
        Background of Their Relation," Caravan (Apr-
        May, Je-Jl, 1959), Nos. 16, 17; 8, 16-17, 42;
        20-23, 26-28.   A two-part article attempting to
        define and discriminate.

1129.   Hoffman, Daniel G.   "Historic Truth and Ballad
        Truth: Two Versions of the Capture of New Or-
        leans," JAF (Jl-Sept, 1952), 65: 295-303.

1130.   Hoffmann, Frank A.   "Yankee Doodle: an Early
        Version," NEF (W, 1958), 1: 55-58.   A version
        collected in 1957 in Pennsylvania is a family tra-
        dition.

1131.   Hostettler, Agnes.   "Symbolic Tokens in a Ballad of
        the Returned Lover," WF (Jan, 1973), 32: 33-38.

1132.   Hudson, Arthur Palmer.   "Glimpses of History in
        Southern Folksongs," SFQ (Sept, 1951), 15: 196-
        202.   Hudson comments on historical pieces in
        general, then concentrates on the North Carolina

Brown collection: 68 historical folksongs in 989
pieces.

1133.   Huntington, E. G.   "Two Songs from Martha's Vineyard, " NEF (Spr, 1959), 2: 1-4.

1134.   Hyman, Stanley Edgar.   "The Raggle-Taggle Ballads
O, " WR (S, 1951), 15: 305-13.   Critical review
of books on ballads by Evelyn Wells and M. J. C.
Hodgart.

1135.   Ives, Edward D.   "'The Bonny Earl of Murray': the
Ballad as History, " MF (F, 1959), 9: 133-38.
Child #181 is not only high folk art but also an
historical document.

1136.   _____ .   "Larry Gorman and 'Old Henry', " NEF
(F, 1959), 2: 40-45.   Includes "The Good Old
State of Maine. "

1137.   _____ .   "Larry Gorman and the Cante Fable, "
NEQ (Je, 1959), 32: 226-37.   Data about the
Maine folk poet, Larry Gorman, and examples of
his habit of making songs about specific incidents.
Gorman's wit and ingenuity were treasured.

1138.   Jackson, Bruce.   "The Glory Songs of the Lord, " in
Our Living Traditions, ed. T. P. Coffin, pp. 108-
119.   Brief discussion of the spirituals, mostly
Negro.

1139.   Jackson, George Pullen.   "American Folksong and
Musical Art, " SFQ (Je, 1953), 17: 140-42.   Folk
songs are sung by recitalists and choruses but
have small place in schools or churches.   Serious composers (Gould, Copland, Harris, Thompson) do use them.

1140.   _____ .   "The 400-Year Odyssey of the 'Captain
Kidd' Song Family--Notably Its Religious Branch, "
SFQ (Dec, 1951), 15: 239-48.   Capt. William
Kidd was executed in London in 1701.   The ballad
was sung to the tune of "Coming Down, " the last
words of another executed criminal (Jack Hall,
chimney-sweep).

1141.   Jones, Louis C.   "Songs of Henry Backus, Sauger-

ties Bard: A Checklist," NYFQ (W, 1955), 11:
301-4. Broadsides and popular songs peddled by
the composer.

1142. Jones, Loyal. "The Minstrel of the Appalachians:
Bascom Lamar Lunsford at 91," JEMFQ (Spr,
1973), 9: no. 29, 2-8. Brief sketch of a famous
folk singer and fiddler from No. Carolina.

1143. Joyner, Charles Winston. "The Craftsmanship of
Frank Proffitt: Tradition and the Individual Talent
in Folklore," TFSB (Mr, 1966), 32: 1-5. Singer,
performer, and maker of dulcimers and banjoes.

1144. Kahn, Ed. "A Texas Folktale Version of 'Get Up
and Bar the Door' (Child 275)," WF (Jl, 1960),
19: 169-71. A Child ballad with a folktale parallel.

1145. _____. "Will Roy Hearne: Peripheral Folk Song
Scholar," WF (Jl, 1964), 23: 173-79. Sketch of
an early collector of race and jazz records, especially 78's.

1146. Kaplan, Israel. "A John Brown Ballad," NYFQ (Spr,
1953), 9: 47-50. Four stanzas of an incomplete
text.

1147. Kealy, J. Kieran. "The Americanization of Horn,"
SFQ (Dec, 1973), 355-84. The ballad "Hind
Horn" (Child #17), has North American variants.
Discussion of basic elements in original Horn
story which recur in later versions.

1148. Kemppinen, Iivar. The Ballad of Lady Isabel and
the False Knight (Helsinki: Suomen Kulttuurira-
hasto, 1954), 301pp. Definitive study of Child
#4, with 1865 variants plus derivative songs.

1149. King, Mary Elizabeth. "More Light on the Ballad
of 'James Bird'," NYFQ (S, 1951), 7: 142-44.
Data about the ballad's subject, a soldier AWOL.

1150. Kirkeminde, Patricia Barclay. "The Confession of
Willis Mayberry," TFSB (Mr, 1964), 30: 7-21.
Data about a Negro murderer, subject of a song
also called "Roane County."

1151. Knoblock, Judith Ann. "'The Gypsy Laddie' (Child
200): An Unrecognized Child of Medieval Romance," WF (Jan, 1960), 19: 35-45. Interesting
comparative study of a Child ballad which has
been extremely popular in the U.S.

1152. Lathrop, Francis P. "Commercial Parlor-Ballad to
Folksong," JAF (Jl-Sept, 1957), 70: 240-46.
Comments on links between "The Ocean Burial"
and "Bury Me Not on the Lone Prairie."

1153. Laufe, Abe. "Sing Along Songs," KFQ (Spr, 1965),
10: 35-42. Interesting survey of popular songs
kept alive by their sprightly tunes and often known
under various names.

1154. Laws, G. Malcolm, Jr. American Balladry from
British Broadsides (Philadelphia: American Folklore Soc., 1957), xiii, 315pp. Chapters on the
types, origin, and variant forms of broadsides are
followed by a long list of ballads arranged the-
matically (no music). An extensive bibliography.

1155. _____. "Anglo-Irish Balladry in North America,"
in Folklore in Action, ed. H. P. Beck, pp. 172-
183. Irish ballads in U.S. are romantic, sentimental, nostalgic.

1156. _____. "Stories Told in Song; the Ballads of
America," in Our Living Traditions, ed. T. P.
Coffin, pp. 83-93. Brief discussion of the bal-
lads commonly sung in U.S.

1157. Leach, MacEdward and Tristram P. Coffin. The
Critics & the Ballad (Carbondale: Southern Illinois U.P., 1961), xii, 284pp. Fifteen essays,
reprinted from various journals, by distinguished
ballad students and authorities. Essays range
from theory and history to meaning and musical
form.

1158. Lee, Hector. "Some Notes on Lead Belly," JAF
(Apr-Je, 1963), 76: 135-40. Anecdotal material
about Lead Belly's visit to Salt Lake City.

1159. Lee, James Ward. "Arkansas Variations of Some
Texas Folksongs," in Singers and Storytellers,
ed. Mody C. Boatright, et al., pp. 212-17.

1160. Livaudais, West. "'Let's Go Hunting': A Nursery
       Song and Its Background," TFSB (Je, 1964), 30:
       61-69. Text from Memphis with historical data
       about the song.

1161. Lodewick, Kenneth. "'The Unfortunate Rake' and His
       Descendants," WF (Apr, 1955), 14: 98-109.
       Verses from many variants of a famous ballad.

1162. Long, Eleanor R. "Thematic Classification and 'Lady
       Isabel,'" JAF (Jan-Mr, 1972), 85: 32-41. The
       ballad contains three different themes.

1163. Loomis, Marjorie C. "Songs: 'Springfield Moun-
       tain,'" NYFQ (Spr, 1955), 11: 66-68. A minor
       variant.

1164. Love, Maggie J. "The Murder of Munroe Bynum,"
       TFSB (Mr, 1954), 20: 9-13. Data about the
       murder of a local figure.

1165. Lumpkin, Ben Gray. "'The Happy Land of Canaan':
       an Unpublished Civil War Song," CWH (Mr, 1965),
       11: 44-57. Variant text of a popular minstrel
       song from Miss. with many allusions to military
       figures. No music.

1166. _____. "Tune for 'Baldy Green,'" SFQ (Mr,
       1970), 34: 12-17. Words and music for one
       well known western ballad.

1167. Lutz, Anne. "The Ballad of 'Brave Paulding and the
       Spy' in the Ramapo Valley," NYFQ (W, 1954),
       10: 279-84. A variant text entitled "Major
       Andre."

1168. Lyle, E. B. "The Opening of 'Tam Lin'," JAF (Jan-
       Mr, 1970), 83: 33-43.

1169. McCarthy, Charles A. "James Bird: The Man and
       the Ballad," KFQ (W, 1961), 6, iv: 2-13. Data
       about Charles Miner, journalist who wrote ballad
       about James Bird, hero of the War of 1812.
       Text of ballad given; it has remained in tradition.

1170. McCormick, Mack. "A Who's Who of 'Midnight
       Special'," Caravan (Jan, 1960), no. 19: 10-21.

Texts and variants of famous Texas prison song
based on Southern Pacific's "The Alamo Special"
from Houston to San Antonio.

1171.   MacCracken, Henry Noble.   "A Ballad for Jenny
         Lind," NYFQ (W, 1957), 13: 277-79.   A doggerel
         ballad welcoming the Sewdish nightingale in 1850.

1172.   MacCurdy, Raymond R. and Daniel D. Stanley.
         "Judaeo-Spanish Ballads from Atlanta, Georgia,"
         SFQ (Dec, 1951), 15: 221-35.   Sephardic Jewish
         ballads in Spanish collected from Atlanta and
         originally preserved on phonograph records; 6
         ballads.

1173.   McIntosh, David S.   "Marching Down to New Orleans,"
         MF (F, 1954), 4: 139-148.   A popular singing
         game with six Illinois texts analyzed.

1174.   Meade, Guthrie T., Jr.   "The Sea Crab," MF (S,
         1958), 8: 91-100.   Comments on a pornographic
         ballad with American variants.

1175.   Millar, Branford P.   "The American Ballad List--
         1952," SFQ (Je, 1953), 17: 158-166.   Survival of
         Child ballads in U.S.   Some 141 individual titles
         have been found, some in fragmentary form.
         Published texts from 30 states.

1176.   _____.   "Three Texts of the 'Death of Queen
         Jane,'" HLB (W, 1951), 5: 99-102.   Two texts
         which appeared after the Child edition and one ms.
         he rejected.

1177.   Montell, Lynwood.   "'My Mother Slew Me; My
         Father Ate Me,'" KFR (Apr-Je, 1973), 19: 42-
         44.   Monroe Co., Ky., ballad version of a
         familiar story (Type #720).

1178.   Moore, Arthur K.   "Neighbors: Kentucky: a Metri-
         cal Version of the Wonderful Hunt," NYFQ (A,
         1951), 7: 236-40.   Unusual rhymed version of
         Thompson's Motif X921.

1179.   _____.   "A Springfield Mountain Composite,"
         SFQ (Dec, 1950), 14: 215-19.   A version sung in
         1948 in New Orleans which is a composite of three
         early versions of "Springfield Mountain."

1180. _____. "Types of the Folk Song 'Father Grum-
          ble'," JAF (Jan-Mr, 1951), 64: 89-94. American
          variants and a long version from Louisiana.

1181. Morris, Alton C. "'The Rolling Stone': the Way of
          a Song," SFQ (Dec, 1973), 37: 331-54. Henry
          Purcell's song of 1695 has survived in popular
          song books and in oral tradition in the U.S.

1182. Nelson, C. E. "The Origin and Tradition of the
          Ballad of 'Thomas Rymer': a Survey," in New
          Voices in American Studies, ed. Ray B. Browne
          et al., pp. 138-150.

1183. Nicolaisen, W. F. H. "Place-Names in Traditional
          Ballads," Folklore (W, 1973), 84: 299-312.
          Place names in Child ballads reveal historical
          events, confer authenticity upon stories, and have
          symbolic value.

1184. Nygard, Holger Olof. The Ballad of Heer Halewijn;
          Its Forms and Variations in Western Europe; a
          Study of the History and Nature of a Ballad Tra-
          dition (Helsinki: Suomalainen Tiedeakatemia,
          1958), 350pp. Careful and elaborate study of
          Child ballad #4, "Lady Isabel and the Elf-Knight,"
          with some French Canadian variants but little
          American material.

1185. _____. "Ballad Source Study: Child Ballad No. 4
          an Exemplar," JAF (Apr-Je, 1955), 68: 141-52.
          Study of "Lady Isabel and the Elf-Knight."

1186. O'Donnell, Thomas F. "'I'm Afloat!' on the Raging
          Erie," NYFQ (A, 1957), 13: 178-80. An Erie
          Canal ballad of the 1840's, possibly by Mrs. F.
          M. Whitcher.

1187. Oliver, Paul. Aspects of the Blues Tradition (New
          York: Oak Publications, 1968), 294pp. Study of
          expurgated material in recorded American blues
          songs.

1188. Oring, Elliott. "Whalemen and Their Songs: A Study
          of Folklore and Culture," NYFQ (Mr, 1971), 27:
          130-52. Whalers in both Greenland and South Pa-
          cific fisheries revealed their own lives and wish
          fulfillments in their songs.

1189. Paredes, Américo. "'El Corrido de Jose Mosqueda'
       as an Example of Pattern in the Ballad," WF
       (Jl, 1958), 17: 154-162. Comments on a ballad
       collected by the Lomaxes in 1939 from a blind
       guitarrero.

1190. Park, John O. "'The Kosciusko Bootlegger's Gripe,'
       A Ballad as History and Argumentation," MSF
       (Spr, 1973), 1: 27-32. Background of ballad
       about arrest of Mississippi bootleggers; the inci-
       dent and its principals are remembered by the
       community.

1191. Pearce, T. M. "What is a Folk Poet?" WF (Oct,
       1953), 12: 242-48. Data about a New Mexican
       folk poet, Prospero S. Baca, and discussion of
       his poetry.

1192. Pinkowski, Edward. "James D. Gay--Lost Bard of
       Pennsylvania," KFQ (A, W, 1962), Part I, 7,
       iii: 2-24; Part II, 7, iv: 18-49. Study of singer
       and composer who peddled his broadsides during
       Civil War and wrote ballads about Col. Ellsworth,
       Gettysburg, Grant, and the "Keystone Brigade."
       Gay lived 1831-1917.

1193. Pleat, Geraldine R. and Agnes N. Underwood. "Pink-
       ster Ode, Albany, 1803," NYFQ (Spr, 1952), 8:
       31-45. A folk poem describing a Negro festival
       in Albany on the day following Pentecost; dedi-
       cated to Negro drummer, "King Charley."

1194. Pound, Louise. "American Folksong," SFQ (Je,
       1953), 17: 114-21. Brief account of origins,
       texts, and modes of diffusion of American folk
       songs. Child ballads and occupational ballads
       touched on.

1195. _____. "Yet Another Joe Bowers," WF (Apr,
       1957), 16: 110-20. Survey of variants of and
       theories about a famous song; its real origin re-
       mains unknown.

1196. Powers, Doris C. "The American Variants of 'Farl
       Brand,' Child No. 7," WF (Apr, 1958), 17: 77-
       96. A study based on 40 texts from printed or
       recorded sources.

1197. Quillin, Brenda Joyce. "Nell Cropsy Died--But
      How?" NCarFJ (May, 1974), 22: 43-54. Local
      ballad about a girl who died in 1910.

1198. Rapp, Marvin A. "A Mohawk Valley Poem," NYFQ
      (W, 1958), 14: 300-4. Mohawk folk tale, "The
      Indian Drum," is part of a poem by Alfred B.
      Street.

1199. Rennick, Robert M. "The Disguised Lover Theme
      and the Ballad," SFQ (Dec, 1959), 23: 215-32.
      An interesting, in-depth discussion. Variants
      peculiar to North America are "Johnny Germany,"
      "William Hall," and "The Banks of the Brandy-
      wine."

1200. _____. "The Pretty Fair Maid in the Garden,"
      SFQ (Sept, 1963), 27: 229-246. Extensive study
      of variants of this ballad theme (lover absent for
      a long period returns to test his sweetheart's
      fidelity).

1201. Richmond, W. Edson. "'Just Sing It Yourself': the
      American Lyric Tradition," in Our Living Tradi-
      tions, ed. T. P. Coffin, pp. 94-107. Brief sur-
      vey of American lyric folksongs: love songs,
      work songs, lullabies, frontier songs, etc.

1202. _____. "Some Effects of Scribal and Typograph-
      ical Error on Oral Tradition," SFQ (Je, 1951),
      15: 159-170. Corrupting forces in the texts of
      ballads are poor human memory and scribal er-
      rors. Examples given.

1203. Robb, J. Donald. "The Sources of a New Mexico
      Folksong," NMFR (1950-1951), 5: 9-16. Spanish
      text and music of a ballad on the death of An-
      tonio Maestas.

1204. _____. "'Whereof I Speak' or Songs of the West-
      ern Sheep Camps," NMFR (1969-70), 12: 17-28.
      Spanish texts and translations of songs sung in
      Mexican sheep camps. Singers are identified.
      Song types are romance, corrido, cancione, dis-
      parate.

1205. Roberts, Leonard. "Beauchamp and Sharp: A Ken-

tucky Legend," KFR (Jan-Mr, 1968), 14: 14-19.
Background for a Kentucky ballad.

1206. Rountree, Thomas J. "Ethnological Implications in
'The Gypsy Laddie'," TFSB (Dec, 1958), 24: 128-
30. Variants of ballad in America change both
the moral and the style.

1207. _____. "'Old Lady Grant,' Another Child Ballad
No. 278," JAF (Oct-Dec, 1970), 83: 458-60. An
American variant.

1208. _____. "'Poor Wayfaring Stranger'; A Note,"
TFSB (Dec, 1957), 23: 106-8. A familiar song
sounds dominantly religious but may also be secular.

1209. Seeger, Peter. "A Contemporary Ballad-Maker in
the Hudson Valley," NYFQ (S, 1954), 10: 133-34.
Les Rice's "Acres of Apples."

1210. Simeone, W. E. "Robin Hood Ballads in North
America," MF (W, 1957), 7: 197-201. Robin
Hood survives as a folk hero even if ballads
about him don't.

1211. Smithyman, Kendrick. "Little Mohee," NYFQ (Mr,
1970), 26: 64-70. Speculations on the origin of
a familiar song.

1212. Stamper, Frances C. and Wm. Hugh Jansen. "'Water Birch': An American Variant of 'Hugh of Lincoln'," JAF (Jan-Mr, 1958), 71: 16-22.

1212a. Stein, Zonweise. "'John Brown's Coal Mine,'" KFR
(Oct-Dec, 1961), 7: 147-58. Aunt Molly Jackson
learned this song about 1885. Variant fragments
listed.

1213. Stephenson, Robert C. "Signature in Ballad and
Story," in Folk Travelers, ed. Mody C. Boatright et al., pp. 97-109. Characters in ballads
are often oddly unidentified (Alice Fry, Billy
Gashade, Crego). But the singers or narrators
often intrude as spectators or honest reporters.

1214. Swetnam, George. "On the Trail of Cherry Tree

Joe," KFQ (Spr, 1962), 7, i: 15-33. Study of
Joe McCreery (1805-1895), the Pennsylvania Paul
Bunyan, a lumberjack and Civil War soldier who
became the subject of a ballad.

1215.   Taylor, Archer. "Trends in the Study of Folksong,
        1937-1950," SFQ (Je, 1953), 17: 97-113. Erudite
        survey of important studies of ballad and folksong
        in several languages during the preceding dozen
        years. Articles generally omitted.

1216.   Thigpen, Kenneth A., Jr. "An Index to the Known
        Oral Sources of the Child Collection," FF (1972),
        5: 55-69.

1217.   Thomason, Jean H. "Ten Broeck and Mollie: New
        Light on a Kentucky Ballad," KFR (Apr-Je, 1970),
        16: 17-34.

1218.   Thornburg, Opal. "The Stillwater Tragedy: A
        Quaker Ballad," MF (Apr, 1951), 1: 55-62.

1219.   Titland, William J. "'The Bitter Withy' and Its Re-
        lationship to 'The Holy Well'," JAF (Jan-Mr,
        1967), 80: 49-70. Comparison of ballad and
        carol.

1220.   Toelken, J. Barre. "The Ballad of the 'Mountain
        Meadows Massacre,'" WF (Apr, 1959), 18: 169-
        172.

1221.   _____. "An Oral Canon for the Child Ballads,"
        JFI (1967), 4: 75-101.

1222.   Tribe, Ivan M. "The Continuing Tradition of Tragedy
        and Disaster Ballads: A Case Study of Silver
        Bridge Songs," JEMFQ (W, 1973), 9: 147-58.
        Article focuses on ballads about an Ohio bridge
        collapse in 1967.

1223.   Urcia, Ingeborg. "The Gallows and the Golden Ball:
        An Analysis of 'The Maid Freed from the Gal-
        lows' (Child 95)," JAF (Jl-Sept, 1966), 79: 463-
        68.

1224.   Vlach, John M. "'Pearl Bryan': Two Ballads in
        One Tradition," JCM (S, 1972), 3: 45-61. An

attempt to differentiate two similar ballads by
textual analysis.

1225. Warner, Anne and Frank Warner. "Frank Noah
Proffitt: Good Times and Hard Times on the
Beaver Dam Road," AJ (A, 1973), 1: 163-93.
Reminiscent article about North Carolina singer
Frank Proffitt (1913-65) with anecdotes, descrip-
tions, excerpts from letters, and illustrations.

1226. Warner, Frank M. Folk Songs and Ballads of the
Eastern Seaboard (Macon, Ga.: Southern P.,
1963), 75pp. Four lectures delivered at Wesleyan
College, Macon. Includes texts and comments on
various songs and ballads by a collector and singer.

1227. Wells, Evelyn Kendrick. "Some Currents of British
Folksong in America, 1916-1958," JEFDSS (1958),
8: 129-141. Survey of archives, collections, and
records plus bibliography of songs and ballads.

1228. Welsch, Roger L. "A 'Buffalo Skinner's' Family
Tree," JPC (S, 1970), 4: 107-129. Comparative
study of ten texts of a famous western ballad.

1229. West, John Foster. The Ballad of Tom Dula; the
Documented Story Behind the Murder of Laura
Foster and the Trials and Execution of Tom Dula
(Durham: Moore Pub. Co., 1970), 212pp.
Background, factual analysis, and 16 versions of
the famous song.

1230. White, Alison. "Children in the Ballads," SFQ (Dec,
1954), 18: 205-11. A study of children in the
Child ballads: pages, swine herds, cabin boys,
school boys, servant girls. The page is ubiquitous
and plays many roles.

1231. White, John I. "'Great Grandma,'" WF (Jan, 1968),
27: 27-31. "Great Grandma" is a popular song
originally the work of the writer.

1232. _____. "A Montana Cowboy Poet," JAF (Apr-Je,
1967), 80: 113-29. Study of D. J. O'Malley
(1867-1943), author of "After the Roundup," etc.

1233. _____. "Owen Wister and the Dogies," JAF (Jan-
        Mr, 1969), 82: 66-69. Owen Wister recorded a
        variant of "Whoopee Ti Yi Yo" in 1893.

1234. Wiatt, William H. "'The Twa Corbies' Again," KFQ
        (F, 1965), 10: 116-26. Excellent close reading
        stressing meaning and diction of a famous ballad.

1235. Wilgus, D. K. "The Individual Song: 'Billy the
        Kid,'" WF (Jl, 1971), 30: 226-234. A particular
        ballad serves as an example of the skill and tech-
        niques needed to study folksong.

1236. _____. "The Oldest (?) Text of 'Edward,'" WF
        (Apr, 1966), 25: 77-92. Speculation about a West
        Virginia text collected by Josiah Combs in 1924.

1237. _____. "Ten Broeck and Mollie: a Race and a
        Ballad," KFR (Jl-Sept, 1956), 2: 77-89. Ballad
        about a famous Kentucky horse race in 1878.

1238. _____. "A Type-Index of Anglo-American Tradi-
        tional Narrative Songs," JFI (1970), 7: 161-176.

1239. _____. "'The White Pilgrim': Song, Legend, and
        Fact," SFQ (Sept, 1950), 14: 177-184. Discus-
        sion of John Ellis's elegy on Joseph Thomas (1791-
        1835), the White Pilgrim, who dressed in white
        robes and died of small pox.

1240. _____ and Lynwood Montell. "Beanie Short: a
        Civil War Chronicle in Legend and Song," in
        American Folk Legend, ed. Wayland D. Hand,
        pp. 133-156. Beanie Short was a Kentucky guer-
        rilla leader celebrated in tale and song.

1241. _____ and _____. "Clure and Joe Williams:
        Legend and Blues Ballad," JAF (Oct-Dec, 1968),
        81: 295-315. Background of a Kentucky-Tennessee
        ballad.

1242. Williams, Cratis D. "Local Ballads: 'John Fergu-
        son,'" KFR (Jan-Mr, 1960), 6: 15-17.

1243. Winkelman, Donald M. "Poetry/Rhythmic Stress in
        the Child Ballads," KFQ (S, 1967), 12: 103-117.
        A study of ballad texts and music.

1244. Wolf, John Quincy. "Aunt Caroline Dye: the Gypsy
       in the 'St. Louis Blues,'" SFQ (Dec, 1969), 33:
       339-346.

1245. _____. "The Sacred Harp in Mississippi," JAF
       (Oct-Dec, 1968), 81: 337-341. Historical sum-
       mary and personal experience from northern Mis-
       sissippi.

1246. _____. "Who Wrote 'Joe Bowers'?" WF (Apr,
       1970), 29: 77-89. Despite careful examination
       the identity of the author is still uncertain.

1247. Woodall, James R. "'Sir Hugh': a Study in Bal-
       ladry," SFQ (Je, 1955), 19: 77-84. Sex and
       mystery make the ballad. Some 25 variants are
       considered.

1248. Yates, Norris W. "Folksongs in the Spirit of the
       Times," SFQ (Dec, 1962), 26: 326-334. Six
       songs printed by W. T. Porter in his famous
       weekly. They include "Bryan O'Lynn," "Kemo
       Kimo," and a version of "Barbara Allen."

1249. Zimm, Louise Hasbrouck. "Songs: Two Ballads of
       the French Indian War, 1763," NYFQ (A, 1955),
       11: 219-221. Ballads by Philip Whitaker tran-
       scribed from mss.

1250. Zug, Charles G., Ill. "Scott's 'Jock of Hazeldean':
       the Recreation of a Traditional Ballad," JAF
       (Apr-Je, 1973), 86: 152-160. A study of the
       composition of Child #293 by Sir Walter Scott,
       who utilized his temperament, experience, and
       knowledge of folklore in treating traditional ma-
       terials.

C. History and Theory

1251. Abrahams, Roger D. "Creativity, Individuality, and
       the Traditional Singer," SLI (Apr, 1970), 3: 5-34.
       Comparison of performance style and repertory of
       two folk singers, one from Virginia, one from
       Arkansas. Texts of 18 songs given, no music.

1252. _____. Deep the Water, Shallow the Shore: Three
Essays on Shantying (Austin: U. of Texas P.,
1974), xiv, 125pp. Brief accounts with examples
of shantying in Tobago, Nevis, St. Vincent (the
last relates to whaling).

1253. _____. "Patterns of Structure and Role Relation-
ships in the Child Ballad in the United States,"
JAF (Jl-Sept, 1966), 79: 448-462.

1254. _____, ed. "Folksong and Folksong Scholarship:
Changing Approaches and Attitudes," in A Good
Tale and a Bonnie Tune, ed. Mody C. Boatright
et al., pp. 199-237. Symposium held at Austin
in 1961: papers by T. P. Coffin, John Greenway, W. E. Richmond, and D. K. Wilgus.

1255. _____ and George Foss. Anglo-American Folksong
Style (Englewood Cliffs, N.J.: Prentice-Hall,
1968), ix, 242pp. Discussions of verse, song
types, meter, melody, musical rhythm, etc.
Material in appendices on collection and classification.

1256. Abrams, W. Amos. "Frank Proffitt: a Legend A-
Borning," NCarF (Nov, 1966), 14: 12-20. A
collector's reminiscences about a folk singer.

1257. Adler, Thomas. "The Ballad in Bluegrass Music,"
FF (Jan, 1974), 7: 3-47. Bluegrass utilizes a
repertoire with deep traditional roots.

1258. Alvey, R. Gerald. "Phillips Barry and Anglo-American Folksong Scholarship," JFI (Je-Aug, 1973),
10: 67-95. Emphasis on Barry's versatility,
private resources, and dedication to the Folk-
Song Society of the Northeast.

1259. Amann, W. F. "Folksong Definitions: a Critical
Analysis," MF (S, 1955), 5: 101-105.

1260. Ames, Russell. "Protest and Irony in Negro Folklore," SS (S, 1950), 14: 193-213.

1260a. _____. The Story of American Folk Song (New
York: Grossett and Dunlap, 1955), xii, 276pp.
Compact study with numerous examples; no music
or index.

1261.   Armistead, Samuel G. and Joseph H. Silverman.
        "Hispanic Balladry among the Sephardic Jews of
        the West Coast," WF (Oct, 1960), 19: 229-244.
        Some 4,000 Sephardic Jews, recent immigrants
        from the Balkans, have preserved Spanish ballads
        in Cal.

1262.   Bailey, Frederick. "The Historical Ballad: a Prob-
        lem of Definition," SFQ (Sept, 1968), 32: 260-
        264. Discussion of historical validity of some of
        the Child ballads.

1263.   Bayard, Samuel P. "American Folksongs and Their
        Music," SFQ (Je, 1953), 17: 122-139.

1263a. _____. "Decline and 'Revival' of Anglo-American
        Folk Music," MF (S, 1955), 5: 69-77. Traces
        of traditional folk music linger in hymns and some
        hillbilly pieces. Reprinted in Folklore in Action,
        ed. Horace P. Beck, pp. 21-29.

1264.   _____. "Prolegomena to a Study of the Principal
        Melodic Families of British-American Folk Song,"
        JAF (Jan-Mr, 1950), 63: 1-44.

1265.   _____. "Two Representative Tune Families of
        British Tradition," MF (Spr, 1955), 4: 13-33.

1266.   Beck, Horace P. "Folksong Affiliations of Maine,"
        MF (F, 1956), 6: 159-166. Beck contends that
        Maine folksong resembles the Maritime rather
        than the New England family. Reprinted in Folk-
        lore in Action, ed. H. P. Beck, pp. 30-36.

1267.   Belz, Carl I. "Popular Music and the Folk Tradi-
        tion," JAF (Apr-Je, 1967), 80: 130-142.

1268.   Ben-Amos, Dan. "The Situation Structure of the Non-
        Humorous English Ballad," MF (F, 1963), 13:
        163-176. Three major kinds of conflicts exist in
        the ballad.

1269.   Benjamin, Harold W. "Tests of Folkloricity Applied
        to Soldier Songs," TFSB (Dec, 1955), 21: 99-105.
        Quotations, somewhat bowdlerized, from many
        army songs, ending with "The Good Old Rebel."

1270.   Bethke, Robert D.   "Narrative Obituary Verse and
        Native American Balladry," JAF (Jan-Mr, 1970),
        83, 61-68.

1270a. Bikel, Theodore.   Folksongs and Footnotes; an In-
        ternational Songbook (New York: Meridian Books,
        1964), 254pp.

1271.   Birdsall, Esther K.   "Some Notes on the Role of
        George Lyman Kittredge in American Folksong
        Studies," JFI (Je-Aug, 1973), 10: 57-66.   An
        assessment of Kittredge's influence on folksong
        studies, out of proportion to his actual published
        work.

1272.   Boswell, George W.   "Folksongs in Northeastern
        Kentucky," KFR (Oct-Dec, 1965), 11: 65-75.
        Mostly a list of song titles.

1273.   _____.   "Metrical Alteration in Folksinging," JAF
        (Jl-Sept, 1972), 85: 248-259.   Valuable chiefly to
        a reader trained in music.

1274.   _____.   "The Operation of Popular Etymology in
        Folksong Diction," TFSB (Je, 1973), 29: 37-58.

1275.   _____.   "Reciprocal Controls Exerted by Ballad
        Texts and Tunes," JAF (Apr-Je, 1967), 80: 169-
        174.

1276.   _____.   "Shaping Controls of Ballad Tunes Over
        Their Texts," TFSB (Mr, 1951), 17: 9-18.
        Musical influences on ballad poetry.

1277.   _____.   "Stanza Form and Music-Imposed Scansion
        in Southern Ballads," SFQ (Dec, 1967), 31: 320-
        331.

1278.   Botkin, B. A.   "The Folksong Revival: a Symposi-
        um," NYFQ (Je, 1963), 19: 83-142.   With inter-
        esting comments by Oscar Brand, Alan Lomax,
        Frank Warner, et al.

1279.   Boyd, Joe Dan.   "Judge Jackson: Black Giant of
        White Spirituals," JAF (Oct-Dec, 1970), 83: 446-
        451.   Judge Jackson, self-educated Alabama
        farmer, published The Colored Sacred Harp with
        77 songs in 1934.

1280. _____. "Negro Sacred Harp Songsters in Mississippi," MFR (F, 1971), 5: 60-83. Careful account of black Sacred Harp singers in Miss. with
helpful illustrations.

1281. Brand, Oscar. The Ballad Mongers: Rise of the
Modern Folk Song (New York: Funk & Wagnalls,
1962), xiv, 240pp. Useful for its comments on
commercial folk and popular singing; unreliable
in its exposition of folksong history.

1282. Brazier, Richard. "The Story of the I.W.W.'s 'Little Red Songbook,'" LH (W, 1968), 9: 91-105.
History of the famous book first published in 1909.

1283. Brewster, Paul G. The Incest Theme in Folklore
(Helsinki: Suomalainen Tiedeakatemia, 1972),
36pp. Discussion of incest in balladry and tale
with almost no American material. Brief list of
literary works employing incest theme.

1284. Bronson, Bertrand Harris. The Ballad as Song
(Berkeley and Los Angeles: U. of California P.,
1969), 324pp. Eighteen essays, mostly reprinted,
on ballads and balladry.

1285. _____. "Cecil Sharp and Folksong: a Review
Article," WF (Jl, 1968), 27: 200-217. Evaluation of Sharp's work in collecting Appalachian
folksong.

1286. _____. "The Morphology of the Ballad Tunes,"
JAF (Jan-Mr, 1954), 67: 1-13.

1287. _____. "On the Union of Words and Music in the
Child Ballads," WF (Oct, 1952), 11: 233-249.
Erudite survey of collections of tunes with stress
on the variants.

1288. _____. "The Riverside Recordings of the Child
Ballads: a Review Article," WF (Jl, 1957), 16:
189-194. Enthusiastic review of five albums of
long-playing records of 82 songs (including 72
Child ballads), sung by Ewan McColl and A. L.
Lloyd.

1289. _____. "Toward the Comparative Analysis of

British-American Folk Tunes," JAF (Apr-Je, 1959), 72: 165-191.

1290. _____. The Traditional Tunes of the Child Ballads, With Their Texts, According to the Extant Records of Great Britain and America (Princeton: Princeton U. P., 1959-1972), four volumes: I, xxxvii, 465pp.; II, xx, 565pp.; III, xvii, 496pp.; IV, xvi, 576pp. Definitive study of the music of the Child ballads with almost endless evidence about tune families, variants, recordings, singers.

1291. Brown, Sterling A. "The Blues," Phylon (4th Q, 1952), 13: 286-292.

1292. _____. "Negro Folk Expression: Spirituals, Seculars, Ballads and Work Songs," Phylon (1st Q, 1953), 14: 45-61.

1293. Browne, Ray B. "Some Notes on the Southern 'Holler,'" JAF (Jan-Mr, 1954), 67: 73-77.

1294. _____, ed. Folksongs and Their Makers (Bowling Green, Ohio: Bowling Green Popular P., 1970), 170pp. Essays by Henry Glassie, Edward D. Ives, and John Szwed on folksinger-songwriters.

1295. Brunvand, Jan Harold. "Folk Song Studies in Idaho," WF (Oct, 1965), 24: 231-248. Survey of collecting in Idaho with many examples.

1296. Buchan, David D. The Ballad and the Folk (London and Boston: Routledge and K. Paul, 1972), xii, 326. Analysis covering social history, folklore, aesthetic qualities, with focus on Scotland.

1297. Burress, Lee A., Jr. "James Jones on Folklore and Ballad," CE (Dec, 1959), 21: 161-165. The possible communal origin of a ballad.

1298. Caldwell, Harry B. "Ballad Tragedy and the Moral Matrix: Observations on Tragic Causation," NYFQ (Sept, 1972), 28: 209-220. Caldwell contends that the tragic flaw in the ballads was a social matter first and an individual matter second.

1299. _____. "The Multiple Effects of the Tragic Event
in the Child Ballad," NYFQ (Mr, 1970), 26: 14-
41. Ballads tell of the tragic sufferings of the
corporate body as well as of individuals.

1300. Cansler, Loman D. "He Hewed His Own Path:
William Henry Scott, Ozark Songmaker," SLI
(Apr, 1970), 3: 37-63. Biographical data and
eight songs.

1301. _____. "Walter Dibben, an Ozark Bard," KFR
(Oct-Dec, 1967), 13: 81-89. Biography and songs
of Walter Dibben (1887-1967).

1302. Carawan, Guy. "Spiritual Singing in the South Carolina Sea Islands," Caravan (Je-Jl, 1960), No. 20,
20-25. Personal experiences plus a list of songs
and bibliography.

1303. Cazden, Norman. "Regional and Occupational Orienta-
tions of American Traditional Song," JAF (Oct-
Dec, 1959), 72: 310-344. Catskill Mts. traditional song represents less a regional culture
than a widespread occupational culture.

1304. Clark, Edgar Regie. "Negro Folk Music in America," JAF (Jl-Sept, 1951), 64: 281-287. A plea
to preserve Negro folk music.

1305. Coffin, Tristram P. "American Balladry: the Term
and the Canon," KF (Spr, 1974), 19: 3-10. Only
about 50 ballads are really pan-American, i.e.,
known nationally.

1306. _____. The British Traditional Ballad in North
America (Philadelphia: Am. Folklore Soc., 1950),
xvi, 188. Rev. ed. 1963. A standard work.

1307. _____. "The Folk Ballad and the Literary Ballad:
an Essay in Classification," MF (Spr, 1959), 9:
5-18. Coffin suggests six categories which should
aid in the literary evaluation of a ballad. Reprinted in Folklore in Action, ed. Horace P.
Beck, pp. 58-70.

1308. _____. "Folksong of Social Protest: a Musical
Mirage," NYFQ (Spr, 1958), 14: 3-9. Strong

argument that social protest songs are not in
oral tradition and not genuine folk songs.

1309. _____. "On a Peak in Massachusetts: the Literary
and Aesthetic Approach," in A Good Tale and a
Bonnie Tune, ed. Mody C. Boatright et al., pp.
201-209. "Springfield Mountain" is evidence that
ballads follow naturally from narrative obituary
verse.

1310. _____. "Remarks Preliminary to a Study of Ballad Meter and Ballad Singing," JAF (Apr-Je,
1965), 78: 149-153.

1311. _____, Cohen, Anne and Norman Cohen. "Tune
Evolution as an Indicator of Traditional Musical
Norms," JAF (Jan-Mr, 1973), 86: 37-47. Examination of 14 songs now in folk tradition which
originally appeared as sheet music.

1312. Cohen, Norman. "The Skillet Lickers: a Study of a
Hillbilly String Band and its Repertoire," JAF
(Jl-Sept, 1965), 78: 229-244. A string band of
the 1920's.

1313. Crawford, Portia Naomi. "A Study of Negro Folk
Songs from Greensboro, North Carolina, and Surrounding Towns," NCarF (Oct, 1968), 16: 66-139.
Whole issue given over to data, texts, and notes
from some 25 songs of various kinds.

1314. Daly, John J. A Song in His Heart (Philadelphia:
Winston, 1951), ix, 102pp. Biography of folk
and minstrel song composer, James A. Bland
(1854-1911).

1315. Danker, Frederick E. "The Repertory and Style of
a Country Singer, Johnny Cash," JAF (Oct-Dec,
1972), 85: 309-329. Biography and excellent
analysis of singing style.

1316. Denisoff, R. Serge. Great Day Coming, Folk Music
and the American Left (Urbana, Ill.: U. of Illinois P., 1971), 219pp. Primarily a history of the
radical movement with special attention to groups
like the Almanac Singers.

1317. _____. "The Proletarian Renascence: the Folkness of the Ideological Folk," JAF (Jan-Mr,
1969), 82: 51-65. Discussion of folksongs per-
formed in an urban setting to achieve political
goals.

1318. _____. Sing a Song of Social Significance (Bowling
Green, Ohio: Bowling Green Popular P., 1972),
200pp. Poorly written restatement of material in
Great Day Coming.

1319. _____. "'Take It Easy, But Take It': the Almanac Singers," JAF (Jan-Mr, 1970), 83: 21-32.
Account of one of America's best known radical
groups: Hays, Seeger, Lampell, Guthrie, et al.

1320. Dunn, James Taylor. "A Century of Song: Popular
Music in Minnesota," MinnH (W, 1974), 44: 122-
141. Study of sheet music written and published
in Minnesota.

1321. Evans, David. "Bubba Brown: Folk Poet," MFR
(Spr, 1973), 7: 15-31. Mississippi Negro musician and blues writer.

1322. _____. "Techniques of Blues Composition among
Black Folksingers," JAF (Jl-Sept, 1974), 87: 240-
249. Comments based on field work in Miss. and
Louisiana.

1323. Ferris, William R., Jr. Blues from the Delta (London: Studio Vista Ltd., 1970), 111pp. Several
short essays on structure, origin, records, etc.

1324. _____. "Folk Song and Culture: Charles Seeger
and Alan Lomax," NYFQ (Sept, 1973), 29: 206-
217. Resumé of folk song views with helpful survey of Lomax's doctrine of cantometrics: singing
styles reflect temperament, personality, social
status.

1325. _____. "Racial Repertoires among Blues Per-
formers," Ethnomusicology (Sept, 1970), 14: 439-
449.

1326. _____. "Railroad Chants: Form and Function,"
MFR (Spr, 1970), 4: 1-14. Interview with Cal
Taylor of Lula, Mississippi.

1327.   _____. "William Billings. The Musical Tanner," KFQ (W, 1967), 12: 261-279. Influence of folk music on the compositions of Billings (1746-1800), the Bostonian author of psalm tunes and anthems.

1328. Field, Arthur Jordan. "Notes on the History of Folk-singing in New York City," Caravan (Je-Jl, 1959), No. 17, 7-17. Anecdotal history with personal reminiscences of 1945-1951 period.

1329.   _____. "Why Is the 'Murdered Girl' So Popular?" MF (Apr, 1951), 1: 113-119. Comments on and examples of murdered girl ballads.

1330. Fife, Austin E. and Francesca Redden. "The Pseudo-Indian Folksongs of the Anglo-American and French-Canadian," JAF (Jl-Sept, Oct-Dec, 1954), 67: 239-251, 379-394. Survey of Indian material in folk and popular songs.

1331. Flanders, Helen Hartness. "Ancient Themes and Characteristics Found in Certain New England Folksongs," JAF (Jan-Mr, 1964), 77: 32-38.

1332. Foss, George. "A Methodology for the Description and Classification of Anglo-American Traditional Tunes," JFI (Je, 1967), 4: 102-126.

1333.   _____. "The Transcription and Analysis of Folk Music," in A Good Tale and a Bonnie Tune, ed. Mody C. Boatright et al., pp. 237-265. Technical analysis by a professional musician.

1334. Fowke, Edith. "American Civil War Ballads in Canada," MF (Spr, 1963), 13: 33-42. Some eight Civil War ballads have survived for various reasons in Canada.

1335. Fowler, David C. A Literary History of the Popular Ballad (Durham: Duke U. P., 1968), 352pp. Excellent discussion of genesis of the popular ballad in Great Britain. No American ballads cited and little attention given to American versions of Child.

1336.   _____. "Toward a Literary History of the Popular Ballad," NYFQ (Je, 1965), 21: 123-141.

Brief scholarly treatment of a big subject, preview of the 1968 book.

1337. Freedman, Morris. "Natural Jazz Rhythms in Folk
Songs," SFQ (Dec, 1957), 21: 194-205.

1338. Gillis, Everett A. "Literary Origin of Some Western
Ballads," WF (Apr, 1954), 13: 101-106. Certain
ballads composed by Badger Clark, Jack Thorp,
and Larry Chittenden have passed into oral circulation.

1339. Goldstein, Kenneth S. "The Ballad Scholar and the
Long-Playing Record," in Folklore & Society, ed.
Bruce Jackson, pp. 35-44. A plea for the use of
recordings in ballad research.

1340. _____. "The Broadside Ballad," KFQ (S, 1964),
9: 34-67. Succinct account of broadsides in general with facsimiles of some 20 examples.

1341. Green, Archie. Only a Miner: Studies in Recorded
Coal-Mining Songs (Urbana: U. of Illinois P.,
1972), xvi, 504pp. Careful study of a handful
of coal-mining songs which appeared on discs between 1925 and 1970--complementary to George
Korson's work.

1342. Greenway, John. "Folksong As An Anthropological
Province: the Anthropological Approach," in A
Good Tale and a Bonnie Tune, ed. Mody C. Boatright et al., pp. 209-217. The aesthetic approach
has become redundant; something different is
needed.

1343. _____. "Jimmie Rodgers--A Folksong Catalyst,"
JAF (Jl-Sept, 1957), 70: 231-234.

1344. Hawes, Bess Lomax. "Folksongs and Function:
Some Thoughts on the American Lullaby," JAF
(Apr-Je, 1974), 87: 140-148.

1345. Hellman, John M., Jr. "'I'm a Monkey': the Influence of the Black American Blues Argot on the
Rolling Stones," JAF (Oct-Dec, 1973), 86: 367-
373. The Rolling Stones from London middle
class families adopted and varied American Negro
diction and rhythm.

1346. Hinton, Sam. "The Singer of Folk Songs and His
      Conscience," WF (Jl, 1955), 14: 170-173. Com-
      ments by a professional singer.

1347. Hodgart, M. J. C. The Ballads (London: Hutchin-
      son's Universal Lib., 1950), 184pp. Hodgart ac-
      cepts Gerould's study, rejects communal theory
      of composition, feels that the literary study of the
      ballads has been disregarded.

1348. Holditch, Kenneth. "The Sacred Harp: a Southern
      Folk Hymnody," LFM (Apr, 1970), 3: 5-15.
      Survey of Sacred Harp singing in Alabama and
      Mississippi.

1349. Horn, Dorothy D. Sing to Me of Heaven (Gainesville:
      U. of Florida P., 1970), xi, 212pp. Study of
      three old harp books.

1350. Hudson, Arthur Palmer. "Folklore Keeps the Past
      Alive," NYFQ (W, 1951), 7: 291-294.

1351. _____. Folklore Keeps the Past Alive (Athens,
      Ga.: U. of Georgia P., 1962), viii, 63pp.
      Three lectures delivered at Mercer University in
      1961 generally concerned with history in southern
      folksong and with folksong in American poetry and
      fiction.

1352. _____. "Glimpses of History in Southern Folk-
      songs," SFQ (Sept, 1951), 15: 196-202. Substan-
      tially the second lecture in the previously cited
      book.

1353. Hyman, Stanley Edgar. "The Child Ballad in Amer-
      ica: Some Aesthetic Criteria," JAF (Jl-Sept,
      1957), 70: 235-239. An attack on American texts
      as bad poetry.

1354. Ives, Edward D. "'Ben Deane' and Joe Scott: a
      Ballad and Its Probable Author," JAF (Jan-Mr,
      1959), 72: 53-66. A Maine woodsman and river
      driver named Joe Scott probably wrote "Ben
      Deane" and several other ballads.

1355. _____. Larry Gorman: the Man Who Made the
      Songs (Bloomington: Indiana U. P., 1964), xv,

225pp. Life and personality of a Maine folk poet.
Some songs included.

1356. _____. Lawrence Doyle, the Farmer Poet of
Prince Edward Island (Orono: U. of Maine P.,
1972), 269pp.

1357. _____. "A Man and His Song: Joe Scott and 'The
Golden Band,'" in Folksongs and Their Makers,
ed. Ray B. Browne, pp. 70-146. Discussion of
ballad composition.

1358. James, Willis Lawrence. "The Romance of the Negro
Folk Cry in America," Phylon (1st Q, 1956), 15-
30. Gospel singing perpetuates the folk cry.

1359. Jansen, William Hugh. "The Folksinger's Defense,"
HF (Jl-Sept, 1950), 9: 65-75. A living folksong
tradition in Kentucky is represented by three
anonymous singers.

1360. _____. "'Ten Broek and Molly' and 'The Rose of
Kentucky,'" KFR (Oct-Dec, 1958), 4: 149-153.
A ballad and a song.

1361. Jones, James H. "Commonplace and Memorization
in the Oral Tradition of the English and Scottish
Popular Ballads," JAF (Apr-Je, 1961), 74: 97-
112. Ballads include couplets and quatrains;
commonplaces memorized by singers explain
change from one to another. Albert B. Friedman refutes argument in following paper, pp. 113-
115.

1361a. Kempf, Barbara. "Meet Doc Williams: Country
Music Star, Country Music Legend," JEMFQ
(Spr, 1974), 10: 1-13. An Ohio-born coal miner
and his music.

1362. Kershaw, Doug and Robin Nelson. Lou'siana Man;
the Doug Kershaw Songbook (New York: Macmillan, 1971), 144pp. Autobiography and songs
of a Cajun performer.

1363. Kmen, Henry A. "Old Corn Meal: a Forgotten Urban Negro Folksinger," JAF (Jan-Mr, 1962), 75:
29-34. Account of New Orleans celebrity who
died in 1842.

1364. Knott, Sarah Gertrude. "Folksongs and Dances,
       U.S.A. The Changing Scene," SFQ (Sept, 1961),
       25: 184-191. Survey of interest in folk festivals
       (New York, Buffalo, St. Paul).

1365. Kurath, Gertrude Prokosch. "Catholic Hymns of
       Michigan Indians," AnthQ (Apr, 1957), 30: 31-44.

1366. _____. "Rhapsodies of Salvation: Negro Respon-
       sory Hymns," SFQ (Sept, 1956), 19: 178-182.

1367. _____. "Syncopated Therapy," MF (F, 1951), 1:
       179-186. Gospel hymns from Michigan with tech-
       nical comment.

1368. Laban, Juana de. "Movement Notation: Its Signifi-
       cance to the Folklorist," JAF (Jl-Sept, 1954),
       67: 291-295.

1369. Laws, G. Malcolm, Jr. "Anglo-Irish Balladry in
       North America," in Folklore in Action, ed. H.
       P. Beck, pp. 172-183.

1370. _____. The British Literary Ballad: a Study in
       Poetic Imitation (Carbondale and Edwardsville,
       Ill.; Southern Illinois U. P., 1972), xii, 180pp.
       Am. ballads excluded.

1371. _____. Native American Balladry. A Descriptive
       Study and Bibliographical Syllabus (Philadelphia:
       Am. Folklore Soc., 1950), xii, 276pp. First
       half of the book discusses ballad types, forms,
       and themes; second half gives specific data about
       185 ballads in oral tradition. Rev. ed., 1964,
       xiv, 298pp.

1372. _____. "The Spirit of Native American Balladry,"
       JAF (Apr-Je, 1951), 64: 163-169. "American
       balladry is characterized by a tender humanity
       toward all who are faced with tragedy."

1373. Leach, MacEdward. "Folksong and Ballad--a New
       Emphasis," JAF (Jl-Sept, 1957), 70: 205-207.
       Introduction to a symposium.

1374. _____. "The Singer or the Song," in Singers and
       Storytellers, ed. Mody C. Boatright, et al., pp.

30-45. Careful analysis of component elements
of ballads with a plea to consider them from the
aesthetic point of view.

1375. List, George. "An Ideal Marriage of Ballad Text
and Tune," MF (S, 1957), 7: 95-112. Careful
study of an American version of "The False
Knight upon the Road," Child #3.

1376. Lomax, Alan. Folk Song Style and Culture (Washington: Am. Assoc. for Advancement of Science,
1968), xix, 363pp. Based on cantometrics, this
book is a contribution to ethnomusicology. North
America is one of six major regions of song
style.

1377. _____. "The Good and the Beautiful in Folksong,"
JAF (Jl-Sept, 1967), 80: 213-235. Technical
development of the thesis that aesthetic style (the
beautiful) has a close relationship to the socially
normative (the good).

1378. _____. Mister Jelly Roll (New York: Duell,
Sloane, and Pearce, 1950), xvii, 318pp. Biography of Ferdinand Morton, jazz pianist, with
considerable jazz folklore.

1379. Long, Eleanor R. "Thematic Classification and 'Lady
Isabel,'" JAF (Jan-Mr, 1972), 85: 32-41.

1380. _____. "Ballad Singers, Ballad Makers, and
Ballad Etiology," WF (Oct, 1973), 32: 225-236.
Four types of folk artists suggested: the per-
severating, confabulating, rationalizing, and in-
tegrative. The jargon is awkward and confusing.

1381. Lovell, John Jr. Black Song: the Forge and the
Flame (New York: Macmillan, 1972), xviii,
686pp. Valuable account of the spirituals: roots,
genesis, rhythms, meaning, and interpretation.
Impressive scholarship.

1382. _____. "Reflections on the Origins of the Negro
Spirituals," NegroALF (F, 1969), 3: 91-97.
Negro spirituals are considered to be folk poems.

1383. Lumpkin, Ben Gray. "Folksongs of the Early

1830's," SFQ (Je, 1969), 33: 116-128. Texts
of five songs from Withers family mss. of Din-
widdie Co., Va., 1831-1832.

1384. McDonald, James J. "Principal Influences on the
Music of the Lilly Brothers of Clear Creek,
West Virginia," JAF (Oct-Dec, 1973), 86: 331-
344. Two brothers influenced by Bill Monroe,
the Blue Sky Boys and the Carter family played
country music for 18 years in Boston.

1385. McLaughlin, Wayman B. "Symbolism and Mysticism
in the Spirituals," Phylon (Spr, 1963), 24: 69-76.

1386. McMillan, Douglas J. "A Survey of Theories Concerning the Oral Transmission of the Traditional
Ballad," SFQ (Dec, 1964), 28: 299-309. Summary of chief ballad theories: oral transmission
is deteriorating or recreating, or there is com-
promise.

1387. McNeil, Brownie. "The Child Ballad in the Middle
West and Lower Mississippi Valley," in Mesquite
and Willow, ed. Mody C. Boatright et al., pp.
23-77. Some 30 Child ballads have been collected
in the specific area. Comments on textual
changes.

1388. McNeil, Norman L. "Origins of 'Sir Patrick
Spens,'" in Hunters & Healers, ed. Wilson M.
Hudson, pp. 65-72.

1389. McNeil, W. K. "Syncopated Slander: the 'Coon
Song,' 1890-1900," KFQ (S, 1972), 17: 63-82.
Popular songs of the 1890's slandered Negroes.

1390. Malone, Bill C. Country Music; U.S.A.: A Fifty
Year History (Austin and London: U. of Texas
P., 1968), xii, 422pp. First scholarly treatment of a commercial phenomenon; ephemeral
periodicals and record jackets sometimes supply
unreliable evidence.

1391. _____. "From Folk to Hillbilly to Country: the
Coming of Age of America's Rural Music," in
Observations & Reflections on Texas Folklore,
ed. F. E. Abernethy, pp. 101-116.

1392.   Marshall, Howard Wright.   "'Keep on the Sunny
        Side of Life'; Pattern and Religious Expression
        in Bluegrass Gospel Music," NYFQ (Mr, 1974),
        30: 3-43.   Bluegrass music conceived of as a
        kind of revival of nativism.   Some 200 song titles
        listed.

1393.   Melnick, Mimi Clar.   "'I Can Peep Through Muddy
        Water and Spy Dry Land': Boasts in the Blues,"
        in Folklore International, ed. D. K. Wilgus, pp.
        139-149.

1394.   Millar, Branford P.   "Eighteenth Century Views of
        the Ballad," WF (Apr, 1950), 9: 124-135.   Dis-
        cussion of critics, broadside peddlers, artists
        who represented ballad singers.

1395.   Miller, E. Joan Wilson.   "The Rag-Bag World of
        Balladry," SFQ (Sept, 1960), 24: 217-225.   So-
        cial conditions and beliefs during period when the
        ballads flourished.

1396.   Morokoff, Gene E.   "Whole Tale Parallels of the
        Child Ballads as Cited or Given by Child or in
        FFC 74," JAF (Apr-Je, 1951), 64: 203-206.

1397.   Murray, Albert.   The Hero and the Blues (Columbia,
        Mo.: U. of Missouri P., 1973), 107pp.   Dis-
        cussion of the sociological origins of blues songs.

1398.   Musick, Ruth Ann.   "Murderers and Cut-Throats in
        Song," TFSB (Je, 1953), 19: 31-36.   Violence in
        the ballads: murder, suicide, theft, rape.

1399.   Nelson, Paul.   "Jug Band! Jug Band!" Sing Out!
        (Dec, 1963-Jan, 1964), 13: 8-14.   Account of
        rise of Negro jug bands in 1920's and their in-
        fluence on northern groups.

1399a. Nettl, Bruno.   An Introduction to Folk Music in the
        United States (Detroit: Wayne State U. P.,
        1962), rev. ed., v, 126pp.   Brief account of
        American ethnic and folk music with stress on
        musical style rather than language.

1400.   Oliver, Paul.   Blues Fell This Morning: the Mean-
        ing of the Blues (London: Cassell, 1960), xx,
        335pp.

1401.   Oring, Elliott. "Whalemen and Their Songs: a Study
        of Folklore and Culture," NYFQ (Mr, 1971), 27:
        130-152. English and American whaling songs
        reflect a particular folk group and also function
        in society.

1402.   Pankake, Jan. "Mike Seeger: the Style of Tradi-
        tion," Sing Out! (Jl, 1964), 14: 6-11. Data
        about Mike Seeger, older brother of Pete Seeger.
        Words and music for two songs.

1403.   Paredes, Américo. "The Bury-Me-Not Theme in the
        Southwest," in And Horns on the Toads, ed.
        Mody C. Boatright et al., pp. 88-92. The dying
        cowboy wished burial in consecrated ground but
        the Mexican vaquero desired a different interment.

1404.   _____. "The Décima on the Texas-Mexican Bor-
        der: Folksong as an Adjunct to Legend," JFI
        (Aug, 1966), 3: 154-167.

1405.   _____. "Folklore and History," in Singers and
        Storytellers, ed. Mody C. Boatright et al., pp.
        56-68. Discussion of two songs from the Mexi-
        can border collected in 1954 but dating from
        1867: "A Grant" and "A Zaragoza."

1406.   _____. "The Legend of Gregorio Cortez," in
        Mesquite and Willow, ed. Mody C. Boatright et
        al., pp. 3-22. Prose summary of the career
        of a ballad hero.

1407.   _____. "The Mexican Corrido: Its Rise and
        Fall," in Madstones and Twisters, ed. Mody C.
        Boatright et al., pp. 91-105. Erudite study of
        the corrido in Greater Mexico with speculation
        of the influence exerted on it by Texas-Mexican
        balladry.

1408.   _____ and George Foss. "The Décima Cantada
        on the Texas Mexican Border: Four Examples,"
        JFI (Aug, 1966), 3: 92-115.

1409.   Pound, Louise. "American Folksong: Origins,
        Texts and Modes of Diffusion," SFQ (Je, 1953),
        17: 114-121.

1410. Ramsey, Frederic, Jr. "Leadbelly: A Great Long Time," Sing Out! (Mr, 1965), 15: i, 7-24. Biographical notes about the Negro folk singer with two songs.

1411. Randolph, Vance and Ruth Ann Musick. "Folksong Hunters in Missouri," MF (Apr, 1951), 1: 23-31. Survey of scholarship in the field.

1412. Reppert, James. "F. J. Child and the Ballad," in The Learned and the Lewed, ed. Larry D. Benson (Cambridge: Harvard U.P., 1974), pp. 197-212. Child's incidental remarks about ballads are interesting but do not provide a coherent theory.

1413. Reuss, Richard A. "Woody Guthrie and His Folk Tradition," JAF (Jl-Sept, 1970), 83: 273-303. Biographical data: Guthrie shown as Dust Bowl singer, people's minstrel, and rustic comedian-sage.

1414. Richmond, W. Edson. "The Comparative Approach: Its Aims, Techniques, and Limitations," in A Good Tale and a Bonnie Tune, ed. Mody C. Boatright et al., pp. 217-227. Discussion of the Finnish historic-geographical method and ballad study.

1415. _____. "The Development of the Popular Ballad: a New Theory," Genre (Je, 1970), 3: 198-204. Review of D. C. Fowler's A Literary History of the Popular Ballad and comparison of various ballad theories.

1416. Robb, John Donald. "H. V. Gonzales: Folk Poet of New Mexico," NMFR (1973-1974), 13: 1-6. Data about a New Mexican author of corridos who died in 1922.

1417. _____. "'Whereof I Speak' or Songs of the Western Sheep Camp," NMFR (1969-1970), 12: 17-28. Discussion of singing by western sheepherders and four types of songs, all based on Spanish originals.

1418. Roberts, Leonard. "The Cante Fable in Eastern

Kentucky," MF (S, 1956), 6: 69-88. Twenty
examples persuade the reader to accept persist-
ence of this form.

1419. _____. "Stella Kenney in Song and Story," KFR
(Oct-Dec, 1962), 8: 116-124. Background material about a Kentucky murder ballad.

1420. Roberts, Warren E. "Ballad Themes in The Fair
Maid of the West," JAF (Jan-Mr, 1955), 68:
19-23. Many American broadside ballads cited.

1421. Rodnitzky, Jerome L. "The Evolution of the American Protest Song," JPC (S, 1969), 3: 25-45.
Discussion of songs by the IWW, Guthrie, Seeger,
et al.

1422. Rooney, James. Bossmen: Bill Monroe & Muddy
Waters (New York: Dial, 1971), 159pp. Information about two important folk musicians based
on interviews.

1423. Sanders, Jean B. "The Ballads as a Source of
Nursery Rhymes," MF (W, 1958), 8: 189-198.
Few nursery rhymes seem to derive from ballads.

1424. Schinhan, Jan Philip. The Music of the Ballads (Durham: Duke U. P., 1957), xliv, 420pp. Volume
IV of the superb Frank C. Brown Collection of
North Carolina Folklore. 517 tunes transcribed
and analyzed.

1425. _____. The Music of the Folk Songs (Durham:
Duke U. P., 1962), xli, 639pp. Volume V of
the Frank C. Brown Collection of North Carolina
Folklore. Music for 786 folk songs plus a number of children's games and rhymes. Singers
are identified and date and place of recording
specified.

1426. Schulman, Steven A. "Howess Dewey Winfrey: the
Rejected Songmaker," JAF (Jan-Mr, 1974), 87:
72-84. A Kentucky folk poet whose community
rejected him.

1427. Seeger, Charles. "Singing Style," WF (Jan, 1958),
·17: 3-11. Discussion of the problems involved in

studying singing style and the kinds of data required.

1428. Seeger, Pete. The Incompleat Folksinger (New York: Simon and Schuster, 1972), viii, 596pp. Personal and anecdotal account of folk singing and songs. Much topical material already outdated but attractively written.

1429. Sellers, William E. "Kinship in the British Ballads; the Historical Evidence," SFQ (Dec, 1956), 20: 199-215. Chiefly a discussion of British society, its debt to feudalism, description of nuclear or stem family or clans. Few ballads cited.

1430. Simpson, Claude M. The British Broadside Ballad and Its Music (New Brunswick, N.J.: Rutgers, 1966), xxxii, 922pp. Primarily a study of the tunes of the British broadside ballads 1550-1700.

1431. Speck, Frank G. and Leonard Broom. Cherokee Dance and Drama (Berkeley and Los Angeles: U. of California P., 1951), xv, 106pp.

1432. Stegner, Page. "Labor History in Fact and Song," Caravan (Je-Jl, 1960), No. 20, 8-16. Brief sketch of American strikes and the songs that reflect them.

1433. Stekert, Ellen. "Cents and Nonsense in the Urban Folklore Movement: 1930-1966," in Folklore & Society, ed. Bruce Jackson, pp. 153-168.

1434. _____. "Tylor's Theory of Survival and National Romanticism; Their Influence on Early American Folksong Collectors," SFQ (Sept, 1968), 32: 209-236. The objective approach of later collectors supersedes earlier trends.

1435. Stephenson, R. C. "Dialogue in Folktale and Song," in Mesquite and Willow, ed. Mody C. Boatright et al., pp. 129-137. Brief but provocative comment on one element of narrative song style. Examples from ballads and tales.

1436. Swetnam, George. "The Church Hymn as a Folklore Form," KFQ (W, 1964), 9: 144-153.

1437.   Szwed, John F.   "Musical Adaptation among Afro-
        Americans," JAF (Apr-Je, 1969), 82: 112-121.

1438.   Tallmadge, William H.   "The Scotch-Irish and the
        Traditional Ballad in America," NYFQ (Dec,
        1968), 24: 261-274.   The Scotch-Irish are held
        to be the chief carriers of the ballad culture to
        the U. S.

1439.   Taylor, Archer.   "Some Recent Studies in Folksongs,"
        MF (W, 1957), 7: 229-236.

1440.   _____.   "Trends in the Study of Folksong, 1937-
        1950," SFQ (Je, 1953), 17: 97-113.

1441.   Thigpen, Kenneth A., Jr.   "A Reconsideration of the
        Commonplace Phrase and Commonplace Theme in
        the Child Ballads," SFQ (Dec, 1973), 37: 385-
        408.   Ballads collected by William Motherwell in
        1825 suggest that ballad clichés are often com-
        munity terms or personal innovations.

1442.   Thurman, Howard.   Deep River; Reflections on the
        Religious Insight of Certain of the Negro Spirituals
        (Port Washington, N.Y.:   Kennikat P., 1969),
        93pp.

1443.   Toelken, J. Barre.   "An Oral Canon for the Child
        Ballads: Construction and Application," JFI (Je,
        1967), 4: 75-101.   An attempt to determine
        which Child ballads existed in oral tradition.

1444.   Tribe, Ivan M.   "The Hillbilly versus the City:
        Urban Images in Country Music," JEMFQ (S,
        1974), 10: 41-51.   Much hillbilly music is un-
        derstandably anti-urban.

1445.   Turner, Judith W.   "A Morphology of the 'True
        Love' Ballad," JAF (Jan-Mr, 1972), 85: 21-31.
        Proposed structural analysis based on eight
        Child ballads.

1446.   Voegelin, C. F. and Robert C. Euler.   "Introduction
        to Hopi Chants," JAF (Apr-Je, 1957), 70: 115-
        136.   Examples and analyses; ethnographic sum-
        mary.

1447. Walton, Ivan H. "Folk Singing on Beaver Island,"
       MF (W, 1952), 2: 243-250. Songs and ballads
       of Irish settlers on a Lake Michigan island.

1448. Weaver, Gordon. "Two Negro Folk-Poems," MFR
       (W, 1970), 4: 98-104. Negro soldier versions
       of "The Signifying Monkey" and "The Pool Shoot-
       ing Monkey." Interpretive errors are corrected
       by D. K. Wilgus in Spring, 1971 issue, 5: 26-27.

1449. Wells, Evelyn Kendrick. The Ballad Tree. A Study
       of British and American Ballads, Their Folklore,
       Verses, Music. Together with Sixty Traditional
       Ballads and Their Tunes (New York: Ronald P.,
       1950), ix, 370pp. Study of ballads in the oral
       tradition from mediaeval times to the present.
       Examples from singers in Maine and Appalachia
       collected in 1916.

1450. West, John O. "Jack Thorp and John Lomax: Oral
       or Written Transmission?" WF (Apr, 1967), 26:
       113-118. Comparison of the work of two early
       collectors.

1451. Wilgus, D. K. Anglo-American Folksong Scholarship
       Since 1889 (New Brunswick, N.J.: Rutgers,
       1959), xx, 466pp. Invaluable survey of ballad
       scholarship, collectors and collections, spirituals;
       plus discography, bibliography, index.

1452. _____. "Ballad Classification," MF (S, 1955),
       5: 95-100. No one index is sufficient; ballads
       must be classified thematically.

1453. _____. "Country-Western Music and the Urban
       Hillbilly," JAF (Apr-Je, 1970), 83: 157-179.
       Survey of the rise in popularity of country-western
       music and its relationship to commercial record-
       ings.

1454. _____. "The Future of American Folksong Schol-
       arship," SFQ (Dec, 1973), 37: 315-329. A plea
       for closer study of ballad texts, tune, perform-
       ance. His example is Andrew Jenkins's ballad of
       automobile race driver "Lee Bible."

1455. _____. "The Rationalistic Approach," in A Good

Tale and a Bonnie Tune, ed. Mody C. Boatright
et al., pp. 227-237. Academic scholarship has
generally ignored commercial recordings. A
focal example is Andrew Jenkins's ballad, "The
Death of Floyd Collins."

1456. _____. "Shooting Fish in a Barrel: the Child
Ballad in America," JAF (Apr-Je, 1958), 71:
161-164. Rebuttal to Hyman's claim that Child
ballads have deteriorated in United States.

1457. _____. "A Syllabus of Kentucky Folksongs," KFR
(Apr.Je, 1955), 1: 31-38. Proposal for a state
collection.

1458. _____. "'The Text Is the Thing,'" JAF (Jl-
Sept, 1973), 86: 241-252. Consideration of text
and performance and a plea for the use of commercial recordings as field texts. Ballad example used: "The Little Grave in Georgia."

1459. Wilgus, D. K. ed. Hillbilly Issue, JAF (Jl-Sept,
1965), 78: 195-286. Entire issue devoted to
hillbilly, country, or bluegrass music. Little
about folk music.

1460. Winkelman, Donald M. "Musicological Techniques of
Ballad Analysis," MF (W, 1960-1961), 10: 197-
205.

1461. _____. "Some Rhythmic Aspects of the Child
Ballad," in New Voices in American Studies, ed.
Ray B. Browne et al., pp. 151-162.

1462. Wolf, John Quincy. "Folksingers and the Re-Creation of Folksong," WF (Apr, 1967), 26: 101-111.
Material from folksingers in the Arkansas Ozarks.

1463. _____. "The Sacred Harp in Mississippi," JAF
(Oct-Dec, 1968), 81: 337-341.

1463a. _____. "The Sacred Harp in Northeast Mississippi," MFR (S, 1970), 4: 58-62. Proof that Sacred Harp singing was prevalent in northern Miss.

1464. Yates, Norris B. "Folksongs in the Spirit of the
Times," SFQ (Dec, 1962), 26: 326-334.

7. TALES AND NARRATIVE MATERIAL

A. Collections (Articles)

1465. Adamson, J. H. "Tales of the Supernatural," WF (Apr, 1959), 18: 79-87. Utah tales including some Nephite stories.

1466. Agogino, George A. and David W. Pickett. "Two Tales of Three Nails," NYFQ (Spr, 1960), 16: 32-36. Traditional stories of Christ from Syracuse, N. Y. gypsies.

1467. Agonito, Rosemary. "Il Paisano: Immigrant Italian Folktales of Central New York," NYFQ (Mr, 1967), 23: 52-64. Eight texts from Italian immigrants residing in the Syracuse area.

1468. Aiken, Riley. "Fifteen Mexican Tales," in A Good Tale and a Bonnie Tune, ed. Mody C. Boatright et al., pp. 3-56. Tales from Mexico and Texas; informants listed.

1469. _____. "More Chisos Ghosts," in Madstones and Twisters, ed. Mody C. Boatright et al., pp. 123-127. Ghost tales from Presidio Co., Texas.

1470. Ainsworth, Catherine Harris. "Some Italian Folktales of the Niagara Frontier," NYFQ (Dec, 1971), 17: 385-392. Tales collected in Buffalo-Niagara area.

1471. Allen, Helen E. "The Jumping Bass of Oak Orchard Creek," NYFQ (S, 1950), 6: 90-95.

1472. Anderson, John Q. "The Haunted Bayou," SFQ (Dec, 1956), 20: 216-224. Ghost story reprinted from

Spirit of the Times; author probably a Louisiana
journalist, H. P. A.

1473. _____. "Old John and the Master," SFQ (Sept,
       1961), 25: 195-197. Five short anecdotes about
       a Negro slave and his master derived from North-
       east Texas.

1474. _____. "'The Waltz of the Wolves,'" SFQ (Dec,
       1957), 21: 206-212. Reprint of an unidentified
       tale from Spirit of the Times with comments on
       folk superstitions.

1475. Arrendondo, Art. "La Llorona in Flagstaff,"
       AFFword (Jan, 1973), 2: 21-29. Sixteen tales
       about the famous Mexican "weeping woman," thir-
       teen from Arizona.

1476. Baker, Ronald L. "The Face in the Wall," IF
       (1969), 2: 29-46.

1477. Ballard, Lou Ellen. "Some Alabama Folktales: an
       Original Collection," LFM (Aug, 1961), 2: 50-68.

1478. _____. "Some Tales of Local Color from South-
       east Alabama," SFQ (Je, 1960), 24: 147-156.
       Eleven tall tales or local anecdotes recorded
       from local informants.

1479. Balys, Jonas. "Lithuanian Ghost Stories from Pitts-
       burgh, Pennsylvania," MF (Spr, 1952), 2: 47-52.

1480. Barnes, Daniel R. "Some Functional Horror Stories
       on the Kansas University Campus," SFQ (Dec,
       1966), 30: 305-312.

1481. Barreras, Ramona. "Spanish-American Belief Tales,"
       AFFword (Jan, 1973), 2: 3-16. Eighteen texts,
       either narratives or beliefs, revealing the ac-
       ceptance of the evil eye tradition, witchcraft,
       etc.

1482. Barrick, Mac E. "Blue Mountain Tales," KFQ (S,
       1964), 9: 74-76. Kentucky tales.

1483. _____. "Folklore in the Library: Old Schuylkill
       Tales," PF (Spr, 1974), 23: iii, 44-48. Dis-

cussion of a volume of Penn. tales published in
1906.

1484. _____. "Numskull Tales in Cumberland County,"
PF (S, 1967), 16: iv, 50-52.

1485. Bastin, Bruce. "The Devil's Goin' to Get You,"
NCarF (Nov, 1973), 21: 189-194. Tales deriving
from a North Carolina Negro family which reflect
beliefs associated with music and the devil.

1486. Batchen, Lou Sage. "Three Tales from Las Placitas,"
WF (Apr, 1956), 15: 89-92. Three tales from
near Bernalillo, N. Mex.

1487. Beck, Horace P. "The Acculturation of Old World
Tales by the American Indian," MF (W, 1958),
8: 205-216. Penobscot Indian tale about a little
person named Jack or N'Jacques.

1488. Bennett, A. L. "Joe Sap, Wit and Storyteller," in
The Golden Log, ed. Mody C. Boatright et al.,
pp. 34-40. Material by and about a small town
Texas newspaperman.

1489. Betts, Leonidas and Richard Walser. "North Carolina Folk Tales from the W. P. A. Writers' Program," NCarF (Jan, 1971), 19: 4-32. Eleven
stories.

1490. Boatright, Mody C. "Aunt Cordie's Ax and Other
Motifs in Oil," in Folk Travelers, ed. Mody C.
Boatright et al., pp. 34-40. Anecdotes about
the discovery of oil wells.

1491. Bosen, Barbara. "Danish Stories from Ephraim,
Utah," AFFword (Oct, 1972), 2: 24-34. Miscel-
laneous material from a Danish Mormon town in
Utah.

1492. Bourque, Darrell. "Cauchemar and Feu Follet,"
LFM (Aug, 1968), 2: 69-84. Two tales of spirits
collected from Negro high school students in
Louisiana.

1493. Bowden, Jim. "Two Oil Tales," in Madstones and
Twisters, ed. Mody C. Boatright et al., pp. 128-
132.

1494.   Brewer, J. Mason. "More of the Word on the
        Brazos," in Observations & Reflections on Texas
        Folklore, ed. F. E. Abernethy, pp. 91-99. Five
        preacher tales in Negro dialect.

1495.   Browne, Ray B. "Negro Folk Tales from Alabama,"
        SFQ (Je, 1954), 18: 129-134. Twelve stories
        from a Negro Methodist minister in 1951. Sparse
        annotation.

1496.   Brunner, Theodore C. "Thirteen Tales from Houston
        County," in The Golden Log, ed. Mody C. Boat-
        right et al., pp. 8-22. Brief tales from the
        Piney Woods of E. Texas.

1497.   Brunvand, Jan Harold. "An Indiana Storyteller Re-
        visited," MF (Spr, 1961), 11: 5-14. Texts from
        Jim Pennington of Bloomington, previously inter-
        viewed by Herbert Halpert in 1942.

1498.   Carlock, Barbara. "Tornado Tales of Northeastern
        Colorado," WF (Apr, 1962), 21: 103-108. Colo-
        rado farmers recall tornado incidents of 1950 and
        1959.

1499.   Carter, Albert Howard. "Some Folk Tales of the
        Big City," AF (Aug 15, 1953), 4: i, 4-6.

1500.   Cheney, Thomas E. "Scandinavian Immigrant Stor-
        ies," WF (Apr, 1959), 18: 99-105. Comic anec-
        dotes and tall tales from Scandinavian Mormon
        converts in Utah.

1501.   Clark, Ella E. "Some Nez Perce Traditions Told by
        Chief Armstrong," OHQ (Sept, 1952), 53: 181-
        191.

1502.   Claudel, Calvin. "Louisiana Folktales and Their
        Background," LHQ (Jl, 1955), 38: 35-56. Brief
        sketch of state history with summaries of typical
        tales from French areas.

1503.   Cobos, Rubén. "Five New Mexican Spanish Folk-
        tales," NMFR (1973-1974), 13: 11-18. Two
        local tales and five traditional tales collected in
        Albuquerque.

1504. Coe, Gayle L. "Tales of the Lost Nigger Mine,"
in Singers and Storytellers, ed. Mody C. Boatright et al., pp. 266-272. Summarized tales
from the Big Bend.

1505. Combs, Josiah H. "Some Kentucky Highland Stories,"
KFR (Apr-Je, 1958), 4: 45-61. Some 23 stories
recollected by the author, mostly from Knott Co.,
Ky.

1506. Cornett, Elizabeth B. "Belief Tales of Knott and
Perry Counties," KFR (Jl-Sept, 1956), 2: 69-76.
Omens, witchcraft, haunts, and ghosts in Eastern
Ky.

1507. Cothran, Kay L. "Talking Trash in the Okefenokee
Swamp Rim, Georgia," JAF (Oct-Dec, 1974), 87:
340-356. Tall tales, personal experiences, practical jokes collected from backwoods folk of
Southeastern Georgia.

1508. Creighton, Helen and Edward D. Ives. "Eight Folktales from Miramichi as Told by Wilmot Mc-
Donald," NEF (1963), 4: 70. Eight tales with
notes occupy entire issue.

1509. Currim, Martha D. and Barbara C. Smetzer.
"'Black-eye, the Intelligent Bird Dog,' and Other
Humorous Stories as Told by Joe D. Currim,"
NCarF (Jl, 1964), 12: 1-6. Nine tales with
types and motifs identified.

1510. Daklugie, Asa and Eve Ball. "Coyote and the Flies,"
NMFR (1955-1956), 10: 12-13. Interesting
Apache story of how Coyote stole fire from its
guardians, the Flies.

1511. Dégh, Linda. "Narratives from Early Indiana," IF
(1970), 3: 229-241.

1512. _____. "The Roommate's Death and Related
Dormitory Stories in Formation," IF (1969), 2:
55-74. Variants of a horror story well known to
female students.

1513. Dobie, J. Frank. "Br'er Rabbit Watches Out for
Himself in Mexico," in Mesquite and Willow, ed.

Mody C. Boatright et al., 113-117.   Mexican addition to Uncle Remus canon.

1514. _____. "Two Treasure Tales," in A Good Tale and a Bonnie Tune, ed. Mody C. Boatright et al., pp. 57-63.

1515. Dodson, Ruth. "South Texas Sketches," in And Horns on the Toads, ed. Mody C. Boatright et al., pp. 214-225.   Tales about ghosts and buried treasure.

1516. Dorman, Artell. "Speak of the Devil," in And Horns on the Toads, ed. Mody C. Boatright et al., pp. 142-146.   Four devil tales from Pyote, Texas.

1517. Dorson, Richard M. "The Astonishing Repertoire of James Douglas Suggs, a Michigan Negro Storyteller," MichH (Je, 1956), 40: 152-166.   Biographical data and analysis of his 160 tales.   No tales given in full but speaker's style discussed.

1518. _____. "Collecting Folklore in Jonesport, Maine," Proceedings APS (1957), 101: 270-289.   Tales, anecdotes, sea legends, all revealing a homogeneous folk tradition.

1519. _____. "The Folktale Repertoires of Two Maine Lobstermen," in Internationaler Kongress der Volkserzählungsforscher in Kiel und Kopenhagen, ed. Kurt Ranke (Berlin: De Gruyter, 1961), pp. 74-83.

1520. _____. "Jewish-American Dialect Stories on Tape," in Studies in Biblical and Jewish Folklore, ed. Raphael Patai et al., pp. 111-174.

1521. _____. "King Beast of the Forest Meets Man," SFQ (Je, 1954), 18: 118-128.   Sixteen variants of Type 157, "Learning to Fear Man," collected from Southern-born Negroes in Michigan.

1522. _____. "Mishaps of a Maine Lobsterman," NEF (Spr, 1958), 1: 1-7.

1523. _____. "More Jewish Dialect Stories," MF (F, 1960), 10: 133-146.   Sixteen stories told by a native of Brooklyn.

1524. _____. "A Negro Storytelling Session on Tape,"
      MF (W, 1953), 3: 201-212. Brief or fragmentary
      tales from three Negro informants in Michigan.

1525. _____. "Negro Tales," WF (Apr, Jl, Oct, 1954),
      13: 77-97, 160-169, 256-259. Tales collected
      from John Blackamore of Benton Harbor, Mich.,
      born 1922. Biographical data and full annotation.

1526. _____. "Negro Tales from Bolivar County, Mis-
      sissippi," SFQ (Je, 1955), 19: 104-116. Some
      20 tales from Mount Bayou, all-Negro town. In-
      formants, tale types, motifs listed.

1527. _____. "Negro Tales of Mary Richardson," MF
      (W, 1952), 6: 1-26. Some 29 brief tales plus
      miscellaneous items.

1528. _____. "Negro Witch Stories on Tape," MF (W,
      1952), 2: 229-241. Material from Southern-born
      Negroes in Calvin, Mich.

1529. _____. "Southern Negro Storytellers in Michigan,"
      MichH (Je, 1953), 37: 197-204. Texts from Cal-
      vin and Benton Harbor, Mich., including Old
      Marster stories, animal tales, hoodoo tales, but
      only one märchen.

1530. _____. "Tales of a Greek American Family on
      Tape," Fabula (1957), 1: i/ii, 114-144. Folk
      narratives, legends, evil eye beliefs, miracles
      told by immigrants from Bambakou, Greece, to
      Iron Mountain, Mich., collected in 1955.

1531. Dow, James R. "'Ah,' He Says, 'I've Heard of
      You.' 'Oh,' I said, 'No Doubt!' Status Seeking
      Through Story Telling," NYFQ (Je, 1973), 29:
      83-96. Tales from retired farmer Ben Kuhn
      about himself and his father-in-law of Bartholo-
      mew Co., Indiana.

1532. Duarte, Guadalupe. "Around the Fire with my
      Abuelitos," in Madstones and Twisters, ed. Mody
      C. Boatright et al., pp. 154-159. Family tales
      from Laredo, Texas.

1533. Edwards, Lawrence. "'The Old Scratch and the

Mean Woman' and 'Warts and Witchery,'" TFSB
(Dec, 1951), 17: 72-80. Two tales without annotation.

1534.   Eggen, Doris. "Indian Tales from Western New
York," NYFQ (W, 1950), 6: 240-245. Three
etiological tales from the Cattaraugus Indian
Reservation.

1535.   Ensor, Wanda. "Tales of the Supernatural Collected
in Mitchell and Yancey Counties, North Carolina," TFSB (Sept, 1972), 38: 61-71.

1536.   Ettawageshik, Jane and Gertrude Kurath, "Three
True Tales from L'Arbre County," MF (Spr,
1957), 7: 39-40.

1537.   Ferris, William R., Jr. "Black Folktales from Rose
Hill," MFR (F, 1973), 7: 70-85. Texts of 13
short tales collected at Vicksburg, 1966.

1538.   _____. "Ray Lum: Muletrader," NCarF (Sept,
1973), 21: 105-119. Tales and anecdotes collected from a veteran livestock trader in North
Carolina.

1539.   Field, Jerome P. "Folk Tales from North Dakota,
1910," WF (Jan, 1958), 17: 29-33. Tales told
by a Norwegian immigrant. No annotation.

1540.   Figh, Margaret Gillis. "Some Alabama Folktales,"
AlaR (Oct, 1963), 16: 270-278.

1541.   Gaston, Edwin W., Jr. "Tall Timber Tales," in
Singers and Storytellers, ed. Mody C. Boatright
et al., pp. 178-184. Anecdotes and folksay from
E. Texas sawmill life.

1542.   Gehman, Henry Snyder. "Ghost Stories and Old
Superstitions of Lancaster County," PF (S, 1970),
19: iv, 48-53. Tales remembered from the
author's childhood.

1543.   George, Philip Brandt. "The Ghost of Cline Avenue:
'La Llorona' in the Calumet Region," IF (1972),
5: 56-91.

1544. Glassie, Henry. "The Greedy Couple: a Folk
      Tale," MLW (S, 1964), 40: 52-56. North Caro-
      lina variant of Aarne-Thompson Type 750A.

1545. _____. "Three Southern Mountain Jack Tales,"
      TFSB (Dec, 1964), 30: 88-102. One Virginia and
      two No. Carolina tales: "Tom and Jack," "Little
      Nippy," and "Billy Peg and His Bull."

1546. Goodbear, Paul Flying Eagle. "Southern Cheyenne
      Ghost Narratives," PM (Jan, 1951), 24: 10-20.

1547. Guthrie, Charles S. "Some Folktales and Legends
      from the Cumberland Valley," KFR (Jl-Sept, 1969),
      15: 61-65.

1548. Hagerty, Gilbert. "The Bull: a Folk Narrative,"
      NYFQ (Spr, 1956), 12: 43-53. A rewritten folk
      tale.

1549. Hale, Meredith. "I Heard It on the Border," in And
      Horns on the Toads, ed. Mody C. Boatright et
      al., pp. 136-141. Panther lore.

1550. Hall, Joseph S. "Bear-Hunting Stories from the
      Great Smokies," TSFB (Sept, 1957), 23: 67-75.
      Four stories told in mountain idiom.

1551. Halpert, Herbert. "Place Name Stories of Kentucky
      Waterways and Ponds," KFR (Jl-Sept, 1961), 7:
      85-101. Some 15 items.

1552. Halpert, Violetta Maloney. "Place Name Stories
      about West Kentucky Towns," KFR (Jl-Sept, 1961),
      7: 103-116. Notes on 15 place names.

1553. Harris, Jesse and Julia Neely. "Southern Illinois
      Phantoms and Bogies," MF (F, 1951), 1: 171-
      178. Variety of brief tales.

1554. Harris, Stanley W. "Stories of Ranch People," in
      Singers and Storytellers, ed. Mody C. Boatright
      et al., pp. 173-177. Five brief tales without
      dates or informants.

1555. Hawes, Bess Lomax. "La Llorona in Juvenile Hall,"
      WF (Jl, 1968), 27: 153-170. Ghost tales from
      girls in a Los Angeles detention home.

1556. Hayes, George McGill. "Tales from the Bristol
          Hills," NYFQ (Spr, 1953), 9: 40-46. Material
          from Ontario Co., N.Y.

1557. Hendricks, George D. "George Washington in Texas,
          and Other Tales, Old Stories in New Surround-
          ings," WF (Oct, 1955), 14: 269-272. Famous re-
          marks perverted for comic effect.

1558. Henning, Marion. "Comic Anecdotes from Santa,"
          WF (Oct, 1965), 24: 249-258. Brief historical
          tales from northern Idaho.

1559. Hiester, Miriam W. "Tales of the Paisanos," in
          Singers and Storytellers, ed. Mody C. Boatright
          et al., pp. 226-243. Nine carefully annotated
          tales from Mission and San Antonio, translated
          from the Spanish.

1560. Howard, James. "Tales of Neiman-Marcus," in
          Folk Travelers, ed. Mody C. Boatright et al.,
          pp. 160-170. Anecdotes of salesmen and cus-
          tomers from the famous Dallas store.

1561. Hurley, Gerard T. "Buried Treasure Tales in
          America," WF (Jl, 1951), 10: 197-216. American
          tales of buried treasure are brief and largely
          factual, but they often have a dual structure and
          end without the treasure being found. 102 such
          tales summarized.

1562. Irvis, K. Leroy. "Negro Tales from Eastern New
          York," NYFQ (A, 1955), 11: 165-176. Rewritten
          stories from Ulster Co.

1563. [Ives, Edward D.] "Malecita and Passamaquoddy
          Tales," NEF (1965), 6: 1-81. Short tales from
          Maine and New Brunswick Indians.

1564. Jackson, Bruce. "'The Greatest Mathematician in
          the World': Norbert Wiener Stories," WF (Jan,
          1972), 31: 1-22. Some 33 anecdotes about MIT
          professor, true or attributed.

1565. Jiménez, Baldemar A. "Cuentos de Sustos," in The
          Golden Log, ed. Mody C. Boatright et al., pp.
          156-164. Three stories from San Antonio dealing
          with fright.

1566.	Johnson, Aili Kolehmainen. "The Eyeturner," MF
		(Spr, 1955), 5: 5-10. Finnish wizard tales from
		upper Michigan.

1567.	Johnson, F. Roy. "Yarns Old and New," NCarFJ
		(Aug, 1974), 22: 102-108.

1568.	Joines, Jerry D. "Twelve Tall Tales from Wilkes
		County," NCarF (Feb, 1972), 20: 3-10.

1569.	Jones, Dazzie Lee. "Some Folktales from Negro
		College Students," TFSB (Sept, 1958), 24: 102-
		111. Stories collected in Memphis and Blackburn
		College, Ill.

1570.	Kellner, Esther. "Token Stories from Indiana," MF
		(W, 1953), 223-230. Early Hoosier stories with
		tokens or warnings.

1571.	Key, Howard C. "Twister Tales," in Madstones
		and Twisters, ed. Mody C. Boatright et al., pp.
		52-68. Factual anecdotes and tales about tor-
		nadoes.

1572.	Kilpatrick, Jack Frederick and Anna Gritts Kilpatrick.
		"Eastern Cherokee Folktales: Reconstructed from
		the Field Notes of Frans M. Olbrechts," (Wash-
		ington: Smithsonian Institution, Bureau of Am.
		Ethnology, 1966), pp. 379-447.

1573.	Kirtley, Bacil F. "'La Llorona' and Related
		Themes," WF (Jl, 1960), 19: 155-168. The
		theme of the Weeping Woman, famous Mexican
		legend, has analogues.

1574.	Lancaster, Richard. "Why the White Man Will Never
		Reach the Sun," in And Horns on the Toads, ed.
		Mody C. Boatright et al., pp. 190-200. Black-
		foot creation story.

1575.	Landar, Herbert J. "Four Navaho Summer Tales,"
		JAF (Apr-Je, Jl-Sept, Oct-Dec, 1959), 72: 161-
		164, 248-251, 298-309. Four tales from Fort
		Defiance, Ariz., collected in 1956. Anecdotal
		and non-ritualistic stories notable for their re-
		alism.

1576.   Lane, Paul K. "Kentucky Folk Narratives," KFR
        (Apr-Je, 1964), 10: 25-34. 14 items.

1577.   Larson, Andrew Karl. "Some Folk Tales from Utah's
        Dixie," WF (Apr, 1959), 18: 89-97. Tales from
        Washington, Utah.

1578.   Larson, Mildred R. "The Taller the Better," NYFQ
        (W, 1961; A, 1962), 17: 271-287; 18: 217-234.
        Student-collected tall tales from various parts of
        New York State.

1579.   Laskowski, Cornelius J. "Polish Tales of the Super-
        natural Collected in Albany, N.Y.," NYFQ (A,
        1954), 10: 165-175.

1580.   Lee, Sara Rhodes. "The Story of Pats Oneal,"
        TFSB (Mr, 1964), 30: 21-26. Ghost story of an
        Overton Co., Tenn. murderer.

1581.   Lohof, Bruce A. "A Morphology of the Modern
        Fable," JPC (S, 1974), 8: 15-27. Short stories
        in Good Housekeeping 1965-69 resemble fables in
        structure and morals.

1582.   Loomis, C. Grant. "Four Gambling Yarns," WF
        (Jan, 1965), 24: 29-31. Reprinted from nine-
        teenth century periodicals.

1582a. Lowie, Robert H. "A Crow Tale," Anth Q. (Jan,
        1954), 27: 1-22.

1583.   Lueg, Maurita Russell. "Russell Tales," in Mad-
        stones and Twisters, ed. Mody C. Boatright et
        al., pp. 160-166. Pioneer tales from a family
        north of Waco, Texas.

1584.   Lunt, C. Richard K. "Jones Tracy: Tall-Tale Hero
        from Mount Desert Island," NEF (1968), 10: 3-
        75. A biography of Tracy and 54 tale texts.

1585.   MacCurdy, Raymond R., Jr. "Spanish Folklore
        from St. Bernard Parish, Louisiana," SFQ (Dec,
        1952), 16: 227-250. Twelve brief tales in
        Spanish without translation, a sequel to collec-
        tions published in 1948-1949.

1586. Mankin, Carolyn. "Tales the German Texans Tell,"
       in Singers and Storytellers, ed. Mody C. Boat-
       right et al., pp. 260-265. Seven tales imported
       from Germany.

1587. Matlock, Grace. "Three Tar Heel Folktales," NCarF
       (Aug, 1972), 20: 128-130.

1588. Milanovich, Anthony. "Serbian Tales from Blanford,"
       IF (1971), 4: i, 1-60. Twelve tales collected
       from emigrants to a small Indiana mining town.

1589. Miles, Elton. "Chisos Ghosts," in Madstones and
       Twisters, ed. Mody C. Boatright et al., pp. 106-
       122. Ghost stories from the Indian country of
       W. Texas.

1590. Miller, Robert J. "Situation and Sequence in the
       Study of Folklore," JAF (Jan-Mr, 1952), 65:
       29-48. Some 21 tales from the Makah Indians
       of Olympic Peninsula.

1591. Montell, Lynwood. "Belief Tales from Barren Coun-
       ty," KFR (Jan-Mr, 1962), 8: 11-17. Nineteen
       brief tales from high school students.

1592. Montgomery, Robert W. "Ghost Stories from Deca-
       tur County," MF (Spr, 1961), 11: 62-64. Trivial
       Indiana tales.

1593. Musick, Ruth Ann. "European Folktales in West
       Virginia," MF (Spr, 1956), 6: 27-37. Four folk
       tales collected from immigrant coal miners.

1594. _____. "Ghost Tales and Unusual Happenings,"
       WFV (F-W, 1964), 15: i-ii, 2-19.

1595. _____. "Indiana Witch Tales," JAF (Jan-Mr,
       1952), 65: 57-65. Tales from the manuscript of
       an Indiana schoolteacher, 1929.

1596. _____. "Juggin' Party Tales," SFQ (Sept, 1951),
       15: 211-219. Indiana tall tales about a bibulous
       hunter.

1597. _____. "The Murdered Pedlar in West Virginia,"
       MF (W, 1961-1962), 11: 247-255. Ten ghost
       stories.

1598. _____. "Omens and Tokens of West Virginia,"
          MF (W, 1953), 2: 263-267. Eleven tales.

1599. _____. "The Trickster Story in West Virginia,"
          MF (F, 1960), 10: 125-132. Three tales brought
          from Europe by W. Virginia miners.

1600. _____. "West Virginia Ghost Stories," MF (Spr,
          1958), 8: 21-28.

1601. Newell, William H. "Schuylkill Folktales," PF (S,
          1958), 9: iii, 18-19.

1602. Nichols, Priscilla Miller. "Greek Lore from Syra-
          cuse, N.Y.," NYFQ (S, 1953), 9: 109-117.

1603. Nolan, Mary Lee. "Stories Told by Refugees from
          the Mexican Revolution (1910-1920)," MSF (W,
          1974), 2: 63-76.

1604. Owens, Ethel. "Five Ghost Tales from Boyle Coun-
          ty, Kentucky," MF (Spr, 1958), 8: 29-36.

1605. _____. "Ghost Tales from Breathitt County,"
          KFR (Jl-Sept, 1959), 5: 81-86.

1606. _____. "Tales of Western Boyle County, Ken-
          tucky," SFQ (Sept, 1957), 21: 149-153. Three
          historical incidents embellished by time.

1607. Padilla, Floy. "Witch Stories from Tapia Azul and
          Tres Fulgores," NMFR (1951-1952), 6: 11-19.
          Tales rewritten from family recollections and
          telling.

1608. Parochetti, Joann Stephens. "Scary Stories from
          Purdue," KFQ (Spr, 1965), 10: 49-57. Versions
          of "The Hook Story."

1609. Pelly, Francine. "Gypsy Folktales from Phila-
          delphia," KFQ (S, 1968), 13: 83-102. Back-
          ground and motifs provided for four tales, one
          legend, and three memorates.

1610. Pennington, Lee and Joy Pennington. "Three Ghost
          Stories from Kentucky," NCarF (May, 1972),
          20: 77-79.

1611.   . "Two Tales from Bloody Harlan," AJ
          (Spr, 1973), 1: 139-142. Brief tales from a
          Kentucky county.

1612. Perdue, Chuck. "'I Swear to God It's the Truth if
          I Ever Told It,'" KFQ (Spr, 1969), 14: 1-54.
          Entire issue given over to tale texts of John and
          Cora Jackson from Rappahannock Co., Va. Data
          about informants given.

1613. Pooler, Lolita Huning. "New Mexican Folk Tales,"
          WF (Jan, 1951), 10: 63-71. Two tales translated
          from the Spanish. "El Diablo" is a variant of
          "Maiden Without Hands," Type 706.

1614.   . "Spanish Folk Tales," WF (Apr, 1956),
          15: 102-105. Four New Mexican tales.

1615. Porter, Kenneth. "Two Ghost Stories of Military
          Life in the Southwest," in And Horns on the
          Toads, ed. Mody C. Boatright et al., pp. 226-
          230.

1616. Poulsen, Richard C. "Mules as Venison," WF (Oct,
          1974), 33: 326-331. Comic hunting stories from
          Utah.

1617. Randolph, Vance. "Bedtime Stories from Missouri,"
          WF (Jan, 1951), 10: 1-10. Ten common fireside
          stories which seem less appropriate as children's
          tales today.

1618.   . "Folktales from Arkansas," JAF (Apr-
          Je, 1952), 65: 159-166. Ten tales with notes on
          informants.

1619.   . "Missouri Folktales," MF (S, 1952), 2:
          77-90. Ten miscellaneous stories.

1620.   . "Ozark Mountain Tales," SFQ (Sept,
          1952), 16: 165-176. Ten stories "not retold or
          rewritten or re-created" but transcribed from in-
          formants as accurately as possible. Dates and
          informants given.

1621.   . "Tales from Arkansas," SFQ (Je, 1955),
          19: 125-136. Stories derived from friends and

neighbors, taken down as notes and then typed.
"I just transcribed each story as accurately as
possible, and let it go at that."

1622. _____. "Tales from Missouri," MF (Spr, 1956),
6: 38-49. "Not one of these tales is an exact
literal transcript, but they are all pretty close
to the mark."

1623. _____. "Tales from South Missouri," SFQ (Je,
1950), 14: 79-86.

1624. _____. "Tales from the Ozark Hills," HF (Apr-
Je, 1950), 9: 37-48.

1625. _____. "Tales from the Ozarks," WF (Jan, 1955),
14: 23-31. Ten stories.

1626. Rattray, Jeanette Edwards. "Rum-Running Tales
from the East End," NYFQ (Mr, 1963), 19: 3-
18. Run-running and bootlegging tales from Long
Island, mostly true.

1627. Reaver, J. Russell. "Legends of the King's Highway," SFQ (Dec, 1956), 20: 225-237. Slight
anecdotes, often edited, about St. Augustine from
a retired surveyor.

1628. _____. "Lithuanian Tales from Illinois," SFQ
(Sept, 1950), 14: 161-168. Six tales from an informant at Benld, Ill.

1629. Rhone, George E. "The Swamp Angel," KFQ (S,
1965), 10: 86-91. Summarized version of Negro
witchcraft tale from Clinton Co., Penn.

1630. Rivers, Richard M. "Homemade Tales," in The
Golden Log, ed. Mody C. Boatright et al., pp.
23-33. Six brief tales from East Texas.

1631. Robe, Stanley L. "Basque Tales from Eastern
Oregon," WF (Jl, 1953), 12: 153-157. Four
tales collected in Burns, Ore., in 1948.

1632. Roberts, Leonard. "The Big Turkle," KFR (Jan-
Mr, 1960), 6: 9-14. Kentucky tall tale.

1633. _____. "Folktales Told in Tennessee," TFSB (Je, 1955), 21: 33-37. Two tales: "Jack and the Beanstalk," and "Bluebonnet." No annotation.

1634. _____. "The King's Well," KFR (Jan-Mr, 1957), 3: 1-8. Type 577 from eastern Ky.

1635. _____. "The Man and the Devil's Daughter," KFR (Jl-Sept, 1959), 5: 87-93. Kentucky version of two tale types, 313 and 563.

1636. _____. "Polly, Nancy, and Muncimeg," KFR (Jan-Mr, 1955), 1: 19-24. Tale collected from Tom Couch of Putney Co., Ky. Type 328.

1637. _____. "Quare Jack," KFR (Jan-Mr, 1958), 4: 1-9. Unusual mountain story with fragments of four story types.

1638. _____. "Tall Tales of Eastern Kentucky," KFR (Jl-Sept, 1962), 8: 68-74. Eight Münchhausen type tales.

1639. Rogers, E. G. "More Tall Tales from Tennessee," SFQ (Sept, 1961), 25: 178-183. Short tales from E. Tennessee; informants given but no dates.

1640. _____. "Tall Tales from Tennessee," SFQ (Dec, 1955), 19: 237-242. Short, rather typical exaggerations. Neither dates nor annotation.

1641. _____. "They Walked by Night," MF (W, 1956), 6: 229-233. Seven brief student-collected tales.

1642. Salzmann, Zdenek and Joy Salzmann. "Arapaho Tales I," HF (Jl-Sept, 1950), 9: 80-96; "Arapaho Tales II," MF (Spr, 1952), 2: 21-42; "Arapaho Tales III," MF (Spr, 1957), 7: 27-37.

1643. Seaman, Gertrude W. "Jesse Alpin Stories," NYFQ (S, 1958), 14: 126-133. Tall tales by a local storyteller.

1644. Shope, James A. "Ghost Tales and Legends, Mainly from Eastern Kentucky," KFR (Apr-Je, 1966), 12: 41-58.

1645. Smith, George K., Jr. "A Sampling of Stories from
         the Area of Machias, Maine," NEF (F-W, 1960),
         3: 39-52. Some 28 brief tales collected in 1960.

1646. Smith, Grace Partridge. "Egyptian 'Lies,'" MF (S,
         1951), 1: 93-97. Brief tall tales from Southern
         Ill.

1647. Smith, James R. "Tales from a Winter Fireside,"
         MFR (Spr, 1968), 2: 9-18. Family data.

1648. Smith, Richard. "Richard's Tales," in Folk Trav-
         elers, ed. Mody C. Boatright et al., pp. 220-
         253. Seventeen animal and Negro tales recounted
         by a Texas dairy worker.

1649. Speck, F. G. and H. P. Beck. "Old World Tales
         among the Mohawks," JAF (Jl-Sept, 1950), 63:
         285-308. Nine tales from two Mohawk women,
         all but two of European provenience.

1650. Splitter, Henry Winfred. "New Tales of American
         Phantom Ships," WF (Jl, 1950), 9: 201-216.

1651. Stephens, James W. "Belief Tales," KFR (Jan-Mr,
         1963), 9: 7-10.

1652. Strong, Leah B. "Neighbors: Humor in the Lehigh
         Valley," NYFQ (S, 1959), 15: 126-130. Anec-
         dotal tales from the Pennsylvania Dutch country.

1653. Studer, Norman. "City Slickers in the Catskill
         Woods," NYFQ (Je, 1964), 20: 110-114. Yarns
         from the Catskill bear hunter and ranger Mike
         Todd.

1654. _____. "Turning Back the Waters of the Ashokan,"
         NYFQ (F, 1959), 15: 165-168. Tales by Elwyn
         Davis from the Ashokan Reservoir area in the
         Catskills.

1655. _____. "Yarns of a Catskill Woodsman," NYFQ
         (A, 1955), 11: 183-192. Stories told by a veteran
         bear-hunter Mike Todd.

1656. Sutherland, Tucker. "Ghost Stories from a Texas
         Ghost Town," in Singers and Storytellers, ed.

Mody C. Boatright et al., pp. 115-122. Tales
from San Patricio.

1657. Tally, Thomas W. "De Wull er de Wust (The Will
o' the Wisp)," TFSB (Sept, 1955), 21: 57-78.
Long tale in Negro dialect with sparse annotation.

1658. Tokar, Elizabeth. "Humorous Anecdotes Collected
from a Methodist Minister," WF (Apr, 1967), 26:
89-100. Sermon anecdotes and jests.

1659. Tollman, Ruth B. "Treasure Tales of the Caballos,"
WF (Jl, 1961), 20: 153-174. Some 32 brief tales
from Caballos Mts. in New Mexico. Informants
listed.

1660. Utech, Eugene. "J. Raymond Bear's Olde Tyme
Ghost Tales of Cumberland County," KFQ (W,
1967), 12: 211-228. Twelve ghost stories recorded in 1966. Introduction and notes by Mac
E. Barrick.

1661. Van Wagenen, Jared, Jr. "An Old-Time Teller of
Tales," NYFQ (W, 1959), 15: 243-251. A man
of 87 recalls a neighborhood tale teller of his
youth.

1662. Vickers, Ovid S. "Five from Gum Swamp," MFR
(S, 1973), 7: 33-38. Georgia tales.

1663. Wade, F. S. "The Adventures of Ad Lawrence," in
Madstones and Twisters, ed. Mody C. Boatright
et al., pp. 133-148. Tales about a Texas pioneer
from the Elgin Courier.

1664. Wallrich, William Jones. "Five Bruja Tales from
the San Luis Valley," WF (Oct, 1950), 9: 359-
362. Witch tales from Southern Colorado.

1665. Walser, Richard. "North Carolina Firearms and
Hunting Stories from the Spirit of the Times,"
KFR (Jl-Sept, 1967), 13: 57-61. Reprints from
a sporting weekly.

1666. Walton, David A. "Folklore as Compensation: a
Content Analysis of the Negro Animal Tale," OF
(1974?), no volume, 1-11.

1667. _____. "Pennsylvania Riverboat Stories," sequels
      entitled "Lou Sesher Stories," KFQ (W, 1966;
      Spr, 1967; F, 1967; W, 1967; Spr, 1968), 11:
      215-237; 12: 81-93, 177-186, 229-232; 13: 3-17.
      Entertaining tall tales and anecdotes by a gifted
      raconteur.

1668. Waugh, Butler H. "Negro Tales of John Kendry from
      Indianapolis," MF (F, 1958), 8: 125-141.

1669. Wellman, Manly Wade. "Folk Yarns and Other Mat-
      ters," NCarFJ (Aug, 1974), 22: 114-118.

1670. White, Vallie T. "Some Folklore from North Louisi-
      ana," SFQ (Sept, 1956), 20: 164-177. Short,
      miscellaneous collection with banshees, fetches,
      morons, Irish bulls.

1671. Whitely, Raymond. "Two Stories from the Maine
      Lumberwoods," NEF (W, 1958), 1: 58-62. "The
      Dungarvon Whooper" and "The Twin Pines."

1672. Williams, Girlene Marie. "Negro Stories from the
      Colorado Valley," in And Horns on the Toads, ed.
      Mody C. Boatright et al., pp. 161-169. Fourteen
      tales from La Grange, Texas, confirming author's
      contention that Negro stories are funny or mysteri-
      ous.

1673. Williams, Marion. "Tales from Tug Hill," NYFQ
      (Spr, 1957), 13: 23-31. Lumberjack tales from
      Tug Hill plateau in northern Adirondack Mts.

1674. Wilson, David, ed. "Boogers, Witches, and Haints,"
      Foxfire (Spr-S, 1971), 5: 28-48, 65-79. Ghost
      stories field-collected by various students, in
      Georgia.

1675. Worthington, Ralph C., Jr. "Five Tar-Pitt Tales,"
      NCarFJ (Feb, 1974), 22: 15-29. Brief tales
      from Tar River country in Pitt Co., No. Car.

1676. Wyant, Betty Jean. "Tales of Kentucky's Cave Re-
      gion," TFSB (Dec, 1954), 20: 82-85.

1677. Wyatt, F. J. "So-Called Tall Tales from Kansas,"
      WF (Spr, 1963), 22: 107-111. Amusing exag-

gerations about Kansas weather but not unique to
that state.

1678.   Yoder, Don. "Witch Tales from Adams County,"
        PF (S, 1962), 12: iv, 29-37. Nineteen texts
        from a single informant.

B. Collections (Books)

1679.   Abernethy, Francis E. Tales from the Big Thicket
        (Austin: U. of Texas P., 1966), xii, 244pp.
        Some tales but mostly miscellaneous essays with
        bits of social history.

1680.   Anderson, John Q. With the Bark On: Popular
        Humor of the Old South (Nashville: Vanderbilt
        U. P., 1967), 337pp. Some 70 reprinted news-
        paper sketches, chiefly from W. T. Porter's
        Spirit of the Times: tall tales, exaggerations,
        etc.

1681.   Angulo, Jaime de. Indian Tales (New York: A. A.
        Wyn, 1953), xii, 246pp. Not true folk tales but
        stories revealing author's saturation in Indian
        material.

1682.   Baker, Betty. Great Ghost Stories of the Old West
        (New York: Four Winds, 1968), 126pp. Popular
        presentation of tales about phantom trains, spooks,
        monsters.

1683.   Beckham, Stephen Dow. Tall Tales from Rogue
        River, the Yarns of Hathaway Jones (Bloomington
        and London: Indiana U. P., 1974), xii, 178pp.
        Jones was a woodsman, hunter, and Oregon mail
        carrier with a talent for wild, Münchhausen-like
        exaggeration.

1684.   Booker, Louise R. Historical and Traditional "Tar
        Heel" Stories from the Colorful Coastal Plains
        (Murfreesboro, N.C.: Johnson Pub. Co., 1968),
        127pp.

1685. Brewer, J. Mason. Dog Ghosts and Other Texas
       Negro Folk Tales (Austin: U. of Texas P.,
       1958), xiv, 124pp. Some 63 short tales collected
       in East Texas by a prominent Negro folklorist and
       told in dialect; they are thinly humorous and re-
       veal traditional life.

1686. _____. The Word on the Brazos (Austin: U. of
       Texas P., 1953), xv, 109pp. Negro preacher
       tales, some by preachers, some about them.
       Negro idiom preserved but the stories are par-
       tially rewritten.

1687. _____. Worser Days and Better Times (Chicago:
       Quadrangle Books, 1965), 192pp. Some 79 tales
       collected in North Carolina, without adequate iden-
       tification or notes.

1688. Campbell, Marie. Tales from the Cloud Walking
       Country (Bloomington: Indiana U. P., 1958),
       270pp. Some 78 tales from Eastern Kentucky
       narrated by six informants who are described.
       They are labeled Am. märchen but have European
       roots.

1689. Canonge, Elliott. Comanche Texts (Norman: Sum-
       mer Institute of Linguistics, 1958), xiii, 156pp.
       Native Comanche texts with English annotations.

1690. Carkin, Helen S. and Norman H. Lerman. Once
       Upon an Indian Tale (New York: Carlton P.,
       1968). Nine short narratives from the Fraser
       River Valley.

1691. Carmer, Carl. The Screaming Ghost and Other
       Stories (New York: Knopf, 1956), xii, 146pp.
       Varied legends, some traditional, some invented.

1692. Chase, Richard. American Folk Tales and Songs
       (New York: New Am. Lib., 1956), 240pp. Re-
       printed by Dover, N.Y., 1971. Convenient
       anthology of tales, ballads, songs.

1693. Coffin, Tristram P. Indian Tales of North America
       (Philadelphia: Am. Folklore Soc., 1961), xvii,
       157pp. Some 45 tales excerpted from JAF with
       some texts rewritten or merged. Inadequate an-

notation. See review by Alan Dundes in JAF,
76: 69-71.

1694. Collins, Earl Augustus. Legends and Lore of Missouri (San Antonio: Naylor, 1951), xvi, 115pp.
Several dozen tales plus other material; popular
and unscholarly.

1695. Corcoran, Jean. Folk Tales of North America (Indianapolis: Bobbs-Merrill, 1962), 123pp. Tales
adapted for a popular audience.

1696. Courlander, Harold. Terrapin's Pot of Sense (New
York: Holt, 1957), 125pp. Some 30 folktales
collected in rural Alabama, New Jersey, Michigan. Casual notes.

1697. Davis, Hubert J. 'Pon My Honor Hit's the Truth:
Tall Tales from the Mountains (Murfreesboro,
N.C.: Johnson Pub. Co., 1973), 112pp.

1698. Dobie, J. Frank. Tales of Old-Time Texas (Boston:
Little, Brown, 1955), xv, 336pp. Tall tales,
legends, historical episodes told by a skilful narrator.

1699. Dorson, Richard M. American Negro Folktales
(Greenwich, Conn.: Fawcett, 1967), 384pp. Reprinted material from earlier books and magazine
articles.

1700. _____. Bloodstoppers and Bearwalkers: Folk
Traditions of the Upper Peninsula (Cambridge:
Harvard, 1952), 305pp. Michigan tales collected
by Dorson from Indian, Cornish, Finnish, and
Canadian sources and carefully annotated.

1701. _____. Negro Folktales in Michigan (Cambridge:
Harvard, 1956), xiv, 245pp. Negro tales from a
northern state; 165 stories with informants listed
and both a motif and tale type index.

1702. _____. Negro Tales from Pine Bluff, Arkansas,
and Calvin, Michigan (Bloomington: Indiana U.
P., 1958), xviii, 292pp. Field-collected Negro
tales which despite their geographical separation
are at times remarkably similar.

1703. Downs, Robert B. The Bear Went Over the Mountain.
       Tall Tales of American Animals (New York:
       Macmillan, 1964), xvii, 358pp. Readable collec-
       tion of fanciful tales reprinted from such authors
       as Twain, Thurber, Saroyan, Stuart, et al.

1704. Feldmann, Susan. The Story Telling Stone: Myths
       and Tales of the American Indians (New York:
       Dell, 1965), 271pp. Useful anthology of printed
       material from various tribes.

1705. Felton, Harold W. The World's Most Truthful Man:
       Tall Tales Told by Ed Grant in Maine (New York:
       Dodd, Mead, 1961), 150pp. Windies from Maine.

1706. Foster, James R. Great Folktales of Wit and Humor
       (New York: Harper, 1955), xiii, 320pp. Liter-
       ary handling of folktales from standard sources.
       Little Am. material. References incomplete or
       missing.

1707. Fulcher, Walter. The Way I Heard It: Tales of the
       Big Bend (Austin: U. of Texas P., 1959), 87pp.
       Reprinted in 1973, notes by Elton Miles.

1708. Graydon, Nell S. South Carolina Ghost Tales (Beau-
       fort, S.C.: Beaufort Book Shop, 1969), xii,
       156pp.

1709. _____. Tales of Beaufort (Beaufort, S.C.: Beau-
       fort Book Shop, 1963), xii, 156pp.

1710. _____. Tales of Edisto (Atlanta: Tupper and
       Love, 1960), 166pp. History of Edisto Island,
       S.C., with tales and Negro folklore.

1711. Grey, Herman. Tales from the Mohaves (Norman:
       U. of Oklahoma P., 1971), 96pp. Introduction
       by Alice Marriott.

1712. Harden, John. Tar Heel Ghosts (Chapel Hill: U.
       of No. Car. P., 1954), xiv, 178pp. Some 38
       stories, many fragmentary, collected and retold
       (spirits, death tokens, lights, etc.).

1713. Harter, Walter. Osceola's Head and Other American
       Ghost Stories (Englewood Cliffs: Prentice-Hall,
       1974), 71pp. Ten stories.

1714. Hughes, Langston, and Arna Bontemps. The Book
       of Negro Folklore (New York: Dodd, Mead,
       1959), xxxi, 624pp. Excellent anthology including
       animal tales, preacher tales, anecdotes, reminis-
       cences, as well as literary material.

1715. Inge, M. Thomas. Sut Lovingood's Yarns (New
       Haven: College and Univ. P., 1966), 336pp.
       Yarns by G. W. Harris, reprinted from books
       and periodicals.

1716. Ives, Burl. Burl Ives' Tales of America (Cleveland:
       World, 1954), 305pp. Rewritten stories.

1717. Jacobs, Elizabeth Derr. Nehalem Tillamook Tales
       (Eugene: U. of Oregon P., 1959), ix, 216pp.
       Melville Jacobs edited this 1934 collection from
       a fullblood Nehalem.

1718. Johnson, F. Roy. How and Why Stories in Carolina
       Folklore (Murfreesboro, No. Car.: Johnson Pub.
       Co., 1971), 112pp.

1719. _____. Tales from Old Carolina (Murfreesboro,
       No. Car.: Johnson Pub. Co., 1965), vii, 248pp.
       Folklore and historical lore, often recorded with-
       out sources.

1720. Jones, Louis C. Things That Go Bump in the Night
       (New York: Hill and Wang, 1959), xii, 208pp.
       200 supernatural tales collected by the writer and
       associates and often rewritten.

1721. Jones, Louis Thomas. So Say the Indians (San An-
       tonio: Naylor, 1970), xix, 191pp. Brief, super-
       ficial tales inserted between historical and geo-
       graphical accounts.

1722. Kilpatrick, Jack F. and Anna Kilpatrick. Friends
       of Thunder: Folktales of the Oklahoma Chero-
       kees (Dallas: So. Methodist U. P., 1964), xviii,
       197pp. Cherokee bird, animal, trickster, and
       humorous tales.

1723. Konitzky, Gustav A. Nordamerikanische Indianer-
       märchen (Düsseldorf: Eugen Diederichs Verlag,
       1963), 304pp.

1724. Lea, Aurora Lucero-White. Juan Bobo, Adapted
      from the Spanish Folktale Bertoldo (New York:
      Vantage, 1962), 44pp. Some 15 adventures of
      Juan the fool in the period of a Mexican governor
      of New Mexico. Juan succeeds by wit.

1725. _____. Literary Folklore of the Hispanic South-
      west (San Antonio: Naylor, 1953), xv, 247pp.
      Some 25 tales in English plus Spanish folk plays,
      ballads, corridos, etc.

1726. Lum, Peter. Folk Tales from America (London:
      Frederick Muller Ltd., 1973), 190pp. Retold
      Indian and Eskimo tales.

1727. Macmillan, Cyrus. Glooskap's Country, and Other
      Indian Tales (Toronto and New York: Oxford,
      1956), 273pp. Some 38 tales, chiefly Canadian,
      pleasantly rewritten. No notes or sources.

1728. McMurry, James. The Catskill Witch and Other
      Tales of the Hudson Valley (Syracuse U. P.,
      1974), viii, 156pp.

1729. Martin, Frances Gardiner. Nine Tales of Raven
      (New York: Harper, 1951), 60pp.

1730. Martin, Margaret Rhett. Charleston Ghosts (Colum-
      bia: U. of So. Carolina P., 1963), x, 105pp.
      Eighteen ghost tales.

1731. Miller, Elaine K. Mexican Folk Narrative from
      the Los Angeles Area (Austin and London: U. of
      Texas P., 1973), 388pp. Some 82 narratives in
      Spanish, not translated.

1732. Musick, Ruth Ann. Green Hills of Magic (Lexing-
      ton: U. P. of Kentucky, 1970), xvi, 312pp.
      Some 79 tales collected from W. Virginia coal
      miners, all of European origin. Notes plus
      motif and tale indexes.

1733. _____. The Telltale Lilac Bush and Other West
      Virginia Ghost Tales (Lexington: U. of Kentucky
      P., 1965), xviii, 189pp. A hundred ghost tales
      reflecting W. Va. history, coal mining, and
      early railroading, told in a banal style. No
      background information given.

1734. Newcomb, Franc Johnson. Navaho Folk Tales (Santa
       Fe: Museum of Navaho Ceremonial Art, 1967),
       xvi, 203pp. Seventeen tales by a specialist in
       Navaho culture but rewritten and sparsely an-
       notated.

1735. Nye, Wilbur Sturtevant. Bad Medicine & Good:
       Tales of the Kiowas (Norman: U. of Oklahoma
       P., 1962), 291pp. Some 44 Kiowa tales collected
       in 1933-1937 by an army officer. Most concern
       war and raids.

1736. Opie, Iona and Peter Opie. The Classic Fairy Tales
       (New York: Oxford, 1974), 255pp. Reprints of
       24 tales familiar to American readers, using the
       earliest English texts.

1737. Patterson, Paul. Pecos Tales (Austin: Encino P.,
       1967), x, 101pp. Tales, anecdotes, legends
       from West Texas, given without documentation.

1738. Post, Lauren C. Cajun Sketches from the Prairies
       of Southwest Louisiana (Baton Rouge: Louisiana
       State U. P., 1962), xiv, 215pp. A few folktales
       and much folk life from the Cajun country.

1739. Rael, Juan R. Cuentos Espanoles de Colorado y de
       Nuevo Mexico: Spanish Tales from Colorado and
       New Mexico (Stanford: Stanford U. P., 1957),
       two volumes, xvi, 559pp. and xv, 819pp. Some
       500 tales in Spanish with brief English summar-
       ies. Mostly of Spanish origin but some show in-
       fluence of Arabian Nights.

1740. Randolph, Vance. The Devil's Pretty Daughter and
       Other Ozark Folk Tales (New York: Columbia U.
       P., 1955), xvi, 239pp. Notes by Herbert Hal-
       pert. Some 91 tales neither retold nor combined
       but obviously blue-pencilled. Adult tales, sexual
       and earthy.

1741. _____. Sticks in the Knapsack and Other Ozark
       Folk Tales (New York: Columbia U. P., 1958),
       xvii, 171pp. Some 96 tales and anecdotes in the
       familiar Randolph pattern. Notes by Ernest
       Baughman.

1742. _____. The Talking Turtle and Other Ozark Folk
Tales (New York: Columbia U. P., 1957), xviii,
226pp. Notes by Herbert Halpert. One hundred
tales, some previously published. Randolph ad-
mits some editorial tampering with dialect and
profanity.

1743. _____. We Always Lie to Strangers (New York:
Columbia U. P., 1951), 309pp. Ozark folk tales
with both understatement and overstatement.

1744. _____. Who Blowed Up the Church House? and
Other Ozark Folktales (New York: Columbia U.
P., 1952), xix, 232pp. Notes by Herbert Halpert. Many familiar tales are given a local setting here. The language is slightly edited.

1745. Rayford, Julian Lee. Whistlin' Woman and Crowin'
Hen (Mobile: Rankin P., 1956), 230pp. Regional
folklore from Bayou la Batre, fishing village
south of Mobile.

1746. Roberts, Leonard. Nippy and the Yankee Doodle:
and Other Authentic Folk Tales from the Southern
Mountains (Berea, Ky.: Council of the Southern
Mountains, 1958), 48pp.

1747. _____. South from Hell-fer-Sartin (Lexington:
U. of Kentucky P., 1955), viii, 287pp. Originally a doctoral dissertation. 100 tales chiefly sup-
plied by children and comprising a domestic tradition.

1748. _____. Up Cutshin and Down Greasy (Lexington:
U. of Kentucky P., 1959), viii, 165pp. Tales
and songs collected from the Couch family of
Southeastern Kentucky. Useful biographical data
and representative selections.

1749. Saucier, Corinne L. Folk Tales from French Louisiana (New York: Exposition P., 1962), 138pp.

1750. Taft, Lewis A. Profile of Old New England, Yankee
Legends, Tales, and Folklore (New York: Dodd,
Mead, 1965), xiii, 271pp. Rewritten tales and
legends without sources given; themes include the
discovery, colonial days, supernaturalism, etc.

1751. Thompson, Stith. One Hundred Favorite Folk Tales
       (Bloomington: Indiana U. P., 1968), xii, 439pp.
       Texts of familiar tales derived from oral tradi-
       tion and localized largely in Europe. The choice
       of the leading American student of the folk tale.

1752. Tidwell, James N. A Treasury of American Folk
       Humor (New York: Crown, 1956), xx, 620pp.
       Some 332 pieces of American humor mostly from
       recognized authors (Thurber, Saroyan, Lardner,
       Sandburg, et al.). Despite the title, not genuine
       folk humor.

1753. Wallis, Wilson D. and Ruth Sawtell Wallis. The
       Micmac Indians of Eastern Canada (Minneapolis:
       U. of Minnesota P., 1955), xv, 515pp. Scholarly
       collection of eastern Indian tales with accounts of
       tribal life and data about informants.

1754. Welsch, Roger. Shingling the Fog and Other Plains
       Lies (Chicago: Swallow P., 1972), vi, 160pp.
       Tall tales chiefly from Nebraska presenting life
       on the prairie.

1755. Whedbee, Charles Harry. The Flaming Ship of the
       Ocracoke and Other Tales of the Outer Banks
       (Winston-Salem, N.C.: John F. Blair, 1971),
       153pp. Retold tales from coastal North Carolina,
       dealing with wrecks, pirates, apparitions, etc.

                  C. Discussions of Individual
                  Tales and Narrative Theory

1756. Abernethy, Francis E. "The Golden Log: an East
       Texas Paradise Lost," in The Golden Log, ed.
       Mody C. Boatright et al., pp. 3-7. Local vari-
       ant of a familiar tale.

1757. Abrahams, Roger D. "The Complex Relations of
       Simple Forms," Genre (Je, 1969), 2: 104-128.
       Discussion of structural analysis of folklore
       forms.

1758. Aiken, Riley. "Don Juan Zurumbete," in The Golden
      Log, ed. Mody C. Boatright et al., pp. 135-140.
      Mexican version of "The Brave Tailor" from Rio
      Grande Valley.

1759. Anderson, George K. The Legend of the Wandering
      Jew (Providence: Brown U. P., 1965), ix,
      489pp. Erudite and thorough study of a large
      subject with attention given to legends, tales,
      verse, and art.

1760. Armstrong, Robert P. "Content Analysis in Folk-
      loristics," in Trends in Content Analysis, ed. I.
      de Sola Pool (Urbana: U. of Illinois P., 1959),
      pp. 151-170.

1761. Arpad, Joseph J. "The Fight Story: Quotation and
      Originality in Native American Humor," JFI (Dec,
      1973), 10: 141-172. Conflict between river boat-
      men and wagoners, common in Am. humor, is
      probably as old as Paulding's 1817 tale.

1762. Barrick, Mac E. "'The Barber's Ghost': a Legend
      Become a Folktale," PF (S, 1974), 23: iv, 36-
      42. An old Pennsylvania legend now familiar as
      a folktale.

1763. Bascom, William. "The Forms of Folklore: Prose
      Narratives," JAF (Jan-Mr, 1965), 78: 3-20.
      An attempt to distinguish myth, legend, and folk
      tale.

1764. Beck, Horace P. "The Acculturation of Old World
      Tales by the American Indian," MF (W, 1958),
      8: 205-216.

1765. Ben-Amos, Dan. "The Americanization of 'The King
      and the Abbot,'" IF (1969), 2: 115-123. An
      American Jewish tale is a variant of the tradi-
      tional story.

1766. Birney, Adrian. "Rumpelstilzchen," NYFQ (Dec,
      1974), 30: 279-285.

1767. Bowen, Elizabeth. "Comeback of Goldilocks et al.,"
      NYTMag (Aug. 26, 1962), pp. 18-19, 74-75.
      Perceptive remarks about the rising popularity
      of fairy tale books.

1768. Boyer, Ruth M. "A Mescalero Apache Tale: the
       Bat and the Flood," WF (Jl, 1972), 31: 189-197.
       An Apache tale which is moralistic and sheds
       light on religion.

1769. Brunvand, Jan Harold. "Some International Folktales
       from Northwest Tradition," NWF (W, 1966), 1:
       7-13. Versions of tale types collected around
       Moscow, Idaho.

1770. _____. "Thor, the Cheechako and the Initiates'
       Tasks: a Modern Parallel for an Old Jest," SFQ
       (Sept, 1960), 24: 235-238. A story from the
       Edda compared to the initiation of a cheechako in-
       to Alaskan sourdough society.

1771. Canning, Ray R. "Mormon Return-from-the-Dead
       Stories: Fact or Folklore?" PUASAL (1965),
       42: i, 29-37.

1772. Clarke, Kenneth. "The Fatal Hairdo and the Em-
       peror's New Clothes Revisited," WF (Oct, 1964),
       23: 249-252. An Indiana tale with structural
       analysis.

1773. Claudel, Calvin. "A Comparison of the Folktales of
       Louisiana and Missouri," SFQ (Dec, 1962), 26:
       296-300. Comparisons of tales in two French-
       speaking areas: animal figures like Bouqui and
       Lapin, numskulls like Jean Sot and Jean Bete.

1774. _____. "The Folktales of Louisiana and Their
       Background," SFQ (Sept, 1955), 19: 164-170.
       Louisiana tales are similar to international tales
       but are full of local color (they deal with Bouqui,
       Lapin, Jean Sot).

1775. _____. "Some Comments on the Bear's Son
       Tale," SFQ (Sept, 1952), 16: 186-191. Com-
       ments on origin and frequency of John the Bear
       tale. J. F. Dobie's version is Mexican.

1776. Coffin, Tristram P. "The Tale Is the Thing," SFQ
       (Je, 1959), 23: 90-94.

1777. Colby, B. N. "Analytical Procedures in Eidochronic
       Study," JAF (Jan-Mr, 1973), 86: 14-24. Pseudo-

scientific jargon applied to an Eskimo tale,
"The Headband."

1778. Cothran, Kay L.   "Woman's Tall Tales: a Problem
       of the Social Structure of Fantasy," SAR (F and
       W, 1972), 2: 21-27.   Field work in Georgia sug-
       gests that women also tell tales or "talk trash."

1779. Davis, M. G.   "American Folk Tales," Horn Book
       (Feb, 1952), 28: 55-62.   Includes a brief bibli-
       ography.

1780. Dégh, Linda.   "Folk Narrative," in Folklore and
       Folklife, ed. R. M. Dorson, pp. 53-83.   Review
       of major trends in scholarship dealing with folk
       narrative.

1781. _____.   "Two Old World Narrators in Urban Set-
       ting," in Kontakte und Grenzen, ed. H. F. Foltin,
       pp. 71-86.   Two Hungarian female immigrants in
       Gary, Ind., are sources of tales, anecdotes,
       jokes, and beliefs.

1782. Desmonde, William H.   "Jack and the Beanstalk,"
       AI (Sept, 1951), 8: 287-288.   An extreme psycho-
       analytic study of a famous folk tale.

1783. Diamond, Stanley.   Culture in History: Essays in
       Honor of Paul Radin (New York: Columbia U.
       P., 1960), xxiv, 1014pp.

1784. Dobie, J. Frank.   "Charm in Mexican Folktales,"
       in The Healer of Los Olmos, ed. Wilson M. Hud-
       son, pp. 1-8.   Mexican tales, as opposed to
       American tall tales, have a natural charm; Dobie
       provides several examples.

1785. Dorson, Richard M.   "Esthetic Form in British and
       American Folk Narrative," in Medieval Literature
       and Folklore Studies, ed. Jerome Mandel and B.
       A. Rosenberg, pp. 305-321.

1786. _____.   "Standards for Collecting and Publishing
       American Folktales," JAF (Jan-Mr, 1957), 70:
       53-57.

1787. _____.   "The Use of Printed Sources," in Folk-

lore and Folklife, ed. R. M. Dorson, pp. 465-
477. The folklorist should consider close repli-
cas of oral texts as well as literary invention
based on oral folklore or literary folklore.

1788. Dundes, Alan. "African Tales among the North
American Indians," SFQ (Sept, 1965), 29: 207-
219. African influences on No. Am. Indian tales
are fairly extensive.

1789. _____. "From Etic to Emic Units in the Structural Study of Folktales," JAF (Apr-Je, 1962),
75: 95-105. Motif and tale types are nonstruc-
tural or "etic," but structural or "emic" units
can also be identified. Another effort to make
folktale study more scientific.

1790. _____. The Morphology of North American Indian
Folktales (Helsinki: Suomalainen Tiedeakatemia,
1964), 134pp. An extension of Propp's method
of analyzing Russian fairy tales to very different
narratives. Terms like "motifeme patterns" may
prove more puzzling than enlightening.

1791. _____. "Structural Typology in North American
Indian Folktales," SJA (Spr, 1963), 19: 121-130.
Dundes applies Propp's theories to Indian narratives and defines folktales as "sequences of mo-
tifemes." He finds clear-cut patterns in this
body of material.

1792. Elmers, Myra Wofford and Azile Wofford. "The
Newby Tales of South Carolina," SFQ (Sept, 1961),
25: 192-194. Summarized tales about an 18th
century landowner and hunter.

1793. Ferris, William R., Jr. "Black Prose Narrative
in the Mississippi Delta; an Overview," JAF (Apr-
Je, 1972), 85: 140-151. Experiences in collecting trickster tales, cante fables, etc. from all
age groups in the Delta.

1794. Figh, Margaret Gillis and Margaret B. Kirkpatrick.
"The Development of an Alabama Folktale," SFQ
(Je, 1974), 38: 109-120. Variants of a story
about a lynching.

1795.   Fischer, J. L. "Sequence and Structure in Folk-
        tales," in Men and Cultures, ed. Anthony F. C.
        Wallace (Philadelphia: U. of Penn. P., 1960),
        pp. 442-446.

1796.   _____. "The Sociopsychological Analysis of Folk-
        tales," CA (Je, 1963), 4: 235-295. Important
        but involved article stressing the need for a
        nexus between form and content of tales and the
        personalities of the bearers.

1797.   "The Folktale: a Symposium," JAF (Jan-Mr, 1957),
        70: 49-65. Papers by Warren E. Roberts, R.
        M. Dorson, Herbert Halpert; a general review
        of projects, indexes, criteria for collecting and
        publishing tales.

1798.   Georges, Robert A. "Toward an Understanding of
        Storytelling Events," JAF (Oct-Dec, 1969), 82:
        313-328. Postulates, a model, and a concept are
        presented.

1799.   Gizelis, Gregory. "A Neglected Aspect of Creativity
        of Folklore Performers," JAF (Apr. Je, 1973),
        86: 167-172. Discussion of Greek storytellers
        in U. S.

1800.   Goldstein, Kenneth A. and Dan Ben-Amos. Thrice-
        Told Tales: Folktales from Three Continents
        (Lock Haven, Penn.: Hammermill Paper Co.,
        158pp. Variants of four famous tales ("Cinderel-
        la," "Tarbaby," "The Magician and His Pupil,"
        "The Three Stolen Princesses") with full discus-
        sion of each tale.

1801.   Hancock, Cecily. "The 'Me All Face' Story," JAF
        (Oct-Dec, 1963), 76: 340-342. Sources suggested
        for the familiar comic Indian anecdote.

1802.   Hand, Wayland D. "Anglo-American Folk Narrative:
        the Old World's Legacy to the New," NFI (Aug-
        Dec, 1970), 7: 136-155.

1803.   Hatcher, Mildred. "Different Versions of 'The Fin-
        gerless Statue,' a Folktale," KFR (Jan-Mr, 1971),
        17: 5-9.

1804. Hatfield, Dorothy Blackman and Eugene Current-
       Garcia. "William Orrie Tuggle and the Creek
       Indian Folk Tales," SFQ (Dec, 1961), 25: 238-
       255. Tuggle's 19th century mss. have recently
       been discovered.

1805. Hendricks, William O. "Folklore and the Structural
       Analysis of Literary Texts," Lang&S (Spr, 1970),
       3: 83-122.

1806. Holloman, William E. "The Ice-Cold Hand," NCarFJ
       (Feb, 1974), 22: 3-8. Old Carolina tale about a
       girl's face appearing on tombstone of man who
       jilted her.

1807. Hoogasian-Villa, Susie. 100 Armenian Tales and
       Their Folkloristic Relevance (Detroit: Wayne
       State, 1966), 602pp. Unusual collection of tales
       from Armenians in Detroit between 1940 and 1942.
       Annotation not always adequate.

1808. Hudson, Arthur Palmer. "Some Versions of 'The
       King of the Cats,'" SFQ (Dec, 1953), 17: 225-
       231. A tale familiar to Scott and Irving; S. R.
       Benét also used it.

1809. Hudson, Wilson M. "Another Mexican Version of the
       Story of the Bear's Son," SFQ (Je, 1951), 15:
       152-158. Careful examination of famous tale
       (Type 301) using J. F. Dobie's version "Juan
       Oso."

1810. _____. "I Want My Golden Arm," in Folk Travel-
       ers, ed. Mody C. Boatright et al., pp. 183-194.
       Discussion of a story (Motif E. 325. 4. 1) made
       famous by Mark Twain.

1811. Hultkranz, Ake. The North American Indian Orpheus
       Tradition: A Contribution to Comparative Reli-
       gion (Stockholm: Ethnographical Museum of Swe-
       den, 1957), 339pp.

1812. Jacobs, Melville. "Areal Spread of Indian Oral
       Genre Features in the Northwest States," JFI
       (Je, 1972), 9: 10-17.

1813. _____. "Our Knowledge of Pacific Northwest In-

dian Folktales," NWF (Nov, 1967), 2: 14-21.
Survey of past collecting and a plea for adequate
linguistic training for future collectors.

1814. Jansen, William Hugh. "Anglo-American Folk Narrative: a Common Trove," JFI (Aug-Dec, 1970),
7: 156-160.

1815. _____. "Classifying Performance in the Study of
Verbal Folklore," in Studies in Folklore, ed.
W. E. Richmond, pp. 110-118.

1816. Jeffrey, Lloyd N. "Snake Yarns of the West and
Southwest," WF (Oct, 1955), 14: 246-258. Texts
and some discussion.

1817. Kearney, Mildred. "La Llorona as a Social Symbol," WF (Jl, 1969), 28: 199-206.

1818. Kirkland, Edwin C. "The American Redaction of
Tale Type 922," Fabula (1961), 4: iii, 248-259.
Study of the familiar tale of the King and the
Abbot from ten Am. variants.

1819. Lanham, Betty B. and Masao Shimura. "Folktales
Commonly Told American and Japanese Children:
Ethical Themes of Omission and Commission,"
JAF (Jan-Mr, 1967), 80: 33-48. Study based
on questionnaires used in Bloomington, Ind., and
Kainan, Japan.

1820. Littleton, C. Scott. "A Two-Dimensional Scheme
for Classification of Narratives," JAF (Jan-Mr,
1965), 78: 21-27. Four criteria suggested:
factual, fabulous, secular, sacred.

1821. Lowie, Robert H. "The Oral Literature of the Crow
Indians," JAF (Apr-Je, 1959), 72: 97-104.

1822. Lumpkin, Ben Gray. "The Fox and the Goose, Tale
Type 62 from South Carolina," NCarF (May,
1970), 18: 90-94. Text and commentary.

1823. _____. "The Hawk and the Buzzard, How Tellers
Vary the Story," NCarF (Nov, 1970), 18: 144-
147. Text given by G. C. Taylor and modified
by J. Frank Dobie.

1824. _____. "'Mr. Fox' (Baughman Type 955C): a
Cante Fable," JAF (Jan-Mr, 1968), 81: 68-70.
Wyoming-Iowa version of an Am. cante fable.

1825. Lüthi, Max. "Parallel Themes in Folk Narrative
and in Art Literature," JFI (Je, 1967), 4: 3-16.
Themes, as well as motifs and motif clusters,
provide possibilities for study and analysis.

1826. Marrant, Doris E. "Variations on a Theme: Some
Northern California Indian Horror Stories," WF
(Oct, 1970), 29: 257-267. Yurok, Hupa, and
Karok tales.

1827. Meese, Elizabeth A. "The Art of the Tale Teller:
a Study of the Suprasegmental Phonemes in a
Folktale," KFR (Apr-Je, 1968), 14: 25-37. Technical analysis of an Indiana ghost tale.

1828. Oster, Harry. "The Afro-American Folktale in
Memphis: Theme and Function," NegroALF (F,
1969), 3: 83-87.

1829. _____. "Negro Humor: John and Old Marster,"
JFI (Je, 1968), 5: 42-57. Five folk tales
transcribed and analyzed.

1830. Pierson, William D. "An African Background for
American Negro Folktales?" JAF (Apr-Je, 1971),
84: 204-214. Persuasive argument supporting
thesis that Negro tales owe more to African than
to European stimuli.

1831. Pope, Polly. "Toward a Structural Analysis of
North American Trickster Tales," SFQ (Sept,
1967), 31: 274-286. Close analysis of 70 variants of the "Bungling Host" tale with an attempt to provide a stable form.

1832. Randle, Martha Champion. "Psychological Types from
Iroquois Folklore," JAF (Jan-Mr, 1952), 65: 13-
21. Material from Cayuga informants in Ontario.

1833. Reaver, J. Russell. "'Embalmed Alive': a Developing Urban Ghost Tale," NYFQ (A, 1952), 8:
217-220. Variant of a tale in Bennett Cerf's
Famous Ghost Stories.

1834. _____. "From Reality to Fantasy: Opening-
       Closing Formulas in the Structures of American
       Tall Tales," SFQ (Dec, 1972), 36: 369-382.

1835. Rich, George W. "Rethinking the 'Star Husbands,'"
       JAF (Oct-Dec, 1971), 84: 436-441. Criticism
       of Stith Thompson's analysis of a famous No.
       Am. Indian tale.

1836. Richmond, W. Edson. "Some Effects of Scribal and
       Typographical Error on Oral Tradition," SFQ
       (Je, 1951), 15: 159-170.

1837. Roberts, Leonard W. "The Cante Fable in Eastern
       Kentucky," MF (S, 1956), 6: 69-88.

1838. _____. "Magic Folktales in America," in Our
       Living Traditions, ed. T. P. Coffin, pp. 142-
       153. Discussion of American variants of well
       known magic tales; text of one Jack tale in full.

1839. Roberts, Warren E. "International Folktales among
       the North American Indians," AE (1966), 15: i-
       ii, 161-166. Tales may have entered North
       America from Asia in pre-Columbian times.

1840. _____. The Tale of the Kind and the Unkind
       Girls (Berlin: Verlag Walter de Gruyter, 1958),
       164pp. Thorough study of Type 480 based on
       examination of some 950 variants. Tale also
       known as "Frau Holle," "Diamonds and Toads,"
       etc.

1841. Rooth, Anna Brigitta. The Cinderella Cycle (Lund:
       Gleerup, 1951), xvi, 269. An exhaustive study
       of what is probably the world's best known folk
       tale.

1842. Rosenberg, Bruce A. and John B. Smith. "The Com-
       puter and the Finnish Historical-Geographical
       Method," JAF (Apr-Je, 1974), 87: 149-154. A
       computer can expedite sorting and classifying
       folktales but a folklorist must still analyze the
       tales.

1843. Rosenberg, Sam. "The Truth about Cinderella (In-
       cest and All!)," Cosmopolitan (Je, 1971), 170:

154-157. Amusingly superficial account of Cinderella theme in cinema.

1844. Schorer, C. E. "Indian Tales of C. C. Trowbridge,"
printed from archives of Wisconsin Hist. Soc. in
various periodicals with careful analysis and comment: "The Toadstool Man," MF (F, 1959), 9:
139-144; "The Red Head," MF (S, 1960), 10:
86-95; "The Star Woman," MF (Spr, 1962), 12:
17-24; "The Gambler," MF (W, 1963-1964), 13:
229-235; "The Man Eater Spirit," SFQ (Dec,
1965), 29: 309-318; "The Giants," SFQ (Sept,
1967), 31: 236-243; "The Ornamented Head," SFQ
(Dec, 1969), 33: 317-332; "Thrown Away," SFQ
(Dec, 1970), 34: 341-352; "The Bad Man," SFQ
(Je, 1972), 36: 160-175; "The Fisherman," SFQ
(Mr, 1974), 38: 63-71; "A Story," SFQ (Sept,
1974), 38: 233-241.

1845. Shoemaker, Henry W. "'May Paul et le Vieux
Charlot,' a Pennsylvania-Huguenot Tale," NYFQ
(W, 1953), 9: 307-313. A Northumberland Co.
tale.

1846. Smith, Grace Partridge. "The Plight of the Folktale
in the Comics," SFQ (Je, 1952), 16: 124-127.
Folktales have been reconditioned for the comics
with stories like "Cinderella," "The Three Little
Pigs," "The Pied Piper" being vulgarized.

1847. Swahn, Jan-Öjvind. The Tale of Cupid and Psyche
(Lund: Gleerup, 1955), 493pp. Meticulous
comparative study of one of the world's greatest
tales. Types 425, 428.

1848. Swart, P. D. "The Diffusion of the Folktale," MF
(S, 1957), 7: 69-84. Theories of diffusion discussed with stress on slaves and early trade
routes.

1849. Taylor, Archer. "Some Recent Trends in Märchen
Anthologies," JFI (Je, 1968), 5: 78-100.

1850. Tedlock, Dennis. "On the Translation of Style in
Oral Narrative," JAF (Jan-Mr, 1971), 84: 114-
133. In publishing folk narratives one must consider oral performance. Frank Cushing's Zuni

Tales (1901), for example, should be treated as dramatic poetry.

1851. Thompson, Stith. "Hypothetical Forms in Folktale Study," in Volksüberlieferung, ed. Fritz Harkort et al., pp. 369-372. Thompson supports the Finnish historical-geographical school but is not dogmatic. Archetypes do not provide all the answers.

1852. _____. "Narrative Motif-Analysis as a Folklore Method," FFC No. 161 (Helsinki: Suomalainen Tiedeakatemia, 1955), 74: 3-9. Comments on the growth of the motif index.

1853. _____. "The Star Husband Tale," StudiaS (1953), 4: 93-163. Some 86 versions of this widely spread North Am. Indian tale without literary or other sources. Origin probably among the Plains Indians of the eighteenth century.

1854. _____. "Story-telling to Story-writing," in Actes du Ve Congrès de l'Association Internationale de Littérature Comparée, Belgrade, 1967, ed. Nikola Banasevic (Amsterdam: Swetz & Zeitlinger, 1969), pp. 433-442.

1855. _____. "Unfinished Business: the Folktale," in Medieval Literature and Folklore Studies, ed. Jerome Mandel and B. A. Rosenberg, pp. 213-231.

1856. Trejo, Judy. "Coyote Tales: a Paiute Commentary," JAF (Jan-Mr, 1974), 87: 66-71. Paiute tales are both entertaining and didactic.

1857. Utley, Francis Lee. "The Migration of Folktales: Four Channels to the Americas," CA (Mr, 1974), 15: 5-27. Folktales migrated from Europe, Africa, and both Northeast Asia and Southeast Asia. Utley pleads for a national folklore archive. The article includes letters from 14 specialists commenting on it.

1858. Wax, Murray. "The Notions of Nature, Man, and Time of a Hunting People," SFQ (Sept, 1962), 26: 175-186. Pawnee Indian ideas as revealed in specific folk tales.

1859.   Witthoft, John.   "The 'Grasshopper War' Folktale,"
        JAF (Oct-Dec, 1953), 66: 295-301.   Study of a
        folktale borrowed from Delaware Indians by the
        whites.

1860.   Yates, Norris W.   William T. Porter and "The Spirit
        of the Times," (Baton Rouge: Louisiana State U.
        P., 1957), xi, 222pp.   Brief biography of Porter
        and an account of his famous sporting paper with
        useful data about contributors and their tales.

1861.   Young, Frank W.   "A Fifth Analysis of the Star
        Husband Tale," Ethnology (Oct, 1970), 9: 389-
        413.   Summaries of four previous analyses and
        a new interpretation.

8. LEGENDS (THEORY, HISTORY, EXAMPLES)

1862. Ainsworth, Catherine Harris. "Polish-American Church Legends," NYFQ (Dec, 1974), 30: 287-294. Material from northwestern New York.

1863. Anderson, John Q. "The Legend of the Phantom Coach in East Texas," WF (Oct, 1963), 22: 259-262. Familiar story proving the vitality of Anglo-American tradition in the southern U.S.

1864. Baker, Ronald L. "The Role of Folk Legends in Place-Name Research," JAF (Oct-Dec, 1972), 85: 367-373. Specialists in onomastics can benefit from folk legends.

1865. Barnouw, Victor. "A Psychological Interpretation of a Chippewa Origin Legend," JAF (Jan-Mr, Apr-Je, Jl-Sept, 1955), 68: 73-85, 211-223, 341-355. Text of a legend obtained from a Mide priest in Wisconsin in 1944 with psychological interpretation involving themes, qualities, and symbols.

1866. Barrere, Dorothy B. The Kumuhonua Legends. A Study of Late 19th Century Hawaiian Stories of Creation and Origins (Honolulu: Bishop Museum, 1969), i, 47pp.

1867. Beauchamp, William M. Folklore and Legends of the Iroquois (Blauvelt, N.Y.: 1973).

1868. Bell, Sandra. "The Legend of Quivira," WF (Apr, 1963), 22: 113-116. Recounting of Coronado's quest for fabulous treasure in the supposed land of Quivira.

1869. Bennett, John Michael. "Folk Speech and Legends of the Trade of House-Painting," SFQ (Dec, 1969), 33: 313-316.

1870. Bennett, Porter K. "Legends and Folklore of Cort-
       land County," NYFQ (Sept, 1964), 20: 163-174.
       Lore from a central New York county.

1871. Bessaignet, Pierre. "Histoires Sioux," JSA (1955),
       n. s. 54: 49-54. Sixteen Sioux legends from Pine
       Ridge, So. Dak., including five ghost tales.

1872. Bianchi, Diane. "Mountain Legend in Eastern Ken-
       tucky," KFR (Jl-Sept, 1973), 19: 58-78. Auto-
       biography of retired coal miner, Hobe Grilles,
       plus some miscellaneous anecdotes. Needlessly
       heavy annotation of folk motifs by William Hugh
       Jansen.

1873. Black, Esther K. "Lawrence County Legends," KFQ
       (Spr, 1962), 7: i, 37-40. Six Penn. legends.

1874. _____. "Legends of Beaver County," KFQ (Spr,
       1963), 8: 16-30. Penn. place names, legends,
       historical anecdotes.

1875. Bond, Eleanor Mitchell. "Legend of the Lad," in
       Singers and Storytellers, ed. Mody C. Boatright
       et al., pp. 166-172. Tales of a cowboy, George
       Sennitt, known as the Irish lad, boastful and
       lusty.

1876. Boyer, L. Bryce. "An Example of Legend Distor-
       tion from the Apaches of the Mescalero Indian
       Reservation," JAF (Apr-Je, 1964), 77: 118-142.

1877. Brown, Raymond L. Phantoms of the Sea: Legends,
       Customs, and Superstitions (New York: Taplinger,
       1973), 192pp.

1878. Brunvand, Jan Harold. "Modern Legends of Mormon-
       dom, or Supernaturalism is Still Alive and Well
       in Salt Lake City," in American Folk Legend, ed.
       Wayland D. Hand, pp. 185-202.

1879. Bullock, Alice. Living Legends of the Santa Fe
       Country (Denver: Green Mountain P., 1970), vii,
       121pp. A Santa Fe journalist summarizes tales
       from New Mexico.

1880. Campa, Arthur. Treasure of the Sangre de Cristo:

Tales and Traditions of the Spanish Southwest
(Norman: U. of Oklahoma P., 1963), xv, 223pp.
Legends of buried treasure retold with honesty but
without panache.

1881. Carey, George G. Maryland Folk Legends and Folk
Songs (Cambridge, Md.: Tidewater Publishers,
1971), viii, 120pp. Mostly legends. Some material edited or paraphrased.

1882. Carranco, Lynwood. "Three Legends of Northern
California," WF (Jl, 1963), 22: 179-185. Two
stories about hidden treasure and one about an
abominable snowman type.

1883. Chamberlain, Samuel. New England Legends and
Folklore, ed. Harry Hansen (New York: Hastings
House, 1967), 192pp. Adapted from a work by
S. A. Drake, 1884.

1884. Clark, Ella E. Indian Legends from the Northern
Rockies (Norman: U. of Oklahoma P., 1966),
xxv, 350pp. 129 legends, myths, tales from
Indian tribes of Northwest.

1885. _____. Indian Legends of Canada (Toronto:
McClelland and Stewart, 1960), viii, 177pp.
Miscellaneous Indian tales assembled by an un-
professional folklorist and often rewritten.

1886. _____. Indian Legends of the Pacific Northwest
(Berkeley and Los Angeles: U. of California P.,
1953), 225pp. Popular collection; native literary
style has not been retained.

1887. Clarke, Kenneth W. Uncle Bud Long: the Birth of
a Kentucky Folk Legend (Lexington: U. Press
of Kentucky, 1973), 78pp. Life and stories of a
Kentucky farmer.

1888. Clements, William M. and William E. Lightfoot.
"The Legend of Stepp Cemetery," IF (1972), 5:
92-141. Variants of a local legend in Indiana.

1889. Collins, Earl Augustus. Legends and Lore of Missouri (San Antonio: Naylor, 1951), xvi, 115pp.
Legends, ghost lore, witchcraft; no data about
informants.

Legends   207

1890. Colum, Padraic. Legends of Hawaii (New Haven:
       Yale, 1960), xvi, 220pp. Nineteen tales of the
       islands, colorfully retold and sometimes conflated.

1891. Combs, Joseph F. Legends of the Pineys (San An-
       tonio: Naylor, 1965), 100pp. Seventeen retold
       legends from E. Texas.

1892. Converse, Harriet. Myths and Legends of the New
       York Iroquois, ed. Arthur C. Parker (Port Wash-
       ington, N.Y.: I. J. Friedman, 1962), 195pp.

1893. Cord, Xenia E. "Department Store Snakes," IF
       (1969), 2: 110-114.

1894. Crawford, Roselle W. Survivals of Legends; Legends
       and Their Relation to History, Literature, and
       Life of the Southwest (San Antonio: Naylor, 1952),
       94pp.

1895. Creighton, Helen. Bluenose Ghosts (Toronto: Ryer-
       son P., 1957), xiv, 280pp. Local legends of
       Nova Scotia; eleven categories with informants
       identified.

1896. De Caro, F. A. "Indiana Miracle Legends: a Sur-
       vey," IF (1969), 2: 36-53.

1897. Dégh, Linda. "The 'Belief Legend' in Modern Soci-
       ety: Form, Function, and Relationship to Other
       Genres," in American Folk Legend, ed. Wayland
       D. Hand, pp. 55-68.

1898. _____ et al. "Folk Legends from Indiana," IF
       (F-W, 1968), 1: 9-109. Sixteen legends collected
       from informants and supplied with notes by six
       field workers.

1899. _____ and Andrew Vázsonyi. "Legend and Belief,"
       Genre (Sept, 1971), 4: 281-304. Definitions at-
       tempted. But almost invariably the legend was
       believed sometime, somewhere, by someone.

1900. Dorson, Richard M. America in Legend (New York:
       Pantheon Books, 1973), 336pp. A large, hand-
       somely illustrated book designed in part for the
       Christmas trade.

1901. _____. "Defining the American Folk Legend," in Forms Upon the Frontier, ed. Austin E. Fife et al., pp. 163-166. Brief survey of problems and collection in legend study.

1902. _____. "How Shall We Rewrite Charles M. Skinner Today?" in American Folk Legend, ed. Wayland D. Hand, pp. 69-95. Skinner published two collections of legends in 1896 and 1903, 437 in all. But he gave them literary polish and provided no sources.

1903. _____. "Legends and Tall Tales," in Our Living Traditions, ed. T. P. Coffin, pp. 154-169. Definitions of legends with examples.

1904. _____. "The UCLA Conference on American Folk Legend," NYFQ (Mr, 1971), 27: 96-112. Summary of papers by 15 participants in a conference held in Los Angeles in 1969.

1905. Douglass, Harry S. "The Legend of the Serpent," NYFQ (Spr, 1956), 12: 27-42. A prized "legend" of Wyoming Co. turns out to be a hoax.

1906. Dundes, Alan. "On the Psychology of Legend," in American Folk Legend, ed. Wayland D. Hand, pp. 21-36. Four American legends serve as examples meriting psychological interpretation.

1907. Eby, Cecil D., Jr., and Jack B. Moore. "The Wizard Clip: an Old Potomac Legend," SFQ (Dec, 1961), 25: 256-260. Summarized composite version of a Va. legend.

1908. Flynn, James J. "The Legend of Breakneck," NYFQ (Spr, 1959), 15: 48-58. Origin of the name of a mountain near West Point and the tale of an Indian suicide.

1909. Georges, Robert A. "The General Concept of Legends: Some Assumptions to be Reexamined and Reassessed," in American Folk Legend, ed. Wayland D. Hand, pp. 1-19. A challenge to the general definition and conception of the legend.

1910. Giddings, Ruth W. Yaqui Myths and Legends (Tuc-

son: U. of Arizona P., 1959), 73pp. 61 stories in English with annotation and biographical
data about narrators.

1911. Goldberg, Christine. "Traditional American Witch
Legends: a Catalog," IF (1974), 7: i-ii, 77-
108. The U.S. is not rich in legends about witchcraft; only 82 cited here.

1912. Greenberg, Andrea. "Drugged and Seduced: a Contemporary Legend," NYFQ (Je, 1973), 29: 131-
158. Familiar tale of freshman college girl
drugged and seduced.

1913. Haden, Walter Darrell. The Headless Cobbler of
Smallett Cave; the Origin and Growth of a
Douglas County, Missouri Legend (Nashville:
Kinfolk P., 1967), 108pp. History of Smallett
Cave area and comparison of the tale with other
stories.

1914. Halpert, Herbert. "Definition and Variation in Folk
Legend," in American Folk Legend, ed. Wayland
D. Hand, pp. 47-54.

1915. _____. "Legends of the Cursed Child," NYFQ
(F, 1958), 14: 233-241. Cursed child legends
from printed sources and oral reports.

1916. Hand, Wayland D., ed. American Folk Legend: A
Symposium (Berkeley, Los Angeles, London: U.
of Cal. P., 1971), vi, 237pp. 14 papers originally presented at UCLA conference in June, 1969.

1917. _____. "Migratory Legend of 'The Cut-Out Pullman'; Saga of American Railroading," NYFQ (Je,
1971), 27: 231-235. Amusing story of pullman
cars being switched from train to train, sepa-
rating passengers, friends, baggage.

1918. _____. "Status of European and American Legend
Study," CA (Oct, 1965), 6: 439-446. Historical
study of legend study on two continents. Types,
areas, and possible indexes considered. Bibliography.

1919. Hathcock, Louise. Legends of East Texas (San Antonio: Naylor, 1957), 156pp.

1920. Hendricks, George D. "Four Southwestern Legends,"
      WF (Oct, 1968), 27: 255-262. Four legends re-
      lated to Texas places.

1921. Huguenin, Charles A. "Neighbors (Connecticut):
      Waramaug and the Indian Legend of Weantinaug,"
      NYFQ (Spr, 1955), 11: 53-65. Early Indian
      legend of New Milford, Conn., versified by Henry
      Sherwood Green, 1875.

1922. Ives, Edward D. "The Man Who Plucked the Gorbey:
      A Maine Woods Legend," JAF (Jan-Mr, 1961),
      74: 1-8.

1923. Ives, Ronald L. "The Sonoran 'Primer Montezuma'
      Legends," WF (Oct, 1950), 9: 321-325. Legends
      of an ancient culture hero, often accompanied by
      a coyote, from Sonora and Arizona.

1924. Jansen, William Hugh. "A Content Classification of
      a Random Sample of Legends, Mostly Local,"
      KFQ (S, 1971), 16: 81-96.

1925. _____. "The Surpriser Surprised, a Modern
      Legend," FF (Jan, 1973), 6: 1-24. Legend col-
      lected originally in 1935 with 28 later variants.

1926. Jason, Heda. "Concerning the 'Historical' and the
      'Local' Legends and Their Relatives," JAF (Jan-
      Mr, 1971), 84: 134-144. No exact definition of
      legend exists; this article examines the Grimms'
      position and adds commentary.

1927. Jeffrey, Adi-Kent Thomas. Ghosts in the Valley:
      True Haunting in the Delaware Valley (New Hope,
      Penn.: New Hope Art Shop, 1971), 72pp. 40
      ghost legends retold.

1928. Johnson, F. Roy. Legends and Myths of North
      Carolina's Roanoke-Chowan Area (Murfreesboro,
      No. Car.: Johnson Publishing Co., 1966), 124pp.
      Reprint of 1962 ed. with slightly different title.
      Material collected and rewritten by the editor.

1929. _____. Witches and Demons in History and Folk-
      lore (Murfreesboro, No. Car.: Johnson Publish-
      ing Co., 1969), 262pp. Historical and field-col-
      lected material.

1930. Kirtley, Bacil F. "Unknown Hominids and New World Legends," WF (Apr, 1964), 23: 77-90. Legends about near-human figures examined (the Sasquatch, Yeti, and Dev).

1931. Little, Ralph B. "Oral Aggression in Spider Legends," AI (S, 1966), 23: 169-179. A study of legends and tales about spiders from a psychoanalytical point of view.

1932. Luomala, Katherine. "Disintegration and Regeneration, the Hawaiian Phantom Hitchhiker Legend," Fabula (1972), 13: 20-59. Connects Pele, Hawaiian volcano goddess, with familiar story.

1933. Lüthi, Max. "Aspects of the Märchen and the Legend," Genre (Je, 1969), 2: 162-178. Distinction between the two forms based on the plot focus.

1934. Lyback, Johanna R. Indian Legends of Eastern America (Chicago: Lyons and Carnahan, 1963), 180pp. Popular retellings.

1935. _____. Indian Legends of the Great West (Chicago: Lyons and Carnahan, 1963), 179pp. More of the same.

1936. McMillan, Douglas J. "The Vanishing Hitchhiker in Eastern North Carolina," NCarF (Aug, 1972), 20: 123-128.

1937. Marcatante, John J. American Folklore and Legends (New York: Globe, 1967), 290pp. Rewritten material for a juvenile audience.

1938. Martin, Margaret Rhett. Charleston Ghosts (Columbia: U. of So. Car. P., 1963), x, 105pp. Eighteen folk legends from Charleston, S.C.

1939. Matson, Emerson N. Longhouse Legends (Camden, N.J.: T. Nelson, 1968), 128pp. Tales from Puget Sound Indians.

1940. Merrill, Arch. "Old Legends Never Die," NYFQ (Spr, 1957), 13: 54-62. Newspaper fillers.

1941. Miller, Elaine K. Mexican Folk Narrative from the

<u>Los Angeles Area</u> (Austin: U. of Texas P.,
1973), xx, 388pp. 82 narratives (largely legends) in colloquial Spanish from some 27 informants. Short English summaries and notes.

1942.   Mitchell, Roger E. "George Knox: from Man to
Legend," <u>NEF</u> (1969), 9: 5-71. Legend about a
Maine woodsman who sold his soul to the devil.

1943.   Morgan, Kathryn L. "Caddy Buffers: Legends of a
Middle Class Negro Family in Philadelphia," <u>KFQ</u>
(S, 1966), 11: 67-88.

1944.   Mullen, Patrick B. "Modern Legend and Rumor
Theory," <u>JFI</u> (Aug-Dec, 1972), 9: 95-109. Theoretical article attempting distinctions between
legend and rumor. The labels seem almost inter-
changeable and the distinctions are nebulous.

1945.   _____. "The Relationship of Legend and Folk Belief," <u>JAF</u> (Oct-Dec, 1971), 84: 406-413. Comparisons based on evidence from Texas Gulf
Coast fishermen.

1946.   Musick, Ruth Ann. "The Murdered Pedlar in West
Virginia," <u>MF</u> (1961-1962), 11: 247-255. Ten
legends about murdered pedlars.

1947.   Olsen, Douglass. "Legends and Tales from Alabama," <u>TFSB</u> (Je, 1962), 28: 31-36.

1948.   Paige, Estelle Jane. "Neighbors: New Hampshire
and Maine: the Isles of Shoals," <u>NYFQ</u> (S, 1952),
8: 143-152. Maritime legends from the well
known islands.

1949.   Paredes, Américo. "Mexican Legendry and the Rise
of the Mestizo: a Survey," in <u>American Folk
Legend</u>, ed. Wayland D. Hand, pp. 97-107.

1950.   Perham, Joseph A. "The Legend of Molly Ockett,"
<u>NEF</u> (Spr, 1960), 3: 1-9. Material about an
Abenaki Indian woman.

1951.   Pound, Louise. "The Legend of the Lincoln Salt
Basin," <u>WF</u> (Apr, 1951), 10: 109-116. Tales of
the now-vanished salt basin near Lincoln, Neb.

One of the first accounts appeared in John T.
Irving's Indian Sketches, 1835.

1952. Preston, Dennis R. "Southern Indiana Place-Name
Legends as Reflections of Folk History," IN (F,
1973), 4: 51-61. Names reflect Indian, pioneer,
French, Civil War past.

1953. Rapp, Marvin A. "Legend of the Stone Giants,"
NYFQ (W, 1956), 12: 280-282. A reprinted
Onondaga Indian legend.

1954. Roach, Joyce Gibson. "The Legend of El Tejano,
the Texan Who Never Was," WF (Jan, 1968),
27: 33-42. El Tejano may have been a minor
desperado named William Brazelton.

1955. Roberts, Roderick J. "Legend and Local History,"
NYFQ (Je, 1970), 26: 83-90. Students of local
history might profitably use legends.

1956. Robertson, Frank. "Some Lost Mines of California,"
WF (Jan, 1951), 10: 26-33. Facts and legends
about some 11 mines, mostly in Northern Cal.
Informants given.

1957. Sapir, Edward. "Indian Legends from Vancouver
Island," JAF (Apr-Je, 1959), 72: 106-114. Post-
humous publication of two stories.

1958. Scanlon, Rosemary. "The Handprint: the Biography
of a Pennsylvania Legend," KFQ (S, 1971), 16:
97-107. A condemned man left a handprint on a
wall as proof of his innocence.

1959. Sengbusch, Beatrice Ebling. "A Comparative Study
of the Themes of Four Major Legends of the New
York State Indians and the Philippine Mountain
Indians," KFQ (W, 1965), 10: 173-190. Comparisons of legends about creation, the first man,
religion and gods, the origins of food.

1960. Shaw, Anna Moore. Pima Indian Legends (Tucson:
U. of Arizona P., 1968), 111pp. Two dozen
narratives told to the author by her father, a
Pima Indian.

1961. Sliney, Deanna. "Haunted Sites in Indiana: a Pre-
       liminary Survey," IF (1974), 7: i-ii, 27-51.
       Place-associated legends as revealed by Blooming-
       ton telephone employees.

1962. Smith, Philip H. Legends of the Shawangunk (Shon-
       Gum) and Its Environs (Syracuse: Syracuse U.
       P., 1965), 212pp. Legends from three New
       York counties.

1963. Snow, Edward Rowe. Fantastic Folklore and Fact;
       New England Tales of Land and Sea (New York:
       Dodd, Mead, 1968), xi, 270pp. Literary versions
       of tales, legends, and factual narratives.

1964. _____. True Tales and Curious Legends: Dra-
       matic Stories from the Yankee Past (New York:
       Dodd, Mead, 1969), 273pp. Rewritten material.

1965. Swetnam, George. "Some Eponymic Legends of
       Southwestern Pennsylvania," KFQ (Spr, 1961),
       6: i, 10-20. Explanatory place names of streams,
       towns (Slippery Rock, etc.).

1966. _____. "Two Southern Beaver Legends," KFQ
       (Spr, 1963), 8: 31-39. Legends long in oral
       tradition based on historical figures. Texts re-
       written from pamphlet versions.

1967. Thigpen, Kenneth A., Jr. "Adolescent Legends in
       Brown County: a Survey," IF (1971), 4: 141-215.
       Some 73 variants of legends told by Indiana high
       school students.

1968. Toelken, Barre. "'Ma'i Joldloshi: Legendary Styles
       and Navaho Myths," in American Folk Legend,
       ed. Wayland D. Hand, pp. 213-211. An examina-
       tion of Coyote narratives shows that Navaho tales
       differ not in content but in style and function.

1969. Vlach, John M. "One Black Eye and Other Horrors:
       a Case for the Humorous Anti-Legend," IF (1971),
       4: 94-100. Nineteen humorous anti-legends col-
       lected by schoolchildren.

1970. Vogel, Virgil J. "Some Illinois Place-Name Leg-
       ends," MF (F, 1959), 9: 155-162. Suggested
       explanations for 15 place names.

1971. Walam Olum, or Red Score: the Migration Legend
       of the Lenni Lenape or Delaware Indians (Indianap-
       olis: Ind. Hist. Soc., 1954), 207pp. Revised
       ed. of the famous text first made available by
       Constantin Rafinesque in 1836.

1972. Wallrich, William Jones. "Five Bruja Tales from
       the San Luis Valley," WF (Oct, 1950), 9: 359-
       362. Old legends involving witches. Beliefs in
       witchcraft now fading.

1973. Wellman, Manly Wade. "Legend of Terror from
       Madison County," NCarF (May, 1972), 20: 68-72.

1974. Westervelt, William D. Hawaiian Legends of Ghosts
       and Ghost-Gods (Rutland, Vt.: Charles E. Tut-
       tle, 1963), xviii, 271pp. Reprint.

1975. _____. Hawaiian Legends of Old Honolulu (Rut-
       land, Vt.: Charles E. Tuttle, 1963), xiv, 284pp.
       Reprint.

1976. _____. Hawaiian Legends of Volcanoes (Rutland,
       Vt.: Charles E. Tuttle, 1963), xix, 210pp. Re-
       print.

1977. Weston, George F. Boston Ways: High, By, and
       Folk (Boston: Beacon P., 1957), xvi, 261pp.
       Popular legends, anecdotes, stories.

1978. Whedbee, Charles H. Legends of the Outer Banks
       and Tar Heel Tidewater (Winston-Salem, N.C.:
       J. F. Blair, 1966), 165pp.

1979. White, Miriam Whitney. "Legends of an Adirondack
       Grandfather," NYFQ (Je, 1966), 22: 132-142.
       Tales and anecdotes of a farmer-blacksmith.

1980. Wilgus, D. K. "The Girl in the Window," WF (Oct,
       1970), 29: 251-256. The motif of a face appear-
       ing on a flat, unobstructed surface assumes the
       character of a legend.

1981. Williams, Mentor L. Schoolcraft's Indian Legends
       (East Lansing, Mich.: Mich. State U. P., 1956),
       xxii, 322pp. Reprint of H. R. Schoolcraft's
       Algic Researches, 1839, and other collections

with useful introduction.   No comparative notes
or motif numbers.

1982.   Wilson, William A.   "Mormon Legends of the Three
        Nephites Collected at Indiana University," IF
        (1969), 2: 3-35.   Background data, a bibliography,
        and 14 texts.

1983.   Wyman, Walker D. and John D. Hart.   "The Legend
        of Charlie Glass," CM (W, 1969), 66: 40-54.
        Local legend about a Negro cattle ranch foreman
        in early 1900's.

1984.   _____. The Legend of Charlie Glass, Negro Cow-
        boy on the Colorado-Utah Range (River Falls,
        Wis.: River Falls State U. P., 1971), no
        pagination.

1985.   Yoder, Don.   "The Saint's Legend in the Pennsylvania
        German Folk-Culture," in American Folk Legend,
        ed. Wayland D. Hand, pp. 157-183.

9. MYTH AND MYTHOLOGY

1986. Alexander, Hartley Burr. The World's Rim (Lincoln: U. of Nebraska P. , 1953), xx, 259pp.
A philosopher's interpretation of Am. Indian ceremonies with constant comparisons with classical examples. Myths, songs, chants quoted.

1987. Alpers, Anthony. Legends of the South Sea (Christchurch, N. Z. : Whitcomb and Tombs, Ltd. , 1970), xv, 416pp. Polynesian legends and myths, a few about Hawaii.

1988. Barnard, Mary. The Mythmakers (Athens, Ohio: Ohio U. P. , 1966), 213pp. A clear, unpretentious exposition of a few types of myths.

1989. Bascom, William. "The Myth-Ritual Theory, " JAF (Apr-Je, 1957), 70: 103-114. Mostly a comment on Lord Raglan's theory in The Hero.

1990. Beckwith, Martha Warren. The Kumulipo: a Hawaiian Creation Chant (Chicago: U. of Chicago P. , 1951), viii, 257pp. A cosmogonic and genealogical chant of the Hawaiian royal family which goes back into Polynesian mythology. Reprinted with foreword by Katharine Luomala (Honolulu: U. of Hawaii P. , 1972).

1991. Berne, Eric. "The Mythology of Dark and Fair: Psychiatric Use of Folklore, " JAF (Jan-Mr, 1959), 72: 1-13. A psychiatrist turns to mythology and folklore to explain the dark-fair (brunette-blond) polarity.

1992. Bidney, David. "The Concept of Myth and the Problem of Psychocultural Evolution, " AA (Jan, 1950), 52: 15-26.

1993.   _____. "Myth, Symbolism, and Truth," JAF (Oct-
         Dec, 1955), 68: 379-392.

1994.   Bierhorst, John. Four Masterworks of American
         Indian Literature: Quetzalcoatl, The Ritual of
         Condolence, Cuceb, The Night Chant (New York:
         Farrar, Straus, Giroux, 1974), xxiv, 371pp.
         New translations of Aztec, Mayan, Iroquois, and Navajo
         myths with useful commentary.

1995.   Boatright, Mody C. "On the Nature of Myth," SWR
         (Spr, 1954), 39: 131-136.

1996.   Brown, Joseph Epes. The Sacred Pipe (Norman: U.
         of Oklahoma P., 1953), xx, 144pp. Account of
         the seven rites of the Oglala Sioux.

1997.   Bruner, Jerome S. "Myth and Identity," Daedalus
         (Spr, 1959), 88: 349-358.

1998.   Buchler, Ira R. and Henry A. Selby. A Formal Study
         of Myth (Austin: U. of Texas P., 1968), iv,
         166pp. Levi-Strauss and Chomsky provide a de-
         parture point.

1999.   Burke, Kenneth. "Myth, Poetry, and Philosophy,"
         JAF (Oct-Dec, 1960), 73: 283-306. Largely an
         examination of Joseph Fontenrose's book Python
         and its exposition of the "combat myth." Written
         in Burke's opaque style.

2000.   Campbell, Joseph. "The Historical Development of
         Mythology," Daedalus (Spr, 1959), 88: 232-253.

2001.   _____. The Masks of God (New York: Viking,
         1959-1968), four volumes:
                  Primitive Mythology (1959), viii, 504pp., first
                  of four volumes on comparative mythology.
                  Learned and interesting but much of it is con-
                  jectural and hypothetical.
                  Oriental Mythology (1962), 561pp.
                  Occidental Mythology (1964), x, 564pp. Psy-
                  chological insights into the meaning of myths
                  but a too ready acceptance of diffusion of ele-
                  ments such as ritual regicide and the hero as
                  sun god.
                  Creative Mythology (1968), xvii, 730pp. Final

volume of the tetralogy. American writers
ignored.

2002.   _____ . Myths to Live By (New York: Viking,
1972), x, 276pp. Originally lectures delivered
at Cooper Union, 1958-1971. A wide coverage
of mythology.

2003. Campbell, T. N. "The Choctaw Afterworld," JAF
(Apr.Je, 1959), 72: 146-154. Version of Choctaw belief from Gideon Lincecum, followed by a
composite statement.

2004. Cata, Regina Alvarado. "Two Stories from San Juan
Pueblo," WF (Apr, 1956), 15: 106-109. Two ancient Pueblo myths.

2005. Chandler, John. "Navaho Mythmakers," Folklore
Annual of the University Folklore Association
(Austin, Texas, 1969), No. 1, 20-27. Analysis
of different versions of the Navaho origin myth.

2006. Christiansen, Reidar Th. "Myth, Metaphor, and
Simile," JAF (Oct-Dec, 1955), 68: 417-427.

2007. Clark, Cora and Texa Bowen Williams. Pomo Indian
Myths and Some of Their Sacred Meanings (New
York: Vantage, 1954), 127pp. Folklore from
California coastal Indians.

2008. Clark, Ella E. "The Mythology of the Indians in the
Pacific Northwest," OHQ (Sept, 1953), 54: 163-
189.

2009. Count, Earl W. "The Earth Diver and the Rival
Twins: a Clue to Time Correlation in North
Eurasiatic and North American Mythology," in
Indian Tribes of Aboriginal America, ed. Sol
Tax (Chicago: U. of Chicago P., 1952), pp. 55-
62. Proof of the wide diffusion of a famous story.

2010.   _____ . "Myth as World View, a Biosocial Syn-
thesis," in Culture in History, ed. Stanley Diamond, pp. 580-627. A wide-ranging study of
myth with examples from many cultures.

2011. Courlander, Harold. The Fourth World of the Hopis:

the Epic Story of the Hopi Indians as Preserved
in Their Legends and Traditions (New York:
Crown, 1971), 239pp. Texts of Hopi myths and
legends gained from informants 1968-1970.

2012. Curtis, Martha E. "The Black Bear and White-
Tailed Deer as Potent Factors in the Folklore of
the Menomini Indians," MF (F, 1952), 2: 177-190.
Tribal cosmology reviewed and some 153 myths
examined, all from printed sources.

2013. Dockstader, Frederick J. The Kachina and the
White Man (Bloomfield Hills, Mich.: Cranbrook
Inst. of Science, 1954), xi, 185pp. Study of the
impact of the white man on Hopi Indian Kachina
religion.

2014. Dorson, Richard M. "The Eclipse of Solar Mythology,"
JAF (Oct-Dec, 1955), 68: 393-416. Summary of
the views of nineteenth century partisans and opponents.

2015. _____. "Theories of Myth and the Folklorist,"
Daedalus (Spr, 1959), 88: 280-290.

2016. Dundes, Alan. "Earth Diver: Creation of the
Mythopoeic Male," AA (Oct, 1962), 64: v, 1032-
1051. A psychoanalytical study of a well known
creation myth.

2017. Durham, Philip. "The Cowboy and the Myth Makers,"
JPC (S, 1967), 1: 58-62.

2018. Eggan, Dorothy. "The Personal Use of Myth in
Dreams," JAF (Oct-Dec, 1955), 68: 445-453.

2019. Elbert, Samuel H. "The Chief in Hawaiian Mythology," JAF (Apr-Je, Oct-Dec, 1956), 69: 99-
113, 341-355. Also see Jl-Sept, Oct-Dec, 1957,
70: 264-276, 306-322.

2020. _____. Selections from Fornander's Hawaiian
Antiquities and Folk-Lore (Honolulu: U. of
Hawaii P., 1959), 297pp. Partly a Hawaiian
reader but containing seven mythical tales.

2021. Feldman, Burton, and Robert D. Richardson. The

Rise of Modern Mythology, 1680-1860 (Bloomington and London: Indiana U. P., 1972), xxvii,
564pp. Extensive anthology of selections dealing
with mythology and relevant subjects.

2022. Fenton, William H. "This Island, the World on the
Turtle's Back," JAF (Oct-Dec, 1962), 75: 283-
300. Discussion of Iroquois tribal cosmology.

2023. Ferris, William R., Jr. "Myth and the Psychological School: Fact or Fantasy," NYFQ (Dec,
1974), 30: 254-66. Brief survey of theories of
Freud, Jung, Rank, and Fromm as they relate
to myth.

2024. Fife, Austin C. "Myth Formation in the Creative
Process," WF (Oct, 1964), 23: 229-39. Auto-
biographical account of the writing of Saints of
Sage & Saddle (1956).

2025. Fisher, Vardis. "The Novelist and His Background,"
WF (Jan, 1953), 12: 1-8. A professional writer
speaks about his background in which, he claims,
myth is the chief thing.

2026. Fishler, Stanley A. In the Beginning: a Navaho
Creation Myth (Salt Lake City: U. of Utah P.,
1953), 130pp.

2027. Fontenrose, Joseph. Python: a Study of Delphic
Myth and Its Origins (Berkeley and Los Angeles:
U. of California P., 1959), xx, 616pp. Elaborate, erudite study of "combat myth" (Apollo vs.
the dragon Python). Little American material.

2028. _____. The Ritual Theory of Myth (Berkeley,
Los Angeles, London: U. of California P., 1971),
77pp. Monograph on a thesis originated by
James Frazer.

2029. Friedman, Albert B. "The Usable Myth: the Legends
of Modern Mythmakers," in American Folk Legend, ed. Wayland D. Hand, pp. 37-46. Discussion of the primary American myth, belief in the
American Eden.

2030. Fromm, Erich, The Forgotten Language: An Intro-

duction to the Understanding of Dreams, Fairy
Tales and Myths (New York: Rinehart, 1951),
viii, 263pp. Freudian interpretation of the language of dreams and myths.

2031. Frye, Northrop. "Myth, Fiction, and Displacement,"
Daedalus (S, 1961), 90: 587-605. Study of place
of myth and folktale in the interpretation of literature.

2032. Georges, Robert A., ed. Studies on Mythology
(Homewood, Ill.: Dorsey P., 1968), vii, 248pp.
Reprinted material from nine anthropologists.

2033. Gibbon, William B. "Asiatic Parallels in North
American Star Lore: Ursa Major," JAF (Jl-
Sept, 1964), 77: 236-50. Erudite examination of
star lore and star myths among the traditions of
the North American Indians.

2034. Giddings, Ruth Warner. Yaqui Myths and Legends
(Tucson: U. of Arizona P., 1968), 180pp.
Some 60 prose narratives from Mexico and Ari-
zona, first published in book form in 1959.

2035. Gresseth, Gerald K. "Linguistics and Myth Theory,"
WF (Jl, 1969), 29: 153-162. The thesis that
"linguistic method can be used as a model for
evaluating instances of convergence in myth"
examined.

2036. Gross, John J. "After Frazer: the Ritualistic Approach to Myth," WHR (A, 1951), 5: 379-391.

2037. Hassan, Ihab H. "Towards a Method in Myth,"
JAF (Jl-Sept, 1952), 65: 205-215.

2038. Hedges, James S. "Attributive Mutation in Cherokee
Natural History Myth," NCarF (Sept, 1973), 21:
147-154. Animal attributes in myths collected
and published by James Mooney in 1900.

2039. Heuscher, Julius E. "A Critique of Some Interpre-
tations of Myths and Fairy Tales," JAF (Apr-Je,
1967), 80: 175-81.

2040. _____. Psychiatric Study of Myths and Fairy Tales

(Springfield, Ill.: Charles C. Thomas, 1974),
vi, 295pp. Revision of a work published in 1963.
Myths, fairy tales, etc., actually deal with problems of childhood and adolescence.

2041. Hudson, Wilson M. "Eliade's Contribution to the
Study of Myth," in Tire Shrinker to Dragster, ed.
Wilson M. Hudson, pp. 219-241. An analysis of
Mircea Eliade's methodological approach to myth.

2042. Hultkranz, Åke. The North American Indian Orpheus
Tradition, a Contribution to Comparative Religion
(Stockholm: Ethnographical Museum of Sweden,
1957), 340pp. Erudite discussion of Orpheus tradition among North Am. Indians and comparisons
with Old World stories.

2043. _____. "Religious Aspects of the Wind River
Shoshoni Folk Literature," in Culture in History,
ed. Stanley Diamond, pp. 552-569. Observations
based on three field trips.

2044. Hyman, Stanley Edgar. "The Ritual View of Myth
and the Mythic," JAF (Oct-Dec, 1955), 68: 462-
472.

2045. Hymes, Dell H. "Myth and Tale Titles of the Lower
Chinook," JAF (Apr-Je, 1959), 72: 139-145.

2046. _____. "The 'Wife' Who 'Goes Out' Like a Man:
Reinterpretation of a Clackamas Chinook Myth,"
in Structural Analysis of Oral Tradition, ed.
Pierre Maranda and Elli Köngäs Maranda (Philadelphia: U. of Pennsylvania P., 1971), pp. 49-
80.

2047. Jacobs, Melville, ed. "The Anthropologist Looks at
Myth," JAF (Jan-Mr, 1966), 79: ix, 1-305.
Whole issue devoted to papers on myth by ten
anthropologists. Little about United States.

2048. _____. The Content and Style of an Oral Literature: Clackamas Chinook Myths and Tales (Chicago: U. of Chicago P., 1959), viii, 285pp.
Careful analysis of tribal myths and extensive
socio-historical interpretation.

2049. _____. "The Fate of Indian Oral Literature in
Oregon," NR (S, 1962), 5: 90-99. Comments
on anthropologists who collect Indian myths.

2050. _____. "A Few Observations on the World View
of the Clackamas Chinook Indians," JAF (Jl-
Sept, 1955), 68: 283-289.

2051. _____. "Humor and Social Structure in an Oral
Literature," in Culture in History, ed. Stanley
Diamond, pp. 181-189. Jacobs perceives sixteen
types of humor situations in Clackamas Chinook
oral literature.

2052. _____. The People Are Coming Soon: Analysis
of Clackamas Chinook Myths and Tales (Seattle:
U. of Washington P., 1960), xii, 359pp. Analysis of the mythology of a Pacific Coast Indian
tribe.

2053. _____. "Psychological Inferences from a Chinook
Myth," JAF (Apr-Je, 1952), 65: 121-137. A
long Chinook myth with interpretation.

2054. _____. "Titles in an Oral Literature," JAF (Apr-
Je, 1957), 70: 157-172. Analysis of titles given
some 59 Clackamas myths and tales field-collected in 1929-1930.

2055. Kluckhohn, Clyde. "Recurrent Themes in Myth and
Mythmaking," Daedalus (Spr, 1959), 88: 268-279.

2056. Köngäs, Elli Kaija. "The Earth Diver (Th. A812),"
Ethnohistory (Spr, 1960), 7: 151-180. Comparative study of what has been termed the most
widely distributed of all North Am. Indian myths.

2057. Kroeber, A. L. More Mohave Myths (Berkeley: U.
of California P., 1972), 182pp. A supplement
to earlier collections. Texts of eleven myths in
English translation.

2058. Kroeber, Theodora. The Inland Whale (Bloomington:
Indiana U. P., 1959), 205pp. Nine California
Indian stories retold with charm and skill.
Comparative literature rather than folklore.

2059. La Farge, Oliver. "Myths That Hide the American Indian," AmH (Oct, 1956), 7: 1-19, 103-107. Certain notions about the aborigines disproved.

2060. Laguna, Frederica de, ed. Selected Papers from the American Anthropologist, 1888-1920 (Evanston and Elmsford, N.Y.: Row, Peterson, 1960), x, 930pp. Anthology of ethnographic material with a surprising attention paid to myths and tales.

2061. Lamphere, Louise. "Symbolic Elements in Navajo Ritual," SJA (A, 1969), 25: 279-305. Discussion of relationship between myth, ritual, and Navajo cosmology.

2062. Landar, Herbert. "Theme of Incest in Navaho Folklore," in Man, Language and Society: Contributions to the Sociology of Language, ed. Samir K. Ghosh (The Hague: Mouton, 1972), pp. 118-133.

2063. Leach, Joseph. The Typical Texan: Biography of an American Myth (Dallas: Southern Methodist U. P., 1952), xiii, 178pp. A composite portrait with examples.

2064. Leach, Maria. The Beginning: Creation Myths around the World (New York: Funk & Wagnalls, 1956), 253pp.

2065. Leeming, David Adams. Mythology: the Voyage of the Hero (Philadelphia: Lippincott, 1973), vii, 338pp. A popularization of myth scholarship with literary texts illustrating the adventures of mythic heroes.

2066. Levin, Harry. "Some Meanings of Myth," Daedalus (Spr, 1959), 88: 223-231.

2067. Lévi-Strauss, Claude. "Four Winnebago Myths: a Structural Sketch," in Culture in History, ed. Stanley Diamond, pp. 351-362. Summary and analysis of four myths first published by Paul Radin.

2068. _____. "The Structural Study of Myth," JAF (Oct-Dec, 1955), 68: 428-444. Cf. Structural Anthropology (Garden City, N.Y.: Doubleday, 1967), pp. 202-228.

2069. Liljeblad, Sven. "The Religious Attitude of the
       Shoshonean Indians," Rendezvous (1969), 4: i,
       47-58. Myths and tales considered as evidence.

2070. Link, Margaret Schevill. "From the Desk of Wash-
       ington Matthews," JAF (Oct-Dec, 1960), 73: 317-
       325. Navajo myth collected by Matthews and
       published posthumously.

2071. _____. The Pollen Path (Stanford: Stanford U.
       P., 1956), 205pp. Twelve retold Navajo myths.
       Psychological commentary by Dr. Joseph L.
       Henderson.

2072. Littleton, C. Scott. "The New Comparative Myth-
       ology," WF (Jan, 1970), 29: 47-52. Chiefly a
       reply to an unfavorable book review.

2073. Lowie, Robert H. Crow Texts (Berkeley and Los
       Angeles: U. of California P., 1960), xiii,
       550pp. Posthumous collection of Lowie's Crow
       texts with interlinear translations.

2074. Luomala, Katherine. "A Dynamic in Oceanic Maui
       Myths," Fabula (1961), 4: i-ii, 137-162. The
       Polynesian mythical hero Maui snared the sun,
       fished up islands, stole fire from the gods,
       raised the sky, and invented tattooing. Hawaiian
       islands preserve visual objects which supposedly
       confirm Maui's existence.

2075. _____. The Menehune of Polynesia and Other
       Little People of Oceania (Honolulu: Bishop Mu-
       seum P., 1951), 95pp.

2076. _____. "Polynesian Myths about Maui and His
       Dog," Fabula (1958), 2: 139-162.

2077. _____. Voices on the Wind: Polynesian Myths
       and Chants (Honolulu: Bishop Museum P., 1955),
       191pp. Outlines of myths, translations of chants,
       and careful exposition of Polynesian culture and
       narrative patterns.

2078. McCullen, J. T., Jr. "Indian Myths Concerning
       the Origin of Tobacco," NYFQ (Dec, 1967), 23:
       264-273. Scattered Indian beliefs.

2079. Marriott, Alice L. and Carol K. Rachlin. American
       Indian Mythology (New York: Crowell, 1968), xii,
       211pp.

2080. Masson, Marcelle. A Bag of Bones: the Wintu
       Myths of a Trinity River Indian (Oakland: no
       publisher, 1966), x, 130pp. Fifteen examples
       collected from Grant Towendolly, a Wintu Indian.

2081. Moon, Sheila. A Magic Dwells: a Poetic and Psy-
       chological Study of the Navajo Emergence Myth
       (Middleton, Conn.: Wesleyan U. P., 1970),
       206pp.

2082. Murray, Henry A. Myth and Mythmaking (New York:
       George Braziller, 1960), 381pp. Enlargement of
       a symposium originally published in Daedalus
       (Vol. 86). 21 essays by a variety of experts in
       anthropology, literature, and folklore.

2083. "Myth: A Symposium," JAF (Oct-Dec, 1955), 68:
       379-488. Reprinted and edited by Thomas A.
       Sebeok (Bloomington: Indiana U. P., 1965),
       180pp. Nine essays.

2084. Neihardt, John G. When the Tree Flowered (New
       York: Macmillan, 1951), 248pp. A fictional
       framework conceals an excellent account of Sioux
       ritual and myth.

2085. Newcomb, Franc Johnson. Hosteen Klah: Navajo
       Medicine Man and Sand Painter (Norman: U. of
       Oklahoma P., 1964), xxxiii, 227pp. Biography
       of prominent Navajo medicine man with material
       on Navajo religion and mythology included.

2086. O'Bryan, Aileen. The Dîné: Origin Myths of the
       Navajo Indians (Washington: U. S. Govt. Printing
       Office, 1956), vii, 187pp. Navajo origin myths
       originally told by Sandoval in 1928.

2087. Ohmann, Richard M., ed. The Making of Myth (New
       York: Putnam, 1962), 179pp. Nine essays all
       previously published.

2088. Opler, Morris E. "Myth and Practice in Jicarilla
       Apache Eschatology," JAF (Apr-Je, 1960), 73:

133-153.   Attitudes and behavioral responses to
death.

2089.   Patai, Raphael.   Myth and Modern Man (Englewood
Cliffs, N.J.:   Prentice-Hall, 1972), xii, 359pp.
A broad definition of myth enables the author to
deal with many areas of modern life (science fiction, television, sex, etc.).

2090.   Radin, Paul.   The Trickster, a Study in American
Indian Mythology (New York: Philosophical Library, 1956), xi, 211pp.   The Winnebago trickster
cycle collected in 1912.   Interpretive essays by
Kerenyi and Jung add little to text.

2091.   Reichard, Gladys Amanda.   Navajo Religion.   A
Study of Symbolism (New York: Bollingen, Pantheon Books, 1950), xxxvi, 800pp.   Monumental
study of tribal religion incorporating a substantial
amount of mythology.

2092.   Rooth, Anna Birgitta.   "The Creation Myths of the
North American Indians," Anthropos (1957), 52:
497-508.

2093.   Rosenberg, Bruce A.   Custer and the Epic of Defeat
(University Park and London: Penn State U. P.,
1974), 313pp.   A study of the history and legendry
surrounding George Armstrong Custer.

2094.   Scharbach, Alexander.   "Aspects of Existentialism in
Clackamas Chinook Myths," JAF (Jan-Mr, 1962),
75: 15-22.

2095.   Skeels, Dell.   "A Classification of Humor in Nez
Perce Mythology," JAF (Jan-Mr, 1954), 67: 57-
63.

2096.   _____.   "The Function of Humor in Three Nez
Perce Indian Myths," AI (F, 1954), 11: 249-261.

2097.   _____.   "Grizzly-Bear Woman in Nez Perce Indian
Mythology," NWF (Nov, 1969), 3: ii, 1-9.   Only
one feminine character plays a principal role
here.

2098.   Spencer, Katherine.   Mythology and Values: an

Analysis of Navaho Chantway Myths (Philadelphia: Am. Folklore Soc., 1957), 240pp.

2099. Spencer, Robert F. "Native Myth and Modern Religion Among the Klamath Indians, " JAF (Jl-Sept, 1952), 65: 217-26. Klamath culture has declined but part of the aboriginal world view remains.

2100. _____ and W. K. Carter. "The Blind Man and the Loon: Barrow Eskimo Variants, " JAF (Jan-Mr, 1954), 67: 65-72. Study of a complex, widely diffused myth.

2101. Stern, Theodore. "Ideal and Expected Behavior as Seen in Klamath Mythology, " JAF (Jan-Mr, 1963), 76: 21-30. Analysis based on 55 tales from Klamath Indians of Southern Oregon. Cf. "Klamath Myth Abstracts, " ibid., pp. 31-41.

2102. _____. "Some Sources of Variability in Klamath Mythology, " JAF (Jan-Mr, Apr-Je, Oct-Dec, 1956), 69: 1-12, 135-46, 377-86. Careful scrutiny of the setting, cultural changes, narrator, and myth.

2103. _____. "The Trickster in Klamath Mythology, " WF (Jl, 1953), 12: 158-74. Discussion of the trickster character and its exemplars: Mink, Weasel, Skunk, etc. Curiously enough Coyote is unimportant.

2104. Stross, Brian. "Serial Order in Nez Perce Myths, " JAF (Jan-Mr, 1971), 84: 104-13.

2105. Thompson, Stith. "Myths and Folktales, " JAF (Oct-Dec, 1955), 68: 482-88.

2106. Townsend, Dabney W., Jr. "Myth and Meaning, " CentR (Spr, 1972), 16: 192-202. Examination of myth in ritual, literature, and folk culture.

2107. Vickery, John B. ed. Myth and Literature. Contemporary Theory and Practice (Lincoln: U. of Nebraska P., 1966), xii, 391pp. Some 34 papers, all reprinted and some already anthologized, dealing with 18 authors.

2108. _____. "Three Masks and a Myth," WHR (A, 1958), 12: 371-378.

2109. Waters, Frank. Book of the Hopi (New York: Viking, 1963), xviii, 347pp. Hopi creation myths, migration legends, and ceremonial cycles.

2110. _____. Masked Gods: Navajo and Pueblo Ceremonialism (Albuquerque: U. of New Mexico P., 1950), 438pp. Tribal myths, legends, and dances.

2111. Watts, Harold H. "Myth and Folk-Tale," ArQ (W, 1955), 11: 293-311. Distinction based on whether the story is connected with a cult or a ritual.

2112. Weisinger, Herbert. "The Proper Study of a Myth," CentR (S, 1968), 12: 237-267.

2113. Wheelwright, Mary C. The Myth and Prayers of the Great Star Chant and the Myth of the Coyote Chant (Santa Fe: Museum of Navajo Ceremonial Art, 1956), 190pp.

2114. _____. "Notes on Some Navajo Coyote Myths," NMFR (1949-1950), 4: 17-19. Three Navajo myths about Coyote related to Navajo religion. Slight.

2115. Wheelwright, Philip. "The Semantic Approach to Myth," JAF (Oct-Dec, 1955), 68: 473-481.

2116. Wherry, Joseph. Indian Masks and Myths of the West (New York: Apollo Eds., 1974), 273pp.

2117. Worley, Ted R. "The Folk Origin of the Arkansas Myth," AF (Aug 15, 1954), 5: i, 1-5.

2118. Wyman, Leland C. ed. Beautyway: a Navaho Ceremonial (New York: Pantheon Books, 1957), xii, 218pp. Myth recorded and transcribed by Father Berard Haile, also by Maud Oakes; sandpaintings by others.

2119. _____. Blessingway (Tucson: U. of Arizona P., 1970), xxviii, 660pp. Texts with commentary on three versions.

2120. Wyman, Walker D. <u>Mythical Creatures of the North Country</u> (River Falls, Wis.: River Falls State U. P., 1969), vi, 65pp.

10.   BELIEFS, CUSTOMS, SUPERSTITIONS, CURES

2121.   Abrahams, Roger D.   "Folk Beliefs in Southern Joke Books," WF (Oct, 1964), 23: 259-261.   44 Negro beliefs reprinted from joke books locally printed by white editors.

2122.   Ainsworth, Catherine Harris.   Superstitions from Seven Towns of the United States (Buffalo: 1973).

2123.   Allen, Lee.   The Superstitions of Baseball Players," NYFQ (Je, 1964), 20: 98-109.   Examples of beliefs and practices from the earlier years of baseball.

2124.   Allison, Lelah.   "Folk Beliefs Collected in Southeastern Illinois," JAF (Jl-Sept, 1950), 63: 309-324.   556 items arranged under different labels and without annotation.

2125.   _____.   "Southern Illinois Tales and Beliefs," HF (Jl-Sept, 1950), 9: 76-79.

2126.   Anderson, John Q.   "The Ghost of the Hutto Ranch," in Mesquite and Willow, ed. Mody C. Boatright et al., pp. 180-186.   Ghost tales from Wheeler Co., Texas.

2127.   _____.   "Magical Transference of Disease in Texas Folk Medicine," WF (Jl, 1968), 27: 191-199.   Beliefs that ailments can be transferred magically from person to person or even to animal or plant.

2128.   _____.   "Popular Beliefs in Texas, Louisiana and Arkansas," SFQ (Dec, 1968), 32: 304-319.   Some 174 beliefs, taboos, sayings, etc.

2129. _____. "Special Powers in Folk Cures and Remedies," in Tire Shrinker to Dragster, ed. Wilson
M. Hudson, pp. 163-174. Beliefs about removing
warts, stopping bleeding, and curing burns.

2130. _____. Texas Folk Medicine: 1,333 Cures, Remedies, Preventives, and Health Practices (Austin:
Encino P., 1970), vii, 91pp. Remedies collected
by students from 133 Texas counties.

2131. Atteberry, Louie. "Rural Traditions of the Snake
River Valley," NWF (W, 1966), 1: 23-30. Customs, superstitions, speech from about 1870-1930.

2132. Baker, James C. "Echoes of Tommy Knockers in
Bohemia, Oregon, Mines," WF (Apr, 1971), 30:
119-122. Gremlins from Great Britain have in-
vaded Oregon mining country.

2133. Barrett, Linda K. and Evon Z. Vogt. "The Urban
American Dowser," JAF (Jl-Sept, 1969), 82:
195-213. Divination continues in U.S.: rural
dowsing from tradition, urban dowsing from written prescriptions.

2134. Barrick, Mac E. "'All Signs in Dry Spells Fails,'"
KFQ (Spr, 1964), 9: 23-28. Weather beliefs
from Penn. and from Baer's Agricultural Almanac published at Lancaster since 1825.

2135. _____. "Folk-Beliefs of a Pennsylvania Preacher," KFQ (W, 1965), 10: 191-193. Seven folk
beliefs of a nineteenth century Lutheran minister.

2136. _____. "Folk Medicine in Cumberland County,"
KFQ (F, 1964), 9: 100-110. Some 137 beliefs
listed and informants identified.

2137. _____. "Moon-Signs in Cumberland County," PF
(S, 1966), 15: iv, 41-43.

2138. Bass, William W. "Dog Days: Some Notes and a
Few Superstitions," TFSB (Sept, 1956), 22: 64-68.
Philological and personal.

2139. Baughman, Ernest W. "Folk Sayings and Beliefs,"
NMFR (1954-1955), 9: 23-27. Cures, omens,

weather predictions, snake beliefs from eight New
Mexico informants.

2140. Beck, Horace P. The Folklore of Maine (Philadelphia and New York: Lippincott, 1957), xvi, 284pp.
Potpourri of superstitions, beliefs, history, songs,
stories, language, material folklore from the Pine
Tree State, much of it maritime.

2141. _____. "Herpetological Lore from the Blue
Ridge," MF (F, 1952), 2: 141-150. Beliefs and
anecdotes about snakes.

2142. Beck, Jane C. "A Traditional Witch of the Twentieth
Century," NYFQ (Je, 1974), 30: 101-116. Folk
medicine and religious ritual used by a Philadelphia negress.

2143. Belting, Natalia Maree. "The Piasa--It Isn't a
Bird!" JISHS (A, 1973), 66: 302-305. The
petroglyphs found by Marquette are water monsters, not a bird.

2144. Betts, Leonidas. "Folk Medicine in Harnett County,"
NCarFJ (May, 1974), 22: 84-94.

2145. Bourgaize, Eidola Jean. "The Unconventional
Ghosts," NYFQ (W, 1957), 13: 295-300. Indian
ghosts in Rhode Island.

2146. Bradford, Gershom. "Sea Serpents? No or May-
be," Am. Neptune (Oct, 1953), 13: 268-274.
Comments about sighting of sea serpents off
coast of Mass. in nineteenth century.

2147. Brandon, Elizabeth. "Superstitions in Vermilion
Parish," in The Golden Log, ed. Mody C. Boatright et al., pp. 108-118. Louisiana beliefs in
conjuration and gris-gris.

2148. Brewster, Paul G. "An Ozark Superstition and Its
World Affinities," AHQ (S, 1950), 9: 76-86. The
Ozark tale of a witch master who made a wooden
doll which he dressed to resemble a local woman
and burned in the fireplace has world-wide analogies.

2149.   Briggs, Harold E.   "Folklore of Southern Illinois,"
        SFQ (Dec, 1952), 16: 207-217.   The Illinois re-
        gion known as "Egypt" has beliefs, weather lore,
        folk medicine, death omens although no great
        folklore figures.

2150.   Brock, Lois.   "Tarantula Lore," in The Golden Log,
        ed. Mody C. Boatright et al., pp. 41-52.   Taran-
        tulas are more dangerous in legend than in fact.

2151.   Brown, Raymond L.   A Book of Superstitions (New
        York: Taplinger, 1970), 123pp.

2152.   Browne, Ray B.   Popular Beliefs and Practices from
        Alabama (Berkeley and Los Angeles: U. of Cal.
        P., 1958), x, 271pp.   Some 4340 items carefully
        numbered and categorized but not representative
        of the whole state.   Notes on informants.

2153.   _____.   "Superstitions Used as Propaganda in the
        American Revolution," NYFQ (A, 1961), 17: 202-
        211.   Use of numbers and omens discussed.

2154.   Brunetti, Michael.   "Italian Folklore Collected from
        Mrs. Stephanie Nappi," NYFQ (Mr, 1973), 28:
        257-262.   Some folk beliefs collected from au-
        thor's grandmother.

2155.   Buley, R. Carlyle.   "Water (?) Witching Can Be
        Fun," IMH (Mr, 1960), 56: 64-77.

2156.   Burridge, Gaston.   "Does the Forked Stick Locate
        Anything?   An Inquiry into the Art of Dowsing,"
        WF (Jan, 1955), 14: 32-43.

2157.   Byington, Robert H.   "Popular Beliefs and Supersti-
        tions from Pennsylvania," KFQ (Spr, 1964), 9:
        3-12.   Miscellaneous beliefs arranged in 13 cate-
        gories.

2158.   _____.   "Powwowing in Pennsylvania," KFQ (F,
        1964), 9: 111-117.   Beliefs in efficacy of pow-
        wowing or Brauche from two widely circulated
        books.

2159.   Campa, Arthur L.   "Herbs and Plants of Early Cali-
        fornia," WF (Oct, 1950), 9: 338-347.   List of

names, often in Spanish, with comments on
proven or supposed efficacy of the plants.

2160. Campbell, Marie. "Folk Remedies from South
Georgia," TFSB (Mr, 1953), 19: 1-4.

2161. Cansler, Loman D. "Madstones and Hydrophobia,"
WF (Apr, 1964), 23: 95-105. Beliefs in curative
powers against dog bites.

2162. Carbo, Terry M. "The Faith Healing Beliefs of a
New Orleans Family," LFM (Aug, 1968), 2: 91-
100. Miraculous cures collected from a relative.

2163. Caroland, Emma Jean. "Popular Beliefs and Superstitions Known to Students of Clarksville High
School," TFSB (Je, 1962), 28: 37-47. Omens,
beliefs, weather lore from a Tennessee high
school.

2164. Carranco, Lynwood. "A Miscellany of Folk Beliefs
from the Redwood Country," WF (Jl, 1967), 26:
169-176. Some 146 items from Humboldt County,
California.

2165. Carrington, Hereward and Nandor Fodor. Haunted
People: Story of the Poltergeist Down the Cen-
turies (New York: Dutton, 1951), 225pp. Data
and analysis of poltergeist activity, including the
famous Bell witch of Tennessee.

2166. Clar, Mimi. "Folk Belief and Custom in the Blues,"
WF (Jl, 1960), 19: 173-189. Blues texts reveal
folk belief, speech, proverbial lore, etc. Many
examples.

2167. Clark, Joseph D. Beastly Folklore (Metuchen, N.J.:
Scarecrow P., 1968), v, 326pp. Derivative
names, superstitions, proverbial phrases associated with common animals and birds: hog, pos-
sum, hawk, sparrow, rabbit, fox, etc.

2168. _____. "Folk Medicine in Colonial North Carolina
as Found in Dr. John Brickell's Natural History,"
NCarF (Nov, 1969), 17: 100-124. Examples of
early beliefs.

2169. _____. "North Carolina Popular Beliefs and Su-
     perstitions," NCarF (Jan, 1970), 18: 1-66. Some
     1683 items arranged in 13 categories, derived
     from printed sources and from county agricultural
     agents.

2170. _____. "North Carolina Superstitions," NCarF
     (Jl, 1966), 14: 3-40. Some 1442 items collected
     from college students in Raleigh, N. Car., 1955-
     1962.

2171. _____. "Superstitions from North Carolina," SFQ
     (Sept, 1962), 26: 198-224. Some 306 items col-
     lected by students from No. Car. State College,
     arranged by theme (good and bad luck, weather,
     animals, etc.).

2172. Clausen, Lucy W. Insect Fact and Folklore (New
     York: Macmillan, 1954), xiv, 194pp. More fact
     than folklore but some interesting beliefs. Bibli-
     ography of 132 items.

2173. Cochran, Robert and Martha Cochran. "Some Men-
     strual Folklore of Mississippi," MFR (W, 1970),
     4: 108-113. Date from interviews in Marion
     County.

2174. Collins, Yandell, Jr. "Superstitions and Belief Tales
     from Louisville," KFR (Apr-Je, 1958), 4: 71-78.
     Some 57 examples.

2175. Cooper, Horton. North Carolina Mountain Folklore
     and Miscellany (Murfreesboro, N.C.: Johnson
     Publishing Co., 1972), 160pp. Miscellaneous
     collection of beliefs and practices assembled by
     an octogenarian mountaineer.

2176. Cordova, Gabriel. "Black and White Magic on the
     Texas-Mexican Border," in Folk Travelers, ed.
     Mody C. Boatright et al., pp. 195-199. Witch-
     craft in the Rio Grande Valley.

2177. Craft, Betty. "Superstitions from Frenchburg, Ken-
     tucky," KFR (Jan-Mr, 1964), 10: 12-17. Some
     97 superstitions arranged according to subjects.

2178. Davidson, Levette J. "Superstitions Collected in

Denver, Colorado," WF (Jl, 1954), 13: 184-189.
Some 75 examples collected from college students
in 1953.

2179. Davis, Kenneth W. "Weather Signs in Central Texas,"
WF (Jl, 1969), 28: 169-174.

2180. De Lys, Claudia. A Treasury of Superstitions (New
York: Philosophical Library, 1957), 317pp.
Collection of popular superstitions; no sources
given.

2181. Dieffenbach, Victor C. "Weather Signs and Calendar
Lore from the 'Dumb Quarter,'" PF (A, 1967),
17: i, 26-30. Some 79 items from Berks County,
Penn.

2182. Dingwall, Iva. "Some Frontier Remedies and Superstitions," MinnH (Spr, 1955), 34: 195-199.

2183. Dinkel, Phyllis A. "Old Marriage Customs in Herzog (Victoria), Kansas," WF (Apr, 1960), 19:
99-105. Customs of Russian-German immigrants
prevalent around 1900.

2184. Dluge, Robert L., Jr. "My Interview with a Pow-
wower," PF (S, 1972), 21: iv, 39-42. An account of a folk-healer in present-day Penn.

2185. Dobie, J. Frank. "Madstones and Hydrophobia
Skunks," in Madstones and Twisters, ed. Mody
C. Boatright et al., pp. 3-17. Speculations on
madstones with evidence of their use in Texas.

2186. Dodson, Ruth. "Don Pedrito Jaramillo: the Curan-
dero of Los Olmos," in The Healer of Los Olmos and Other Mexican Lore, ed. Wilson M.
Hudson, pp. 9-70. Biographical data and tales
about the therapy and cures of the healer.

2187. Dow, James R. "Folklore of the Wyoming Territory
from Printed Sources," WR (W, 1971), 8: 23-28.
Tall tales from Wyoming, mostly from Jim
Bridger.

2188. Dundes, Alan. "Brown County Superstitions," MF
(Spr, 1961), 11: 25-56. Some 219 items from
one Indiana county with extensive annotations.

2189. Elliot, Frances. "Stagestruck Luck; Beliefs From and About the Theatre," KFR (Jan-Mr, 1964), 10: 18-21. Superstitions held by actors and theater people.

2190. Fendrich, Nathan. "Superstitions and Popular Beliefs of Oregon," NWF (S, 1965), 1: 24-28. Weather, luck, taboos, signs, etc.

2191. Ferm, Virgilius. A Brief Dictionary of American Superstitions (New York: Philosophical Lib., 1959), x, 259pp. Brief, subjectively selected list of American superstitions, largely from the East and South. Indians and Spanish Americans neglected.

2192. Fife, Austin E. "Pioneer Mormon Remedies," WF (Jl, 1957), 16: 153-162. An amazing variety of frontier remedies mostly garnered from interviews in Utah.

2193. Firestone, Melvin M. "Sephardic Folk-Curing in Seattle," JAF (Oct-Dec, 1962), 75: 301-310. Rituals, cures, dietary practices among Seattle Jews.

2194. Fish, Lydia. "The Old Wife in the Dormitory--Sexual Folklore and Magical Practices from State University College," NYFQ (Mr, 1972), 28: 30-36.

2195. Flory, Claude R. "A Hazard of Good Fortunes," JAF (Jan-Mr, 1969), 82: 71-72. Brief account of fortune-telling in Virginia.

2196. Foster, James R. "Brooklyn Folklore," NYFQ (S, 1957), 13: 83-91. Superstitions and tales.

2197. Foster, Jerry. "Varieties of Sea Lore," WF (Oct, 1969), 28: 260-266. Superstitions, rites, language.

2198. Fowler, David C. and Mary Fowler. "More Kentucky Superstitions," SFQ (Sept, 1950), 14: 170-176. Supplement to Daniel L. and Lucy B. Thomas, Kentucky Superstitions, 1920.

2199.   Frazier, Paul. "Some Lore of Hexing and Powwow-
        ing," MF (S, 1952), 2: 101-107. Pennsylvania
        material collected from a resident of Allentown.

2200.   Freud, Ralph. "George Spelvin Says the Tag: Folk-
        lore of the Theater," WF (Oct, 1954), 13: 245-
        250. An experienced actor and play director re-
        ports on stage folklore.

2201.   Friedman, Albert B. "The Scatological Rites of
        Burglars," WF (Jl, 1968), 27: 171-179. The
        traditional habit of burglars leaving fecal calling
        cards.

2202.   Garcia, Alfredo R. "Spanish Folklore from South
        Texas," in Mesquite and Willow, ed. Mody C.
        Boatright et al., pp. 187-191. Beliefs in the
        evil eye and fortune telling.

2203.   Garza, Humberto. "Owl-Bewitchment in the Lower
        Rio Grande Valley," in Singers and Storytellers,
        ed. Mody C. Boatright et al., pp. 218-225.
        Texas Mexicans are inclined to associate owls
        with brujas and witchcraft.

2204.   Georges, Robert A. "Matiasma: Living Folk Be-
        lief," MF (S, 1962), 12: 69-74. Belief in the
        evil eye is prevalent among immigrant Greeks
        in the U. S.

2205.   Gifford, Edward S. "The Evil Eye in Pennsylvania
        Medical History," KFQ (A, 1960), 5: iii, 3-8.
        Brief account of popular belief in the evil eye.

2206.   _____. The Evil Eye; Studies in the Folklore of
        Vision (New York: Macmillan, 1958), 216pp.
        Full account of beliefs in the evil eye by a Penn-
        sylvania ophthalmologist.

2207.   Gilbert, Lanvil. "The Prairie Dog," in Madstones
        and Twisters, ed. Mody C. Boatright et al., pp.
        69-80. Tales and rumors about a familiar west-
        ern rodent.

2208.   Gillis, Everett A. "Weather Talk from the Cap
        Rock," in Folk Travelers, ed. Mody C. Boat-
        right et al., pp. 200-204. Familiar weather lore
        from West Texas.

2209. Gizelis, Gregory. "The Function of the Vision in
       Greek-American Culture," WF (Jan, 1974), 33:
       65-76. Immigrant Greeks in Philadelphia experi-
       ence visions as a result of religious doctrines,
       austerities, dancing, or folk narratives.

2210. _____. "The Use of Amulets among Greek-
       Philadelphians," PF (Spr, 1971), 20: iii, 30-37.

2211. Gourley, Norma Mae. "About Powwowing," PD (Mr
       15, 1954), 5: xiv, 7-8. Part of a master's
       thesis on witchcraft among the Penn. Germans.

2212. Granger, Byrd Howell. "Folklore Along the Colorado
       River," WR (W, 1969), 6: 3-11. Brief historical
       account with mention of buried treasure and lost
       mines.

2213. _____. "Witchcraft in the Southwest," WR (S,
       1968), 5: 3-12. Mexican Americans retain be-
       liefs in the evil eye, effigies, hexing, and witches.

2214. Gross, Dan. "Folklore of the Theater," WF (Oct,
       1961), 20: 257-263. Some 61 beliefs and super-
       stitions compiled by a veteran in show business.

2215. Hall, Ella R. "A Comparison of Selected Mississippi
       and North Carolina Remedies," MFR (W, 1971),
       5: 94-113. Some 195 remedies cited from Mis-
       sissippi.

2216. Hall, Joseph S. "Witchcraft and Ghostlore in the
       Great Smokies," TFSB (Mr, Je, 1970), 36: 1-6,
       31-36. Beliefs in witchlore and means of counter-
       acting it.

2216a. Halpert, Violetta Maloney. "Death Beliefs from
       Indiana," MF (W, 1952), 2: 205-219. Death
       omens and taboos collected from Indiana Univer-
       sity students.

2217. _____. "Folk Cures from Indiana," HF (Jan-Mr,
       1950), 9: 1-12.

2218. Hand, Wayland D. "American Superstitions and Popu-
       lar Beliefs," in Folklore in Action, ed. H. P.
       Beck, pp. 151-172. Based on Hand's introduction

to Vol. VI of <u>Frank C. Brown Collection of North Carolina Folklore</u>.

2219. _____. "Curative Practice in Folk Tales," <u>Fabula</u> (1967), 9: i-iii, 264-269. Discussion of the treatment of illness in folk tales. Both magical cures and actual folk medicine are used. Many examples.

2220. _____. "The Curing of Blindness in Folk Tales," in <u>Volksüberlieferung</u>, eds. Fritz Harkort <u>et al.</u>, pp. 81-87. Blindness has been cured by plants, animal products, water, unguents, human secretions (saliva, blood, tears).

2221. _____. "'The Devil Beating His Wife' and Other Folk Beliefs about the Sun's Shining While It Rains," <u>KFR</u> (Oct-Dec, 1957), 3: 139-142.

2222. _____. "'The Fear of the Gods': Superstition and Popular Belief," in <u>Our Living Traditions</u>, ed. T. P. Coffin, pp. 215-227. Rapid survey with illustrations.

2223. _____. "Folk Beliefs and Customs of the American Theater; a Survey," <u>SFQ</u> (Mr, 1974), 38: 23-48. Fascinating list of good and bad luck tokens accepted by actors.

2224. _____. "Folk Medical Magic and Symbolism in the West," in <u>Forms Upon the Frontier</u>, ed. Austin Fife <u>et al.</u>, pp. 103-118.

2225. _____. "Hangmen, the Gallows, and the Dead Man's Hand in American Folk Medicine," in <u>Medieval Literature and Folklore Studies</u>, ed. Jerome Mandel and Bruce A. Rosenberg, pp. 323-329.

2226. _____. "Jewish Popular Beliefs and Customs in Los Angeles," in <u>Studies in Biblical and Jewish Folklore</u>, ed. Raphael Patai, Francis Lee Utley, and Dov Noy (Bloomington: Indiana U. P., 1960), pp. 309-326. A large Jewish population with well defined beliefs and customs merits study.

2227. _____. "'Measuring' with String, Thread, and

Fibre: a Practice in Folk Medical Magic," SAV (1972-1973), 68-69: 240-251.

2228. _____. "A Miscellany of Nebraska Folk Beliefs," WF (Oct, 1962), 21: 257-278. Some 209 beliefs, informants identified; with annotation.

2229. _____. "More Popular Beliefs and Superstitions from Pennsylvania," in Two Penny Ballads... ed. Kenneth S. Goldstein and Robert H. Byington, pp. 137-164.

2230. _____. "North Carolina Folk Beliefs and Superstitions Collected in California," NCarF (Nov, 1970), 18: 117-123. 145 beliefs from students.

2231. _____. "'Passing Through': Folk Medical Magic and Symbolism," Proceedings of the APS (Dec, 1968), 112: 379-402. Survey of almost universal practice of curing patients by having them pass through apertures of various kinds. Extensive documentation.

2232. _____. "Physical Harm, Sickness, and Death by Conjury: a Survey of the Sorcerer's Evil Art in America," AE (1970), 19: 169-177. Magic practiced in association with injury or death in the southern U.S.

2233. _____. "Plugging, Nailing, Wedging, and Kindred Medical Practices," in Folklore & Society, ed. Bruce Jackson, pp. 63-75. The magic treatment of disease.

2234. _____. Popular Beliefs and Superstitions from North Carolina (Durham: Duke U. P., 1961, 1964), lxxi, 664pp.; xxxiii, 677pp. Vols. VI and VII of the Frank C. Brown Collection of North Carolina Folklore. Some 8,569 items in 14 categories ranging from birth and the human body to death, witchcraft, and weather. Vol. VII contains an excellent index; both volumes include bibliography.

2235. _____. "Popular Beliefs and Superstitions from Pennsylvania," KFQ (F, 1958; Spr and S, 1959), Part I, 3: 61-74; Part II, 4: 106-120. Some 234 superstitions arranged by subject categories (infancy, human body, folk medicine, animals, weather, etc.).

2236. Handelman, Don. "Aspects of the Moral Compact of a Washo Shaman," AnthQ (Apr, 1972), 45: 84-101. A study of shamanistic beliefs and practices of Nevada Indians.

2237. Hatcher, Mildred. "Superstitions in Middle Tennessee," SFQ (Sept, 1955), 19: 150-155. Clarksville, Tenn. beliefs (omens, good luck, remedies, etc.). No annotation.

2238. Helfman, Elizabeth S. Maypoles and Wood Demons: the Meaning of Trees (New York: Seabury, 1972), 128pp.

2239. Hendricks, George D. Mirrors, Mice, and Mustaches (Austin: Texas Folklore Soc., 1966), 110pp. Folk remedies, superstitions, popular beliefs.

2240. _____. "Misconceptions Concerning Western Wild Animals," WF (Apr, 1953), 12: 119-127. Insufficient knowledge about the cougar, opossum, grizzly, mountain sheep has produced serious misconceptions and exaggerated beliefs.

2241. _____. "More Texas Superstitions," WF (Apr, 1965), 24: 111-113. Some 27 examples.

2242. _____. "Superstitions Collected in Denton, Texas," WF (Jan, 1956), 15: 1-18. Some 408 superstitions collected by 71 students arranged by subjects. Informants listed.

2243. Hertzog, Phares H. "Snakes and Snakelore of Pennsylvania," PF (A, 1967), (W, 1967-8), 17: i, 14-17; ii, 24-26. Beliefs, names for, and tales about snakes.

2244. Hicks, Sam. Desert Plants and People (San Antonio: Naylor, 1966), 75pp. Texas folk medicine.

2245. Hill, Carole E. "Black Healing Practices in the Rural South," JPC (Spr, 1973), 6: 849-853. Negroes in rural South go to healers because of

poverty rather than to doctors for curing of
warts, burns, bleeding, toothache, the thrash.

2246. Hilliard, Addie Suggs. "I Remember, I Remember,"
TFSB (Dec, 1966), 32: 121-128. Personal
reminiscences of Scotch-Irish family in Chester
Co., Tenn.

2247. _____. "A Lick o' Lemon," KFR (Jl-Sept, 1973),
19: 79-86. Survey of the uses of the lemon:
medicinal, culinary, beauty.

2248. _____. "On Swallowing Punkin Seed," TSFB (Dec,
1974), 40: 119-121. Euphemisms about pregnancy and beliefs concerning birth and child care.

2249. _____. "What'll We Give the Baby-O?" TFSB
(Je, 1974), 40: 41-46.

2250. Hines, Donald M. "Superstitions from Oregon," WF
(Jan, 1965), 24: 7-20. Some 216 examples from
various informants.

2251. Hinton, Sam. "Further Notes on Snake Yarns," WF
(Jl, 1956), 168-171. Data on coral snakes, rat-
tlesnakes, and apocryphal glass and hoop snakes.

2252. Hudson, Lois Phillips. "The Water Witch," Report-
er (Jl 23, 1959), 21: 34-37. A North Dakota
dowser in operation.

2253. Huguenin, Charles A. "The Ghost of Ticonderoga,"
NYFQ (Spr, 1959), 15: 4-24. Historical data
about a Scotch major in a Black Watch regiment.

2254. Hunter, Earl D. "Folk Remedies of Man and Beast,"
KFR (Jl-Sept, 1962), 8: 97-108. Mostly from
Cumberland Co., Kentucky.

2255. Hyatt, Harry Middleton. Folklore from Adams County, Illinois (New York: Alma Hyatt Egan Foundation, 1935), xvi, 723pp. Sec. ed., 1965, of
this amazing compilation for a single state lists
16,537 items.

2256. _____. Hoodoo, Conjuration, Witchcraft, Root-
work (Hannibal, Mo.: Western Publishing Co.,

1972), two volumes, 1857pp. Extensive material
mostly from black informants in 1930's transcribed verbatim and from cylinders. Long personal introduction but scanty data about informants.

2257. Jack, Phil R. "Folk Medicine from Western Pennsylvania," PF (Oct, 1964), 14: i, 35-37.

2258. Jeffrey, Lloyd N. "Snake Yarns of the West and
Southwest," WF (Oct, 1955), 14: 246-248. Some
61 misconceptions about reptiles with scientific
corrections.

2259. Johnson, Clifton E. God Struck Me Dead (Philadelphia: Pilgrim P., 1969), xix, 172pp. Ex-
slave interviews from archives of Fisk University.

2260. Johnson, F. Roy. Supernaturals among Carolina
Folk and Their Neighbors (Murfreesboro, No.
Car.: Johnson Pub. Co., 1974), 256pp.

2261. Jones, Janice S. "Folk Beliefs Popular in the Lower
Snake Valley," NWF (Nov, 1969), 3: 12-15. Be-
liefs about illness and cures from rural Idaho.
Informants named.

2262. Jones, Louis C. "The Devil in York State," NYFQ
(Spr, 1952), 8: 5-19. Devil lore collected by
students 1940-1946, now part of Cooperstown
folklore archives.

2263. _____. "The Evil Eye among European-Ameri-
cans," WF (Jan, 1951), 10: 11-25. Discussion
of possessors of the evil eye, diagnosis, preventives, cures, impact.

2264. Jones, Michael Owen. "Folk Beliefs: Knowledge and
Action," SFQ (Dec, 1967), 31: 304-309. An attempt to organize beliefs in a triple division; data
from Kansas.

2265. _____. "Toward an Understanding of Folk Medical
Beliefs in North Carolina," NCarF (May, 1967),
15: 23-27. Discussion of items in the North Car.
Brown collection.

2266. Joyner, Charles W. "Soul Food and the Sambo

Stereotype: Foodlore from the Slave Narrative Collection," KFQ (W, 1971), 16: 171-178.

2267. Kawamoto, Fumi. "Folk Beliefs among Japanese in the Los Angeles Area," WF (Jan, 1962), 21: 13-26. 216 folk beliefs with explanatory comments; informants listed.

2268. Kell, Katherine T. "Tobacco in Folk Cures in Western Society," JAF (Apr. Je, 1965), 78: 99-114.

2269. Ketner, Kenneth L. "Superstitious Pigeons, Hydrophobia, and Conventional Wisdom," WF (Jan, 1971), 30: 1-18. Analysis of "superstitious"; account of a madstone cure.

2270. Koch, Edwin E. "G.I. Lore; Lore of the Fifteenth Air Force," NYFQ (Spr, 1953), 9: 59-70. Eight superstitions from the 485th Heavy Bomb Group.

2271. Koch, William E. "Hunting Beliefs and Customs from Kansas," WF (Jl, 1965), 24: 165-175. Some 200 items relating to animals, birds, and hunting practices.

2272. Kordal, Leland. Natural Folk Remedies (New York: Putnam, 1974), 284pp.

2273. Labarbera, Michel. "An Ounce of Prevention, and Grandma Tried Them All," NYFQ (Je, 1964), 20: 126-129. Family folk remedies and their efficacy.

2274. Lathrop, Amy. "Pioneer Remedies from Western Kansas," WF (Jan, 1961), 20: 1-22. Common remedies many of which seem to have neither rhyme nor reason.

2275. Lawson, O. G. and Kenneth W. Porter. "Texas Poltergeist," JAF (Oct-Dec, 1951), 64: 371-382. A tale from the Humble Oil Company records.

2276. Lestz, Gerald S. "How Much Snow Next Winter?" KFQ (A, 1961), 6: iii, 12-14. Goose bones, onion skins, the size of icicles may predict the duration of winter.

2277. Lett, Anna. "Some West Tennessee Superstitions
       about Conjurers, Witches, Ghosts, and the Devil,"
       TFSB (Je, 1970), 36: 37-45. Collected from a
       Negro sorceress.

2278. Linton, Ralph and Adeline Linton. Halloween Through
       Twenty Centuries (New York: Henry Schuman,
       1950), 108pp.

2279. Long, Eleanor R. "Aphrodisiacs, Charms, and
       Philtres," WF (Jl, 1973), 32: 153-163. Examin-
       ation of belief that such items can bring about
       sexual complaisance.

2280. Long, Grady M. "Folk Customs in Southeast Ten-
       nessee," TFSB (Dec, 1961), 27: 76-84. Agri-
       cultural practices and beliefs, especially in re-
       gard to planting crops.

2281. _____. "Folk Medicine in McMinn, Polk, Bradley,
       and Meigs Counties, Tennessee, 1910-1927,"
       TFSB (Mr, 1962), 28: 1-8. Herbal remedies,
       potions, teas, etc.

2282. Lyman, Thomas G., Jr. "Water Dowsing as a Sur-
       viving Folk Tradition," KFQ (S, 1967), 12: 133-
       142. Methods of dowsing described and attitudes
       discussed. Bibliography.

2283. McAtee, W. L. "Home Medication in Grant County,
       Indiana, in the 'Nineties'," MF (W, 1955), 5:
       213-216. Cf. supplement, MF (F, 1958), 8:
       151-153.

2284. _____. "Some Folklore of Grant County, Indiana,
       in the Nineties," MF (W, 1951), 1: 243-267.
       Games, ditties, sayings, superstitions, etc.

2285. McKinney, Ida Mae. "Superstitions of the Missouri
       Ozarks," TFSB (Dec, 1952), 18: 104-109. Su-
       perstitions about the weather, farming, medicine,
       courtship, salt.

2286. McLean, Patricia S. "Conjure Doctors in Eastern
       North Carolina," NCarF (Feb, 1972), 20: 21-29.

2287. McNeil, Brownie. "Curanderos of South Texas," in

And Horns on the Toads, ed. Mody C. Boatright
et al., pp. 32-44. Belief in folk healing remains
prevalent although methods may vary.

2288. Maley, Suzanne. "North Carolina Animal and Weather
       Superstitions," NCarFJ (Feb, 1974), 22: 21-25.
       Some 82 rural beliefs from college students.

2289. Métraux, Alfred. Voodoo in Haiti (New York:
       Schocken, 1972), 426pp., trans. by Hugo Char-
       teris. Extensive treatment of origins of voodoo,
       its relationship to artistic expression, the atti-
       tudes of the populace toward it.

2290. Meyer, Clarence. American Folk Medicine (New
       York: Crowell, 1973), 296pp. Beliefs and prac-
       tices.

2291. Miles, Elton R. "Christ in the Big Bend," in Mes-
       quite and Willow, ed. Mody C. Boatright et al.,
       pp. 171-179. Christ vs. the Devil on the Texas-
       Mexican frontier.

2292. _____. "The Devil in the Big Bend," in Folk
       Travelers, ed. Mody C. Boatright et al., pp.
       205-216. Devil lore from La Junta at confluence
       of Conchos and Rio Grande.

2293. Monteiro, Lois. "Nursing Lore," NYFQ (Je, 1973),
       29: 121-130. Beliefs prevalent among nurses and
       to some extent found in hospitals generally.
       Author a nurse.

2294. Montell, Lynwood. "Death Beliefs from the Kentucky
       Foothills," KFR (Jl-Sept, 1966), 12: 81-86.
       Some 63 beliefs collected from Eastern Kentucky.

2295. Moody, Clara Moore. "Some Folk Beliefs and Su-
       perstitions," MFR (1967), 1: 25-33.

2296. Mook, Maurice A. "Quaker Campus Lore," NYFQ
       (W, 1961), 17: 243-252. Amusing anecdotes
       from Haverford, Swarthmore, Pendle Hill, and
       Westtown.

2297. Morton, Julia F. Folk Remedies of the Low Coun-
       try (Miami: E. A. Seamann, 1974), 176pp.
       Folk cures in use in the U.S. today.

2298. Mullen, Patrick B. "Department Store Snakes," IF (1970), 3: 214-228.

2299. _____. "The Function of Folk Belief among Negro Fishermen of the Texas Coast," SFQ (Je, 1969), 33: 80-91.

2300. _____. "The Function of Magic Folk Belief among Texas Coastal Fishermen," JAF (Jl-Sept, 1969), 82: 214-225. Customs, beliefs, taboos considered.

2301. Mullins, Gladys. "Herbs of the Southern Highlands and Their Medicinal Uses," KFR (Apr-Je, 1973), 19: 36-41. 22 plants found in Pike Co., Kentucky.

2302. Murphy, Charles H. "A Collection of Birth Marking Beliefs from Eastern Kentucky," KFR (Apr-Je, 1964), 10: 36-38. Evidence from the author's own family.

2303. Musick, Ruth Anne. "Omens and Tokens of West Virginia," MF (W, 1952), 2: 263-267.

2304. _____. "Witchcraft and the Devil in West Virginia," AJ (Spr, 1974), 1: 271-276. Accounts of the evil eye, witchcraft, and confrontations with the Devil.

2305. Naff, Alixia. "Belief in the Evil Eye among the Christian Syrian-Lebanese in America," JAF (Jan-Mr, 1965), 78: 46-51.

2306. Neighbors, Keith A. "Mexican-American Folk Diseases," WF (Oct, 1969), 28: 249-259. Some Californians believe in the skill of curanderos in controlling the evil eye, empacho (indigestion), etc.

2307. Newman, Lucile F. "Folklore of Pregnancy: Wives' Tales in Contra Costa County, California," WF (Apr, 1969), 28: 112-135. Pregnancy beliefs of Negro and white women, "signs" against "magic."

2308. Norris, Ruby R. "Folk Medicine of Cumberland County," KFR (Jl-Sept, 1958), 4: 101-110. Miscellaneous cures.

2309. Odell, Ruth W. "Before You Call the Doctor," TSFB (Je, 1951), 17: 29-31. Home cures.

2310. _____. "Mid-Western Saliva Lore," SFQ (Dec, 1950), 14: 220-223. Cures, sayings, charms, superstitions relating to saliva (fishing, for example).

2311. Opler, Marvin K. "Japanese Folk Beliefs and Practices, Tule Lake, California," JAF (Oct-Dec, 1950), 63: 385-397. Omens, taboos, beliefs, legends.

2312. Owens, William A. "Seer of Corsicana," in And Horns on the Toads, ed. Mody C. Boatright et al., pp. 14-31. Account of visit to Annie Buchanan, clairvoyant Negress.

2313. Parkinson, John, Jr. "Outwitting Davy Jones," Yachting (Mr, 1959), 105: iii, 80-81, 127. Common sea superstitions relating to wind, whistling women, witches, cats.

2314. Parr, Jerry S. "Folk Cures of Middle Tennessee," TFSB (Mr, 1962), 28: 8-12. Panaceas for some 25 ailments.

2315. Parsely, Coy Harlan. "Ollie Oddities: Folklore of a Kentucky Ridge," KFR (Jl-Sept, 1955), 1: 61-79. Superstitions, cures, witchcraft, etc.

2316. Paulsen, Frank M. "A Hair of the Dog and Some Other Hangover Cures from Popular Tradition," JAF (Apr-Je, 1961), 74: 152-168. Amazing number of suggested cures, gathered largely from Detroit bars.

2317. Pearce, T. M. "The Bad Son (El Mal Hijo) in Southwestern Spanish Folklore," WF (Oct, 1950), 9: 295-301. Bad son theme is preserved in stories told for moral reasons or as an example of divine wrath.

2317a. Pelton, Robert M. Voodoo Charms and Talismans (New York: Drake Pub., 1973), 220pp.

2318. Penrod, James H. "Folk Beliefs About Work,

Trades, and Professions from New Mexico," WF
(Jl, 1968), 27: 180-183. Some 57 beliefs from
the sea, the rodeo, the theater.

2319. Pérez, Soledad. "Mexican Folklore from Austin,
Texas," in The Healer of Los Olmos, ed. Wilson
M. Hudson, pp. 71-127. Ghost, devil, buried
treasure tales, etc. collected from Mexican informants in 1948-1949. Also some proverbs and
riddles.

2320. Periman, Kenneth I. "Don Cacahuate to La Bruja:
Hispanic Folklore of the Four Corners," WR (W,
1969), 6: 64-70. Beliefs, tales, anecdotes from
the corner of New Mexico and Colorado.

2321. Peterson, Tracey. "The Witch of Franklin," SFQ
(Dec, 1969), 33: 297-312. Divination, hoodoo,
spells, cures associated with a maternal ancestor.

2322. Pope, Genevieve. "Superstitions and Beliefs of
Fleming County," KFR (Jl-Sept, 1965), 11: 41-
51. Beliefs about children, foods, cures, etc.

2323. Pound, Louise. "The John G. Maher Hoaxes," NH
(Dec, 1952), 33: 203-219. Tales about a petri-
fied man, a soda spring, an alkali lake monster
perpetrated by an early Nebraska politician and
newspaperman.

2324. Powe, Marilyn. "Black 'Isms,'" MFR (F, 1972),
6: 76-82. Some 200 beliefs gathered from Mississippi Negroes (dreams, bad luck, death signs,
predictions).

2325. Radbill, Samuel X. "The Folklore of Teething,"
KFQ (W, 1964), 9: 123-143. Sampling of world-
wide beliefs.

2326. Randolph, Vance. "Fabulous Monsters of the Ozarks,"
AHQ (S, 1950), 9: 65-75. Amusing essay introducing the gowrow, snawfus, pimplicute, king-
doodle, etc.

2327. _____. "Nakedness in Ozark Folk Belief," JAF
(Oct-Dec, 1953), 66: 333-339. Nudity in the
Ozarks is disapproved save in magic and folk
religion.

2328. Rayburn, Otto Ernest. "Animal Wisdom in the
      Ozarks," SFQ (Dec, 1954), 18: 239-241. Beaver,
      crow, rooster, fox, squirrel, dove, and wild tur-
      key.

2329. _____. "Some Fabulous Monsters and Other Folk
      Beliefs from the Ozarks," MF (Spr, 1960), 10:
      27-32.

2330. Reecer, Kathleen. "Folklore in Graves County,"
      KFR (Oct-Dec, 1959), 5: 121-126. Anecdotes,
      cures, and superstitions from a Kentucky county.

2331. Rice, George W. and David F. Jacobs. "Saltpeter:
      a Folkloric Adjustment to Acculturation Stress,"
      WF (Jl, 1973), 32: 164-179. Discussion of the
      belief that saltpeter (potassium nitrate) serves
      as a sexual depressant.

2332. Riddick, Thomas M. "Dowsing Is Nonsense," HM
      (Jl, 1951), 203: 62-68. A professional engineer
      ridicules claims for the validity of dowsing.

2333. Robacker, Earl F. "Long-Lost Friend," NYFQ (Spr,
      1956), 12: 25-31. Pennsylvania Dutch black and
      white magic.

2334. Roberts, Kenneth L. Henry Gross and His Dowsing
      Rod (Garden City: Doubleday, 1951), 310pp. A
      well known novelist expresses his faith in dowsing.

2335. Rogers, E. G. "Some Animal Superstitions from
      Marshall County, Tennessee," SFQ (Dec, 1954),
      18: 233-238. Some 155 superstitions collected
      by high school students in 1934-1936: weather,
      sickness, courtship and marriage, luck, taboos,
      death.

2336. Ryan, Lawrence V. "Some Czech-American Forms
      of Divination and Supplication," JAF (Jl-Sept,
      1956), 69: 281-285. Evidence of survivals of
      Czech beliefs and practices in Iowa and Minne-
      sota.

2337. Saucier, Corinne L. Traditions de la Paroisse des
      Avoyelles en Louisiane (Philadelphia: Am. Folk-
      lore Soc., 1956), vii, 162pp. Historical and

economic data plus oral traditions. Careful in-
clusive study.

2338. Sayre, Robert F. "Vision and Experience in Black
       Elk Speaks," CE (Feb, 1971), 32: 509-535. Auto-
       biography of an Oglala Sioux medicine man as
       rendered by John G. Neihardt.

2339. Schedler, Paul W. "Folk Medicine in Denton County
       Today; or, Can Dermatology Displace Dishrags?"
       in Hunters & Healers, ed. Wilson M. Hudson,
       pp. 11-17. Most home remedies don't work.

2340. Schwartz, Alvin. Cross Your Fingers, Spit in Your
       Hat (Philadelphia: Lippincott, 1974), 161pp. List
       of familiar superstitions.

2341. Scully, Virginia. A Treasury of American Indian
       Herbs: Their Lore and Their Use for Food,
       Drugs, and Medicine (New York: Crown, 1970),
       xiv, 306pp.

2342. Sears, Jean Sarrazin. "A Garland of Louisiana Wart
       Cures," LFM (Apr, 1971), 3: 27-33.

2343. Shaner, Richard H. "Recollections of Witchcraft in
       the Oley Hills," PF (Folk Festival Supplement,
       1972), 21: 39-42. Comments on witchcraft,
       hexes, etc.

2344. Shepard, Brooks. "Firsthand Report on Dowsing,"
       HM (Sept, 1951), 203: 69-75. A modified belief
       in the validity of dowsing.

2345. Shoemaker, Henry W. "The Ghost of the Buckhorn,"
       NYFQ (S, 1950), 6: 82-85. A ghost story in Al-
       toona, Penn., turns out to be a hoax.

2346. _____. "Neighbors: The Werewolf in Pennsyl-
       vania," NYFQ (S, 1951), 7: 145-155.

2347. Sloane, Eric. Folklore of American Weather (New
       York: Duell, Sloan & Pearce, 1963), 63pp.

2348. Smith, Grace Partridge. "Negro Lore in Southern
       Illinois," MF (F, 1952), 2: 159-162. Some 28
       omens, tokens, superstitions.

2349. Smith, M. Estellie. "Folk Medicine among the
        Sicilian-Americans of Buffalo, New York," UA
        (Spr, 1972), 1: 87-106. Traditional elements in
        the native pharmacopeia have been eliminated but
        supernatural elements remain.

2350. Snellenburg, Betty. "Four Interviews with Pow-
        wowers," PF (S, 1969), 18: iv, 40-45. Discus-
        sion of charms, procedures, and success in
        treatment.

2351. Snow, Loudell F. "'I Was Born Just Exactly with
        the Gift,'" JAF (Jl-Sept, 1973), 86: 272-281.
        Profile of a black woman in a Southwestern city
        who is a practicing folk healer and who believes
        she inherited voodoo power from her grandmother.

2352. Snyder, Perry A. "Remedies of the Piney Woods
        Pioneer," MFR (Spr, 1973), 7: 11-14. Back-
        woods Mississippi cures for 17 ailments.

2353. Spears, James E. "Negro Folk Maternal-Natal Care,
        Practices, and Remedies: a Glossary," MFR
        (Spr, 1971), 5: 19-22. Data from a Negro mid-
        wife.

2354. _____. "Some Negro Folk Pregnancy Euphemisms
        and Birth Superstitions," MFR (Spr, 1970), 4:
        24-27.

2355. Splitter, Henry Winfred. "New Tales of American
        Phantom Ships," WF (Jl, 1950), 9: 201-216.
        Five tales of ships, one on L. Erie, one on
        Devil's L., No. Dak.

2356. Steese, Charles. "Hoopsnakes and Huckleberries,"
        KFQ (F, 1956), 1: 33-36. Accounts of hoop-
        snakes in Penn. tales.

2357. Stekert, Ellen J. "Focus for Conflict: Southern
        Mountain Medical Beliefs in Detroit," JAF (Apr-
        Je, 1970), 83: 115-147. Folk medicine and be-
        liefs about birth and infancy gathered from South-
        ern mountain women in Detroit.

2358. Stephens, Claude E. "Witching for Water in Ore-
        gon," WF (Jl, 1952), 11: 204-207. Miscellaneous
        details about Oregon dowsing.

2359. Stewart, Kenneth M. "The Owl in Mohave Indian
        Culture," AFFword (Oct, 1972), 2: 17-23. Owls
        are associated with witchcraft and stimulate many
        beliefs.

2360. _____. "Witchcraft among the Mohave Indians,"
        Ethnology (Jl, 1973), 12: 315-324. Witchcraft
        is a waning belief in this tribe.

2361. Stuart, Jesse. "New Wine in Old Bottles," KFR (Oct-
        Dec, 1966), 12: 105-107. Kentucky folk medicine
        and traditional therapy. Cf. sequel in KFR (Jan-
        Mr, 1967), 13: 20-24.

2362. Tally, Frances. "American Folk Customs of Court-
        ship and Marriage: the Bedroom," in Forms upon
        the Frontier, ed. Austin Fife et al., pp. 138-158.

2363. Tanner, Jeri. "The Teeth in Folklore," WF (Apr,
        1968), 27: 97-105. Dental lore from many coun-
        tries and periods.

2364. Tantaquidgeon, Gladys. Folk Medicine of the Dela-
        ware and Related Algonquin Indians (Harrisburg,
        Penn.: Penn. Historical and Museum Commis-
        sion, 1972), vi, 145pp.

2365. Taylor, Dorothy Bright. "Indian Medicinal Herbs
        and the White Man's Medicine," NYFQ (Dec,
        1967), 23: 264-273. Mostly Iroquois practices.

2366. Taylor, Walter. "Home Remedies for Arthritis,"
        in Mesquite and Willow, ed. Mody C. Boatright
        et al., pp. 192-200. Remedies from Texas.

2367. Terbovich, John B. "Religious Folklore among the
        German-Russians in Ellis County, Kansas," WF
        (Apr, 1963), 22: 79-88. Superstitions and be-
        liefs collected from German-Russian Catholics
        and linked chiefly with Easter and Christmas.

2368. Thompson, Lawrence S. "Hogs in Ohio Valley
        Superstition," KFR (Oct-Dec, 1964), 10: 59-61.

2369. _____. "The Moon in Kentucky and Elsewhere,"
        KFR (Jan-Mr, 1973), 19: 7-10. Moon-related
        beliefs about planting and behavior from Kentucky
        Negroes.

2370. _____. "Some Notes on the Folklore of Tobacco
       and Smoking," KFR (Jl-Sept, 1964), 10: 43-46.

2371. _____. "A Vanishing Science," KFR (Jl-Sept,
       1959), 5: 95-105. The richness of Kentucky folk
       medicine.

2372. Touchstone, Blake. "Voodoo in New Orleans," LH
       (F, 1972), 13: 371-386. Brief account of voo-
       dooism and attempts to suppress it.

2373. Viitanen, Wayne. "Folklore and Fakelore of an
       Earthquake," KFR (Oct-Dec, 1973), 19: 99-111.
       Careful examination of history of New Madrid
       earthquake, 1811-1812, and separation of factual
       record from fakelore associated with it.

2374. Vogel, Virgil J. American Indian Medicine (Norman:
       U. of Oklahoma P., 1970), 583pp. Discussion of
       shamanism, theories of disease, folk medicine,
       etc.

2375. Vogt, Evon Z. and Peggy Golde. "Some Aspects of
       the Folklore of Water Witching in the United
       States," JAF (Oct-Dec, 1958), 71: 519-531.

2376. _____ and Ray Hyman. Water Witching U.S.A.
       (Chicago: U. of Chicago P., 1959), xi, 248pp.
       Study of motivation and practice of dowsing.
       Some 25,000 diviners are apparently active in
       U.S.

2377. Walker, Deward E., Jr. "Nez Perce Sorcery,"
       Ethnology (Jan, 1967), 6: 66-96. Informants
       over fifty years of age confirmed earlier beliefs
       in sorcery but only a minority of Indians of this
       tribe accept it today.

2378. Walker, John. "A Sampling of Folklore from Ruther-
       ford County [N.C.]," NCF (Dec, 1955), 3: 6-16.
       Principally superstitions and beliefs.

2379. Walker, Warren S. "Water Witching in Central
       Illinois," MF (W, 1956), 6: 197-203. Beliefs
       and methods described.

2380. Waller, Tom and Gene Killion. "Georgia Folk Medi-

cine," SFQ (Mr, 1972), 36: 71-92.   Folk remedies
compiled from Georgia Writers' Project papers.

2381.   Wallrich, William Jones.   "Some Variants of the
'Demon Dancer,'" WF (Apr, 1950), 9: 144-146.
Some San Luis Valley tales of a girl who
danced with the Devil.

2382.   _____.   "Spanish American Devil Lore in Southern
Colorado," WF (Jan, 1950), 9: 50-55.   Twelve
tales about El Diablo and brujas (witches) in San
Luis Valley collected in 1949.

2383.   _____.   "Superstition and the Air Force," WF
(Jan, 1960), 19: 11-16.   Material collected from
personal experience in two wars.

2384.   Webb, Hilda.   "Water Witching as Part of Folklife
in Southern Indiana," JFI (Je, 1966), 3: 10-29.
Beliefs in dowsing, cures, and healing.

2385.   Weiner, Harvey.   "Folklore in the Los Angeles Gar-
ment Industry," WF (Jan, 1964), 23: 17-21.   Discussion of customs and beliefs of Europeans work-
ing in Los Angeles.

2386.   Welch, Charles E., Jr.   "Some Drugs of the North
American Indian--Then and Now," KFQ (F, 1964),
9: 83-99.   Some 25 drugs utilized by Indians;
their value discussed.

2387.   Wellborn, Grace Pleasant.   "The Magic Art of Removing Warts," in Singers and Storytellers, ed.
Mody C. Boatright et al., pp. 205-211.   A healer in Wise Co., Texas.

2388.   Welsch, Roger L.   "'We Are What We Eat':   Omaha
Food as Symbol," KFQ (W, 1971), 16: 165-170.
Food habits and beliefs of an Indian tribe.

2389.   Welsh, Jack.   "The Bell Witch," KFR (Oct-Dec,
1973), 19: 112-116.   Interviews with the descend-
ants of the Bell family of Tenn. confirm the
familiar witch story.

2390.   Westermeier, Thérèse S.   "Old-Time Commercial
Cure-Alls," WF (Oct, 1953), 12: 257-265.   Newspaper ads 1881-1898 ballyhooed patent medicines.

2391. Westkott, Marcia. "Powwowing in Berks County,"
PF (W, 1969-1970), 19: ii, 2-9. Rural beliefs
in healing in Penn.

2392. Whitehurst, Bruce W. "Plant and Animal Husbandry
Beliefs from Daughtry's Crossroads," NCarFJ
(Feb, 1974), 22: 9-14. Some 54 specific beliefs
from one family.

2393. Whiting, Beatrice B. Paiute Sorcery (New York:
Viking Fund Publications in Anthropology, No.
15, 1950), 110pp.

2394. Whitten, Norman E., Jr. "Contemporary Patterns
of Malign Occultism among Negroes in North
Carolina," JAF (Oct-Dec, 1962), 75: 311-325.
Evidence field-collected to support contention that
Negroes believe in maleficia.

2395. Whittlesey, Wes. "On the Etiology of Werewolves,"
NYFQ (Dec, 1966), 22: 261-268. Survey of beliefs in werewolves with suggestion that a medical
disease called prophyria develops from symptoms
associated with lycanthropy.

2396. _____. "The Ritual of the Surgical Scrub," NYFQ
(Je, 1964), 20: 122-125. Survey of practical and
symbolic reasons for handwashing prior to opera-
tions.

2397. Wilgus, D. K. "The Girl in the Window," WF (Oct,
1970), 29: 251-256. Local variants of tale about
a girl's image on glass.

2398. Williams, Cratis D. "Lawrence County Superstitions:
Pregnancy, Childbirth, and Infancy," KFR (Oct-
Dec, 1956), 2: 137-140. Twenty-five examples.

2399. Wilson, Eddie W. "The Onion in Folk Belief," WF
(Apr, 1953), 12: 94-104. Weather, agricultural,
and medical beliefs.

2400. _____. "Some American Fishing Superstitions,"
MF (W, 1955), 5: 217-220. A sampling of common beliefs.

2401. _____. "The Spider and the American Indian,"

WF (Oct, 1951), 10: 290-297.   Indians appreciate
the cleverness and helpfulness of spiders; they
appear in creation stories, myth, magic, and
medicine.

2402.   Wine, Martin L.   "Superstitions Collected in Chicago, "
MF (F, 1957), 7: 149-159.   Some 175 items from
Austin High School.

2403.   Winkler, Louis and Carol Winkler.   "A Reappraisal
of the Vampire, " NYFQ (Sept, 1973), 29: 194-
205.   Superficial survey of beliefs about vampires,
considered more formidable than ghosts, witches,
or demons.

2404.   Winslow, David J.   "Occupational Superstitions of
Negro Prostitutes in an Upstate New York City, "
NYFQ (Dec, 1968), 24: 294-301.   From Saratoga
Springs, N. Y.

2405.   Wolf, John Quincy.   "Two Folk Scientists in Action, "
TSFB (Mr, 1969), 35: 6-10.   Chiefly a discussion
of water witching and cures for warts.

2406.   Wright, Lillian Mayfield.   "Mountain Medicine, "
NCarF (Jl, 1964), 12: 7-12.   Reminiscences
about cures, beliefs, superstitions prevalent in
the mountains.

11.   FOLK HEROES

2407.   Abrahams, Roger D.   "The Changing Concept of the Negro Hero," in The Golden Log, ed. Mody C. Boatright et al., pp. 119-134.   The bad man has replaced the trickster as the hero of American Negro folklore.

2408.   _____.   "Some Varieties of Heroes in America," JFI (Dec, 1966), 3: 341-362.   Definition and description of folk hero; types distinguished, sometimes fuzzily.

2409.   _____.   "Trickster, the Outrageous Hero," in Our Living Traditions, ed. Tristram P. Coffin, pp. 170-178.   Brief account of character of Trickster, with examples from Negro and No. American Indian tales.

2410.   Adams, Ramon F.   A Fitting Death for Billy the Kid (Norman: U. of Oklahoma P., 1960), ix, 310pp. Analysis of the material published about Billy the Kid.

2411.   Adams, Samuel Hopkins.   Grandfather Stories (New York: Random House, 1955), 312pp.   Tales of Erie Canal, Sam Patch, etc.

2412.   Adler, Alfred,   "Billy the Kid: A Case Study in Epic Origins," WF (Apr, 1951), 10: 143-152. With some wrenching of evidence Billy the Kid fits into Lord Raglan's type of legendary hero.

2413.   Anderson, John Q.   "Belle Starr and the Biscuit Dough," in Singers and Storytellers, ed. Mody C. Boatright et al., pp. 156-165.   Data about a notorious woman bandit.

2414.   Ashabranner, Brent.   "Pecos Bill--An Appraisal,"

WF (Jan, 1952), 11: 20-24. E. J. O'Reilly invented Pecos Bill in Century Magazine article in
1923.

2415. Ball, Larry D. "Black Jack Ketchum; the Birth of a
Folk Hero," MSF (Spr, 1973), 1: 19-25. Ketchum, a Texas-New Mexico outlaw executed in 1901,
is remembered by the folk as a Robin Hood type
and personally attractive.

2416. Barrick, Mac E. "Lewis the Robber in Life and
Legend," PF (A, 1967), 17: i, 10-13. David
Lewis (1790-1820) was a Robin Hood type of hero
in central Penn.

2417. Beath, Paul S. Febold Feboldson: Tall Tales from
the Great Plains (Lincoln: U. of Nebraska P.,
1962), xi, 138pp. Good example of what Richard
Dorson calls fakelore.

2418. Beck, E. C. They Knew Paul Bunyan (Ann Arbor:
U. of Michigan P., 1956), 255pp. Little about
Paul Bunyan but a host of logging lore, chiefly
from Michigan.

2419. Beck, Horace P. "The Making of the Popular Legendary Hero," in American Folk Legend, ed.
Wayland D. Hand, pp. 121-132. Examples:
Ethan Allen, Davy Crockett, Joshua Barney (naval
hero).

2420. Benson, Ivan. Paul Bunyan and His Men (Rutland:
Charles E. Tuttle, 1955), 231pp. More about
Paul's men than about Paul Bunyan and much of
it the author's fancy.

2421. Bentley, James M. "William F. Cody, Buffalo Bill,
an Iowa-born Folk Hero," AnI (W, 1968), 39:
161-168. Biographical sketch primarily.

2422. Blair, Walter and Franklin J. Meine. Half Horse
Half Alligator: the Growth of the Mike Fink Legend (Chicago: U. of Chicago P., 1956), ix,
289pp. Documents about and allusions to the
famous river boatman.

2423. Boatright, Mody C. "The American Myth Rides the

Range; Owen Wister's Man on Horseback," SWR
(S, 1951), 36: 157-163.

2424. _____. "The American Rodeo," AQ (S, 1964), 16:
195-202. Excellent account of transformation of
cowboy into folk hero: historical data about cowboys.

2425. _____. "The Formula in Cowboy Fiction and
Drama," WF (Apr, 1966), 18: 135-145. Article
based on movies, books, pulp magazines. Author
identifies seven standard plot types.

2426. _____. "The Morality Play on Horseback: Tom
Mix," in Tire Shrinker to Dragster, ed. Wilson
M. Hudson, pp. 63-71. A Western movie star
and his horse helped to establish a stereotype.

2427. _____. "The Oil Promoter as Trickster," in
Singers and Storytellers, ed. Mody C. Boatright
et al., pp. 76-91. The trickster is a familiar
figure in all cultures; at the beginning of the twentieth century he was often an oil promoter.

2428. _____. "The Petroleum Geologist: A Folk
Image," in The Golden Log, ed. Mody C. Boatright et al., pp. 58-72. The geologist or rock
hound becomes a folk figure.

2429. _____. "The Western Bad Man as Hero," in
Mesquite and Willow, ed. Mody C. Boatright et
al., pp. 96-104. Criteria for western bad men
with examples.

2430. Bock, Dean Frederic. "Huckleberry Charlie and
Nick the Fiddler," NYFQ (S, 1952), 8: 92-103.
Anecdotes about two minor folk heroes from
vicinity of Watertown, N.Y.

2431. Braddy, Haldeen. Cock-of-the-Walk, Qui-Qui-Ri-Qui!
the Legend of Pancho Villa (Albuquerque: U. of
New Mexico P., 1955), 174pp. Life of Pancho
Villa stressing his quest for violence, women,
and gold.

2432. _____. "Dorotello Arango, alias Pancho Villa,"
NMFR (1949-1950), 5: 4-8. Facts and rumors

about Arango, who rebaptized himself Pancho
Villa.

2433. _____. "Myths of Pershing's Mexican Campaign,"
SFQ (Je, 1963), 27: 181-195. Stories and quotations from Mexican corridos about Pancho Villa
and Pershing.

2434. Brent, William. The Complete and Factual Life of
Billy the Kid (New York: Frederick Fell, 1964),
ix, 213pp. A romantic figure reduced to a con-
scienceless killer.

2435. Brooks, John Lee. "Paul Bunyan: Oil Man," in
Texas Folk and Folklore, ed. Mody C. Boatright
et al., pp. 315-322. Brooks worked in Texas
oil fields and heard transplanted Paul Bunyan
tales.

2436. Browne, Ray B. et al., eds. Heroes of Popular
Culture (Bowling Green, Ohio: Bowling Green U.
Popular P., 1972), 190pp. Miscellaneous es-
says on folk and popular heroes.

2437. Brunvand, Jan Harold. "Len Henry: North Idaho
Münchausen," NWF (S, 1965), 1: 11-19. Data
about an Idaho squawman (1852?-1946), notable
for tall tales. Eight printed.

2438. Byington, Robert H. "The Frontier Hero: Refine-
ment and Definition, in Singers and Storytellers, ed.
Mody C. Boatright et al., pp. 140-155. Attempt
to identify the archetypal frontier hero by Cain
motifs, Ishmael motifs, Hamlet motifs, etc.

2439. Byrne, Clifford. "Jesse James: Folk Hero," TFSB
(Sept, 1954), 20: 47-52. Jesse James considered as a hero to die-hard Confederates.

2440. Cawelti, John G. "Cowboys, Indians, Outlaws," AW
(Spr, 1964), 1: ii, 28-35, 77-79. Brief study
of the cowboy image. A Stephen Crane story
sums up the myth of the West.

2441. Chamberlain, Robert F. "The Febold Feboldson
Legend," NH (Je, 1952), 33: 95-102.

2442. Clare, Warren. "The Slide-Rock Bolter, Splinter
       Cats and Paulski Bunyanovitch," Idaho Yesterdays
       (F, 1971), 6: 245-250. Deals with the James
       Stevens stories about Paul Bunyan.

2443. Corle, Edwin. "Billy the Kid in Arizona," AH (Feb,
       1954), 30: 34-35. Folklore versions of alleged
       killings by Billy in Arizona.

2444. Cray, Ed. "The Rabbi Trickster," JAF (Oct-Dec.,
       1964), 77: 331-345. Jewish anecdotal folklore
       pits Jewish rationalism against Catholic and Prot-
       estant dogmatism.

2445. Davis, David B. "Ten-Gallon Hero," AQ (S, 1954),
       6: 111-125. Excellent composite portrait of cow-
       boy hero: physical traits, idealized traits.

2446. De Nio, Pierre. "A Delaware River Raftsman,"
       NYFQ (W, 1960), 16: 287-294. Data about
       George (Boney) Quillen (1845-1918), raftsman,
       soldier, jester.

2447. Dobie, J. Frank. The Ben Lily Legend (Boston:
       Little, Brown, 1950), xv, 237pp.

2448. _____. "Coyote, Hero-God and Trickster," SWR
       (A, 1967), 32: 336-344. A paean to the coyote
       with two tales from Indian mythology to confirm
       the tribute.

2449. Dorson, Richard M. "The Career of 'John Henry.'"
       WF (Jl, 1965), 24: 155-163. Helpful study of
       the ramifications of the John Henry story in
       balladry and song.

2450. _____. "Cowboy Folktales about Cowboys," SAV
       (1972-1973), 68-69, 72-82.

2451. _____. "Folklore and Fakelore," AM (Mr, 1950),
       70: 335-343. Famous article which scorns syn-
       thetic folk heroes like Paul Bunyan and pleads
       for collecting folklore with an oral viability.
       Dorson attacks James Stephens and B. A. Botkin.

2452. _____. "Mishaps of a Maine Lobsterman," NEF
       (Spr, 1958), 1: 1-7. Stories from Curt Morse,
       a local raconteur.

2453. _____. "Paul Bunyan in the News," WF (Jan, Jl, Oct, 1956), 15: 26-39, 179-193, 247-261. Material from a clipping bureau supporting Dorson's contention that Bunyan is the "pseudo folk hero of twentieth-century mass culture."

2454. _____. "The Sources of Davy Crockett, American Comic Legend," MF (F, 1958), 8: 143-149.

2455. DuBose, Robert W., Jr. "Updating the Cowboy," SFQ (Sept, 1962), 26: 187-197. The cowboy as he is in history, myth, and the cinema. The cowboy is a hero, not a god.

2456. Durham, Philip. "The Cowboy and the Myth Makers," JPC (S, 1967), 1: 58-62. Facts about cowboy history, then a survey of the writers who idealized him. Today the six gun is a sex gun and the horse a phallic symbol.

2457. _____. "The Lost Cowboy," MJ (S, 1955), 7: 176-182. Brief account of Negro cowboy.

2458. _____ and Everett L. Jones. The Negro Cowboys (New York: Dodd, Mead, 1965), x, 278pp. Negroes did exist in the cattle kingdom.

2459. Dykes, J. C. Billy the Kid: the Bibliography of a Legend (Albuquerque: U. of New Mex. P., 1952), 186pp. Some 437 items (books, articles, ballads, plays, records) about Billy the Kid (1859-1881).

2460. Felton, Harold W. Fire-Fightin' Mose (New York: Knopf, 1955), 173pp. Foreword by B. A. Botkin. Juvenile.

2460a. _____. John Henry and His Hammer (New York: Knopf, 1950), 82pp. Juvenile.

2461. Fife, Austin and Alta Fife. "Spurs and Saddlebags," AW (Sept, 1970), 7: v, 44-47. Compact, informative article on cowboys with incidental folklore.

2462. Figh, Margaret Gillis. "Nineteenth Century Outlaws in Alabama Folklore," SFQ (Je, 1961), 25: 126-

135.   Anecdotes about the Murrell gang, Jesse
       James, et al.

2463.   Fishwick, Marshall W.   "American Heroes: Colum-
        bia's Path," WF (Jl, 1954), 13: 153-159. Many
        American heroes were not of folk origin but were
        created by publicists.

2464.   _____. American Heroes: Myth and Reality
        (Washington: Public Affairs P., 1954), viii,
        242pp. Amorphous study of the hero type with
        examples from politics, business, and western
        life (Buffalo Bill, Daniel Boone, etc.).

2465.   _____. "Billy the Kid: Faust in America," SRL
        (Oct 11, 1952), 35: 11-12, 34-36.

2466.   _____. "The Cowboy: America's Contribution to
        the World's Mythology," WF (Apr, 1952), 11:
        77-92. General data about cowboy plus survey
        of writers like Owen Wister and Zane Grey.

2467.   _____. The Hero, American Style (New York:
        McKay, 1969), vii, 270pp. Series of popular es-
        says on various kinds of American heroes.

2468.   _____. "Paul Bunyan: the Folk Hero as Tycoon,"
        YR (W, 1952), 41: 264-274.

2469.   _____. "Sons of Paul: Folklore or Fakelore?"
        WF (Oct, 1959), 18: 277-286. Spurious folk
        heroes imitating Paul Bunyan: Pecos Bill, Joe
        Magarac, Tony Beaver.

2470.   _____. "Uncle Remus vs. John Henry: Folk
        Tension," WF (Apr, 1961), 20: 77-85. Contrast
        of two symbolic Negroes.

2471.   _____. "What Ever Happened to John Henry?"
        SHR (S, 1971), 5: 231-236. The black revolu-
        tionist has replaced John Henry as a folk hero.

2472.   Frantz, Joe B. "Cowboy Philosophy: A Cold
        Spoor," in The Frontier Reexamined, ed. John F.
        McDermott (Urbana: U. of Illinois P., 1967),
        pp. 170-180. Descriptions and interpretations
        of the cowboy supported by ample evidence.

2473. _____ and Julian Ernest Choate. The American
          Cowboy (Norman: U. of Oklahoma P., 1955),
          232pp. Full dress history of the cowboy.

2474. Friedman, Ralph. "The Montez Legend," WF (Oct
          1951), 10: 273-284. Factual data about Lola
          Montez, the most glamorous woman of northern
          California.

2475. Fulton, Maurice G. "Billy the Kid in Life and
          Books," NMFR (1949-1950), 4: 1-6. Survey of
          works about the desperado; suggestion that he
          lives in legend.

2476. Gartenberg, Max. "W. B. Laughead's Great Ad-
          vertisement," JAF (Oct-Dec, 1950), 63: 444-449.
          Laughead's advertising pamphlet about Paul Bun-
          yan's exploits.

2477. Gillis, Everett A. "The Cowboy Boast, Ballad
          Style," NMFR (1954-1955), 9: 1-3. In western
          balladry the cowboy frequently bragged like the
          backwoods roarer.

2478. Greenway, John. "Aunt Molly Jackson and Robin
          Hood: A Study in Folk Re-Creation," JAF (Jan-
          Mr, 1956), 69: 23-38. Interesting account of
          Aunt Molly's handling of Robin Hood material.

2479. Hall, C. Eleanor. "Joe Call, the Lewis Giant,"
          NYFQ (Spr, 1953), 9: 5-27. Facts and legends
          about a local lumberman and wrestler from Essex
          Co., N. Y.

2480. Hamlin, William Lee. The True Story of Billy the
          Kid (Caldwell, Idaho: Caxton Printers, 1959),
          364pp. An attempt at a documentary work into
          which romance and folklore occasionally creep.

2481. Hampton, Bill R. "On Identification and Negro
          Tricksters," SFQ (Mr, 1967), 31: 55-65. Analy-
          sis of the Negro's identification with the spider,
          rabbit, and slave John.

2482. Harrison, Lowell H. "Davy Crockett: the Making
          of a Folk Hero," KFR (Oct-Dec, 1969), 15: 87-
          90.

2483. Haverstick, John. "The Two Davy Crocketts," SR
(Jl 9, 1956), 38: xxviii, 19, 30.

2484. Hoffman, Daniel. "Folk Tales of Paul Bunyan:
Themes, Structure, Style, and Sources," WF
(Oct, 1950), 9: 302-320. Preview of 1952 book.

2485. _____. Paul Bunyan, Last of the Frontier Demi-
gods (Philadelphia: U. of Penn. P., 1952), xiv,
213pp.

2486. _____. "Robert Frost's Paul Bunyan: a Frontier
Hero in New England Exile," MF (Apr, 1951),
1: 13-18. Chiefly about Frost's poem, "Paul's
Wife."

2487. _____. "Sandburg and 'The People': His Literary
Populism Reappraised," AR (S, 1950), 10: 265-
278. Paul Bunyan as an incongruous folk symbol.

2488. Hoig, Stan. The Humor of the American Cowboy
(Caldwell, Idaho: Caxton Printers, 1958), Re-
printed 1970 (U. of Nebraska Press), 193pp.
Tall tales, yarns, incidents.

2489. Hutchinson, W. H. "The Caesarean Delivery of Paul
Bunyan," WF (Jan, 1963), 22: 1-15. Mostly an
interview with W. H. Laughead, author of advertising pamphlets.

2490. Jackson, Bruce. "Stagolee Stories: a Badman Goes
Gentle," SFQ (Sept, 1965), 29: 228-233. Stories
told by John Hurt in which Stagolee becomes a
Good Guy, possibly even white.

2491. Jones, Archie H. "Cops, Robbers, Heroes and Anti-
Heroines; the American Need to Create," JPC
(F, 1967), 1: 114-127. No. American heroes,
actual and fictional, enact mythical roles.

2492. Jones, Michael Owen. "(PC plus CB) x SD (R plus
I plus E) equals Hero," NYFQ (Sept, 1971), 27:
243-260. An ingenious argument is offered to
identify a folk hero.

2493. Karni, Michael G. "Otto Walta: Finnish Folk Hero
of the Iron Range," MinnH (W, 1967), 40: 391-

402. Tall tales spliced together about a local strong man in St. Louis Co., Minn.

2494. Kavanagh, Kathleen M. "The Limited Fame of Sam Patch," NYFQ (Je, 1972), 28: 118-134. Sam Patch, a typical American comic hero, has been forgotten.

2495. Kennedy, Mary Jean. "The Gold Cup of Joaquin Murieta," WF (Apr, 1954), 13: 98-100. One more legend about California's most famous bandit.

2496. Ketchum, Alton. Uncle Sam: the Man and the Legend (New York: Hill and Wang, 1959), xiii, 143pp. Popular history of the famous American symbol with chapters on Yankee Doodle, Samuel Wilson, and Thomas Nast. Pictures, cartoons, posters.

2497. Kirtley, Bacil F. "John Ellis--Hunter, Guide, Legend," NEF (Spr, 1958), 1: 13-17. Maine figure who lived 1784-1867.

2498. _____. "Theories and Fantasies Concerning Robin Hood," SFQ (Je, 1956), 20: 108-115. Outlaw has been interpreted by theorists, solar mythologists, historians. Most data reflect not history but the ballad muse.

2499. Klapp, Orrin E. "The Clever Hero," JAF (Jan-Mr, 1954), 67: 21-34. Tyl Eulenspiegel to Will Rogers.

2500. _____. Heroes, Villains, and Fools; the Changing American Character (Englewood Cliffs, N. J.: Prentice-Hall, 1962), x, 176pp. The "hero" analyzed through language and epithet.

2501. Koch, William E. "The Sioux Trickster," KM (1960), pp. 18-26. Seven tales relating the exploits of Iktomi, the spider trickster of the Dakota.

2502. Leach, MacEdward. "John Henry," in Folklore & Society, ed. Bruce Jackson, pp. 93-106. Discussion of tales, ballads, legends; comparison with a Jamaican hero.

2503.   Lightfoot, William E. "Charlie Parker: a Contem-
        porary Folk Hero, " KFQ (S, 1972), 17: 51-62.

2504.   Linneman, William R. "Colonel Bill Snort, a Texas
        Jack Downing, " SHQ (Oct, 1960), 64: 185-199.
        A Texas comic figure created by Alex Sweet.

2505.   Loehr, Rodney C. "Some More Light on Paul Bun-
        yan, " JAF (Oct-Dec, 1951), 64: 405-407. Lum-
        berjack tales suggest that Bunyan might have been
        known in camps before 1910.

2506.   McCracken, Henry Noble. "Andre: a Case of Mod-
        ern Folklore, " NYFQ (Spr, 1959), 15: 58-65.
        The folk adulation of Major John Andre is un-
        justified.

2507.   McDowell, Bart. The American Cowboy in Life and
        Legend (Washington: National Geographic Soc.,
        1972), 211pp. A literary survey with excellent
        photographs by William Albert Allard.

2508.   McMullen, J. T., Jr. "Symposium: 'The Making
        of the Hero,'" NYFQ (Je, 1968), 24: 83-87. In-
        troduction to four papers on the folk hero.

2509.   Makarius, Laura. "The Crime of Manabozho, " AA
        (Je, 1973), 75: 663-675. Analysis of Algonkin
        trickster myths. Extensive notes and bibliography.

2510.   Marshall, George O., Jr. "Epic Motifs in Modern
        Football, " TFSB (Dec, 1958), 24: 123-128. The
        unpromising player sometimes becomes a hero on
        the gridiron.

2511.   Maunder, Elwood R. "An Interview with James
        Stevens: the Making of a Folklorist, " FH (W,
        1964), 7: 2-19. Stevens discusses his role in
        the publication of the Paul Bunyan tales.

2512.   Mickel, Jere C. "The Genesis of Toby: a Folk
        Hero of the American Theater, " JAF (Oct-Dec,
        1967), 80: 334-340. Stage history of Toby, the
        country bumpkin who satisfied rural audiences for
        many years.

2513.   Miller, Ernest C. Tintypes in Oil (Rutland, Vt.:

Charles E. Tuttle, 1961), 186pp. Brief history
of oil industry with attention to its legends.
Chapter 8 concerns Gib Morgan.

2514. Mitchell, Merlin P. "Tales of Bone Mizell, Folk
Character of South Florida," SFQ (Mr, 1971),
35: 34-43. Comic escapades of a cowboy from
South Florida around the turn of the century.

2515. Monteiro, George. "Fenimore Cooper's Yankee
Woodsman," MF (W, 1962), 12: 209-216. Cooper
drew an early folk type in Billy Kirby in The
Pioneers.

2516. _____. "Histoire de Montferrand: L'Athlete
Canadien and Joe Mufraw," JAF (Jan-Mr, 1960),
73: 24-34. Suggested genealogy of Joe Mufraw,
Paul Bunyan's cook.

2517. _____. "The Unhistorical Uses of Peter Francisco," SFQ (Je, 1963), 27: 139-159. Portuguese
Revolutionary War hero has become a legendary
figure through the accretion of legendary details.

2518. Moody, James W., Jr. "Casey Jones Railroad Museum," THQ (Spr, 1966), 25: 3-21. Biography
of famous railroad engineer plus Casey Jones as
a ballad and folk hero.

2519. Mullin, Robert N. and Charles E. Welsh, Jr. "Billy
the Kid: the Making of a Hero," WF (Apr, 1973),
32: 104-111. Publicity and advertising did much
to establish Billy the Kid as a folk hero. Other
western bad men were actually more sinister.

2520. Mullin, Susan. "Huckleberry Finn in Oregon," OFB
(W-Spr, 1963), 2: 1-3.

2521. _____. "Oregon's Huckleberry Finn: a Münchhausen Enters Tradition," NWF (1967), 2: i, 19-
25. Windy stories about an Oregon pioneer,
Benjamin Franklin Finn.

2522. Nussbaum, Martin. "The 'Adult Western' as an Art
Form," Folklore (Sept, 1959), 70: 460-467. The
western hero is a genuine contribution to the
world's folk types with definite traits. Television
shows exemplify this contention well.

2523. Paredes, Américo. With His Pistol in His Hand: a Border Ballad and Its Hero (Austin: U. of Texas P., 1958), 262pp. Excellent account of Gregorio Cortez, a Mexican border figure.

2524. Parker, Arthur C. "Who Was Hiawatha?" NYFQ (W, 1954), 10: 285-288. An effort to identify Longfellow's hero.

2525. Parsons, Gerald. "Sam Patch Falls Again: Second Thoughts on a Folk Hero," NYFQ (Je, 1969), 25: 83-92. Sam Patch was a temporary sensation but not greatly admired; he has not survived in oral tradition.

2526. Penrod, James H. "The Folk Hero as Prankster in the Old Southwestern Yarns," KFR (Jan-Mr, 1956), 2: 5-12.

2527. Pickering, James H. "Shube Merritt: Freebooter of the Neutral Ground," NYFQ (Mr, 1965), 21: 31-39. A New York state desperado in the late 18th century was a local folk hero.

2528. Price, Robert. Johnny Appleseed, Man and Myth (Bloomington: Indiana U. P., 1954), 320pp. Definitive biography of John Chapman, folk figure and horticulturist of the Ohio Valley.

2529. Radin, Paul. The Trickster, a Study in American Indian Mythology (New York: Bell Pub. Co., 1925), 211pp. Winnebago trickster myth with commentary by Radin, Jung, and Kerenyi.

2530. Richman, Hyman. "The Saga of Joe Magarac," NYFQ (W, 1953), 9: 282-293. Sharp evaluation of the Joe Magarac story, which is denied authenticity as a folktale.

2531. Robins, John D. Logging with Paul Bunyan (Toronto: Ryerson P., 1957), ed. Edith Fowke, xvii, 97pp. Canadian tales about Paul Bunyan, slightly refurbished.

2532. Roheim, Géza. "Culture Hero and Trickster in North American Indian Mythology," in Indian Tribes of Aboriginal America (Chicago: U. of Chicago P.,

1952), ed. Sol Tax, pp. 190-194. The real
hero of these myths, the author contends, is the
Id.

2533. Rosa, Joseph G. The Gunfighter: Man or Myth?
(Norman: U. of Oklahoma P., 1969), xv, 229pp.
The gunfighter as a kind of legendary folk hero:
fact vs. fiction.

2534. Rosenberg, Bruce A. "Custer: the Legend of the
Martyred Hero in America," JFI (Aug-Dec, 1972),
9: 110-132. Study of the facts and legends about
Gen. Custer, who is called the most popular hero
of the American people.

2535. Russell, Don. The Lives and Legends of Buffalo
Bill (Norman: U. of Oklahoma P., 1960), 514pp.
Facts and legends about Bill Cody.

2536. Settle, William A. Jesse James Was His Name
(Columbia: U. of Missouri P., 1966), 263pp.
Facts separated from folklore; extensive notes and
bibliography.

2537. Shackford, James Atkins. David Crockett: the Man
and the Legend (Chapel Hill: U. of No. Car. P.,
1956), xiv, 338pp. Ed. John B. Shackford.
Some attention paid to the Crockett myth but
chiefly a factual life about his political and military career.

2538. Shapiro, Irwin. Heroes in American Folklore (New
York: J. Messner, 1962), 256pp. Popular retellings.

2539. Simeone, William E. "The Mythical Robin Hood,"
WF (Jan, 1958), 17: 21-28. Survey of some of
the theories about the famous outlaw, historical
or mythical.

2540. _____. "Robin Hood and Some Other Outlaws,"
JAF (Jan-Mr, 1958), 71: 27-33. Robin Hood's
exploits and traits are reflected in tales of other
outlaws.

2541. Slotkin, Richard. Regeneration Through Violence:
the Mythology of the American Frontier (Middle-

town, Conn.: Wesleyan U. P., 1973), 670pp.
Heroes and anti-heroes.

2542. Smith, Donnal V. "'Pants' Lawrence of the Adirondacks," NYFQ (S, 1953), 9: 85-93. Tales of an
Adirondack guide.

2543. Smith, Helena Huntington. "Sam Bass and the Myth
Machine," AW (Jan, 1970), 7: i, 31-35. Folklore has created a major outlaw out of an inept
and unlucky robber.

2544. Stanford, Raney. "The Return of Trickster: When
a Not-A-Hero is a Hero," JPC (W, 1967), 1:
228-242. An article which links the folkloristic
trickster, the picaro, and the modern anti-hero
(cf. the "hero" of Ellison's The Invisible Man).

2545. Steckmesser, Kent L. "Joaquin Murieta and Billy
the Kid," WF (Apr, 1962), 21: 77-82. Legends
of the two desperadoes are similar and owe their
inceptions to imaginative journalists.

2546. _____. "The Oklahoma Robin Hood," AW (Jan,
1970), 7: i, 38-41. Brief discussion of Pretty
Boy Floyd, a bragging, overbearing desperado.

2547. _____. "Robin Hood and the American Outlaw:
a Note on History and Folklore," JAF (Apr-Je,
1966), 79: 348-355. "The outlaw hero, from
Robin Hood to Sam Bass, is a thoroughly folkloric
product."

2548. _____. The Western Hero in History and Legend
(Norman: U. of Oklahoma P., 1965), xiii, 281.
Four types of heroes identified: Kit Carson,
Billy the Kid, Wild Bill Hickok, Gen. Custer.

2549. Stevens, James. "Folklore and the Artist," AM
(Mr, 1950), 70: 343-349. Reply to R. M. Dorson's strictures with the admission that Stevens
invented many Paul Bunyan tales.

2550. Stiffler, Stuart A. "Davy Crockett: the Genesis of
a Heroic Myth," THQ (Je, 1957), 16: 134-140.
Brief survey of Crockett's life with focus on how
his legend developed.

2551. Studer, Norman. "Boney Quillen of the Catskills,"
       NYFQ (W, 1951), 7: 276-282. A raftsman and
       teamster known as a singer and wit.

2552. Thomas, W. Stephen. "Folklore Figures of Roches-
       ter, N.Y.," NYFQ (Spr, 1954), 10: 9-17. De-
       scriptions and anecdotes of local figures.

2553. Thompson, Vivian L. Aukele the Fearless: a Leg-
       end of Old Hawaii (Chicago: Golden Gate, 1972),
       79pp. Hero who slays monsters.

2554. Tinkle, Lon and Allen Maxwell. The Cowboy Reader
       (New York: Longmans, Green, 1959), xi, 307pp.
       Anthology of cowboy material from some 32 con-
       tributors. Prose.

2555. Tuthill, Barbara. "Hatfield the Rainmaker," WF
       (Apr, 1954), 13: 107-112. A rain maker in San
       Diego area succeeded so well that he passed into
       legend.

2556. Vlach, John M. "Fenimore Cooper's Leatherstocking
       as Folk Hero," NYFQ (Dec, 1971), 27: 323-338.
       Covers familiar ground in a repetitious way.

2557. Waldmeier, Joseph J. "The Cowboy, the Knight, and
       Popular Taste," SFQ (Sept, 1958), 22: 113-120.
       Impact of knightly tradition on the cowboy theme.
       Lone Ranger stories provide a good example of
       adaptation of mediaeval romance to the Am. West.

2558. Walker, Warren S. "Buckskin West: Leatherstock-
       ing at High Noon," NYFQ (Je, 1968), 24: 88-102.
       Some of the traits of Natty Bumppo as archetypal
       frontiersman were preserved by the western cow-
       boy, who also developed other qualities.

2559. _____. "Dan'l Stamps: Tall Tale Hero of the
       River Country," MF (F, 1954), 4: 153-160. Tall
       tales from the lower Illinois River Valley.

2560. Walle, Alf. "The Western Hero--a Static Figure in
       an Evolving World," KF (W, 1974), 19: 207-224.
       The western hero in current fiction and cinema.

2561. Weldon, Fred O., Jr. "Negro Folktale Heroes," in

And Horns on the Toads, ed. Mody C. Boatright
et al., pp. 170-189. John Henry is the one con-
test hero of the Negroes. The two major Negro
folktale cycles deal with Brer Rabbit and John the
trickster.

2562. Westermeier, Clifford P. "The Cowboy--Sinner or
Saint?" NMHR (Apr, 1950), 25: 89-108. The
cowboy as he appeared in historical literature before 1900 and in dime novels and westerns, also
the origins of his folk role.

2563. Wiggins, William H. "Jack Johnson as Bad Nigger:
the Folklore of His Life," Black Scholar (1971),
2: 35-46. The heavyweight champion revealed
many of the traits of the bad nigger as seen by
whites.

2564. Wisbey, Herbert A., Jr. "Jemima Wilkinson: Historical Figure and Folk Character," NYFQ (Mr,
1964), 20: 5-13. Jemima Wilkinson (1752-1819)
is better known in legend than in history.

2565. Wood, Leslie C. Holt! T'Other Way! (Middletown,
N.Y.: Leslie C. Wood, 1950), 252pp. Ac-
counts of rafters and fiddlers in Delaware Co.,
New York.

2566. Woodward, Robert H. "Moore's St. Nick: Model
and Motif," NYFQ (W, 1959), 15: 251-254.
Irving's portrait of a Dutch governor influenced
Moore's St. Nick.

2567. Wyld, Lionel D. "The Horse Ocean," KFQ (Spr,
1962), 7: i, 7-14. Anecdotes and folk heroes of
the Erie Canal.

2568. _____. Low Bridge! Folklore and the Erie Canal
(Syracuse: Syracuse U. P., 1962), 212pp. Extensive treatment of the history and lore of the
famous ditch based primarily on printed sources.

12.   FOLKLORE IN LITERATURE

2569. Abrams, W. Amos. "Time Was: Its Lore and Language," NCarF (Mr, 1971), 19: 40-46. Folklore in a novel by John F. West.

2570. Anderson, John Q. "Emerson and the Ballad of George Nidever--'Staring Down' a Grizzly Bear," WF (Jan, 1956), 15: 40-45. A ballad attached to Emerson's essay "Courage" was written by Elisabeth Hoar. In it a hunter stares down a bear.

2571. _____. "Emerson and the Language of the Folk," in Folk Travelers, ed. Mody C. Boatright et al., pp. 152-59. Comments on how Emerson's theory of language affected his own choice of diction.

2572. _____. "Folklore in the Writings of 'The Louisiana Swamp Doctor'," SFQ (Dec, 1955), 19: 243-51. The work of Henry Clay Lewis examined.

2573. _____. "Folklore in Two Northeast Louisiana Novels," LFM (Aug, 1961), 2: 28-43.

2544. _____. Louisiana Swamp Doctor; the Life and Writings of Henry Clay Lewis. (Baton Rouge: La. S. U. P. , 1962), 296pp. Biography of a man who made extensive use of folklore in his regional writings.

2575. _____. "Mike Hooter--The Making of a Myth," SFQ (Je, 1955), 19: 90-100. Stories about Michael Hooter (1791-1865), as told by William C. Hall and Henry Clay Lewis.

2576. Arner, Robert D. "Of Snakes and Those Who Swallow Them: Some Folk Analogues for Hawthorne's

278

'Egotism; or the Bosom Serpent'," SFQ (Dec, 1971), 35: 336-46.

2577. Arpad, Joseph J. "The Fight Story: Quotation and Originality in Native American Humor," JFI (Dec, 1973), 10: 141-172. The conflict between river boatman and wagoner as depicted by Paulding, Crockett, Twain, etc.

2578. _____. "John Wesley Jarvis, James Kirke Paulding and Colonel Nimrod Wildfire," NYFQ (Je, 1965), 21: 92-106. Details about the genesis of the play The Lion of the West.

2579. Babcock, C. Merton. "Americanisms in the Novels of Sinclair Lewis," AS (May, 1960), 35: 110-16. Points out that Lewis was conspicuously successful in recording the expressions of the 1920's, many of which are now listed in dictionaries.

2580. _____. "Melville's Backwoods Seamen," WF (Apr, 1951), 10: 126-33. Material from Moby Dick illustrating Melville's knowledge of whaleman traditions and also of other traditions from the American frontier.

2581. _____. "The Vocabulary of Moby Dick," AS (May, 1952), 27: 91-101.

2582. _____. "A Word-List from Zora Neale Hurston," PADS (Nov, 1963), No. 40, 1-11. Words and phrases from South Florida garnered from five books.

2583. Baker, Houston A., Jr. "Black Folklore and the Black American Literary Tradition," in Long Black Song, Essays in Black American Literature and Culture (Charlottesville: U.P. of Virginia, 1972), pp. 18-41. Comments on animal and religious tales, folksongs, ballads, proverbs. Dunbar, Chesnutt, McKay, Himes, and Wright cited.

2584. Baker, Ronald L. "Folk Medicine in the Writings of Rowland E. Robinson," VH (S, 1969), 37: 184-193. Potions, drugs, practices cited in Robinson's Vermont fiction.

2585. _____. "Folklore in the Prose Sketches of James
Whitcomb Riley," IEJ (Spr, 1970), 4: 3-19, 27.
Riley employed proverbs, superstitions, tales,
songs, and customs.

2586. _____. Folklore in the Writings of Rowland E.
Robinson (Bowling Green, Ohio: Bowling Green
U. Popular Press, 1974), xi, 240pp. Excellent
treatment of folklore in the fiction of a minor
Vermont writer.

2587. Barbour, Frances M. "William Gilmore Simms and
the Brutus Legend," MF (F, 1957), 7: 159-62.
Sources of an episode in The Yemassee.

2588. Barnes, Daniel R. "The Bosom Serpent, A Legend
in American Literature and Culture," JAF (Apr-
Je, 1972), 85: 111-22. Hawthorne, Thoreau, and
Hortense Calisher all used the theme of a serpent
or newt in a man's stomach.

2589. _____. "'Physical Fact' and Folklore: Hawthorne's 'Egotism; or the Bosom Serpent'," AL
(Mr, 1971), 43: 117-21. Hawthorne most likely
used folklore as the basis of one of his more
famous stories.

2590. Barrick, Mac E. "Proverbs and Sayings from Gibbs-
ville, Pa.; John O'Hara's Use of Proverbial Materials," KFQ (Spr, 1967), 12: 55-80.

2591. Beard, Anne. "Games and Recreations in the Novels
of Edward Eggleston," MF (S, 1961), 11: 85-104.
Eggleston incorporated at least a dozen folk
games into his fiction.

2592. Beck, Horace P. "Melville as a Folklife Recorder
in Moby-Dick," KF (F, 1973), 18: 75-88. Beck's
1971 experience with whalers near Caribbean island of Bequia confirms his belief that Melville's
novel is accurate documentation.

2593. Bennett, Paul L. "Folklore and the Literature to
Come," JAF (Jan-Mr, 1952), 65: 23-27. Brief
paper suggesting how folklore might be utilized in
future literature.

2594. Bennett, S. M. "Ornament and Environment: Uses
      of Folklore in Willa Cather's Fiction," TSFB
      (Sept, 1974), 40: 95-102. The Nebraska novels
      used folklore to aid characterization and local
      color; the New Mexico and Quebec novels used
      religious folklore to underscore the mixture of
      cultures.

2595. Bigelow, Gordon E. "Marjorie Kinnan Rawlings'
      'Lord Bill of the Suwannee River'," SFQ (Je,
      1963), 27: 113-31. Previously unpublished sketch
      of a legendary Florida cracker whose character
      and exploits intrigued Mrs. Rawlings.

2596. Bluestein, Gene. "'The Arkansas Traveler' and the
      Strategy of American Humor," WF (Jl, 1962), 21:
      153-60. The basic confrontation of rural and
      urban culture with special examples from Mark
      Twain.

2597. _____. "Constance Rourke and the Folk Sources
      of American Literature," WF (Apr, 1967), 26:
      77-87. Praise for Rourke's insight into the
      merging of folk and popular traditions.

2598. Boatright, Mody C. "The Formula in Cowboy Fiction
      and Drama," WF (Apr, 1969), 28: 136-45. Ex-
      tensive survey of magazine stories reveals some
      7 basic plots.

2599. Boswell, George W. "The Folklore Basis of Litera-
      ture," TFSB (Sept, 1961), 27: 43-45.

2600. _____. "Folkways in Faulkner," MFR (1967), 1:
      83-90. Brief discussion of Faulkner's use of
      proverbs, dialect, song fragments, rituals, etc.

2601. Brookes, Stella Brewer. Joel Chandler Harris--
      Folklorist (Athens: U. of Georgia P., 1950), xv,
      182pp. Not a source study but a description of
      Negro songs and stories used by Harris with dis-
      cussion of dialect and proverbs.

2602. Brown, Calvin S. "Faulkner's Use of the Oral Tradi-
      tion," GR (S, 1968), 22: 160-169. Faulkner
      adapted southern tale-telling technique to literary
      purposes.

2603. Browne, Ray B. "The Affirmation of 'Bartleby,'" Folklore International, ed. D. K. Wilgus, pp. 11-21. Melville's story was aided by the use of myth and folklore.

2604. _____. "The Oft-Told Twice Told Tales: Their Folklore Motifs," SFQ (Je, 1958), 22: 69-85. Hawthorne's use of folklore themes (the returning champion, water of life, pride before a fall) and folklore allusions discussed.

2605. _____. "'Popular' and Folk Songs: Unifying Force in Garland's Autobiographical Works," SFQ (Sept, 1961), 25: 153-66. The role of songs in Garland's autobiographical tetralogy of the middle-western border studied.

2606. Brunvand, Jan Harold. "From Western Folklore to Fiction in the Stories of Charles M. Russell," WR (S, 1965), 5: 41-49. Russell published 44 stories, full of cowboy lingo, snatches of songs, and tall tales.

2607. _____. "Sailors' and Cowboys' Folklore in Two Popular Classics," SFQ (Dec, 1965), 29: 266-83. Discussion of folklore (songs, tales, speech) in Andy Adams' Log of a Cowboy and R. H. Dana's Two Years Before the Mast.

2608. Budd, Louis J. "Gentlemanly Humorists of the Old South," SFQ (Dec, 1953), 17: 232-40. Five antebellum Southern humorists: Longstreet, Hooper, Baldwin, W. T. Thompson, and G. W. Harris.

2609. Byrd, James W. "Zora Neale Hurston: A Novel Folklorist," TFSB (Je, 1955), 21: 27-41. Random quotations of folk speech confirm Hurston's importance as a folklorist.

2610. Cannon, Agnes Dicken. "Melville's Use of Sea Ballads and Songs," WF (Jan, 1964), 23: 1-16. Melville used balladry to reenforce his descriptions of sea life, to indicate the moods of characters, to give deeper meaning to original verse.

2611. Carey, George G. "Folklore from the Printed Sources of Essex County, Massachusetts," SFQ

(Mr, 1968), 32: 17-43. Folklore material preserved in local newspapers and histories. Motifs
identified.

2612. _____. "John Greenleaf Whittier and Folklore:
the Search for a Traditional American Past,"
NYFQ (Mr, 1971), 27: 113-129. Whittier was
concerned with witchcraft, demonology, and the
Indian heritage.

2613. _____. "Whittier's Roots in a Folk Culture,"
Essex Institute Historical Collections (1968), 104:
3-18. Whittier's Legends of New England and
other verse derive from folk roots.

2614. Clagett, John H. "The Maritime Works of James
Fenimore Cooper as Sources for Sea Lore, Sea
Legend, and Sea Idiom," SFQ (Dec, 1966), 30:
323-331. A big subject sketchily treated.

2615. Clark, Joseph D. "Burke Davis as Folklorist,"
NCarF (Mr, 1971), 19: 59-65. Discussion of
folklore in the fiction of Burke Davis.

2616. Clarke, Mary Washington. "As Jesse Stuart Heard
It in Kentucky," KFR (Jl-Sept, 1963), 9: 75-86.
Dialectal words and proverbial sayings gleaned
from Stuart's work.

2617. _____. "Jesse Stuart Reflects Kentucky Lore of
Tokens and Ghosts," KFR (Jl-Sept, 1963), 9:
41-46. Stuart's use of folk themes in his books.

2618. _____. "Jesse Stuart's Writings Preserve Passing
Folk Idiom," SFQ (Sept, 1964), 28: 157-98. A
careful selection of folk phrases and terms familiar to the Cumberland region which Stuart
used in his writings.

2619. Claudel, Calvin A. "Louisiana's Jean Sot in Folklore
and Literature," RLLR (1972), 1: 55-64.

2620. Clayton, Lawrence. "Hamlin Garland's Negative Use
of Folk Elements," FF (Apr, 1973), 6: 107-8.
Garland introduced folk motifs, songs, games, and
speech into his writings but often negatively as a
condemnation of rural life.

2621.   Coffin, Tristram P. "Gatsby's Fairy Lover," WF
        (S, 1960), 10: 79-85. Fitzgerald's novel may
        be indebted to an old Celtic fairy tale.

2622.   _____. "Real Use and Real Abuse of Folklore in
        the Writer's Subconscious: F. Scott Fitzgerald,"
        in New Voices in American Studies, ed. Ray B.
        Browne et al., pp. 102-112.

2623.   Cohen, Hennig. "American Literature and American
        Folklore," in Our Living Traditions, ed. T. P.
        Coffin, pp. 238-247. A very brief treatment.

2624.   _____. "Twain's Jumping Frog: Folktale to
        Literature to Folktale," WF (Jan, 1963), 22: 17-
        18. Cites a parallel tale about a gamecock from
        a San Francisco newspaper.

2625.   Costello, Donald P. "The Language of The Catcher
        in the Rye," AS (Oct, 1959), 34: 172-81. Salin-
        ger's diction is seen as an authentic rendering of
        colloquial teenage American speech.

2626.   Cuff, Roger Penn. "Mark Twain's Use of California
        Folklore in His Jumping Frog Story," JAF (Apr-
        Je, 1952), 65: 155-58. Sources: a tale heard in
        a California barroom and his own imagination.

2627.   Davidson, James. "The Post-Bellum Poor-White as
        Seen by J. W. DeForest," SFQ (Je, 1960), 24:
        101-8. DeForest's experiences in Greenville, So.
        Carolina aided him in portraying southern poor
        whites accurately and vividly.

2628.   Davis, Rose M. "How Indian Is Hiawatha?" MF
        (Spr, 1957), 7: 5-25. Longfellow's version of
        the Hiawatha story lacks psychological truth.

2629.   De Caro, Rosan Jordan. "A Note about Folklore and
        Literature (The Bosom Serpent Revisited)," JAF
        (Jan-Mr, 1973), 86: 62-65.

2630.   DeFalco, Joseph M. "Frost's 'Paul's Wife': the
        Death of an Ideal," SFQ (Dec, 1965), 29: 259-
        265. Robert Frost in a neglected poem provided
        Paul Bunyan with a wife.

2631. Deming, Robert H. "The Use of the Past: Herrick
       and Hawthorne," JPC (F, 1968), 2: 278-291.
       Study of the artistic use of customs in a Herrick
       poem and a Hawthorne tale.

2632. Dinn, James M. "A Novelist's Miracle: Structure
       and Myth in Death Comes for the Archbishop,"
       WAL (Spr, 1972), 7: 39-46. Willa Cather's use
       of myth and symbols.

2633. Dorson, Richard M. "Indian Mythology Since 'Hi-
       awatha,'" MichH (Dec, 1955), 39: 464-465.
       Summary of a speech.

2634. Drake, Carlos G. "Literary Criticism and Folklore,"
       JPC (F, 1971), 5: 289-297.

2635. Dresser, Norine. "The Metamorphosis of the Humor
       of the Black Man," NYFQ (Sept, 1970), 26: 216-
       28. Printed and orally reported jokes confirm
       theory that black humor has grown much more
       sophisticated since the days of Old Master and
       John jokes.

2636. Eby, Cecil D., Jr. "Americanisms in the Down-
       East Fiction of George D. Wasson," AS (Dec,
       1962), 37: 249-54. Wasson's three books of fic-
       tion are a neglected reservoir of Americanisms.

2637. Edmondson, Munro S. Lore: an Introduction to the
       Science of Folklore and Literature (New York:
       Rinehart and Winston, 1971), xv, 456pp. De-
       signed as a text for both fields, the book touches
       on many topics, cites examples, and includes
       charts and indexes.

2638. Englekirk, John E. "The Source and Dating of New
       Mexican Spanish Folk Plays," WF (Oct, 1957),
       16: 232-55. The story of the Spanish folk theater
       in New Mexico based on field work and textual
       study.

2639. Ferguson, Robert C. "Folklore References in
       Faulkner's The Hamlet and As I Lay Dying,"
       JOFS (Spr, 1972), n.s. 1: 1-10.

2640. Field, Leslie A. "Wolfe's Use of Folklore," NYFQ

(A, 1960), 16: 202-15. Thomas Wolfe included
considerable folklore, though fragmentary, in The
Hills Beyond.

2641. Figh, Margaret Gillis. "Folklore in the 'Rufus
Sanders' Sketches," SFQ (Sept, 1955), 19: 185-
95. Tales by Francis Bartow Lloyd, Alabama
journalist.

2642. Flanagan, John T. "Folk Elements in John Brown's
Body," NYFQ (Dec, 1964), 20: 243-56.

2643. _____. "The Folk Hero in Modern American
Drama," MD (Feb, 1964), 6: 402-16.

2644. _____. "Folklore in Minnesota Literature,"
MinnH (Sept, 1958), 36: 73-83.

2645. _____. "Folklore in the Novels of Conrad Richter," MF (Sept, 1952), 2: 5-14. Concerned
chiefly with Richter's trilogy of Ohio settlement.

2646. _____. "Folklore in the Stories of James Hall,"
MF (F, 1955), 5: 159-68.

2647. _____. "The Impact of Folklore on American
Literature," JA (1962), 7: 67-76. General survey of folklore themes in American writing.

2648. _____. "John G. Neihardt, Chronicler of the
West," ArQ (Spr, 1965), 21: 7-20. Occasional
reference to Neihardt as a folklorist.

2648a. _____ and Arthur Palmer Hudson. The American
Folklore Reader (New York: Barnes, 1958), xvi,
511pp. Anthology of familiar and unfamiliar selections with strong folklore content.

2649. Fleming, Robert E. "'Playing the Dozens' in the
Black Novel," SBL (A, 1972), 3: 23-24. The
use of the familiar insult game by three black
novelists.

2650. "Folklore in Literature: A Symposium," JAF (Jan-
Mr, 1957), 70: 1-24. Papers by Daniel G. Hoffman, Richard M. Dorson, Carvel Collins. Valuable comment and bibliographical material. Cf.

Dorson, "Folklore in American Literature: A Postscript," JAF (Apr-Je, 1958), 71: 157-59. Additional items.

2651. Ford, Thomas W. "Ned Brace of Georgia Scenes," SFQ (Sept, 1965), 29: 220-227. Identification of a Southern-born Yankee trickster in Longstreet's Georgia Scenes.

2652. Foster, Charles W. "The Phonology of the Conjure Tales of Charles W. Chesnutt," PADS (Apr, 1971), No. 55, pp. 1-43. Examination of Chesnutt's dialect tales and praise for his accurate and artistic use of Negro speech.

2653. Franklin, H. Bruce. The Wake of the Gods (Stanford: Stanford U. P., 1963), xvi, 270pp. Melville's use of myths in his fiction: an erudite and perceptive analysis.

2654. Frantz, Ray W. "The Role of Folklore in Huckleberry Finn," AL (Nov, 1956), 28: 314-327.

2655. Franz, Eleanor. "Hunting the Hunter: Nat Foster Today," NYFQ (Dec, 1964), 20: 270-275. Additional details about one of the putative models for Cooper's Leatherstocking.

2656. Gillis, Everett A. "Southwestern Literary Balladry," NMFR (1953-1954), 8: 1-5. Brief survey of "ballad poems" written by Stanley Vestal, S. Omar Barker, Charles Badger Clark, and N. Howard Thorp.

2657. Glassie, Henry. "The Use of Folklore in David Harum," NYFQ (Sept, 1967), 23: 163-85. Folklore in E. N. Westcott's familiar popular novel. 71 proverbs cited.

2658. Goodwyn, Frank. "A Proposed Terminology for Clarifying the Relationship Between Folklore and Literature," SFQ (Sept, 1950), 14: 143-49.

2659. Gray, Richard. "Signs of Kinship: Thomas Wolfe and His Appalachian Background," AJ (Spr, 1974), 1: 309-19. Wolfe's last novel, The Hills Beyond, used mountain legends and traditions.

2660. Greenberg, Alvin. "Shaggy Dog in Mississippi," SFQ
       (Dec, 1965), 29: 284-87. Faulkner uses a kind of
       shaggy dog story in Light in August.

2661. Grimes, Geoffrey A. "'Brandy and Water': Ameri-
       can Folk Types in the Works of Artemus Ward,"
       NYFQ (Sept, 1969), 25: 163-74. Ward used the
       Yankee, southern Negro, backwoodsman, and Indi-
       an in his work.

2662. _____. "'Muels,' 'Owls,' and Other Things:
       Folk Material in the Tobacco Philosophy of Josh
       Billings," NYFQ (Dec, 1970), 26: 283-96. Ma-
       terial quoted from Old Farmer's Allminax. Bil-
       ling's cacography is no longer appreciated.

2663. Hall, Wade. "Humor and Folklore in Vinnie Wil-
       liams' Walk Egypt," SFQ (Sept, 1962), 26: 225-
       31. Discussion of folk elements in a popular
       novel of 1960.

2664. Hansen, Chadwick. "The Metamorphosis of Tituba,
       or Why American Intellectuals Can't Tell an Indi-
       an Witch from a Negro," NEQ (Mr, 1974), 47:
       3-12. Longfellow, William Carlos Williams, and
       Arthur Miller attribute Negro blood to Tituba.

2665. Harrell, Laura D. S. "Irwin Russell and 'The Blue-
       Tail Fly Grange'," MFR (W, 1968), 2: 113-21.
       Memories of the Port Gibson poet.

2666. Harris, George Washington. Sut Lovingood (New
       York: Grove Press, 1954), pp. xxiv, 262.
       Modern edition, somewhat simplified, of famous
       tales with introduction by Brom Weber.

2667. Hatley, Donald W. "Folklore in the Fiction of Barry
       Benefield," MQ (W, 1967-1968), 21: 63-70. Dis-
       cussion of E. Texas folklore in Benefield's stories
       and novels.

2668. Hendricks, William O. "Folklore and the Structural
       Analysis of Literary Texts," LangS (Spr, 1970),
       3: 83-121. Attempt to relate the folklore research
       and theories of V. Propp and A. Olrik to litera-
       ture. A Faulkner story used as example.

2669. Hess, Judith W. "Traditional Themes in Faulkner's
       'The Bear'," TFSB (Je, 1974), 40: 57-64. One
       more argument that "The Bear" was indebted to
       folk themes, especially Thorpe's "Big Bear of
       Arkansas."

2670. Hoadley, Frank M. "Folk Humor in the Novels of
       William Faulkner," TFSB (Sept, 1957), 23: 75-82.
       Sketchy treatment of humor in Faulkner's major
       novels.

2671. Hoffman, Daniel G. Form and Fable in American
       Fiction (New York: Oxford, 1961), xvi, 368pp.
       Excellent study of the influence of oral tradition,
       myth, and folklore on the work of Irving, Haw-
       thorne, Melville, and Twain.

2672. _____. "Irving's Use of American Folklore in
       'The Legend of Sleepy Hollow'," PMLA (Je, 1953),
       68: 425-35. Careful analysis.

2673. _____. "Jim's Magic: Black or White?" AL (Mr,
       1960), 32: 47-54. The witchcraft and omens of
       Twain's Jim, although widely prevalent among
       southern Negroes, were primarily of European
       white origin.

2674. _____. "Thoreau's 'Old Settler' and Frost's
       Paul Bunyan," JAF (Jl-Sept, 1960), 73: 236-38.

2675. Howell, Elmo. "Faulkner's Sartoris and the Mis-
       sissippi Country People," SFQ (Je, 1961), 25:
       136-46. Survey of characters and scenes in
       Faulkner's first Mississippi novel--his emotional
       return to his native state.

2676. _____. "William Faulkner's 'Christmas Gift',"
       KFR (Apr-Je, 1967), 13: 37-40. Faulkner's use
       of an old southern term and custom.

2677. Huddleston, Eugene L. "Place Names in the Writ-
       ings of Jesse Stuart," WF (Jl, 1972), 31: 169-
       177. Kentucky names used by the novelist and
       poet.

2678. Hudson, Arthur Palmer. "The Impact of Folklore on
       American Poetry," in A Tribute to George Coffin

Taylor, ed. Arnold Williams (Chapel Hill: U. of
N. Carolina P. , 1952), pp. 142-147.

2679. Huguenin, Charles A. "The Truth About the Schooner
Hesperus," NYFQ (Spr, 1960), 16: 48-53. The
chief event in Longfellow's famous ballad did not
occur as he described it but other schooners were
wrecked in the storm.

2680. Hyde, Stuart W. "The Ring-Tailed Roarer in American Drama," SFQ (Sept, 1955), 19: 171-78.

2681. Ives, Sumner. "The Phonology of the Uncle Remus
Stories," PADS (Nov, 1954), no. 22, 3-59.
Scholarly study of Harris's Negro dialect: Harris has given us literature suffused with life and
obviously true.

2682. Ivey, Saundra Keyes. "Aunt Mahalia Mullins in Folklore, Fakelore, and Literature," TFSB (Mr,
1975), 41: 1-8. Data about an enormous Melun-
geon moonshiner of Hancock Co. , Tenn. , who
figures in books by James Aswell and Jesse Stuart.

2683. Jaskoski, Helen. "Power Unequal to Man: the Significance of Conjure in Works by Five Afro-
American Authors," SFQ (Je, 1974), 38: 91-108.
Chiefly Frederick Douglass, Charles W. Chesnutt,
and Ann Petry.

2684. Jones, Bartlett C. "American Frontier Humor in
Melville's Typee," NYFQ (W, 1959), 15: 283-88.
Folk hyperbole and rustic speech in Melville's
first novel.

2685. Jones, Charles W. "Knickerbocker Santa Claus, "
NYHSQ (Oct, 1954), 38: 357-83. Irving got his
initial idea about St. Nicholas from the state historical society and embellished it with folk legends.

2686. Jones, Kyra. "Myth in The Winter of Our Discon-
tent, " in Diamond Bessie & the Shepherds, ed.
Wilson M. Hudson, pp. 93-102. Analysis of the
Steinbeck novel.

2687. Jones, Michael Owen. "'Ye Must Contrive Allers to
Keep Jest the Happy Medium Between Truth and

Falsehood': Folklore and the Folk in Mrs.
Stowe's Fiction, " NYFQ (Dec, 1971), 27: 357-69.
One of Mrs. Stowe's best characters, Sam Law-
son, speaks monologues rich in popular belief and
Yankee idiom.

2688.   Jones, William M.   "Eudora Welty's Use of Myth in
        'Death of a Traveling Salesman', " JAF (Jan-Mr,
        1960), 73: 18-23.

2689.   _____.   "Name and Symbol in the Prose of Eudora
        Welty, " SFQ (Dec, 1958), 22: 173-85.   Welty
        drew heavily on the world of myth and folklore in
        both short stories and novels.   Cf. A Curtain of
        Green and The Robber Bridegroom.

2690.   Keim, Charles J. and Jack Bernet.   "From String
        Stories to Satellites: Portrayal of the Native
        Alaskan in Literature and Folklore, " BRMMLA
        (Sept, 1973), 27: 167-173.   Fiction and verse
        present native Alaskans as disreputable figures;
        native folklore is more accurate.

2691.   Kent, George E.   "Langston Hughes and Afro-Ameri-
        can Folk and Cultural Tradition, " Blackness and
        the Adventure of Western Culture (Chicago: Third
        World Press, 1972), pp. 53-75.   Study of
        Hughes's use of folk speech, spirituals, blues,
        folk speech in novel Not Without Laughter, verse,
        and plays.

2692.   _____.   "Ralph Ellison and Afro-American Folk
        and Cultural Tradition, " Blackness and the Adven-
        ture of Western Culture, pp. 152-63.   Discussion
        of Ellison's theories and use of folk material in
        literature with special stress on Invisible Man.

2693.   Kestin, Diane.   "Western Folklore in Modern Ameri-
        can Opera, " WF (Jan, 1957), 16: 1-7.   Survey
        of operatic treatments of folklore themes by such
        composers as Douglas Moore, Lukas Foss,
        George Gershwin, Kurt Weill, and Benjamin Brit-
        ten.

2694.   Kime, Wayne R.   "Washington Irving and Frontier
        Speech, " AS (Feb, 1967), 42: 5-18.   A list of
        approximately 100 terms gleaned from Irving's

three western books, proof of his awareness of
western terminology and colloquialisms.

2695. Klotman, Phyllis R. "An Examination of the Black
Confidence Man in Two Black Novels: The Man
Who Cried I Am and dem," AL (Jan, 1973), 44:
596-611. The role of the confidence man in
novels by William M. Kelley and John A. Williams.

2696. Knox, George. "The Totentanz in Ellison's Invisible
Man," Fabula (1971), 12, ii-iii, 168-78. Ellison's novel is many things: a journey, a
parody, a Bildungsroman plus rites of passage,
a rebirth ritual, but basically it treats the dance
of death motif.

2697. Laughlin, Rosemary M. "Attention, American Folklore: Doc Craft Comes Marching In," SAF (A,
1973), 1: 220-27. Analysis of James Alan Mac-
Pherson's short story, "A Solo Song; For Doc,"
with the contention that Doc Craft, a Negro dining
car waiter, resembles more famous occupational
folk heroes.

2698. Leach, MacEdward. "Folklore in American Regional
Literature," JFI (Dec, 1966), 3: 376-397.

2699. Leisy, Ernest E. "Folklore in American Prose,"
SRL (Jl 21, 1951), 34: 6-7, 32. Rapid survey
of folklore in prose narrative.

2700. Light, Martin. "Lewis's 'Scarlet Sign,' Accom-
modating to the Popular Market," JPC (F, 1967),
1: 106-113. Sinclair Lewis introduced folklore
motifs into an early story (1917), but used them
ineffectively.

2701. Linneman, William R. "Southern Punch: A Draught
of Confederate Wit," SFQ (Je, 1962), 26: 131-36.
Discussion of a Richmond, Va., comic weekly.

2702. Long, E. Hudson. "Social Customs in O. Henry's
Texas Stories," in A Good Tale and a Bonnie
Tune, ed. Mody C. Boatright et al., pp. 148-67.
Texas folklife and folklore recorded by O. Henry
in his fiction after two years on a ranch.

2703. Loomis, C. Grant. "Bret Harte's Folklore," WF
       (Jan, 1956), 15: 19-22. Brief account of Harte's
       use of legends, superstitions, tall tales, etc.

2704. _____. "Folk Language in William MacLeod
       Raine's West," TFSB (Dec, 1958), 24: 131-48.
       186 proverbs and 201 proverbial expressions--all
       arranged alphabetically from some 80 western
       novels.

2705. _____. "Henry David Thoreau as Folklorist,"
       WF (Apr, 1957), 16: 90-106. Tales, customs,
       beliefs, weather lore, superstitions, proverbs,
       and aphorisms are listed.

2706. Lydenberg, John. "Nature Myth in Faulkner's 'The
       Bear'," AL (Mr, 1952), 24: 62-72.

2707. Lynch, James J. "The Devil in the Writings of
       Irving, Hawthorne, and Poe," NYFQ (S, 1952),
       8: 111-31. Irving's devil is comic, Hawthorne's
       psychologically treated, Poe's grotesque.

2708. McAtee, W. L. Studies in the Vocabularies of Hoo-
       sier Authors: Baynard Rush Hall (1793-1863),
       (Chapel Hill: p.p., 1960), iii, 90ff.

2709. McCloskey, John C. "Back-Country Folkways in
       Mrs. Kirkland's A New Home--Who'll Follow?"
       MichH (Sept, 1956), 40: 297-308.

2710. McCullen, J. T., Jr. and Jeri Tanner. "The Devil
       Outwitted in Folklore and Literature," NCarF
       (May, 1969), 17: 15-20. Sketchy account of
       Devil's discomfiture in literature.

2711. MacDougald, Duncan Jr. "The 'Uncle Remus
       Stories,'" Fabula (1957), 1: i/ii, 159-161. Ap-
       preciative review of new ed. of Joel Chandler
       Harris.

2712. McGhee, Nancy B. "Langston Hughes: Poet in the
       Folk Manner," in Langston Hughes, Black Genius:
       a Critical Evaluation, ed. Therman B. O'Daniel
       (New York: Morrow, 1971), pp. 39-64.

2712a. Marsh, Philip M. "Indian Folklore in Freneau,"

New Jersey Historical Society Proceedings (Apr, 1953), 71: 125-135.

2713. Martin, Wendy. "The Rogue and the Rational Man: Hugh Henry Brackenridge's Study of a Con Man in Modern Chivalry," EAL (F, 1973), 8: 179-192. Teague O'Regan is the earliest confidence man in American fiction.

2714. Metzger, Deena Posy. "Hart Crane's Bridge: the Myth Active," ArQ (Spr, 1964), 20: 36-46. Crane employed two Middle American myths: Quetzalcoatl and the Eagle and the Serpent.

2715. Milledge, Luetta Upshur. "Light Eternal: An Analysis of Some Folkloristic Elements in Faulkner's Go Down, Moses," TFSB (Dec, 1963), 29: 86-93. Humorous exaggeration, the folk exemplum, folk speech, custom, and ritual appear in Faulkner.

2716. Millichap, Joseph R. "Carson McCullers' Literary Ballad," GR (F, 1973), 27: 329-39. Carson McCullers' novella Ballad of the Sad Cafe has some of the qualities found in the old ballads even though it is a conspicuously literary performance.

2717. Millward, Celia and Cecilia Tichi. "Whatever Happened to Hiawatha?" Genre (Sept, 1973), 6: 313-332. Longfellow strove to write a folk epic (certain folklore elements are discussed).

2718. Moore, Jack B. "A Traditional Motif in Early American Fiction," MF (W, 1962), 12: 197-203. Use of the theme, "The Boy Who Had Never Seen a Woman."

2719. Moore, Robert. "Hawthorne's Folk-Motifs and The House of the Seven Gables," NYFQ (Sept, 1972), 28: 221-233. A variety of folklore motifs support Hawthorne's notion of witchcraft and were derived from experience and reading.

2720. Morris, Robert L. "The Arkansan in American Folklore," AHQ (S, 1960), 9: 99-107. The Arkansan in American cultural history is a symbol like the Kentucky colonel, Texas ranger, and California gold miner.

2921. Moyne, Ernest J. Hiawatha and Kalevala (Helsinki:
       Suomalainen Tiedeakatemia, 1963), FF Communi-
       cations, no. 192, 146pp. Hiawatha is not basical-
       ly a plagiarism of the great Finnish epic, al-
       though Longfellow used the metre and structure of
       Kalevala.

2722. _____. "Manabozho, Tarenyawagon, and Hiawatha,"
       SFQ (Sept, 1965), 29: 195-203. Schoolcraft, not
       Longfellow, was to blame for the confusion of Al-
       gonquin and Iroquois legends.

2723. Mullen, Patrick B. "Myth & Folklore in The Ord-
       ways," in Hunters & Healers, ed. Wilson M.
       Hudson, pp. 133-145. Analysis of William
       Humphreys's 1965 novel.

2724. Noyes, Sylvia Gray. "Mrs. Almira Todd, Herbalist-
       Conjurer," CLQ (Dec, 1972), Series IX, 12: 643-
       649. Account of a character in Sarah Orne
       Jewett's novel, The Country of the Pointed Firs.

2725. O'Donnell, Richard W. "'On the Eighteenth of April,
       in Seventy-five ...' Longfellow Didn't Know the
       Half of It," Smithsonian (Apr, 1973), 4: 72-77.
       A facetious article about Paul Revere's ride and
       the errors made in describing it.

2726. O'Donnell, Thomas F. "More Apologies: the Indian
       in New York Fiction," NYFQ (Dec, 1967), 23:
       243-53. More literary history than folklore.

2727. Owen, Guy. "The Use of Folklore in Fiction,"
       NCarF (Mr, 1971), 19: 73-79. A novelist com-
       ments on his own practices.

2728. Payne, Mildred Y. "Folk Characters in Two Kroll
       Novels," TFSB (Mr, 1965), 31: 16-22. Fury in
       the Earth and Rogues' Company analyzed for folk
       elements.

2729. _____. "A Tennessee Judge Revised: A Study
       of Folk Elements in One of Opie Read's Best-
       Known Novels," TFSB (Sept, 1966), 32: 82-87.

2730. _____. "The Vanishing Folklorist," TFSB (Dec,
       1965), 31: 105-8. Brief mention of novelists

like Jesse Stuart, Opie Read, H. H. Kroll,
Elizabeth Roberts, and Mary N. Murfree.

2731. Pearce, T. M. "The New Mexican 'Shepherds'
Play'," WF (Apr, 1956), 15: 77-88. Discussion
of various texts of the traditional Los Pastores
and the basic episodes synthesized.

2732. Peavy, Charles D. "Faulkner's Use of Folklore in
The Sound and the Fury," JAF (Jl-Sept, 1966),
79: 437-47.

2733. Pedrini, Lura and Duilio T. Pedrini. "Similes and
Metaphors in Cooper's The Pathfinder," NYFQ (Je,
1967), 23: 99-108. Animals, the sea, the forest
provide figurative language for the novelist.

2734. Penrod, James H. "The Folk Hero as Prankster in
the Old Southwestern Yarns," KFR (Jan-Mr,
1956), 2: 5-12. Characters from Longstreet,
Cobb, Field, etc.

2735. _____. "Folk Humor in Sut Lovingood's Yarns,"
TFSB (Dec, 1950), 16: 76-84. Good analysis of
George W. Harris's rural humor with stress on
folk customs, tall talk, and rough comedy.

2736. _____. "The Folk Mind in Early Southwestern
Humor," TFSB (Mr, 1952), 18: 49-54. Folk
humor in George W. Harris, William T. Thompson, and Johnson J. Hooper.

2737. _____. "Folk Motifs in Old Southwestern Humor,"
SFQ (Je, 1955), 19: 117-24. Southwestern humor
is not unique but is related to international
themes. Examples: origins of colored races,
animal heroes, mythical beasts, and unusual men
(dirt eaters, ugly men).

2738. _____. "Harden Taliaferro, Folk Humorist of
North Carolina," MF (F, 1956), 6: 147-53.

2739. _____. "Military and Civil Titles in the Old
Southwestern Yarns," TFSB (Mr, 1953), 19: 13-
19. Satire of pretentious titles by Longstreet,
Baldwin, Harris, et al.

2740. _____. "Minority Groups in Old Southwestern
       Humor," SFQ (Sept, 1958), 22: 121-28. Treat-
       ment of Negroes and Indians by Longstreet, G.
       W. Harris, Thompson, and others. Too ambi-
       tious a study for brief discussion.

2741. _____. "Teachers and Preachers in the Old
       Southern Yarns," TFSB (Dec, 1952), 18: 91-96.
       Character types in A. B. Longstreet, G. W.
       Harris, et al.

2742. _____. "Two Types of Incongruity in Old South-
       western Humor," KFR (Oct-Dec, 1958), 4: 163-
       73. Burlesques and shifts of diction or usage
       discussed.

2743. _____. "Women in the Old Southwestern Yarns,"
       KFR (Apr-Je, 1955), 1: 41-47.

2744. Peterson, Richard F. "The Grail Legend and Stein-
       beck's 'The Great Mountains'," StQ (W, 1973),
       6: 9-15. Steinbeck uses rapier and grail sym-
       bolism in the middle part of The Red Pony.

2745. Pickering, James H. "Fenimore Cooper and Pink-
       ster," NYFQ (Mr, 1966), 22: 15-19. Cooper's
       use of Albany material in his New York City
       scenes in Satanstoe.

2746. Plater, Ormonde. "Before Sut: Folklore in the
       Early Works of George Washington Harris," SFQ
       (Je, 1970), 34: 104-115. Folk motifs in eight
       early works, by the creator of the trickster Sut
       Lovingood.

2747. _____. "The Lovingood Patriarchy," AJ (Spr,
       1973), 1: 82-93. G. W. Harris's Sut Lovingood
       yarns include erotic humor and folklore as well
       as Sut himself (a trickster).

2748. Pollack, Vivian R. "Emily Dickinson's Valentines,"
       AQ (Mr, 1974), 26: 60-78. Emily Dickinson
       wrote three early "valentine" poems showing Eng-
       ligh conventions.

2749. Poulsen, Richard C. "Black George, Black Harris,
       and the Mountain Man Vernacular," Rendezvous

(S, 1973), 8: 15-23. The literary use of mountain men's speech in George Ruxton's autobiography and Emerson Bennett's fiction.

2750. Pronechen, Joseph S. "The Making of Hiawatha," NYFQ (Je, 1972), 28: 151-60. A superficial survey of familiar material.

2751. Pugh, Griffith T. "George W. Cable's Theory and Use of Folk Speech," SFQ (Dec 1950), 24: 287-93. Brief survey of Cable's handling of dialect in fiction.

2752. Rael, Juan B. "More Light on the Origin of Los Pastores," NMFR (1951-52), 6: 1-6. Three important Spanish nativity plays: Texas and New Mexico versions published, Colorado text unpublished.

2753. Randall, Dale J. B. "Dialect in the Verse of 'the Hoosier Poet'," AS (Feb, 1960), 35: 36-50. Riley's dialect, although an amalgam necessitated by his desire to write verse, is generally accurate.

2754. Randel, William. "Edward Eggleston on Dialect," AS (May, 1955), 30: 111-14. Brief discussion showing that Eggleston was accurate in using Negro and Hoosier dialect.

2755. Rayson, Ann L. "The Novels of Zora Neale Hurston," SBL (W, 1974), 5: 1-10. Hurston filled her novels with folk idioms and folkways derived from Negro folklore in Georgia and Florida.

2756. Read, Allen Walker. "The World of Joe Strickland," JAF (Oct-Dec, 1963), 76: 277-308. Study of George W. Arnold (1783-1838), whose Joe Strickland letters appeared in the National Advocate and preceded Seba Smith's Jack Downing.

2757. Reaver, J. Russell. "Emerson's Use of Proverbs," SFQ (Dec, 1963), 27: 280-99. Emerson's views and uses of proverbs may have influenced his style.

2758. _____. "Mythic Motivation in Willa Cather's O

Pioneers!" WF (Jan, 1968), 27: 19-25. Mythic
heroes and heroines may have served the novelist
as models.

2759. Reeves, Paschal. "The Humor of Thomas Wolfe,"
        SFQ (Je, 1960), 24: 109-20. Wolfe has not al-
        ways been found funny but he did use tall tales,
        satire, and bawdy material.

2760. _____. "Thomas Wolfe and His Scottish Heritage,"
        SFQ (Je, 1964), 28: 134-41. Wolfe's maternal
        ancestry was Scotch and he used Scotch folk
        strains in his fiction.

2761. Reichart, Walter A. "Washington Irving's Interest
        in German Folklore," NYFQ (A, 1957), 13: 181-
        92. Careful account of Irving's German sources.

2762. Render, Sylvia Lyons. "North Carolina Dialect:
        Chesnutt Style," NCarF (Nov, 1967), 15: 67-70.
        Discussion of regional dialect in the fiction of
        Charles W. Chesnutt.

2763. _____. The Short Fiction of Charles W. Chesnutt
        (Washington: Howard U. P., 1974), lvi, 422pp.
        Some 55 tales and sketches published here.

2764. Richards, Lewis A. "Frank Dobie's Use of Folklore:
        The Lost Adams Digging Story," WR (Spr, 1970),
        7: 29-49. Dobie's story of a mine in New Mexi-
        co, a substantial part of Apache Gold and Yaqui
        Silver, is mostly folklore.

2765. Rickels, Milton. Thomas Bangs Thorpe: Humorist
        of the Old Southwest (Baton Rouge: La. S. U. P.,
        1962), x, 275pp. Valuable study of the author
        of "The Big Bear of Arkansas" and other tall
        tales.

2766. Robb, J. D. "The Music of Los Pastores," WF (Oct,
        1957), 16: 263-80. Transcriptions and evaluations
        of some of the music of the famous folk play.

2767. Roberts, Warren E. "Some Folksong References in
        Kennedy's Swallow Barn," SFQ (Dec, 1953), 17:
        249-54. Hafen Blok, a German in the novel,
        sings folk songs around 1800. Some 11 ballads
        or songs used.

2768. Rodes, Sara Puryear. "Washington Irving's Use of
      Traditional Folklore," SFQ (Sept, 1956), 20: 143-
      153. Reprinted in NYFQ (Spr, 1957), 13: 3-15.
      Irving used ghosts, buried treasure, and local
      legends. Diffuse and not very analytical.

2769. Rubin, Louis D., Jr. "Uncle Remus and the Ubiqui-
      tous Rabbit," SR (Oct, 1974), 10: 787-804. The
      rabbit is a Negro and the animals are colored
      folk. Harris's stories are comic, not tragic.

2770. Samuels, Charles E. "Folklore in Eben Holden,"
      NYFQ (S, 1957), 13: 100-3. Tall tales in an
      Irving Bacheller novel.

2771. Sands, Donald B. "Holman Day: His Ballad Books
      (1900-1904) and Their Lexical Features," AS
      (Feb, 1965), 41: 17-27. A minor Maine poet had
      an ear for dialect and regional folk speech; cf.
      Up in Maine, 1900.

2772. Schwendinger, Robert J. "The Language of the Sea:
      Relationships Between the Language of Herman
      Melville and Sea Shanties of the 19th Century,"
      SFQ (Mr, 1973), 37: 53-73. Texts of familiar
      sea shanties reveal Melville's accuracy in depict-
      ing conditions of sea life in the nineteenth century.

2773. Sears, Donald A. "Folk Poetry in Longfellow's Boy-
      hood," NEQ (Mr, 1972), 45: 96-105. Convincing
      proof that folk poetry in the Portland of Long-
      fellow's youth influenced his own writing.

2774. Stein, William Bysshe. Hawthorne's Faust: A Study
      of the Devil Archetype (Gainesville: U. of Fla.
      P., 1953), pp. vii, 172. Study of the Faust
      theme in Hawthorne's Scarlet Letter and some of
      the short stories. Not always convincing.

2775. Stokely, Wilma Dykeman. "The Literature of the
      Southern Appalachian Mountains," MLW (W, 1964),
      40: 7-18. Mostly literary in content but with
      some attention paid to ballads and tall tales.

2776. Stuckey, Sterling. "Through the Prism of Folklore:
      The Black Ethos in Slavery," MR (S, 1968), 9:
      417-37. Careful analysis of attitudes and beliefs
      of slaves as evidenced in their folklore.

2777. Sullivan, Philip E. "Buh Rabbit: Going Through the Changes," SBL (S, 1973), 4: 28-32. The briar patch rabbit survives as Old Gray Goose, Stagolee, Mr. Jiveass Nigger, and in the works of Ellison and Cecil Brown.

2778. Thompson, Lawrence S. "Folklore in the Kentucky Novel," MF (F, 1953), 3: 137-45. Rapid survey of titles and authors.

2779. _____. "The Rediscovery of Kentucky," ABC (Dec, 1957), 8: 19-24. Cursory survey of folklore and tradition in Kentucky fiction.

2780. Thompson, Stith. "The Indian Legends Since 'Hiawatha'," MichH (Dec, 1955), 39: 462-63. Summary of speech.

2781. Utley, Francis Lee. "Folk Literature: An Operational Definition," JAF (Jl-Sept, 1961), 74: 193-206. Definition of folk literature as "orally transmitted literature wherever found."

2782. _____. "From the Dinnsenchas to Proust: the Folklore of Placenames in Literature," Names (Sept, 1968), 16: 273-293. Irish, French, and American examples confirm the universality of interest and charm in placenames.

2783. [No entry]

2784. Vickers, Ovid S. "The Gourd and Regional Writing," MFR (Spr, 1972), 6: 5-8. Deals with allusions to gourds in novels by Carolyn Miller and Vinnie Williams.

2785. Walker, Warren S. "The Frontiersman as Recluse and Redeemer," NYFQ (S, 1960), 16: 110-122. Speculations on the models for and character of Cooper's Natty Bumppo.

2786. _____. James Fenimore Cooper: An Introduction and Interpretation (New York: Barnes and Noble, 1962), pp. xvii, 142. Walker states (p. 27): "No other writer in his own time and few since have used folklore so extensively or as effectively as Cooper did," but does not always provide the evidence.

2787.   Walser, Richard. "Ham Jones: Southern Folk Hu-
        morist," JAF (Oct-Dec, 1965), 78: 295-316.
        Study of a North Carolina writer, author of "Cous-
        in Sally Dilliard" and other well known sketches.

2788.   _____. "Negro Dialect in Eighteenth-Century
        American Drama," AS (Dec, 1955), 30: 269-76.

2789.   Walters, Thomas N. "Thad Stem, Jr., and Folk-
        lore," NCarF (May, 1969), 17: 40-52. Interview
        with a practicing writer.

2790.   Walton, David A. "Joel Chandler Harris as Folklor-
        ist; a Reassessment," KFQ (Spr, 1966), 11: 21-
        26. Although not a trained folklorist Harris used
        the Negro tales reliably.

2791.   Walton, Ivan H. "Eugene O'Neill and the Folklore
        and Folkways of the Sea," WF (Jl, 1955), 14:
        153-69. Sailors' shanties, superstitions, tales,
        and folkways.

2792.   Ward, Jerry W. "Folklore and the Study of Black
        Literature," MFR (F, 1972), 6: 83-90. Analysis
        of folklore in various writers: Ellison, Killens,
        Hughes, etc.

2793.   Watkins, Floyd C. "Indian Folklore in the Fiction
        of James Kirke Paulding," NYFQ (A, 1951), 7:
        217-25. Paulding was the first important Ameri-
        can novelist to use comparatively authentic Indian
        folklore.

2794.   _____. "James Kirke Paulding's Early Ring-
        Tailed Roarer," SFQ (Sept, 1951), 15: 183-87.
        Letters from the South, 1817, contains a sketch
        of a ring-tailed roarer, possibly the earliest of
        its type known.

2795.   _____. "Thomas Wolfe and the Southern Moun-
        taineer," SAQ (Jan, 1951), 50: 58-71.

2796.   Waugh, Butler. "Structural Analysis in Literature
        and Folklore," WF (Jl, 1966), 25: 153-64.
        Analysts should consider language, plot, scene,
        and theme.

2797. Wellborn, Grace Pleasant. "The Golden Thread in
       The Scarlet Letter," SFQ (Je, 1965), 29: 169-78.
       Symbolic values of yellow (gold) and red in Haw-
       thorne's novel.

2798. _____. "Plant Lore and The Scarlet Letter,"
       SFQ (Je, 1963), 27: 160-67. Hawthorne used
       plants with both good and evil connotations: rose,
       oak, pine, lily, dogwood, henbane.

2799. Wentersdorf, Karl P. "The Element of Witchcraft
       in The Scarlet Letter," Folklore (S, 1972), 83:
       132-53. A close study of Mistress Hibbins and
       the Black Man references in the novel.

2800. Wess, Robert C. "The Use of Hudson Valley Tradi-
       tions in Washington Irving's Knickerbocker His-
       tory of New York," NYFQ (Sept, 1974), 30: 212-
       25. Mostly repetitious.

2801. West, Harry C. "Negro Folklore in Pierce's Novels,"
       NCarF (Mr, 1971), 19: 66-72. Folklore in the
       fiction of Ovid Williams Pierce.

2802. West, James L. W., III. "Early Backwoods Humor
       in the Greenville Mountaineer, 1826-1840," MissQ
       (W, 1971-1972), 25: 69-82. Backwoods humor in
       a Greenville, S.C., periodical. Tales of frontier
       fights, courtship and marriage customs, religious
       humor.

2803. Wiggins, Eugene. "Benét's 'Mountain Whippoorwill':
       Folklore and Folklore," TFSB (Sept, 1975), 41:
       99-114. Benét's use of a mountain fiddlers'
       contest in a celebrated poem.

2804. William, Cratis D. "Mountain Customs, Social Life,
       and Folk Yarns in Taliaferro's Fisher's River
       Scenes and Characters," NCarF (Nov, 1968), 16:
       143-52. Excellent study of an 1859 book which
       is rich in folk materials.

2805. Williams, Leonard. "An Early Arkansas 'Frolic':
       A Contemporary Account," MSF (S, 1974), 2:
       39-42. Reprint with comment of a Spirit of the
       Times sketch by Noland.

2806. Wilson, George P. "Lois Lenski's Use of Regional Speech," NCarF (Dec, 1961), 9: 1-3. Dialect defended in a writer of children's books.

2807. _____. "Shakespeare and Southern Folklore," GR (W, 1967), 21: 508-20. Comparison of southern beliefs about ghosts, witches, the moon, and numbers with citations of appropriate passages from the plays.

2808. Winkelman, Donald M. "Goodman Brown, Tom Sawyer, and Oral Tradition," KFQ (Spr, 1965), 10: 43-48. Perfunctory examination of a tale and a novel confirms the contention that Hawthorne and Twain used folklore consciously and effectively.

2809. _____. "Three American Authors as Semi-Folk Artists," JAF (Apr-Je, 1965), 78: 130-135. Brief studies of Twain, Manly Wellman, and Charles W. Chesnutt.

2810. Winslow, David J. "Hawthorne's Folklore and the Folklorists' Hawthorne: A Reexamination," SFQ (Mr, 1970), 34: 34-52.

2811. Woodbridge, Hensley C. "Americanisms in Felix Holt's Gabriel Horn," KFR (Jan-Mr, 1956), 2: 15-22. Folk speech in an historical novel of Kentucky.

2812. Woodward, Robert H. "Harold Frederic and New York Folklore," NYFQ (S, 1960), 16: 83-89. Folklore material in the fiction of a nineteenth century novelist.

2813. _____. "Harold Frederic's Use of British and Irish Folklore," NYFQ (Spr, 1961), 17: 51-55. Frederic's use of local folklore in British tales.

2814. _____. "Harold Frederic's Woodchuck Story," NYFQ (A, 1961), 17: 197-99. Frederic used a traditional anecdote from printed sources.

2815. _____. "Mohawk Valley Folk Life During the Civil War," NYFQ (S, 1962), 18: 107-18. Folk life reflected in the fiction of Harold Frederic.

2816. Wyld, Lionel D. "Fiction, Fact, and Folklore: the
       World of Chad Hanna," EJ (May, 1967), 56: 716-
       719. Folklore in Walter Edmonds' 1940 novel
       about the circus.

2817. Yates, Norris W. William T. Porter and the Spirit
       of the Times (Baton Rouge: La. S. U. P. , 1957),
       pp. xi, 222. Definitive biography of Porter and
       useful study of his sporting magazine.

2818. Young, Philip. Three Bags Full: Essays in Ameri-
       can Fiction (New York: Harcourt, Brace, Jovano-
       vich, 1972), pp. xvi, 231. Substantial discus-
       sions of myths of Pocahontas and Rip Van Winkle,
       among other reprinted essays.

2819. Yu, Beong-Cheon. "Lafcadio Hearn's Twice-Told
       Legends Reconsidered," AL (Mr, 1962), 34: 56-
       71. Comments on Stray Leaves from Strange
       Literature, Some Chinese Ghosts, and various
       Japanese legends.

2820. Zug, Charles G. , III. "The Construction of 'The
       Devil and Tom Walker': A Study of Irving's
       Later Use of Folklore," NYFQ (Dec, 1968), 24:
       243-60.

13. PROVERBS, RIDDLES, WELLERISMS, LIMERICKS

2821. Abrahams, Roger D. "The Bigger They Are, the Harder They Fall," TFSB (Dec, 1963), 29: 94-102. Elephant jokes told as riddles or conundrums.

2822. _____. "Ghastly Commands: the Cruel Joke Revisited," MF (W, 1961-1962), 11: 235-246.

2823. _____. "Introductory Remarks to a Rhetorical Theory of Folklore," JAF (Apr.Je, 1968), 81: 143-158. Discussion of structure and performance with stress on riddles and proverbs.

2824. _____. "The Literary Study of the Riddle," TSLL (Spr, 1972), 14: 177-197. Criticism of previous riddle scholarship. Examples of riddles chosen from island of St. Vincent.

2825. _____. "Some Riddles from the Negro of Philadelphia," KFQ (W, 1962), 7: iv, 10-17. Riddles collected from So. Philadelphia.

2826. _____ and Alan Dundes. "Riddles," in Folklore and Folklife, ed. R. M. Dorson, pp. 129-143. Brief survey of riddles and variants.

2827. _____ and Joseph C. Hickerson. "Cross-Fertilization Riddles," WF (Oct, 1964), 23: 253-257.

2828. Ainsworth, Catherine Harris. "Black and White and Said All Over," SFQ (Dec, 1962), 26: 263-295. Some 535 riddles from ninth grade students from different towns.

2829. Arner, Robert D. "Proverbs in Edward Taylor's Gods Determinations," SFQ (Mr, 1973), 37: 1-13. The colonial poet Taylor used proverbs and figurative verse extensively.

306

2830.   Arora, Shirley L. "More Spanish Proverbial Exaggerations from California," WF (Apr, 1971), 30: 105-118. Supplement to a previous list.

2831.   _____. "Proverbial Exaggerations in English and Spanish," Proverbium (1973), 18: 675-683.

2832.   _____. "Some Spanish Proverbial Comparisons from California," WF (Oct, 1961), 20: 229-237. Spanish texts with translations, mostly from Los Angeles.

2833.   _____. "Spanish Proverbial Exaggerations from California," WF (Oct, 1968), 27: 229-253. Some 150 Spanish texts with translations from Los Angeles area.

2834.   Ashton, John W. "Popular Wisdom in Indiana in the 1830's," JOFS (Spr, 1968), 3: 41-44. Collection of 18 proverbs and sayings plus beliefs and household hints.

2835.   Babcock, C. Merton. "Melville's Proverbs of the Sea," WF (Oct, 1952), 11: 254-265. Classified list of proverbs, sayings, etc. from 11 Melville works.

2836.   _____. "Some Expressions from Herman Melville," PADS (Apr, 1959), No. 31, 3-13.

2837.   Baldwin, L. Karen. "A Sampling of Housewives' Proverbs and Proverbial Phrases from Levittown, Pennsylvania," KFQ (F, 1965), 10: 127-148. 249 items from 11 housewives.

2838.   Balys, Jonas. "Fifty Lithuanian Riddles," JAF (Jl-Sept, 1950), 63: 325-327. Translated riddles from a Lithuanian housewife in Chicago.

2839.   Barbour, Frances M. "Embellishment of the Proverb," SFQ (Dec, 1964), 28: 291-298. Proverbs frequently show alterations: expansion, changes of words or similes, weightier diction. Some 89 examples of such changes from Illinois, 1944-1950.

2840.   _____. Proverbs and Proverbial Phrases in

Illinois (Carbondale: So. Illinois U. P., 1965),
213pp. Data gathered from students and arranged
alphabetically by key words. Much of it not
unique to Illinois. Some definitions seem naive.

2841. _____. "Some Foreign Proverbs in Southern
Illinois," MF (F, 1954), 4: 161-164. Many German proverbs remain in circulation; translations
given.

2842. _____. "Some Uncommon Sources of Proverbs,"
MF (S, 1963), 13: 97-100. Proverbs may come
from songs, advertisements, or sayings.

2843. Barrick, Mac E. "Early Proverbs from Carlisle,
Pennsylvania (1788-1821)," KFQ (F, 1968), 13:
193-217.

2844. _____. "The Newspaper Riddle Joke," JAF (Jl-
Sept, 1974), 87: 253-257.

2845. _____. "Popular Comparisons and Similes," KFQ
(Spr, 1965), 10: 3-34. Common comparisons
from Cumberland Co., Penn. arranged alphabetically.

2846. _____. "Proverbs and Sayings from Cumberland
County," KFQ (W, 1963), 8: 139-203. Long list
of Penn. proverbial material derived from con-
versations and questionnaires. Items listed alphabetically by key words; informants given.

2847. _____. "Racial Riddles and the Polack Joke,"
KFQ (Spr, 1970), 15: 3-15. Some 52 examples
which exaggerate alleged qualities of Polish
Americans for comic effect.

2848. _____. "Riddles from Cumberland County," KFQ
(S, 1963), 8: 59-74. Riddles classified according
to Archer Taylor's thematic arrangement. Informants listed.

2849. _____. "The Shaggy Elephant Riddle," SFQ (Dec,
1964), 28: 266-290. Comments on the 1962-1963
craze for elephant jokes with 245 examples.
Most items are ridiculously irrelevant to the
pachyderms.

2850.   Bauman, Richard. "The Turtles: an American
        Riddling Institution," WF (Jan, 1970), 29: 21-25.
        Riddles used as an initiation rite.

2851.   _____ and Neil McCabe. "Proverbs in an LSD
        Cult," JAF (Jl-Sept, 1970), 83: 318-324. Ten
        proverbs used in a ritual in a Dallas initiation
        cult.

2852.   Blackwell, Louise. "Eudora Welty: Proverbs and
        Proverbial Phrases in The Golden Apples," SFQ
        (Dec, 1966), 30: 332-341. Analysis of the story
        "Shower of Gold."

2853.   Boshears, Frances. "Proverbial Comparisons from
        an East Tennessee County," TFSB (Je, 1954), 20:
        27-41. 1,045 items from Scott Co. from col-
        lector's own memory.

2854.   Boswell, George W. "Folk Wisdom in Northeastern
        Kentucky," TFSB (Mr, 1967), 33: 10-17. Some
        99 student-collected proverbs; informants listed
        but no annotation.

2855.   _____. "Riddles in the WPA-Collected Folklore
        Archives," MFR (Spr, 1969), 3: 33-52. Some
        48 true riddles from eight collectors plus some
        trick questions.

2856.   Brooks, Bill and Ray B. Browne. "Riddles from
        Tippecanoe County, Indiana," MF (F, 1961), 11:
        155-160. True riddles and arithmetical puzzles.

2857.   Brown, Waln K. "Cognitive Ambiguity and the 'Pre-
        tended Obscene Riddle,'" KF (F, 1973), 18: 89-
        101. Some true riddles utilize sexual or obscene
        allusions but because of intentional ambiguity end
        harmlessly.

2858.   Browne, Ray B. "'The Wisdom of Many': Proverbs
        and Proverbial Expressions," in Our Living Tradi-
        tions, ed. Tristram P. Coffin, pp. 192-203.
        Brief survey with the usual definitions; many ex-
        amples. Benjamin Franklin's work cited.

2859.   Brunvand, Jan Harold. Dictionary of Proverbs and
        Proverbial Phrases from Books Published by In-

diana Authors Before 1890 (Bloomington: Indiana
U. P., 1961), xxxiv, 168pp. Material from such
authors as Eggleston, Riley, Lew Wallace.

2860. _____. "Some Thoughts on the Ethnic-Regional
Riddle Jokes," IF (1970), 3: 128-142. Old jokes
are often adapted to new situations.

2861. Bryant, Margaret M. "Proverbial Lore in American
Life and Speech," WF (Apr, 1951), 10: 134-142.
Survey of proverbs in cartoons, headlines, ad-
vertising, etc.

2862. _____. "Proverbs: Proverb Lore in American
Life and Speech," NYFQ (A, 1952), 8: 221-226.
Brief discussion with many examples.

2863. Cerf, Bennett A. Out on a Limerick (New York:
Harper, 1960), 125pp. Carefully chosen collection dry-cleaned by the author.

2864. _____. Riddle-de-dee; 458, Count Them (New
York: Random House, 1962), 119pp. Of no
scholarly value.

2865. Clark, Joseph D. "Proverbs and Sayings from North
Carolina," SFQ (Je, 1962), 26: 145-173. Some
710 items collected by No. Car. State College
students. Arranged alphabetically by key words;
inconsistent annotations.

2866. _____. "Riddles from North Carolina," SFQ (Je,
1961), 25: 113-125. Some 132 riddles and two
riddle songs with annotations.

2867. Clarke, Mary Washington. "Proverbs, Proverbial
Phrases, and Proverbial Comparisons in the
Writings of Jesse Stuart," SFQ (Je, 1965), 29:
142-163. Extensive list of proverbial material
from a Kentucky regionalist; meticulous annotation.

2868. Cobos, Rubén. "New Mexico Spanish Proverbs,"
NMFR (1969-1970), 12: 7-11. Some 73 Spanish
proverbs with literal translations and approximate
meanings from Bernalillo and Santa Fe counties.

2869. Cole, Arthur H. "The Social Significance of New

England Idiomatic Phrases, " Proceedings of the
American Antiquarian Society (1960), 70: 21-68.
Some 2,000 proverbial comparisons which are
said to characterize New England speech.

2870. Cray, Ed. "Wellerisms in Riddle Form," WF (Apr,
1964), 23: 114-116. Some 22 items.

2871. _____ and Marilyn Eisenberg Herzog. "The Ab-
surd Elephant: a Recent Riddle Fad, " WF (Jan,
1967), 26: 27-36. 116 elephant riddles and jokes
from Los Angeles.

2872. Dann, Flora H. "The Counties: Lore from Chautau-
qua County, " NYFQ (W, 1951), 7: 306-318.
Mostly proverbs and riddles.

2873. Davidoff, Henry. A World Treasury of Proverbs
from Twenty-Five Languages (London: Cassell,
1953), 492pp. First ed. New York, 1946. Proverbs arranged alphabetically and largely from
English and American sources; Emerson cited
66 times, Franklin 45.

2874. Dundes, Alan. "The Elephant Joking Question, "
TFSB (Je, 1963), 29: 40-42. 14 examples.

2875. Dunlap, A. R. "More Delaware Sayings, " DFB
(1952), 1: 11. Some 27 examples.

2876. Dunn, James Taylor. "'Steal Not This Book,'"
NYFQ (A, 1952), 8: 206-209. Autographs in
books warning against theft.

2887. French, Florence Healy. "Cooper the Tinkerer, "
NYFQ (Sept, 1970), 26: 229-239. Partial repetition of an earlier article. Cooper changed
original form of proverbs.

2878. _____. "Cooper's Use of Proverbs in the Anti-
Rent Novels, " NYFQ (Mr, 1970), 26: 42-49. History of the controversy; 206 proverbs of which
77 are literary.

2879. Fuller, Beverly. "Epitaphs: Hartsdale Canine
Cemetery, Westchester County, " NYFQ (A, 1953),
9: 221-228.

2880.   Georges, Robert A. and Alan Dundes. "Toward a
        Structural Definition of the Riddle," JAF (Apr-Je,
        1963), 76: 111-118. Structural analysis applied
        to the riddle. Riddles classified as "opposition-
        al" and "nonoppositional."

2881.   Grambo, Ronald. "Paremiological Aspects," FF (Jl,
        1972), 5: 99-105. Chiefly a discussion of Wel-
        lerisms.

2882.   Guthrie, Charles S. Riddles from the Cumberland
        Valley (Bowling Green, Ky.: Kentucky Folklore
        Soc., 1973), 35pp. 104 riddles from Cumber-
        land Co. with data about informants and notes.

2883.   Haberly, Lewis. "Here Lies Schroon Lake," NYFQ
        (W, 1962), 18: 265-272. Epitaphs from Schroon
        Lake, N.Y. collected by a high school student.

2884.   Halpert, Herbert. "East Tennessee Question-and-
        Answer Tall Tales," TFSB (Dec, 1952), 18: 101-
        103. Six riddle questions, two true riddles.

2885.   _____. "More Proverbial Comparisons from West
        Tennessee," TFSB (Mr, 1952), 18: 15-21.

2886.   _____. "A Pattern of Proverbial Exaggerations
        from West Kentucky," MF (Apr, 1951), 1: 41-47.
        Some 162 examples from Murray State College
        students.

2887.   _____. "Proverbial Comparisons from West Ten-
        nessee," TFSB (Sept, 1951), 17: 49-61. Some
        658 examples mostly from seven W. Tenn. coun-
        ties reported by students.

2888.   _____. "Riddles from West Tennessee," TFSB
        (Je, 1952), 18: 29-42. Sixty true riddles re-
        ported by students.

2889.   _____. "Some Wellerisms from Kentucky and
        Tennessee," JAF (Apr-Je, 1956), 69: 115-122.
        Some 62 examples of student-collected Weller-
        isms.

2890.   Hand, Wayland D. "Folk Beliefs in Proverbial
        Form," Proverbium (1970), 15: 48-50.

2891. _____. "Writings of Archer Taylor on Proverbs and Proverbial Lore," Proverbium (1970), 15: 4-8. A bibliography.

2892. Harder, Kelsie B. "Proverbial Snopeslore," TFSB (Sept, 1958), 24: 89-95. Examination of Faulkner's use of proverbs and proverbial lore, especially in The Hamlet and The Town and the character of I. O. Snopes.

2893. Hendricks, George D. "Don't Look Back," in Singers and Storytellers, ed. Mody C. Boatright et al., pp. 69-75. A kind of proverbial fugue on the basic theme.

2894. Hilliard, Addie Suggs. "Shakespeare Proverbs in Chester County, Tennessee," NCarFJ (May, 1974), 22: 63-74.

2895. Hindman, Darwin Alexander. 1800 Riddles, Enigmas and Conundrums (New York: Dover, 1963), 154pp. A compilation.

2896. Hines, Donald M. "Rare Blooms from a Rude Land: Frontier Riddles from the Inland Pacific Northwest," IF (1973), 6: 205-240. Some 230 riddles from weekly newspapers.

2897. _____. "Wry Wit and Frontier Humor--the Wellerism in the Inland Pacific Northwest," SFQ (Mr, 1971), 35: 15-26. Wellerisms appeared frequently in frontier weekly newspapers as fillers.

2898. Hughes, Muriel Joy. "Vermont Proverbial Comparisons and Similes," VH (Oct, 1958), 26: 257-293. Compiled from print, newspaper queries, teachers, students.

2899. _____. "Vermont Proverbs and Proverbial Sayings," VH (Apr, Je, 1960), two parts, 28: 113-142, 200-230. A compilation, no informants listed.

2900. Jablow, Alta and Carl Withers. "Social Sense and Verbal Nonsense in Urban Children's Folklore," NYFQ (Dec, 1965), 21: 243-257. Riddles, rhymes, tongue twisters, etc.

2901. Jansen, William Hugh. "Riddles: 'Do-It-Yourself Oracles,'" in Our Living Traditions, ed. T. P. Coffin, pp. 204-214. The characteristics, types, and uses of riddles.

2902. Jason, Heda. "Proverbs in Society: the Problem of Meaning and Function," Proverbium (1971), 17: 617-623.

2903. Kin, David. Dictionary of American Proverbs (New York: Philosophical Lib., 1955), 290pp. Brief preface by Mark Van Doren. Hastily selected collection.

2904. Kirshenblatt-Gimblett, Barbara. "Toward a Theory of Proverb Making," Proverbium (1973), 22: 821-827.

2905. Kreiger, Amo T. "Epitaphs of Bristol Pioneers," NYFQ (F, 1956), 12: 207-209.

2906. Kroll, Harry Harrison. "How I Collect Proverbial Material for My Novels," TFSB (Mr, 1957), 23: 1-5. A novelist describes his professional procedure.

2907. Kuusi, Matti. Towards an International Type-System of Proverbs (Helsinki: Suomalainen Tiedeakatemia, 1972), 41pp. Attempt to systematize proverb study with types and sub-classes based on proverbs from the whole world.

2908. Leach, Maria. Riddle Me, Riddle Me, Ree (New York: Viking, 1970), 142pp. Riddles collected from all over the world, arranged by subjects. Sources given in notes.

2909. Legman, G[ershon]. The Limerick (New York: Bell, 1954), 517pp. Some 1700 limericks with notes, index of rhymes and subjects. Mostly obscene or erotic, with themes including sex, disease, pornography.

2910. Lethin, Joyce Bynum. "Syriac Proverbs from California," WF (Apr, 1972), 31: 87-101. Thirty Syriac masale (proverbs) with literal and free translations.

2911. Lewis, Mary Ellen B. "The Feminists Have Done
       It: Applied Folklore," JAF (Jan-Mr, 1974), 87:
       85-87. Proverbs about women are often negative;
       the feminists rebel.

2912. Loomis, C. Grant. "American Limerick Traditions,"
       WF (Jl, 1963), 22: 153-157. Examples from
       such Am. magazines as Puck, Argonaut, Life,
       etc.

2913. _____. "Emerson's Proverbs," WF (Oct, 1958),
       17: 257-262. Rather sketchy analysis of Emer-
       son's aphoristic style with selective examples.

2914. _____. "Names in American Limericks," Names
       (Dec, 1954), 2: 229-233. Based on limericks
       published in American periodicals.

2915. _____. "Proverbial Phrases in Journalistic Word-
       play," WF (Jl, 1964), 23: 187-189. Examples
       largely from pre-Civil War journalism.

2916. _____. "Proverbs in Business," WF (Apr, 1964),
       23: 91-94. An old collection of commercial anec-
       dotes reveals that maxims about thrift and busi-
       ness remain current.

2917. _____. "Proverbs in The Farmer's Almanack,"
       WF (Jl, 1956), 15: 172-178. Chronological list
       of proverbs 1795-1834. Some may be the earliest
       printed form in the U.S.

2918. _____. "Proverbs in the Golden Era," WF (Jl,
       1955), 14: 196-199. A hundred texts from a San
       Francisco periodical, 1866-1868.

2919. _____. "Traditional Riddles in American Peri-
       odicals," WF (Jl, 1955), 14: 210-212.

2920. _____. "Wellerisms in California Sources," WF
       (Oct, 1955), 14: 229-245. Some 326 texts from
       various San Francisco periodicals, 1855-1945.

2921. McAllester, David P. "Riddles and Other Verbal
       Play Among the Comanches," JAF (Jl-Sept,
       1964), 77: 251-257. Comanche riddles suggest
       that riddling was at least known in aboriginal
       America.

2922. McNeil, W. K. "Proverbs Used in New York
       Autograph Albums 1820-1900," SFQ (Dec, 1969),
       33: 352-359.

2923. McReynolds, Douglas. "'Mysterious Names' Riddles
       in the Ozarks," BMHS (Apr, 1974), 30: 205-207.

2924. Mann, Thomas C. and Janet Greene. Over Their
       Dead Bodies: Yankee Epitaphs and History
       (Brattleboro, Vt.: Stephen Greene, 1962), xii,
       103pp. Some 215 epitaphs memorializing Yankees,
       most of them observed by the editors.

2925. Maranda, Elli Köngäs. "Theory and Practise of
       Riddle Analysis," in Toward New Perspectives
       in Folklore, ed. Américo Paredes and Richard
       Bauman, pp. 50-61. Theories supported by ex-
       amples from the Solomon Islands.

2926. Meister, Charles W. "Franklin as a Proverb
       Stylist," AL (May, 1952), 24: 157-166.

2927. Mieder, Wolfgang. "The Essence of Literary
       Proverb Studies," NYFQ (Mr, 1974), 30: 66-76.
       Serious collection of proverbs is badly needed;
       proverb studies in the U.S. apparently limited to
       regional writers. Same article in Proverbium
       (1974), 23: 888-894.

2928. _____. "The Proverb and Anglo-American Litera-
       ture," SFQ (Mr, 1974), 38: 49-62. A plea for
       further work in the study of the proverb.

2929. _____. "Proverbs in Carl Sandburg's Poem The
       People, Yes," SFQ (Mr, 1973), 37: 15-36. At
       least 322 proverbs appear in the Sandburg poem;
       his folk speech is "a valid replica of common
       life between the two world wars."

2930. Millard, Eugenia L. "A Sampling of Guessing
       Games," NYFQ (S, 1957), 13: 135-143. Child-
       ren's riddles and games.

2931. Moldenhauer, Joseph J. "The Rhetorical Function
       of Proverbs in Walden," JAF (Apr-Je, 1967),
       80: 151-159.

2932. Monteiro, George. "Proverbs and Proverbial Phrases
of the Continental Portuguese," WF (Jan, 1963),
22: 19-45. Some 457 proverbs from Rhode Island Portuguese with English translations.

2933. Montgomery, Evelyn. "Proverbial Materials in The
Politician Out-Witted and Other Comedies of Early
American Drama, 1789-1829," MF (W, 1961-
1962), 11: 215-224. About 100 expressions taken
from four early plays.

2934. Mook, Maurice A. "Tongue Tanglers from Central
Pennsylvania," JAF (Oct-Dec, 1959), 72: 291-296.
Student-collected examples from Centre and con-
tiguous counties.

2935. Moore, Danny W. "The Deductive Riddle: an
Adaptation to Modern Society," NCarFJ (Aug,
1974), 22: 119-125. Sixteen riddles from college
students which require deductive reasoning and
contain modern elements.

2936. Paredes, Américo. "Proverbs and Ethnic Stereotypes," Proverbium (1970), 15: 95-97.

2937. Pedrini, Lura and Duilio T. Pedrini. "Similes and
Metaphors in Cooper's The Pathfinder," NYFQ
(Je, 1967), 23: 99-108. Sources of figurative
language.

2938. Person, Henry A. "Proverbs and Proverbial Lore
from the State of Washington," WF (Jl, 1958),
17: 176-185. Some 369 items arranged by subjects without annotation.

2939. Porter, Kenneth W. "Humor, Blasphemy, and Criticism in the Grace Before Meat," NYFQ (Mr,
1965), 21: 3-18. Amusing examples of grace at
dinner tables. Cf. addendum: "More Examples
of Humor, Blasphemy, and Criticism in the Grace
Before Meat," NYFQ (Mr, 1968), 24: 64-67.

2940. Randolph, Vance and Mary Celestia Parler. "Riddles
from Arkansas," JAF (Jl-Sept, 1954), 67: 253-
259.

2941. Raymond, Joseph. "Tensions in Proverbs: More

Light on International Understanding," WF (Jl,
1956), 15: 152-158. Proverbs reveal crises and
tensions in the group mind.

2942. Reynolds, Horace. "A Proverb in the Hand,"
NYTMag (Sept. 13, 1959), p. 74. Popular article
with standard definitions and Irish, Russian,
French, Spanish examples.

2943. Roberts, Leonard. "Additional Exaggerations from
East Kentucky," MF (F, 1952), 2: 163-166.

2944. Rogers, E. G. "Some East Tennessee Figurative
Exaggerations," TFSB (Je, 1953), 19: 36-40.
Ninety comparisons.

2945. Sackett, S. J. "E. W. Howe as Proverb Maker,"
JAF (Jan-Mr, 1972), 85: 73-77. Howe used
many proverbs or aphorisms, which often lacked
compactness.

2946. Schlesinger, Marilyn Ruth. "Riddling Questions from
Los Angeles High School Students," WF (Jl, 1960),
19: 191-195. Material collected at Fremont High
School in 1957.

2947. Scott, Charles T. "New Evidence of American Indian
Riddles," JAF (Jl-Sept, 1963), 76: 236-241.
Article contends that riddling was familiar to In-
dians of both Americas.

2948. _____. "On Defining the Riddle: the Problem of
a Structural Unit," Genre (Je, 1969), 2: 129-142.

2949. _____. "Some Approaches to the Study of the
Riddle," in Studies in Language, Literature, and
Culture of the Middle Ages and Later, ed. E. B.
Atwood and Archibald A. Hill (Austin: U. of
Texas P., 1969), pp. 111-127.

2950. Seely, Marcia Wells. "Neighbors (Massachusetts):
Epitaphs from Taunton," NYFQ (S, 1955), 11:
137-145.

2951. Seitel, Peter. "Proverbs: a Social Use of Metaphor," Genre (Je, 1969), 2: 143-161. Examples
taken mostly from the Ibo people of Eastern Ni-
geria.

2952.   Simmons, Donald C.   "Anti-Italian-American Riddles
            in New England," JAF (Jl-Sept, 1966), 79: 475-
            478.   Some 26 examples given.

2953.   Simon, Gwladys H.   "Riddles from Hawaii," WF (Jl,
            1959), 19: 254-255.

2954.   Stroup, Thomas.   "Three Biblical Riddles from
            North Carolina," SFQ (Dec, 1952), 16: 255-256.
            Riddles about Eve, Jonah, the rooster.

2955.   Taylor, Archer.   English Riddles from Oral Tradi-
            tion (Berkeley and Los Angeles: U. of California
            P., 1951), xxxi, 959pp.   Monumental collection
            of 1,749 riddles by the acknowledged specialist
            in the field.   Rich comparative notes.   Arrange-
            ment by types of comparison (man, animal, plant,
            thing, etc.).

2956.   _____.   "Investigations of English Proverbs,
            Proverbial and Conventional Phrases, Oaths, and
            Cliches," JAF (Jl-Sept, 1952), 65: 255-265.
            Primarily Am. material.

2957.   _____.   "More Proverbial Comparisons from
            California," WF (Jan, 1958), 17: 12-20.   Over
            200 texts from oral California tradition.

2958.   _____.   Proverbial Comparisons and Similes from
            California (Berkeley and Los Angeles: U. of
            Cal. P., 1954), 97pp.

2959.   _____.   "Proverbial Comparisons and Similes in
            On Troublesome Creek," KFR (Jl-Sept, 1962),
            8: 87-96.   Some 170 examples taken from James
            Still's 1941 novel.

2960.   _____.   "Proverbial Materials in Edward Eggle-
            ston, The Hoosier Schoolmaster," in Studies in
            Folklore, ed. W. Edson Richmond, pp. 262-270.

2961.   _____.   "Proverbial Materials in Two More Novels
            by Harry Harrison Kroll," TFSB (Sept, 1956),
            22: 73-84.   Proverbs from Rogues' Company,
            1943, and Fury in the Earth, 1945.

2962.   _____.   "Proverbial Materials in Two Novels by

Harry Harrison Kroll," TFSB (Je, 1956), 22: 39-
52.

2963. _____. "Proverbs and Proverbial Phrases in the
Writings of Mary N. Murfree," TFSB (Mr, 1958),
24: 11-50.

2964. _____. "The Riddle as a Primary Form," in
Folklore in Action, ed. Horace P. Beck, pp.
200-217. Discussion of riddles stimulated by
Andre Jolles's theories of 1929.

2965. _____. "Riddles in Dialogue," Proceedings APS
(Feb. 14, 1953), 97: i, 61-68.

2966. _____. "The Study of Proverbs," Proverbium
(1965), 1: 10.

2967. _____. "'This Too Will Pass (Jason 910Q)," in
Volksüberlieferung, ed. Fritz Harkort et al.,
pp. 345-350. A widely known phrase which is
also a tale.

2968. Taylor, Archer and Bartlett Jere Whiting. A Dictionary of American Proverbs and Proverbial
Phrases 1820-1880 (Cambridge: Belknap P. of
Harvard U. P., 1958), xxii, 418pp. Impressive
scholarship, the standard work in the field.

2969. _____. "The Use of Proper Names in Wellerisms
and Folk Tales," WF (Oct, 1959), 18: 287-293.

2970. [Thompson, Harold W.] "Epitaphs: Inscriptions Collected by a Cornell Class," NYFQ (S, 1953), 9:
142-152.

2971. Tidwell, James N. "Adam's Off Ox. A Study in the
Exactness of the Inexact," JAF (Oct-Dec, 1953),
66: 291-294. Proverbial expressions about the
inexact used by the folk.

2972. _____. "Wellerisms in Alexander's Weekly Mes-
senger, 1837-1839," WF (Jl, 1950), 9: 257-262.
Chronological list of Wellerisms from a Philadelphia periodical which show a strong Dickens
influence.

2973. Toelken, J. Barre. "Riddles Wisely Expounded,"
       WF (Jan, 1966), 25: 1-16. Discussion of riddles
       and their ambiguities in a number of Child bal-
       lads.

2974. Tolman, Ruth B. "Proverbs and Sayings in Eight-
       eenth-Century Almanacs," WF (Jan, 1962), 21:
       35-42. Role of almanacs in Revolutionary times.
       Also a bibliography.

2975. Vatuk, Ved Prakash. "Panjabi Riddles from the
       West Coast," WF (Jan, 1970), 29: 35-46. Indian
       riddles collected in California; original texts plus
       translations.

2976. Walker, Warren S. "Proverbs in the Novels of
       James Fenimore Cooper," MF (S, 1953), 3: 99-
       107.

2977. Wallis, Charles L. "Epitaphs: New York Stories
       in Stone," NYFQ (Spr, 1954), 10: 54-56.

2978. _____. Stories on Stone, A Book of American
       Epitaphs (New York: Oxford, 1954). Republished
       as American Epitaphs Grave and Humorous (New
       York: Dover, 1973), xv, 272pp. Many examples,
       over 750 epitaphs.

2979. Weiner, Meryl. "The Riddle Repertoire of a Massa-
       chusetts Elementary School," FF (Jan, 1970),
       3: 7-38. Some 300 riddles collected from chil-
       dren in an Auburn, Mass. elementary school.

2980. West, Harry C. "Simon Suggs and His Similes,"
       NCarF (May, 1968), 16: 53-57. The folk speech
       of Johnson J. Hooper's famous "shifty" character.

2981. Whiting, Bartlett Jere. "Proverbs in Cotton Mather's
       Magnalia Christi Americana," NM (1972), 73:
       477-484.

2982. Wilson, Gordon. "Similes from the Mammoth Cave
       Region with a Farm Flavor," KFR (Apr-Je, Jl-
       Sept, Oct-Dec, 1968), 14: 44-50, 69-75, 94-99.

2983. _____. "Studying Folklore in a Small Region,
       VIII: Proverbial Lore," TFSB (Dec, 1965), 31:
       99-104.

14. SPEECH, NAMES, CRIES, ETC.

2984. Ackerman, Louise C. "Naming the Nags," Names (Dec, 1953), 1: 262-65. Names for race horses.

2985. Adams, Charles C. Boontling; an American Lingo (Austin and London: U. of Texas P., 1971), ix, 275pp. Secret language of Boonville, California.

2986. Adams, James N. Illinois Place Names (Springfield, Ill.: Ill. State Hist. Soc., 1968), ed. William E. Keller, viii, 321pp. Reprint of material published in Illinois Libraries, 1968. Sources rarely given but useful for data about vanished places.

2987. Adams, John F. "Ranching Terms from Eastern Washington," AS (Dec, 1958), 33: 266-73. Ranch slang alphabetically arranged; some obsolete, some current.

2988. Adams, Ramon F. The Cowman Says It Salty (Tucson: U. of Arizona P., 1971), ix, 163pp. A complement to Adams' earlier compendium, Western Words.

2989. _____. Western Words: a Dictionary of the American West (Norman: U. of Oklahoma P., 1968), xviii, 355pp. Revision and extension of a 1945 book.

2990. Alderson, William L. "Carnie Talk from the West Coast," AS (May, 1953), 28: 112-119. Carnival talk from Pacific Coast in the late 1940's. Billboard is carnies' Bible.

2991. Allen, Harold B. "Pejorative Terms for Midwest Farmers," AS (Dec, 1958), 33: 260-65. 86 terms from "appleknocker" to "yokel" gathered by interviews and questionnaires.

2992.   Allen, Philip F. "A New Sample of New Hampshire
        Dialect," PADS (Apr, 1951), no. 15, 65-68.
        Personal memories from Grafton County, N.H.,
        in the 1920-1930 period.

2994.   Allen, Ward. "'You Don't Have to Be Crazy ...'"
        WF (Jan, 1954), 13: 7-12. Language of the grips
        (scene shifters, operators of camera equipment,
        etc.). Many examples.

2995.   Anderson, E. N., Jr., and Marja L. Anderson.
        "The Social Context of a Local 'Lingo,'" WF
        (Jl, 1970), 29: 153-65. More Boontling material
        from Mendocino Co., Cal.

2996.   Anderson, John Q. "From Flygap to Whybark; Some
        Unusual Texas Place Names," in The Golden Log,
        ed. Mody C. Boatright et al., pp. 73-98. Fas-
        cinating collection of names representing geo-
        graphical descriptions, euphemisms, personalities,
        humor.

2997.   _____. "Texas Stream Names," in A Good Tale
        and a Bonnie Tune, ed. Mody C. Boatright et al.,
        pp. 112-47. Inventory of names given Texas
        rivers and derived from family names, trees,
        animals, minerals, Spanish, and the Indians.

2998.   Atwood, E. Bagby. The Regional Vocabulary of Texas
        (Austin: U. of Texas P., 1962), xiv, 274pp.
        English words arranged according to customs and
        material culture; also a section on border Span-
        ish. Commentary on locale and linguistic changes.
        Reissued 1969.

2999.   _____. "Shivarees and Charivaris: Variations
        on a Theme," in A Good Tale and A Bonnie
        Tune, ed. Mody C. Boatright et al., pp. 64-71.
        Definition of term with examples.

3000.   Auser, Cortland P. "Westchester Place Names:
        Strata of Folk-Life and History," NYFQ (Mr,
        1968), 24: 44-49. Mostly a compilation.

3001.   Ayres, Lucille et al. "Expressions from Rural
        Florida," PADS (Apr, 1950), no. 14, 74-80.
        Brief list of student-collected terms.

3002.   Babcock, C. Merton. "The Echo of a Whistle,"
        WF (Jan, 1960), 19: 47-51. Railroad and hobo
        jargon.

3003.   _____. "Herman Melville's Whaling Vocabulary,"
        AS (Oct, 1954), 29: 161-74. Moby Dick and other
        sea stories include words, chiefly from New Eng-
        land, not found in dictionaries or earlier in use
        than those cited. 177 items.

3004.   _____. "The Language of Melville's 'Isolatoes,'"
        WF (Oct, 1951), 10: 285-89.

3005.   _____. "Melville's World's-Language," SFQ
        (Sept, 1952), 16: 177-82. Melville used folk
        language in his sea tales to dramatize his demo-
        cratic theme.

3006.   _____. "The Vocabulary of Social Life on the
        American Frontier," WF (Apr, 1950), 9: 136-43.
        Material from domestic life, dress, diet, amuse-
        ments and social gatherings.

3007.   Babington, Mima and E. Bagby Atwood. "Lexical
        Usage in Southern Louisiana," PADS (Nov, 1961),
        no. 36, 1-24. Words from six parishes in the
        Acadian section.

3008.   Barker, George C. Pachuco: An American-Spanish
        Argot and Its Social Functions in Tucson, Arizona
        (Tucson: U. of Arizona P., 1950), 38pp. Study
        of the linguistic deterioration of Spanish in one
        area. Sec. ed., 1958.

3009.   Barnes, Daniel R. "An Early American Collection
        of Rogues' Cant," JAF (Oct-Dec, 1966), 79: 600-
        607. Data from a Pennsylvania penitentiary in
        1848, recorded by a Methodist minister and pub-
        lished in The Ladies' Repository.

3010.   Barnes, Will C. Arizona Place Names (Tucson: U.
        of Arizona P., 1960), extensively revised by
        Byrd H. Granger, xix, 519pp. Originally pub-
        lished in 1935.

3011.   Barrick, Mac E. "The Folklore Repertory of a
        Pennsylvania Auctioneer," KF (Spr, 1974), 19:

27-42. Auctioneer uses proverbs, rhymes, comparisons.

3012. Berkovits, Rochele. "Secret Languages of School Children," NYFQ (Je, 1970), 26: 127-52. Sixth and seventh graders reveal their speech.

3013. Berrey, Lester V. and Melville Van den Bark. The American Thesaurus of Slang: A Complete Reference Book of Colloquial Speech (New York: Crowell, 1953), xxxv, 1272pp. Useful and substantially revised edition of work published in 1942.

3014. Birnbaum, Mariana D. "On the Language of Prejudice," WF (Oct, 1971), 30: 247-68. Extensive compilation of European and American verbal ethnic slurs; with commentary.

3015. Boone, Lalia Phipps. "Florida: the Land of Epithets," SFQ (Je, 1958), 22: 87-92.

3016. _____. "Folk Names for Blooming Plants," SFQ (Dec, 1955), 19: 230-36. Botanical and popular names for plants around Gainesville, Florida.

3017. _____. "Names of Idaho Counties," Names (Mr, 1968), 16: 19-26.

3018. Boroff, David. "A Study of Reformatory Argot," AS (Oct, 1951), 26: 190-95. Brief list of racy, irreverent terms not unlike any slang and prison argot.

3019. Boswell, George W. "A Dialect Sampling of Mississippi Speech," MFR (1967), 1: 15-19.

3020. Botkin, Benjamin A. "The Spiels of New York," NYFQ (A, 1953), 9: 165-75. Street cries.

3021. Braddy, Haldeen. "The Anonymous Verses of a Narcotic Addict," SFQ (Sept, 1958), 22: 129-38. Six poems rich in argot by a Creole woman; glossary appended.

3022. _____. "Narcotic Argot Along the Mexican Border," AS (May, 1955), 30: 84-90. Supplementary

list of English and Spanish terms in international
dope speech.

3023. _____. "The Pachucos and Their Argot," SFQ
(Dec, 1960), 24: 255-71. Language of the
Pachucos (Latin-American youths) in El Paso.
Alphabetized vocabulary in Spanish with English
translations.

3024. _____. "Riding the White Horse," SFQ (Sept,
1961), 25: 167-77. Language used by addicts of
heroin, marijuana, morphine, opium in El Paso.

3025. _____. "Smugglers' Argot in the Southwest," AS
(May, 1956), 31: 96-101. Mostly from El Paso.

3026. Bradley, F. W. "Supplementary List of South Carolina Words and Phrases," PADS (Apr, 1954), no.
21, 16-41.

3027. _____. "A Word-List from South Carolina,"
PADS (Nov, 1950), no. 14, 3-73. Extensive list
resulting from newspaper inquiries in 1949-1950.

3028. Brinegar, Bonnie. "Metaphorical Expressions from
Adams County, Mississippi," MFR (W, 1971), 5:
124-31. Some 124 folk similes and metaphors.

3029. Browne, Ray B. "Children's Taunts, Teases, and
Disrespectful Sayings from Southern California,"
WF (Jl, 1954), 13: 190-98. Some 61 examples.

3030. Brunvand, Jan Harold. "A Note on Names for Cars,"
Names (Dec, 1962), 10: 279-84. Examples of
the fad for baptizing jalopies and trucks with
singular names.

3031. _____, (guest editor). Special Issue on Names
in Folklore, Names (Sept, 1968), 16: 197-298.
Introduction by Brunvand, pp. 197-206.

3032. Bryant, Margaret M. "Names and Terms Used in
the Fashion World," AS (F-W, 1970), 45: 168-
94. Compilation derived from fashion magazines,
arranged in various categories.

3033. _____. "Names in Everyday Speech," Names (Mr,

1957), 5: 47-58. Sources of common names with
fascinating examples.

3034. _____. "Space Exploration Terms," AS (Oct,
1968), 43: 163-81. Largely technical.

3035. Byrd, James W. "Current Jazz Lingo," TFSB (Mr,
1956), 22: 21-28. Including a jazz version of
Little Red Riding Hood tale.

3036. Carlson, Helen S. Nevada Place Names; A Geographical Dictionary (Reno: U. of Nevada P.,
1974), xiv, 282pp.

3037. Carranco, Lynwood. "Americanisms in the Redwood
Country," WF (Oct, 1963), 22: 263-267. Lum-
ber industry argot in Humboldt Co., Cal.
Terms defined.

3038. _____. "Logging Railroad Language in the Redwood Country," AS (May, 1962), 37: 130-136.
Terms from Humboldt Co., Cal.

3039. _____. "More Logger Talk of the Redwood Region," AS (Feb, 1959), 34: 76-80.

3040. _____ and Wilma Rawles Simmons. "The Boonville Language of Northern California," AS (Dec,
1964), 39: 278-286. Vocabulary list plus two
stories.

3041. Chadbourne, Ava Harriet. Maine Place Names and
the Peopling of Its Towns (Freeport, Me.: Bond
Wheelwright, 1955), 530pp.

3042. Cheney, Roberta Carkeek. "Montana Place Names,"
Montana (Jan, 1970), 20: 48-61. Brief sketch
of names derived from local geography, old settlers, Indian words.

3043. _____. Names on the Face of Montana: the
Story of Montana (Missoula: U. of Montana Publications in History, 1971), xix, 275pp. An extension of the preceding article.

3044. Clark, Joseph D. "Folk Speech from North Carolina," NCarF (Jl, 1962), 10: 6-21. 649 words,

many not listed in the Frank C. Brown collection
of No. Car. folklore.

3045. _____. "Folk Speech from North Carolina," SFQ
(Dec, 1962), 26: 301-25. Material collected
from college students and labeled dialect, slang,
etc.

3046. Clements, William M. "The Rhetoric of the Radio
Profession," JAF (Oct-Dec, 1974), 87: 318-27.
Radio broadcasts of Pentecostal ministers from
two Ark. counties.

3047. Clough, Wilson O. "Some Wyoming Speech Patterns,"
AS (Feb, 1954), 29: 28-35. Differences in idiom
and nomenclature within the state.

3048. Cohen, Hennig. "The Terminology of Mardi Gras,"
AS (May, 1951), 26: 110-15. Definition of terms
used in New Orleans spectacle; origin of "krewes"
explained.

3049. Combs, Josiah H. "Spellin' 'Em Down in the Highlands," KFR (Apr-Je, 1957), 3: 69-73. Amusing
examples of mountain speech.

3050. _____. "The Vocabulary of Marble Playing,"
PADS (Apr, 1955), no. 23, 3-33. Citations from
print or orally recorded in Tennessee.

3051. Cray, Ed. "Ethnic and Place Names as Derisive
Adjectives," WF (Jan, 1962), 21: 27-34.

3052. Cummings, G. Clark. "The Language of Horse
Racing," AS (Feb, 1955), 30: 7-29. An area
which H. L. Mencken neglected. Names of
animals, races, and track figures.

3053. Davidson, Levette J. "A Folk Speech Miscellany,"
CF (1954), 2: 19-23. Ranch talk, jargon, riddles, etc.

3054. Davis, Wilbur A. "Logger and Splinter-Picker Talk,"
WF (Apr, 1950), 9: 111-23. Role of logger defined and an alphabetical list of his occupational
speech given from Northwest Oregon.

3055.   Davison, Zeta C.   "A Word-List from the Appalachian
        and the Piedmont Area of North Carolina," PADS
        (Apr, 1953), no. 19, 8-14.

3056.   Day, Donald, ed.   Uncle Sam's Uncle Josh (Boston:
        Little, Brown, 1953), lx, 244pp.   Unscholarly
        anthology of the humor of Josh Billings (Henry
        Wheeler Shaw).

3057.   De Camp, David and Thomas Stell Newman.   "Smoke-
        jumping Words," AS (Oct, 1958), 33: 180-84.
        Technical terms used by parachuting fire-fighters
        in forest areas.

3058.   De Lannoy, William C. and Elizabeth Masterson.
        "Teen-Age Hophead Jargon," AS (Feb, 1952), 27:
        23-31.   Terms gained from newspapers, inter-
        views, letters.

3059.   Dempsey, Don.   "The Language of Traffic Police-
        men," AS (Dec, 1962), 37: 266-73.

3060.   Dietterle, Otto C.   "Road Talk," NYFQ (F, 1959),
        15: 190-93.   Railroad jargon from the New
        York Central Railroad.

3061.   Directory of Geographic Names in Nevada (Carson
        City, Nev.: n.p., 1971), 192pp.   Some 7,000
        names listed: place names, descriptions, zones,
        counties, coordinates.

3062.   Drew, Shelley.   "Place Names in Ten Northeastern
        Counties of Florida," AS (Dec, 1962), 37: 255-
        65.   Proof that Florida is rich in toponymic vari-
        ety.

3063.   Duckert, Audrey R.   "Place Nicknames," Names
        (Sept, 1973), 21: 153-60.   Nicknames originate
        from abbreviations, shibboleths, slurs, compass
        points, and special promotions.

3064.   Dundes, Alan.   "The Henny-Penny Phenomenon,"
        SFQ (Mr, 1974), 38: 1-9.   Emphasis on common
        pairs of words and reduplicatives.

3065.   _____ and C. Fayne Porter.   "American Indian
        Student Slang," AS (Dec, 1963), 38: 270-277.
        Material from Haskell Institute, Lawrence, Kan.

3066.   _____ and Manuel R. Schonhorn. "Kansas Univer-
         sity Slang: a New Generation," AS (Oct, 1963),
         38: 163-177. Slang suggesting both social and
         academic status.

3067.   Eliason, Norman E. Tarheel Talk: an Historical
         Study of the English Language in North Carolina
         to 1860 (Chapel Hill: U. of No. Carolina P.,
         1956), xii, 324pp. Study based on a manuscript
         collection at Chapel Hill, intelligently used.

3068.   Emrich, Duncan. "A Manuscript of the Folk Lan-
         guage," WF (Oct, 1952), 11: 266-283. A folk
         autobiography.

3069.   Eschholz, Paul A. and Alfred F. Rosa. "Course
         Names: Another Aspect of College Slang," AS
         (Spr-S, 1970), 45: 85-90. Data from the Univ.
         of Vermont.

3070.   Eubanks, Ralph T. "The Basic Derivation of 'O.K.,'"
         AS (Oct, 1960), 35: 188-92. The old "Oll Kor-
         rect" explanation resuscitated.

3071.   Evers, Alf. "We Call It the Rickey," NYFQ (Spr,
         1959), 15: 36-47. Apple lore and the origin of
         the Jonathan apple.

3072.   Feinsilver, Lillian Mermin. "Yiddish Idioms in
         American English," AS (Oct, 1962), 37: 200-206.
         Translations or equivalent idioms from Yiddish.

3073.   Field, Thomas P. A Guide to Kentucky Place Names
         (Lexington: U. of Kentucky P., 1961), 264pp.

3074.   _____. "The Indian Place Names of Kentucky,"
         Names (Sept, 1959), 7: 154-66. Few Indian
         names survive in Kentucky.

3075.   Fields, Mary C. "The View From the Water Table:
         Folklore of the Offshore Oilfield Workers," MSF
         (W, 1974), 2: 63-76. Ritual and customs on the
         drilling rigs plus definitions of unusual terminology
         employed.

3076.   Fife, Austin E. "Similes From Moab, Utah," WF
         (Apr, 1966; Jl, 1966), 25: 126-27, 195-96. 144
         similes in alphabetical order.

3077. _____. "Wordplay in Highway-Side Nomenclature,"
AS (Dec, 1950), 25: 274-79. Names of motels
and highway businesses reflect alliteration, puns,
etc.

3078. Finnie, W. Bruce. "Ohio Valley Localisms: Topo-
graphical Terms, 1750-1800," AS (Oct, 1963),
38: 178-87. Material derived from accounts of
early travelers, diaries, etc.

3079. _____. "Topographic Terms in the Ohio Valley,
1748-1800," PADS (Apr, 1970), No. 53, pp. 1-
119. Alphabetical list with definitions; sources
mostly diaries and journals.

3080. Fitzpatrick, Lilian Linder. Nebraska Place-Names,
ed. G. Thomas Fairclough (Lincoln: U. of Nebraska P., 1960), x, 227pp. Originally published
1925.

3081. Flanagan, John T. "A Pound of Pyrus Malus,
Please," Names (Mr, 1966), 14: 18-25. Survey
of names given the varieties of apples grown in
U. S.

3082. Franklyn, Julian. A Dictionary of Nicknames (London: Hamish Hamilton, 1962), xx, 132pp. Some
300 of the 2,000 items are American but the annotations do not show great familiarity with American usage.

3083. Frazier, Marshall W. "Truck Drivers' Language,"
AS (May, 1955), 30: 91-94. Truckers' language
derived from industry sources and drivers. Many
terms are standard but others are freakish.

3084. Freeman, Sidney L. "Carnival and Circus," NYFQ
(W, 1950), 6: 213-20. The jargon and superstitions of the travelling shows.

3085. Fuson, Robert H. "The Origin of the Word Gringo,"
in Singers and Storytellers, ed. Mody C. Boatright et al., pp. 282-84. Philology vs. folk
etymology.

3086. Gard, Robert E. and L. G. Sorden. The Romance
of Wisconsin Place Names (New York: October

House, 1968), xiii, 144pp. Amateurish contribution to onomastics.

3087. Garrett, Kim S. "Family Stories and Sayings," in Singers and Storytellers, ed. Mody C. Boatright et al., pp. 273-81. Family lore from Wilson Co., Texas.

3088. Gold, Robert S. A Jazz Lexicon (New York: Knopf, 1964), xxvi, 363pp.

3089. _____. "The Vernacular of the Jazz World," AS (Dec, 1957), 32: 271-82. Language is a fusion of Negro talk and musicians playing jazz in "dives."

3090. Gonzales, Rafael Jésus. "Pachuco: the Birth of a Creole Language," ArQ (W, 1967), 23: 343-56.

3091. Granger, Byrd Howell. "Methodology Used in the Revision of Arizona Place Names," Names (Dec, 1962), 10: 265-73. Editorial practise explained.

3092. _____. "Naming: in Customs, Beliefs and Folk Tales," WF (Jan, 1961), 20: 27-37. A widely ranging survey.

3093. Granville, Wilfred. Sea Slang of the Twentieth Century (New York: Philosophical Lib., 1950), vix, 271pp. Largely a glossary of British Navy slang; American and colonial sea terms are generally omitted.

3094. Green, Archie. "'Dutchman': An On-the-Job Etymology," AS (Dec, 1960), 35: 270-74. Comments on a term familiar in construction work which is not pejorative.

3095. Grise, George C. "Patterns of Child Naming in Tennessee During the Depression Years," SFQ (Sept, 1959), 23: 150-54. Parents often employed sports, political, and motion picture heroes and heroines but Biblical names still appeared.

3096. Gudde, Erwin G. California Place Names: the Origin and Etymology of Current Geographical Names (Berkeley and Los Angeles: U. of California P., 1960), xiv, 383pp. Second rev. ed. of a 1949 work.

3097. _____. "Naming Storms," Names (Mr, 1955), 3:
34-37. Girls' names for tropical storms began
in 1954.

3098. _____. 1000 California Place Names: Their Origin and Meaning (Berkeley and Los Angeles: U.
of California P., 1959), second rev. ed., viii,
96pp. Minor additions and revisions in a book
published in 1949.

3099. Gunn, Larry. "Some Slang Terms of the South Mississippi Sawmill Industry," MFR (F, 1971), 5:
84-86.

3100. Haber, Tom Burns. "Polysemantic Expressions of
Dog and Allied Terms," AS (Feb, 1961), 36: 5-
16; "The Use of Canine Terms in the Names of
Other Animals," AS (Oct, 1962), 37: 189-99;
"Canine Terms in Popular Names of Plants," AS
(Feb, 1963), 38: 28-41; "Canine Terms Applied
to Human Beings and Human Events: Part I,"
AS (May, 1965), 40: 83-101; "Canine Terms Applied to Human Beings and Human Events: Part
II," AS (Dec, 1965), 40: 243-71. All articles relate to terms like dog, bitch, hound, etc., as
they appear in proverbs, analogies, and verbal
combinations. Many examples.

3101. Hall, Edith Thompson. "Cattle Nomenclature and
Genealogy," Names (Je, 1954), 2: 113-120.
Origin of names like Hereford, Aberdeen-Angus,
and Shorthorn breeds.

3102. Hall, Joseph S. Sayings from Old Smoky (Asheville:
Cataloochee P., 1972), 149pp. Collection of
mountain phrases, sayings, aphorisms, folk
names, idioms, etc.

3103. Halpert, Herbert. "'Egypt'--A Wandering Place-
Name Legend," MF (F, 1954), 4: 165-68.

3104. _____. "Place Name Stories of Kentucky Water-
ways and Ponds," KFR (Jl-Sept, 1961), 7: 85-101.
15 names explained with extensive notes.

3105. Halpert, Violetta Maloney. "Place Name Stories
about West Kentucky Towns," KFR (Jl-Sept,

1961), 7: 103-16.   15 examples of unusual names and their origins.

3106.   Hanley, Robert.   "Truck Drivers' Language in the Northwest," AS (Dec, 1961), 36: 271-74.   Comparison of trucker lingo east and west with some unique terms.

3107.   Hanna, Phil Townsend.   Dictionary of California Land Names (Los Angeles: Automobile Club of So. California, 1951), sec. ed., xxi, 392pp.

3108.   Hanson, Raus McDill.   Virginia Place Names: Derivations, Historical Uses (Verona, Va.:   McClure P., 1969), ix, 253pp.   Interesting and entertaining but uncritical collection.

3109.   Harder, Kelsie B.   "Hay-Making Terms in Perry County," TFSB (Je, 1967), 33: 41-48.

3110.   _____.   "The Jake Leg," TFSB (Sept, 1961), 27: 45-47.   Term defined, derivative from Jamaica ginger; also an ailment suffered from drinking contaminated alcohol.

3111.   _____.   "Pert Nigh Almost: Folk Measurement," TFSB (Mr, 1957), 23: 6-12.   Miscellaneous examples of folk measurement of size, height, distance, etc.

3112.   _____.   "Rhyming Names in Tennessee," SFQ (Je, 1955), 19: 101-3.   Rhyming names, chiefly girls', from oral recordings and print.   Trivial.

3113.   _____.   "The Vocabulary of Hog-Killing," TFSB (Dec, 1959), 25: 111-15.   Technical and rather obvious list from Perry Co., Tenn.

3114.   _____.   "The Vocabulary of Marble Playing," PADS (Apr, 1955), no. 23, 3-33.   Terms defined and game rules explained.

3115.   _____.   "A Vocabulary of Wagon Parts," TFSB (Mr, 1962), 28: 12-20.   Definitions of terms.

3116.   _____.   "Weather Expressions and Beliefs in Perry County, Tennessee," TFSB (Sept, 1957),

23: 83-86. A wealth of descriptive expressions
for weather.

3117. Harper, Jared and Charles Hudson. "Irish Traveler
Cant in Its Social Setting," SFQ (Je, 1973), 37:
101-14. Argot used by Irish tinkers and livestock
traders in the Deep South. Lingo derived from
Gaelic is gradually disappearing.

3118. Harris, Jesse W. "The Humorous Yarn in Early
Illinois Local Histories," MF (F, 1952), 2: 167-
75. Examples from printed sources, often fan-
tastically rhetorical.

3119. _____. "Illinois Place Name Lore," MF (W,
1954), 4: 217-20.

3120. Heflin, Woodford A. "'O. K.' and Its Incorrect
Etymology," AS (Dec, 1962), 37: 243-48. Survey
of past scholarship; the exact origin is still unknown.

3121. Hemperley, M. R. "Indian Place Names in Georgia,"
GHQ (W, 1973), 57: 562-579. Some 200 place
names with brief notes.

3122. Hendricks, George D. "The Names of Western Wild
Animals," in Folk Travelers, ed. Mody C. Boatright et al., pp. 40-46. Explanation of names
of cougar, bighorn, etc.

3123. _____. "Ranch Country Metaphors," ArQ (Spr,
1954), 10: 30-41.

3124. _____. "Texas Folk Similes," WF (Oct, 1960),
19: 245-62. Some 639 examples collected at
Denton, Texas, and listed alphabetically by key
words.

3125. Hines, Donald M. "Painter Jargon of the Pacific
Northwest," AS (Feb, 1969), 44: 5-32.

3126. Hinton, Norman D. "The Language of Jazz Musicians,"
PADS (Nov, 1958), no. 30, 38-48. Basic terms
include cool, dig, cat, goof, hip, square, swing.

3127. Hoffman, Frank A. "Place Names in Brown County,"

MF (Spr, 1961), 11: 57-62. Report of a team
project to collect folklore in an Indiana county.

3128. Howard, Donald. "United States Marine Corps Slang,"
       AS (Oct, 1956), 31: 188-94.

3129. Hubbard, Claude. "The Language of Ruxton's Moun-
       tain Man," AS (Oct, 1968), 43: 216-21. Jargon
       originally recorded in 1848.

3130. Huden, John C. Indian Place Names in Vermont
       (Burlington, Vt.: p.p. [Lane P.], 1957), 32pp.
       Some interesting folk etymologies.

3131. _____. Indian Place Names of New England (New
       York: Museum of the Am. Indian, 1962), xiv,
       408pp. Some 4,000 names included with a useful
       introduction.

3132. Hughes, Herbert L. "A Word-List from Louisiana,"
       PADS (Apr, 1951), No. 15, 69-71. Items from
       No. Louisiana where French influence is scant.

3133. Hughes, Muriel Joy. "A Word-List from Vermont,"
       VH (Apr, 1959), 27: 123-67. A compilation
       with comments on pronunciation, frequency, and
       parallels.

3134. Hunt, Elmer Munson. New Hampshire Town Names
       and Whence They Came (Peterborough, N.H.:
       Noone House, William Bauhan Publisher, 1970),
       xx, 282pp. Essay-biographies of towns.

3135. Hurvitz, Nathan. "Blacks and Jews in American
       Folklore," WF (Oct, 1974), 33: 301-25. Thought-
       ful article on attitudes toward two minority groups.

3136. Ives, Sumner. The Phonology of the Uncle Remus
       Stories (Gainesville, Fla.: Am. Dialect Soc.,
       1954), 59pp. Negro dialect analyzed.

3137. Jakle, John A. "Salt-Derived Place Names in the
       Ohio Valley," Names (Mr, 1968), 16: 1-5. Com-
       pounds of lick, licking, mahoning, and salt or
       saline.

3138. Jarka, Horst. "The Language of Skiers," AS (Oct,

Speech, Names, Cries, etc.

1963), 38: 202-208. German predominates in
the language of American skiers.

3139. Jett, Stephen C. "An Analysis of Navajo Place-
Names," Names (Sept, 1970), 18: 175-184. Most
Navajo names refer to features of the natural
landscape.

3140. Johnson, Thesba N. "Vermont Town Names and
Their Derivatives," VH (Oct, 1952), 20: 260-77.

3141. Kane, Joseph Nathan and Gerard L. Alexander.
Nicknames of Cities and States of the United
States (New York: Scarecrow P., 1965), 341pp.
Directory with few explanations or notes. Second
ed., somewhat enlarged, in 1970; vi, 456pp.

3142. Kay, Donald. "British Influence on Kentucky Muni-
cipal Place Names," KFR (Jan-Mr, 1974), 20:
9-13. 131 place names given in dual columns.

3143. Keen, Ruth. "A Word Study of Musical Americana,"
AS (May, 1965), 40: 127-33. Technical terms
or colloquialisms from 222 comic songs and ballads, 1800-1900.

3144. Kell, Katherine T. "Folk Names for Tobacco,"
JAF (Oct-Dec, 1966), 79: 590-99. Compilation
of euphemisms, slang, and idiomatic expressions
from print and observation.

3145. Kelly, Ray T. "The Spuyten Duyvil Enigma,"
NYFQ (W, 1960), 16: 255-65. Speculations on
the origin of a famous New York place name.

3146. Kenny, Hamill Thomas. Origin and Meaning of the
Indian Place Names of Maryland (Baltimore:
Waverly P., 1961), xix, 186pp.

3147. Knapp, Mary and Herbert Knapp. "Tradition and
Change in American Playground Language," JAF
(Apr-Je, 1973), 86: 131-41. Generalizations
about children's speech, based on inadequate evidence from Monroe Co., Ind., and the Canal Zone.

3148. Kratz, Henry. "What Is College Slang?" AS (Oct,
1964), 39: 188-95. Campus slang often spreads

beyond the campus but technical academic language may not be slang.

3149. Krueger, John R. "Indiana Limestone Industry
       Terms," AS (Dec, 1967), 42: 289-96.

3150. Krumpelman, John T. "More Americanisms from
       C. F. Hoffman," AS (May, 1954), 29: 119-21.
       25 expressions from A Winter in the West, 1835.
       and another book.

3151. _____. "Timothy Flint, Contributor of American-
       isms, 1826," AS (May, 1969), 44: 135-38. Ex-
       amples from Flint's autobiography and one novel.

3152. Kuhm, Herbert W. "Indian Place Names in Wiscon-
       sin," WA (Mr-Je, 1952), 33: 1-157.

3153. Larsen, Sven A. "The Vocabulary of Poker," AS
       (May, 1951), 26: 96-102. Terminology taken
       generally from Western America but generally
       familiar.

3154. Larson, Cedric. "Terms of the Men's Apparel
       Industry," AS (Dec, 1952), 27: 261-67. Tech-
       nical terms used by men's garment workers.
       Familiar words newly applied.

3155. Leigh, Rufus Wood. Five Hundred Utah Place
       Names: Their Origin and Significance (Salt Lake
       City: n. p. , 1961), 109pp.

3156. _____. Nevada Place Names; Their Origin and
       Significance (Salt Lake City: Deseret News P. ,
       1964), xi, 149pp.

3157. Leland, J. A. C. "Indian Names in Missouri,"
       Names (Dec, 1953), 1: 266-73. An extension
       of a list compiled by Robert L. Ramsay.

3158. Lewis, Arthur H. Carnival (New York: Trident,
       1970), 315pp. Personal account of the traveling
       show and midway entertainment with considerable
       use of argot and slang.

3159. Lewis, Margaret Jane. "Some Nicknames and Their
       Derivations," MFR (S, 1970), 4: 52-57. Mis-

sissippi nicknames mostly reflecting physical appearance.

3160. Lighter, Jonathan. "The Slang of the American Expeditionary Forces in Europe, 1917-1919: An Historical Glossary," AS (Spr-S, 1972), 47: 5-142. Folk speech of the American soldier abroad. Informative compilation with extensive bibliography.

3161. Lindsey, David. "New England Origins of Western Reserve Place Names," AS (Dec, 1955), 30: 243-55. Yankees moving west brought personal and place names with them.

3162. Lish, T. G. "Word List of Construction Terms," PADS (Nov, 1961), no. 36, pp. 25-31. Compilation based on personal experience in Alaska and the western states.

3163. Lomax, John A. "Cowboy Lingo," in The Sunny Slopes of Long Ago, ed. Wilson M. Hudson and Allen Maxwell, pp. 12-25. An early paper revised and enlarged.

3164. Loomis, C. Grant. "The Hell You Did Not Say," Names (Sept, 1961), 9: 163-64. Euphemisms for mild profanity.

3165. _____. "Names in American Limericks," Names (Dec, 1954), 2: 229-33. Strained rhymes in periodical limericks suggest local or former pronunciations.

3166. _____. "Some Call It Money," Names (Sept, 1956), 4: 160-65. Interesting list of substitutes for the word "money" from recent books.

3167. _____. "Traditional American Wordplay," WF (Apr, 1950), 9: 147-52. Material from newspapers and periodicals 1820-1880. List of puns, cliches, and occupational jokes.

3168. Lowry, Lillian. "Christian Names in Western Kentucky," MF (F, 1953), 3: 131-36.

3169. Lumiansky, R. H. "New Orleans Slang in the 1880s,"

AS (Feb, 1950), 25: 28-40. Some 325 terms
selected from the New Orleans weekly, The Lan-
tern; many unrecorded.

3170. McAtee, W. L. "American Bird Names, Two Studies," Names (Je, 1959), 7: 110-21. Supernaturalism in bird names and folk names for the bittern.

3171.   . "Bird Names Connected with Weather,
Seasons, and Hours," AS (Dec, 1951), 26: 268-
78. Many folk variants for common birds, e.g.,
the cuckoo.

3172.   . "Bird Names with Animal or Plant Com-
ponents," AS (Oct, 1955), 30: 176-85.

3173.   . "Facetious Monickers for American Birds,"
AS (Oct, 1956), 31: 180-87.

3174.   . "Folk Etymology in North American Bird
Names," AS (May, 1951), 26: 90-95. Example:
pileated woodpecker is commonly called the log
cock.

3175.   . "Gleanings from the Dialect of Grant
County, Indiana," PADS (Apr, 1951), no. 15,
51-64.

3176.   . "Naming Wild Birds as if They Were
Poultry," AS (Dec, 1953), 28: 276-84. Names
of domestic fowl applied to ducks, grouse, upland
game.

3177.   . "Nationality Names for American Birds,"
AS (Oct, 1957), 32: 180-85. Examples: English
sparrow, Hungarian partridge, Chinese pheasant.

3178.   . "Some Folk and Scientific Names for
Plants," PADS (Apr, 1951), no. 15, 3-25.

3179.   . "Some Pioneer Indiana Terms," AS (Dec,
1961), 36: 299-301.

3180. McClung, Barbara Lynette. "Americanisms from
Horse Racing Accounts in the Spirit of the Times,"
AS (Oct, 1965), 40: 178-85. Supplementary list
of 108 items.

3181. _____. "Horse Racing Accounts in the Spirit of
the Times," AS (Feb, 1965), 40: 20-31. Folk
speech of the race track from an American sporting weekly.

3182. McCulloch, Walter F. Woods Words (Portland: Oregon Hist. Soc. and Champoeg P., 1958), vi,
219pp. Useful listing and definitions of logging
terms.

3183. McDavid, Raven I., Jr. "Folk Speech," in Our
Living Traditions, ed. T. P. Coffin, pp. 228-37.
General comments with regional examples and
variations.

3184. _____. "The Folk Vocabulary of New York State,"
NYFQ (A, 1951), 7: 173-92. Five dialect areas
identified with many examples.

3185. _____. "The Positions of the Charleston Dialect,"
PADS (Apr, 1955), no. 23, 35-49.

3186. _____ and Virginia McDavid. "Cracker and
Hoosier," Names (Sept, 1973), 21: 161-67. Linguistic discussion of two well known pejorative
names.

3187. _____ and Sarah Ann Witham. "Poor Whites and
Rustics," Names (Sept, 1974), 22: 93-103.
Terms used for inhabitants of rural regions.

3188. McIntyre, Terry L. "The Language of Railroading,"
AS (W, 1969), 44: 243-62. Railroad practices
explained and glossary provided.

3189. McMullen, Edwin Wallace, Jr. English Topographic
Terms in Florida (Gainesville: U. of Florida P.,
1953), vi, 227pp.

3190. _____. "The Term Prairie in the United States,"
Names (Mr, 1957), 5: 27-46. Exhaustive study
of the term based on geographical evidence.

3191. Madison, Virginia and Hallie Stillwell. How Come
It's Called That? Place Names in the Big Bend
Country (Albuquerque: U. of New Mexico P.,
1958), 129pp. Some local and uncritical topony-
my from three Texas counties.

3192. Mansell, Don and Joseph S. Hall. "Hot Rod Terms
       in the Pasadena Area," AS (May, 1954), 29: 89-
       104. Technical, vernacular, and obscene terms
       used by hot rodders.

3193. Maurer, David W. "The Argot of the Racetrack,"
       PADS (Nov, 1951), no. 16, 3-70. Extensive list
       of language used in horse racing, with definitions.

3194. _____. "Whiz Mob," PADS (Nov, 1955), no. 24,
       3-199. The argot of pickpockets, developed
       through essays on theft and thieves, skills, mobs,
       the law, ethics, and "the mark."

3195. _____. "A Word-Finder List for Whiz Mob,"
       PADS (Apr, 1959), no. 31, 14-30. Index to
       Nov., 1955, article.

3196. Meredith, Mamie. "The Nomenclature of American
       Pioneer Fences," SFQ (Je, 1951), 15: 109-51.

3197. Millard, Eugenia L. "What Does It Mean?--the Lore
       of Secret Languages," NYFQ (S, 1954), 10: 103-
       10. Children's use of pig Latin, Tuttin, and other
       arcane speech.

3198. Mills, Hazel E. "The Constant Webfoot," WF (Jl,
       1952), 11: 153-64. Discussion of origin and use
       of the term webfoot, an epithet applied to Ore-
       gonians.

3199. Mills, Randall. "Oregon Speechways," AS (May,
       1950), 25: 81-90. Terms from agriculture, lum-
       bering, cattle raising. Meaning varies but pro-
       nunciation remains standard.

3200. Mockler, William R. and Burns D. Goodwin. "San
       Diego's Poker Vocabulary," WF (Jl, 1950), 9:
       268-70. Journalistic report; terms not unique
       to San Diego.

3201. Moe, Albert J. "Leatherneck: a Borrowed Nick-
       name," Names (Dec, 1965), 13: 225-57. Rumors
       dispelled about a familiar name, originally
       British.

3202. Monteiro, George. "Alcunhas Among the Portuguese

in Southern New England," WF (Apr, 1961), 20:
103-7. Nicknames and substitute surnames discussed.

3203. _____. "Truckers Language in Rhode Island,"
AS (Feb, 1963), 38: 42-46.

3204. Mook, Maurice. "Nicknames Among the Amish,"
KFQ (W, 1960), 5, iv, 3-12. Nicknames are
often abbreviated first names or are suggested
by personal habits and traits.

3205. _____. "Tongue Tanglers from Central Pennsylvania," JAF (Oct-Dec, 1959), 72: 291-96. Student-collected tongue twisters in both rhyme and
prose.

3206. Musick, Ruth Ann and Vance Randolph. "Children's
Rhymes in Missouri," JAF (Oct-Dec, 1950), 63:
425-37.

3207. Nelson, Mildred M. "Folk Etymology of Alabama
Place-Names," SFQ (Dec, 1950), 14: 193-214.
Selected names discussed (Selma, Eufaula, Burnt-
corn, Alabama itself).

3208. Neuffer, Claude Henry. "Folk Etymology in South
Carolina Place Names," AS (Dec, 1966), 41: 274-
77.

3209. _____. Names in South Carolina (Columbia: U.
of So. Carolina P., 1965), 55pp. Thirteen articles about specific geographical terms with origins and legends.

3210. _____. Names in South Carolina, Volumes I-XII,
1954-1965 (Columbia: State Printing Co., 1967),
v. 271pp. Compilation of material published in
first state onomastic journal.

3211. Newman, Thomas Stell. "Air Refueling Words," AS
(May, 1963), 38: 117-20. Technical terms
emanating from a new operation.

3212. Nooy, Amy Ver. "Place-Names and Folklore in
Dutchess County," NYFQ (Mr, 1964), 20: 42-46.
Legends associated with a New York county.

3213. Norman, Arthur M. Z. "Army Speech and the Fu-
       ture of American English," AS (May, 1956), 31:
       107-12. Influence of military ellipses, substitu-
       tions, and obscenities.

3214. Nye, Hermes. "Folksay of Lawyers," in Singers
       and Storytellers, ed. Mody C. Boatright et al.,
       pp. 92-97. Legal fallacies, cliches, mispro-
       nunciations collected by a practicing attorney.

3215. _____. "T-Bones and Cheater Slicks: the Folk-
       say of the Drag Strip," in Tire-Shrinker to Drag-
       ster, ed. Wilson M. Hudson, pp. 11-25. Exten-
       sive collection of language of hot rod cars and
       drag races with definitions.

3216. Oliver, Raymond. "More Carnie Talk from the West
       Coast," AS (Dec, 1966), 41: 278-83. Supplement
       to William L. Alderson's list.

3217. Orth, Donald J. Dictionary of Alaska Place Names
       (Washington: U. S. Govt. P. O., 1967), xi, 1084
       pp., plus 12 pp. of maps.

3218. Osborn, Lettie. "Fiddle-Tunes from Orange County,
       New York," NYFQ (A, 1952), 8: 211-15. Inter-
       esting collection of names of fiddle tunes (no
       music).

3219. Overman, William D. Ohio Place Names; the Origin
       of the Names of Over 500 Ohio Cities, Towns
       and Villages (Akron: p. p., 1951), xii, 86pp.

3220. _____. Ohio Town Names (Akron: Atlantic P.,
       1958), ix, 155pp. An amateurish work which
       has some utility.

3221. Palmer, Francis W. "Gold Rush Language," AS
       (May, 1968), 43: 83-113. Extensive list of
       mining, outfitting, clothing terms gleaned from
       printed sources.

3222. Paredes, Américo. "On Gringo, Greaser, and Other
       Neighborly Names," in Singers and Storytellers,
       ed. Mody C. Boatright et al., pp. 285-90. Mu-
       tual epithets along the Rio Grande.

3223. Partridge, Eric. A Dictionary of the Underworld, British and American... (New York: Macmillan, 1950), xv, 804pp. Language of crooks, beggars, tramps, convicts, etc.

3224. Pearce, Thomas M. New Mexico Place Names: A Geographical Dictionary (Albuquerque: U. of New Mexico P., 1965), xv, 187pp. About 5,000 place names given.

3225. _____. "The New Mexico Place-Name Dictionary: A Polyglot in Six Languages," Names (Dec, 1958), 6: 217-25. Problems encountered in compiling a lexicon.

3226. _____. "Religious Place Names in New Mexico," Names (Mr, 1961), 9: 1-7.

3227. _____. "Spanish Place Names in the Southwest," Names (Dec, 1955), 3: 201-9. Pearce suggests a place name category: "names which transfer terms of folk imagination, affection, and humor to localities and landmarks."

3228. _____. "Three Rocky Mountain Terms: Park, Sugan, and Plaza," AS (May, 1958), 33: 99-107. Three widely used terms of variant meanings.

3229. Peden, Ann. "Place Names in Humphreys County," MFR (S, 1971), 5: 39-49.

3230. Pederson, Lee. "Chicago Words: the Regional Vocabulary," AS (F-W, 1971), 46: 163-92. Material gathered from 37 carefully selected informants.

3231. Penrod, James H. "Two Aspects of Folk Speech in Southwestern Humor," KFR (Oct-Dec, 1957), 3: 145-52. Wise sayings and comic imagery.

3232. Phillips, George L. "Street Cries of American Chimney-Sweepers," NYFQ (A, 1952), 8: 191-98. Cries of chimney sweepers from New York and New Orleans.

3233. Phillips, James W. Alaska-Yukon Place Names (Seattle: U. of Washington P., 1973), 149pp. Some 2,000 place names annotated.

3234. _____. Washington State Place Names (Seattle:
       U. of Washington P., 1971), xv, 167pp.

3235. Poston, Lawrence III. "Some Problems in the Study
       of Campus Slang," AS (May, 1964), 39: 114-23.
       Various meanings of campus slang and their ori-
       gins explored.

3236. Preston, Dennis Richard. "Bituminous Coal Mining
       Vocabulary of the Eastern United States," PADS
       (Apr, 1973), no. 59, pp. 1-128. Some 489
       terms from twelve states arranged alphabetically
       with definitions and annotations. Maps showing
       distribution included.

3237. Pukui, Mary Kawena and Samuel H. Elbert. Place
       Names of Hawaii (Honolulu: U. of Hawaii P.,
       1966), 53pp. Some 1,125 place names listed
       and defined.

3238. Ramsay, Robert L. Our Storehouse of Missouri
       Place Names (Columbia: U. of Missouri P.,
       1952), 160pp. Five main categories: borrowed
       names from outside Missouri, local, historical
       and political, topographical, and cultural.

3239. _____. "The Place Names of Boone County,
       Missouri," PADS (Nov, 1952), no. 18, 3-52.

3240. _____. The Place Names of Franklin County,
       Missouri (Columbia: U. of Missouri P., 1954),
       55pp.

3241. Randle, William. "Payola," AS (May, 1961), 36:
       104-16. Variety of usages for sub rosa pay-
       ments.

3242. Randolph, Vance. "The Names of Ozark Tunes,"
       MF (S, 1954), 4: 81-86. Names of tunes
       played in the Ozarks, 1920-1950.

3243. _____ and George P. Wilson. Down in the Holler:
       A Gallery of Ozark Folk Speech (Norman: U. of
       Oklahoma P., 1953), ix, 320pp. Ozark linguistic
       evidence in its social context.

3244. Rawles, Myrtle Read. "'Boontling'--Esoteric Speech

of Boonville, California," WF (Apr, 1966), 25:
93-103. Brief account with glossary.

3245. Rea, J. "Seeing the Elephant," WF (Jan, 1969), 28:
21-26. Suggested etymology for a colorful phrase.

3246. Read, Allen Walker. "The First Stage in the History
of 'O. K. '," AS (Feb, 1963), 38: 5-27; "The Second Stage in the History of 'O. K. '," AS (May,
1963), 38: 83-102.

3247. _____. "The Folklore of 'O. K. '," AS (Feb, 1964),
39: 5-25. Various accounts of the genesis of this
famous expression; "Later Stages in the History
of 'O. K. '," AS (May, 1964), 39: 83-101; additional evidence; "Successive Revisions in the Explanations of 'O. K. '," AS (Dec, 1964), 39: 243-67;
history of the scholarship.

3248. _____. "'G. T. T. '--Gone to Texas," SFQ (Sept,
1963), 27: 223-28. History of a famous American acronym; its heyday, 1839-1840.

3249. Reed, Carroll E. "English Archaisms in Pennsylvania German," PADS (Apr, 1953), no. 19, 3-7.

3250. _____. "Washington Words," PADS (Apr, 1956),
no. 25, 3-11. Regional list from state of Washington.

3251. Reed, David W. "Eastern Dialect Words in California," PADS (Apr, 1954), No. 21, 3-15.

3252. Reid, Bessie M. "Vernacular Names for Texas
Plants," PADS (Apr, 1951), No. 15, 26-50.

3253. Rennick, Robert M. "The Folklore of Curious and
Unusual Names," NYFQ (Mr, 1966), 22: 5-14.
Name-changes by persons seeking to avoid ob-
scene or harsh-sounding names.

3254. _____. "The Inadvertent Changing of Non-English
Names by Newcomers to America: a Brief Historical Survey and Popular Presentation of Cases,"
NYFQ (Dec, 1970), 26: 263-82. Immigrant name
changes imposed by substitution or translation.

3255. _____. "Obscene Names and Naming in Folk Tradition," Names (Sept, 1968), 16: 207-29. Many
examples of personal names (with etymologies or
conjectural origins).

3256. _____. "Successive Name-Changing: a Popular
Theme in Onomastic Folklore and Literature,"
NYFQ (Je, 1969), 25: 119-28. Variants on basic
story of a man who changed his name twice to
hide his origins.

3257. Reynolds, Anthony M. "Urban Negro Toasts: a
Hustler's View from L. A.," WF (Oct, 1974), 33:
267-300. Texts and comments about urban toasts.

3258. Reynolds, Horace. "All Mines, Fellas, All Mines!"
AS (Feb, 1956), 31: 35-39. The childish word
"hosie" (lay claim to) leads to comment on other
juvenile terms.

3259. _____. "A Nest of Unnoticed Americanisms," WF
(Apr, 1953), 12: 114-18. List published by a
Yankee pastor in 1836 including pawn party,
spinning bevy, quilting bevy, etc.

3260. Rippy, Pauline. "Language Trends in Oil Field
Jargo," PADS (Apr, 1951), no. 15, 72-80.
Technical terms defined in running comment.

3261. Roach, Joyce Gibson. "Diesel Smoke & Dangerous
Curves: Folklore of the Trucking Industry," in
Hunters & Healers, ed. Wilson M. Hudson, pp.
45-53. Songs, speech, and vehicle names.

3262. Robacker, Earl F. "Victorian Wall Mottoes," PF
(Spr, 1974), 23, iii, 2-10.

3263. Roberts, Leonard. "Additional Exaggerations from
East Kentucky," MF (F, 1952), 2: 163-66. Some
92 proverbial expressions.

3264. Rogers, E. G. "Figurative Language the Folkway,"
TFSB (Dec, 1950), 16: 71-75. Long list of folk
similes and metaphors without annotation.

3265. _____. "Guideposts to Fortune," TFSB (Je,
1950), 16: 31-37. Two lists of beliefs or super-

stitions, 179 in all; guarantees of good fortune
and avoidance of bad.

3266.   Rogers, P. Burwell.   "Place Names on the Virginia
        Peninsula," AS (Dec, 1954), 29: 241-56.   Place
        names between York and James rivers come from
        history and biography.

3267.   Romig, Walter.   Michigan Place Names (Grosse
        Point, Mich.:   Walter Romig Publisher, n. d.),
        673pp.   Some 5,000 place names arranged alpha-
        betically with data about origins and locations.

3268.   Rowe, H. D.   "New England Terms for Bull: Some
        Aspects of Barnyard Bowdlerism," AS (May,
        1957), 32: 110-16.   Linguistic folklore about
        the "male cow."

3269.   Rudolph, Robert S.   Wood County Place Names (Madi-
        son: U. of Wisconsin P., 1970), ix, 121pp.

3270.   Runcie, John F.   "Truck Drivers' Jargon," AS (F,
        1969), 44: 200-9.   Truckers use jargon to explain
        technical problems quickly, to exclude outsiders,
        to impose on neophytes.

3271.   Rutherford, Phillip A.   Dictionary of Maine Place-
        Names (Freeport, Me.:   Bond Wheelwright, 1970),
        xx, 283pp.

3272.   Rydjord, John.   Indian Place Names, Their Origin,
        Evolution and Meaning, Collected in Kansas
        (Norman: U. of Oklahoma P., 1968), xi, 380pp.
        Kansas Indian names, rather anecdotal in style.

3273.   _____.   Kansas Place-Names (Norman: U. of
        Oklahoma P., 1972), xii, 613pp.   Etymological
        and geographical study of 3,000 Kansas names
        with impressive documentation.

3274.   Sackett, S. J.   "Simile in Folksong," MF (Spr, 1963),
        13: 5-12.   Some 82 folksongs in a Kansas archive
        suggest that similes are less common in folksong
        than in poetry.

3275.   Sagarin, Edward.   The Anatomy of Dirty Words (New
        York: Lyle Stuart, 1962), 220pp.   Discussions

and examples of language often represented in
print by asterisks. Excellent analysis of verbal
taboos. Useful bibliography.

3276. Schulman, Steven A. "Logging Terms from the Upper
      Cumberland River," TFSB (Je, 1973), 39: 35-36.
      27 commonly used logging terms, a few regional.

3277. Schwartz, Alvin. Tomfoolery: Trickery and Foolery
      with Words (Philadelphia and New York: Lippin-
      cott, 1973), 127pp. Verbal twists taken from
      folklore books and journals.

3278. _____. A Twister of Twists, a Tangler of Tongues
      (Philadelphia and New York: Lippincott, 1972),
      126pp. 186 tongue twisters, some in other lan-
      guages than English.

3279. Scott, Clayton S., Jr. "Corporate Nicknames in the
      Stock Market," AS (Oct, 1960), 35: 193-202.
      Parodies and amalgamations produce Fanny Mae,
      Katy, Big Steel, Monkey Ward.

3280. Seymour, Richard K. "Collegiate Slang: Aspects of
      Word Formation and Semantic Change," PADS
      (Apr, 1969), no. 51, 13-22. Examples from
      Duke University, 1964-1967.

3281. Shain, Samson A. "Old Testament Place Names in
      Pennsylvania," KFQ (A, 1961), 6, iii, 3-11.
      Biblical names of places and people are reflected
      on Penn. map.

3282. Shankle, George Earlie. American Nicknames, Their
      Origin and Significance (New York: Wilson,
      1955), vii, 524pp. Sec. ed. of a book first pub-
      lished in 1937.

3283. Sheldon, Esther M. "Some Pun among the Huck-
      sters," AS (Feb, 1956), 31: 13-20. Amusing ex-
      amples of punning in advertising.

3284. Shirk, George H. Oklahoma Place Names (Norman:
      U. of Oklahoma P., 1965), xv, 233pp. Essen-
      tially a sec. ed. of C. N. Gould, Oklahoma
      Place Names, 1933.

3285. Shulman, David. "Baseball's Bright Lexicon," AS
       (Feb, 1951), 26: 29-34. Alphabetical list of
       common baseball terms and phrases.

3286. _____. "Culinary Americanisms," AS (Feb, 1959),
       34: 26-32. Mostly items from nineteenth century
       magazines and books.

3287. _____. "Nicknames of States and Their Inhabi-
       tants," AS (Oct, 1952), 27: 183-85. Brief list
       of historical and current terms.

3288. Shuy, Roger W. "Tireworker Terms," AS (Dec,
       1964), 39: 268-77. Specialized vocabulary of
       the rubberworker; data from Firestone plant in
       Akron, Ohio.

3289. Smith, Elsdon C. Dictionary of American Family
       Names (New York: Harper, 1956), xxxiv, 244pp.
       Useful book but limited in space.

3290. _____. The Story of Our Names (New York:
       Harper, 1950), x, 296pp.

3291. _____. Treasury of Name Lore (New York and
       Evanston: Harper & Row, 1967), 246pp.

3292. Smith, Grace Partridge. "They Call It Egypt,"
       Names (Mr, 1954), 2: 51-54. Explanations of
       "Egypt" as a term for Southern Illinois.

3293. Smith, Jack A. "The Mississippi Place-Name
       Repository," MFR (Spr, 1968), 2: 9-18. An
       archive of state place names.

3294. _____. "Some Notes on the Dialect of Key West,"
       MFR (S, 1968), 2: 55-64. Place names, food
       names, weather lore.

3295. Snook, Sydney. "Echoes on the River," MF (S,
       1960), 10: 70-78. Selection of names from old
       river steamboats on the Mississippi, Ohio, and
       other rivers.

3296. Sonkin, Robert. "Bleeding Betty's Brakes: or, the
       Army Names a Jeep," AS (Dec, 1954), 29: 257-
       62. Names given army vehicles during World
       War II.

3297. Sorden, L. G. Lumberjack Lingo (Spring Green,
       Wis.: Wisconsin House, 1969), 149pp.

3298. Spears, James E. "Folk Children's Pejorative Nick-
       names and Epithets," KFR (Jl- Sept, 1972), 18:
       70-74.

3299. _____. "The Metaphor in American Folk Speech,"
       NYFQ (Mr, 1973), 29: 50-57. Brief comments
       about 112 folk metaphors and similes collected by
       questionnaire.

3300. _____. "A Note on Folk Cures," NYFQ (Je,
       1974), 30: 157-60. Trivial.

3301. Sperber, Hans and James N. Tidwell. "Words and
       Phrases in American Politics," AS (May, 1950),
       25: 91-100.

3302. _____ and _____. "Words and Phrases in
       American Politics: Facts and Fiction About Salt
       River," AS (Dec, 1951), 26: 241-47.

3303. _____ and Travis Trittschuh. American Political
       Terms: a Historical Dictionary (Detroit: Wayne
       State U. P., 1962), viii, 516pp. Political history
       and folklore intermingled.

3304. Splitter, Henry Winfred. "Miner's Luck," WF (Oct,
       1956), 15: 229-46. California gold mining ac-
       counts from contemporary periodicals.

3305. Stanley, Julia P. "Homosexual Slang," AS (Spr-S,
       1970), 45: 45-59. Core vocabulary of homosexual
       terms derived from theatre, prostitutes, crimin-
       als, and stock phrases.

3306. Stewart, George R. American Place-Names (New
       York: Oxford, 1970), xl, 544pp. Invaluable
       study by the leading student of Am. toponyms.
       Pronunciation of unusual names not always indi-
       cated.

3307. _____. "A Classification of Place Names,"
       Names (Mr, 1954), 2: 1-13. Nine categories of
       place names suggested with vivid illustrations.

3308. _____. Names on the Land (Boston: Houghton Mifflin, 1958), 511pp. Substantially rev. ed. of a book first published in 1945.

3309. Straubinger, O. Paul. "Names in Popular Sayings," Names (Sept, 1955), 3: 157-64.

3310. Tak, Montie. Truck Talk: the Language of the Open Road (Philadelphia: Chilton, 1971), xiv, 191pp. Alphabetically arranged list including occupational, descriptive, and humorous terms.

3311. Tamony, Peter. "Coca-Cola; the Most-Lawed Name," Names (Dec, 1969), 17: 278-283. Legal, chemical, and folk history of a famous label.

3302. _____. "'Hootenanny'; the Word, Its Context and Continuum," WF (Jl, 1963), 22: 165-170. Suggested etymology with examples from Seattle (1940) and New York.

3313. _____. "Western Words: the Wobblies," WF (Jan, 1971), 30: 49-54. Etymology of "Wobblies" plus some history.

3314. Tarpley, Fred. Place Names of Northeast, Texas (Commerce, Texas: East Texas St. U.P., 1969), xxi, 245pp. Some 2,693 names listed from 26 counties. Extensive field work but sources limited and information spotty.

3315. _____. "Southern Cemeteries: Neglected Archives for the Folklorist," SFQ (Dec, 1963), 27: 323-33. Tombstone epitaphs reveal interesting linguistic material.

3316. _____ and Ann Moseley, eds. Of Edsels and Marauders (Commerce, Tx.: Names Institute P., 1971), 126pp. Miscellaneous collection of names including sections on ethnic and place names.

3316a. Tidwell, James N. "A Neglected Source of Americanisms," AS (Dec, 1960), 35: 266-69.

3317. _____. "Political Words and Phrases: Card-Playing Terms," AS (Feb, 1958), 33: 21-28.

3318. Tillson, William. "How the Boilermakers Did Not
       Get Their Name," MF (S, 1961), 11: 105-14.
       Origin of nickname of Purdue athletic teams ques-
       tioned.

3319. Tinkler, Mary Crawford. "Newspaper English of
       Marshall County, Alabama," SFQ (Sept, 1957),
       21: 154-59. Colloquialisms, solecisms, dialect
       reflect current usage.

3320. Tucker, H. Clay. "The Language of Jazz," TFSB
       (Dec, 1954), 20: 77-81.

3321. Underwood, Gary N. "Midwestern Terms for the
       Ground Squirrel," WF (Jl, 1970), 29: 167-74.

3322. Upham, Warren. Minnesota Geographic Names (St.
       Paul: Minn. Hist. Soc., 1969), xxiv, 7888pp.
       Reprint of one of the best state collections
       (originally published in 1920). Slightly enlarged
       and still valuable despite Upham's lack of ono-
       mastic training.

3323. Utley, Francis Lee. "Onomastic Variety in the High
       Sierra," Names (Je, 1972), 20: 73-82. Mountain
       names reflect legends, history, humor, and fancy.

3324. Vickers, Ovid S. "Word Watching in Red Neck
       Country," MFR (F, 1968), 2: 69-75.

3325. Vogel, Virgil J. Indian Place Names in Illinois
       (Springfield, Ill.: Ill. State Hist. Lib., 1963),
       176pp.

3326. Wallrich, William J. "Barroom Slang from the Upper
       Rio Grande," WF (Jan, 1951), 10: 80-82; (Apr,
       1951), 170-72; (Jl, 1951), 249-50; (Oct, 1951),
       324.

3327. Walton, Gerald W. "A Word List of Southern Farm
       Terms from Faulkner's The Hamlet," MFR (S,
       1972), 6: 60-75. Quotations and definitions.

3328. Walton, Ivan H. "Indian Names in Michigan," MF
       (Spr, 1955), 5: 23-34.

3329. Warshaver, Gerald. "Schlop Scholarship; a Survey

of Folkloristic Studies of Lunchcounter and Soda
Jerk Operatives," JFI (Dec, 1971), 4: 134-145.
The jargon of the counter man.

3330. Welsh, James M. "Addenda to the Vocabulary of
Railroading," AS (Dec, 1968), 43: 282-290.

3331. White, Edward Mitchell. "The Vocabulary of Marbles
in Eastern Kentucky," KFR (Jl-Sept, 1963), 9:
57-74. Terminology of a favorite game with
distribution of terms by counties.

3332. Williams, Cratis D. "Mountain Speech," MLW
(1961-1964), Vols. 37-40. A ten-part series
running serially from Spr, 1961, through Spr,
1964. Williams deals with pronunciation, syntax,
vocabulary, and metaphor, supplying many examples. The articles are brief and rich in folk
meaning.

3333. Wilson, Gordon. "Place Names in the Mammoth Cave
Region," KFR (Jan-Mr, 1968), 14: 8-13.

3334. _____. "Regional Words," KFR (Jan-Mr, Apr-
Je, 1971), 10-18, 31-39. Terms from the Mammoth Cave region.

3335. _____. "Similes from the Mammoth Cave Region
with a Farm Flavor," KFR (Apr-Je, Jl-Sept,
Oct-Dec, 1969), 19: 44-50, 69-75, 94-99.
Many of these are generally found rather than being limited to a single region.

3336. Winslow, David J. "Children's Derogatory Epithets,"
JAF (Jl-Sept, 1969), 82: 255-63. Data from
children in Rochester, Cooperstown, Philadelphia.

3337. Wolfe, Charles K. "Southwestern Humor and Old-
Time Music: Lunsford's 'Speaking the Truth',"
JEMFQ (Spr, 1974), 10: 31-34. A folk sermon,
used for parody.

3338. Wood, Gordon R. "A List of Words from Tennessee," PADS (Apr, 1958), no. 29, 3-18. Words
contributed by Tennessee newspaper readers,
1952-1953.

3339.   _____. "Some Sources of Information on Tennes-
             see Folk Speech," TFSB (Mr, 1955), 21: 20-26.
             Scholars need to consider newspapers, letters,
             government reports, etc.

3340.   Woodbridge, Hensley C. "Eleven Kentucky Tobacco
             Words," KFR (Apr-Je, 1957), 3: 59-66. Techni-
             cal words in tobacco culture.

3341.   _____. "Some Unrecorded Hunting Terms Found
             in Kentucky," KFR (Oct-Dec, 1957), 3: 153-58.
             Many appear in Harriette Arnow's novel Hunter's
             Horn, 1949.

3342.   Wright, Martha R. "Hootenanny: More of Its Past,"
             AS (Feb, 1966), 41: 56-58. Addenda to Peter
             Tamony's 1963 article.

3343.   Wyld, Lionel D. "Notes for a Yorker Dictionary of
             Canalese," NYFQ (W, 1959), 15: 264-73. Erie
             Canal terms.

3344.   Yates, Norris. "Children's Folk Plays in Western
             Oregon," WF (Jan, 1951), 10: 55-62. Discussion
             of fragments of 11 playlets or pantomimes pre-
             served orally by children in Oregon and Washing-
             ton.

15. MINOR GENRES

(Including jokes, rhymes, verses, graffiti, games, etc.)

3345. Abrahams, Roger D. "The 'Catch' in Negro Philadelphia," KFQ (F, 1963), 8: 107-111. Negro
children recite rhymes which surprise others and
stimulate aggressive behavior.

3346. _____. Deep Down in the Jungle: Negro Narrative
Folklore from the Streets of Philadelphia (Chicago:
Aldine Pub. Co., 1970), ix, 278pp. Considerably
revised sec. ed. of a book published in 1964.
In Robert Wildhaber's words, "a primary collec-
tion of slum-lore" based on field experience.

3347. _____. "Ghastly Commands: the Cruel Joke Revisited," MF (W, 1961-1962), 11: 235-246.

3348. _____. Jump-Rope Rhymes: a Dictionary (Austin
and London: U. of Texas P., 1969), xxiv, 228pp.
Excellent annotations and a bibliography.

3349. _____. "Jump-Rope Rimes From Texas," SFQ
(Sept, 1963), 27: 196-213. Miscellaneous rhymes
from various parts of the state and from Texas
archives of folklore. Extensive bibliography in
a footnote.

3350. _____. "'Playing the Dozens'," JAF (Jl-Sept,
1962), 75: 209-20. Discussion and examples of
the famous Negro game of exchanging insults.

3351. _____. "Some Jump-Rope Rhymes From South
Philadelphia," KFQ (Spr, 1963), 8: 3-15. Rhymes
collected from Negro children in 1958-60.

357

3352.   _____. "The Toast: A Neglected Form of Folk Nar-
        rative," in Folklore in Action, ed. H. P. Beck, pp.
        1-11. Negro "toasts" from South Philadelphia.

3353. Agar, Michael H. "Folklore of the Heroin Addict:
        Two Examples," JAF (Apr-Je, 1971), 84: 175-85.
        Texts and analysis of two "toasts" related to drug
        addiction.

3354. Ainsworth, Catherine Harris. "Jump Rope Verses
        Around the United States," WF (Jl, 1961), 20:
        179-99. Material from seventh-grade pupils
        (mostly girls) from public schools in nine dif-
        ferent states. Remarkable similarities in verses
        and content.

3355. Anderson, John Q. "For the Ugliest Man: An Exam-
        ple of Folk Humor," SFQ (Sept, 1964), 28: 199-
        209. Tradition of the ugly man in life and litera-
        ture examined and now found moribund. Long-
        street, Hooper, DeVoto cited.

3356.   _____. "Some Migratory Anecdotes in American
        Folk Humor," MQ (F, 1972), 25: 447-457. Sur-
        vey of humorous anecdotes which are found in
        oral tradition and in print in many parts of the
        U. S.

3357. Atkinson, Robert M. "Songs Little Girls Sing: An
        Orderly Invitation to Violence," NWF (1967), 2:
        i, 2-8. Children's parodies of jump rope rhymes.

3358. Ayoub, Millicent R. and Stephen A. Barnett. "Ritu-
        alized Verbal Insult in White High School Culture,"
        JAF (Oct-Dec, 1965), 78: 337-44. Authors con-
        tend that playing the "Dozens" is not limited to
        Negroes. Limited evidence from Ohio. Cf.
        Bruce Jackson, "White Dozens and Bad Sociology,"
        JAF (Apr-Je, 1966), 79: 374-77, a refutation.

3359. Barakat, Robert A. "Arabic Gestures," JPC (Spr,
        1973), 6: 749-93. General discussion of ges-
        tures--their purpose, meaning, variety. Exam-
        ples taken from Arab world but many are familiar
        to Western Europe and U. S.

3360. Barrick, Mac E. "Jump-Rope Rhymes," PF (S,

1970), 19: iv, 43-47.   Some 20 rhymes collected
at Harrisburg, Penn.

3361. _____. "Pulpit Humor in Central Pennsylvania,"
PF (A, 1969), 19: i, 28-36.   Jokes told by and
about preachers, a form worth more study.

3362. _____. "Some Nineteenth Century Autograph
Verses," KFQ (F, 1963), 8: 112-114.   Several
examples from an autograph book in the family's
possession.

3363. _____. "The Typescript Broadside," KFQ (Spr,
1972), 17: 27-38.   Typed broadsides circulated
in Penn. in 1950's were eagerly read because of
their erotic or obscene material.

3364. Ben-Amos, Dan. "The 'Myth' of Jewish Humor,"
WF (Apr, 1973), 32: 112-131.   Perceptive analysis which disproves Freud's theory that Jewish
humor is largely masochistic and self-critical.
Collected anecdotes show Jewish protagonists
often as victors.

3365. Bieter, Pat. "Folklore of the Boise Basques," WF
(Oct, 1965), 24: 262-270.   Miscellaneous material
from immigrant sheepherders in Idaho.

3366. Boswell, George W. "Autograph Album Verses,"
TFSB (Dec, 1971), 38: 97-104.   105 rhymes.

3367. Brewster, Paul G. American Nonsinging Games
(Norman: U. of Oklahoma P., 1953), xxii, 218
pp.   Texts and descriptions of 150 games with
extensive annotations.

3368. _____. "'Witchdoctor Advertising': Folklore in
the Modern Advertisement," NYFQ (S, 1958), 14:
140-144.   About Cold Lemons and Peter Pain.

3369. Brewton, John E. "Folk Rimes of Southern Children,"
TFSB (Dec, 1960), 26: 92-99.   Traditional nursery rhymes and playground rhymes; also parodies.

3370. Browne, Ray B. "Children's Taunts, Teases, and
Disrespectful Sayings from Southern California,"
WF (Je, 1954), 13: 190-198.

3371. _____. "Southern California Jump-Rope Rhymes:
       a Study in Variants," WF (Jan, 1955), 14: 3-22.
       41 examples from So. California with variants
       from elsewhere.

3372. _____. "Two Alabama Nonsense Orations," SFQ
       (Sept, 1953), 17: 213-15. A style of oratory
       popular in the South. Delivery is more important
       than content (sometimes the speech made no
       sense). Two examples given.

3373. Brunvand, Jan Harold. "As the Saints Go Marching
       By: Modern Jokelore Concerning Mormons,"
       JAF (Jan-Mr, 1970), 83: 53-60. Miscellaneous
       parodies, anecdotes, acronyms, nicknames, rid-
       dles, etc.

3374. _____. "The Study of Contemporary Folklore:
       Jokes," Fabula (1972), 13: i-ii, 1-19. There
       is a need to study jokes on a comparative basis.
       Pairs of jokes from U.S. and Romania are quoted
       to stress their cultural, social, ethnic values.

3375. Buckley, Bruce R. "Jump-Rope Rhymes: Sugges-
       tions for Classification and Study," KFQ (S,
       1966), 11: 99-111. Five types of jumping identi-
       fied.

3376. Buffington, Albert F. "Pennsylvania German Humor:
       Some Representative Examples," KFQ (S, 1963),
       8: 75-80. Three preacher stories.

3377. Butler, Francella. "International Variations in Skip-
       Rope Rhymes," TFSB (Mr, 1965), 31: 1-7.

3378. Cabaniss, Allen. "Some Examples of Masonic Lore,"
       MFR (S, 1969), 3: 7-18.

3379. Cansler, Loman D. "Midwestern and British Chil-
       dren's Lore Compared," WF (Jan, 1968), 27: 1-
       18. Children's rhymes show more similarities
       than differences.

3380. Castagna, Barbara. "Some Rhymes, Games, and
       Songs from Children in the New Rochelle Area,"
       NYFQ (Sept, 1969), 25: 221-237. Material col-
       lected in 1969 from children aged 3-12. Bibli-
       ography of references.

3381. Childers, William C. "Some Themes and Variations in Georgia Cemetery Epitaphs," SFQ (Je, 1956), 20: 97-107. Most epitaphs are routine but these examples are humorous, careless, or even defiant.

3382. Clarke, Kenneth. "Folklore of Negro Children in Greater Louisville Reflecting Attitudes Towards Race," KFR (Jan-Mr, 1964), 10: 1-11. Tape-recorded sayings and rhymes support thesis that racial lore clarifies identity and attitudes.

3383. Clements, William M. "The Polack Joke in 1970: an Addendum," FF (Jan-Mr, 1971), 4: 19-29. Supplement to a 1969 compilation. See Bibliography.

3384. Cohen, Hennig. "A Negro 'Folk Game' in Colonial South Carolina," SFQ (Sept, 1952), 16: 183-185. Negroes parody their white masters in a description taken from the South Carolina Gazette, Charleston (Sept. 17, 1772).

3385. Cooke, Jean. "A Few Gestures Encountered in a Virtually Gestureless Society," WF (Jl, 1959), 18: 233-237. California examples of facial and muscular gestures.

3386. Cray, Ed. "Jump-Rope Rhymes from Los Angeles," WF (Apr, 1970), 29: 119-127. Texts of rhymes collected 1958-1963.

3387. _____. "The Soldier's Deck of Cards Again," MF (W, 1961-1962), 11: 225-234.

3388. Cross, Paulette. "Jokes and Black Consciousness, a Collection with Interviews," FF (Nov, 1969), 2: 140-161. Jokes told by blacks about whites with interpretation.

3389. Curry, Timothy. "One-Liners as a Folklore Genre," KFQ (S, 1970), 15: 88-92.

3390. Davidson, Levette J. "Some Current Folk Gestures and Sign Language," AS (Feb, 1950), 25: 3-9.

3391. Davis, O. L., Jr. "A Note on Autograph Book

Verses," TFSB (Sept, 1956), 22: 69-72.   Sexual
references in childish rhymes.

3392.   Dirks, Martha.   "Teen-Age Folklore from Kansas,"
        WF (Apr, 1963), 22: 89-102.   Material collected
        from high school students in a small unnamed
        town includes sick jokes, little moron jokes,
        historical character jokes, and knock-knock jokes.

3393.   Dobie, J. Frank.   "The Traveling Anecdote," in
        Folk Travelers, ed. Mody C. Boatright et al.,
        pp. 1-17.   A variety of evidence proves that
        some familiar anecdotes cling to celebrities in
        different parts of the country.

3394.   Dow, James R.   "Folklore from the Frontier Index
        Wyoming Territory 1867-68," KF (Spr-S, 1973),
        18: 15-44.   A frontier Wyoming newspaper which
        followed the track of the Union Pacific R.R.
        printed tall tales, anecdotes, and marvel stories.

3395.   Dresser, Norine.   "Telephone Pranks," NYFQ (Je,
        1973), 29: 121-130.   Author contends that prank-
        ish telephone calls by children serve a practical
        purpose: admiration comes from the peer group.

3396.   _____.   "The Metamorphosis of the Humor of the
        Black Man," NYFQ (Sept, 1970), 26: 216-228.

3397.   Dundes, Alan.   "Chain Letter: a Folk Geometric
        Progression," NWF (W, 1966), 1: ii, 14-19.

3398.   _____.   "Advertising and Folklore," NYFQ (Je,
        1963), 19: 143-151.   Discussion of advertising
        puns, jingles, and jokes.

3399.   _____.   "Here I Sit--A Study of American
        Latrinalia," KASP (1966), 34: 91-105.

3400.   _____.   "Mnemonic Devices," MF (F, 1961), 11:
        139-147.   Proof that mnemonic devices are folk-
        lore although often neglected.

3401.   _____.   "On Game Morphology: a Study of the
        Structure of Non-Verbal Lore," NYFQ (Dec,
        1964), 20: 276-288.   Dundes contends that struc-
        turally children's games (nonverbal) are similar
        to verbal folklore (the folktale).

3402. _____. "Some Examples of Infrequently Reported Autograph Verse," SFQ (Je, 1962), 26: 127-130. A few unusual inscriptions and a useful brief bibliography.

3403. _____. "Some Minor Genres of American Folklore," SFQ (Mr, 1967), 31: 20-36. Unimportant but traditional oral materials: acronyms, telephone answers, etc.

3404. _____. "A Study of Ethnic Slurs: the Jew and the Polack in the United States," JAF (Apr-Je, 1971), 84: 186-203. Jewish and Polish stereotypes in American culture and the jokes associated with them. Excellent examples.

3405. _____ and Robert A. Georges. "Some Minor Genres of Obscene Folklore," JAF (Jl-Sept, 1962), 75: 221-226. Six minor genres analyzed; 54 examples given.

3406. Estes, Phoebe Beckner. "The Reverend Peter Vinegar," SFQ (Dec, 1959), 23: 239-252. Account of Peter Vinegar (1942-1905), Kentucky Negro preacher, and his famous folk sermons. Doubts about his personality but none about his impact.

3407. Evans, Patricia. Jump Rope Rhymes, 1955; Hopskotch, 1955; Jacks, 1956; Who's It, 196? (San Francisco: Porpoise Bookshop), all brochures of 32 pp. each.

3408. _____. Rimbles (New York: Doubleday, 1961).

3409. Evers, Alf. "Some Ulster Fly-Leaf Rhymes and Games," NYFQ (W, 1957), 13: 204-209. Autographs and inscriptions in school books.

3410. Faulk, John Henry. "Joe Whilden, One of the People," in And Horns on the Toads, ed. Mody C. Boatright et al., pp. 45-47. Anecdotes and tales about a gifted liar.

3411. Ferris, William R., Jr. "Prison Lore: a Neglected Tradition," MFR (W, 1971), 5: 114-120. Examples of poems and letters written by convicts.

3412. _____. "Railroad Chants: Form and Function,"
      MFR (1970), 4: 1-14.

3413. Flanagan, John T. "Folklore in the Newspapers,"
      JQ (Spr, 1958), 35: 205-211. Folklore themes
      considered newsworthy by editors (superstitions,
      legends, etc.).

3414. Ford, Nancy K. "A Garland of Playground Jingles,"
      KFQ (W, 1957-1958), 2: 109-111.

3415. Fowler, Bill F. "Hell-Fire and Folk Humor on the
      Frontier," in Tire Shrinker to Dragster, ed.
      Wilson M. Hudson, pp. 51-62. Preacher anec-
      dotes, mostly from the Spirit of the Times.

3416. Ganim, Mary. "A Study of Children's Folklore,"
      NYFQ (Mr, 1970), 26: 50-63. Children's folk-
      lore, especially games, is the acting out of life
      situations.

3417. Gibbs, Iris and Alonzo Gibbs. "Jump Rope Songs,"
      NYFQ (W, 1958), 14: 312-316. Jump rope songs
      from the past.

3418. Gillis, Everett A. "Almanac Lore," in Madstones
      and Twisters, ed. Mody C. Boatright et al., pp.
      81-90. Weather and astrological lore from
      famous almanacs.

3419. Glanz, Rudolph. The Jew in Early American Wit
      and Graphic Humor (New York: KTAV Pub.
      House, 1973), 269pp. Caricatures of the Jew
      versus the American economy and American so-
      ciety. Helpful illustrations.

3420. Golden, Harry. The Golden Book of Jewish Humor
      (New York: Putnam, 1972), 252pp. A miscellany
      of Jewish jokes from printed sources which are
      not always identified. It is rich in ethnic humor.

3421. Gonzalez, Rosalind. "Work and Play on a Border
      Ranch," in The Golden Log, ed. Mody C. Boat-
      right et al., pp. 141-155. Family history,
      ranch work, songs, riddles.

3422. Gordon, David. "Rhymes," WVF (S, 1962), 12: 50-
      53.

3423. Greenberg, Andrea. "Form and Function of the
      Ethnic Joke," KFQ (W, 1972), 17: 144-161.

3424. Hall, Wade. The Smiling Phoenix: Southern Humor
      from 1865 to 1914 (Gainesville: U. of Florida
      P., 1965), xv, 375pp. Includes considerable
      folklore material.

3425. Harder, Kelsie B. "Jingle Lore of Pigtails, Pals,
      and Puppy Love," TFSB (Mr, 1956), 22: 1-9.
      Rhymes from autograph books and love letters.

3426. Hardin, William Henry. "Grandpa Brown," in And
      Horns on the Toads, ed. Mody C. Boatright et
      al., pp. 58-68. Family tales, somewhat em-
      broidered, from East Texas.

3427. Hawthorne, Ruth. "Classifying Jump-Rope Games,"
      KFQ (S, 1966), 11: 113-126.

3428. Heimbuecher, Ruth. "Jump-Rope Rhymes," KFQ
      (W, 1962), 7: iv, 2-9. Children's rhymes col-
      lected in Pittsburgh.

3429. Hendricks, George D. "Adam's Rib," in A Good
      Tale and a Bonnie Tune, ed. Mody C. Boatright
      et al., pp. 176-187. Folklore about women,
      mostly from male sources.

3430. Hickerson, Joseph C. and Alan Dundes. "Mother
      Goose Vice Verse," JAF (Jl-Sept, 1962), 75:
      249-259. Parodies of Mother Goose rhymes from
      the Indiana U. collection.

3431. Hirsch, Robin. "Wind-Up Dolls," WF (Apr, 1964),
      23: 107-110. 52 wind-up doll jokes.

3432. Horn, Dorothy. "Tune Detecting in 19th Century
      Hymnals," TFSB (Dec, 1960), 26: 99-109. Deals
      with origins of hymn tunes; 73 have variant titles.

3433. Howard, James H. "Peyote Jokes," JAF (Jan-Mr,
      1962), 75: 10-14. Jokes collected from printed
      sources and from personal experiences in the
      Middle West.

3434. Hurley, Elizabeth. "Come Buy, Come Buy," in

<u>Folk Travelers</u>, ed. Mody C. Boatright et al.,
pp. 115-38. Chants and cries of street vendors
with examples mostly from Texas.

3435. Hurvitz, Nathan. "Blacks and Jews in American
Folklore," <u>WF</u> (Oct, 1974), 33: 301-25. Examination of white Christian folklore concerning two
minority groups often linked together. Author
labels this folklore either bland and amusing or
hostile and vicious.

3436. _____. "Jews and Jewishness in the Street Rhymes
of American Children," <u>Jewish Social Studies</u>
(Apr, 1954), 16: 135-150.

3437. Jackson, Bruce. "Circus and Street: Psychosocial
Aspects of the Black Toast," <u>JAF</u> (Apr-Je, 1972),
85: 123-139. Discussion of the Negro toast with
a comparison of circus activities and the behavior
described in the toast. Texts of the familiar
"Titanic" and "Signifying Monkey" given.

3438. _____. "Folk Ingenuity Behind Bars," <u>NYFQ</u> (Dec,
1966), 22: 243-250. Ingenuity of Texas convicts
in making knives and brewing "chock" discussed.

3439. Jagendorf, Moritz. "The Rich Lore of a Rich Hotel,
the Plaza," <u>NYFQ</u> (A, 1953), 9: 176-182. Anecdotes and superstitions from a New York hotel.

3440. Jason, Heda. "The Jewish Joke: the Problem of
Definition," <u>SFQ</u> (Mr, 1967), 31: 48-54. Chiefly
a criticism of recent articles and a plea for more
field work.

3441. John, Teri. "A Collection of Jump Rope Rhymes,"
<u>NCarF</u> (Apr, 1973), 21: 15-17.

3442. Katz, Naomi and Eli Katz. "Tradition and Adaptation in American Jewish Humor," <u>JAF</u> (Apr-Je,
1971), 84: 215-220. Stories told by Jews are
often anti-immigrant, anti-greenhorn, and anti-
Old World.

3443. Köngäs, Elli Kaija. "A Finnish Schwank Pattern:
the Farmer-Servant Cycle of the Kuusisto Family,"
<u>MF</u> (W, 1961-1962), 11: 197-211. Jokes col-

lected from members of an immigrant Finnish
family in Minn., Ore., and Illinois.

3444. Krelove, Harold. "New Year's Verses of the Print-
er's Boy," KFQ (S, 1964), 9: 68-73. Four
facsimiles from two 18th century newspapers, the
Pennsylvania Gazette and the Ledger.

3445. Kroll, Harry Harrison. "Licking River Revisited,"
SFQ (Sept, 1962), 26: 246-251. Description of a
visit to an outdoor church service in Floyd Co.,
Ky. Samples of a folk sermon given.

3446. Krueger, John R. "On the Rimes in Nursery Rimes,"
SFQ (Dec, 1967), 31: 291-295.

3447. Leach, Joseph. "Crockett's Almanacs and the Typical
Texan," SWR (Spr, 1950), 35: 88-95.

3448. Legman, Gershon. "Rationale of the Dirty Joke,"
Neurotica (1951), no. 9, 49-64. Summaries of
tales. Sexual humor and castration themes.

3449. _____. Rationale of the Dirty Joke: an Analysis
of Sexual Humor (New York: Grove P., 1968),
811pp. Needlessly long study of a subject which
has heretofore escaped print by the folklorist best
qualified to undertake it. Valuable bibliography
but a faulty indexing system.

3450. Leventhal, Nancy C. "Depth Collecting from a
Sixth-Grade Class," ed. Ed Cray, WF (Oct,
1963), 22: 231-257. Riddles, jokes, and rhymes
from Hawthorne, Cal.

3451. Loomis, C. Grant. "Mary Had a Parody: a Rhyme
of Childhood in Folk Tradition," WF (Jan, 1958),
17: 45-51. Ample evidence that the famous
rhyme has satirical and often blasphemous commentary.

3452. _____. "Some Rope-Jumping Rhymes from
Berkeley, 1943," WF (Oct, 1954), 13: 278-280.

3453. McDowell, Flora. "Friendship Verses," TFSB (Mr,
1952), 18: 22-24. Sentimental verses written in
friendship albums.

3454.   McDowell, John H.   "Performance and the Folkloric
        Text: a Rhetorical Approach to 'The Christ of
        the Bible,'" FF (Jl, 1973), 6: 139-148.   A plea
        to study performance style plus an analysis of a
        folk sermon delivered in Delano, Cal., in 1967.

3455.   McNeil, W. K.   "The Autograph Album Custom: a
        Tradition and Its Scholarly Treatment," KFQ
        (Spr, 1968), 13: 29-40.   Twelve examples given.

3456.   _____.   "From Advice to Laments: New York
        Autograph Album Verse: 1820-1850," NYFQ
        (Sept, 1969), 25: 175-194.   Discussion of auto-
        graph album verse with attention given to themes
        and style.

3457.   _____.   "From Advice to Laments Once Again:
        New York Autograph Album Verse: 1850-1900,"
        NYFQ (Sept, 1970), 26: 163-203.   More of the
        same from a later period.

3458.   Mankins, Jerilyn.   "Children's Games and Rhymes,"
        WVF (S, 1962), 12: 53-58.

3459.   Mason, Julian.   "Some Uses of Folklore in Adver-
        tising," TFSB (Sept, 1954), 20: 58-61.   Exam-
        ples of tales, heroes, and folksay in magazine
        advertising.

3460.   Mastick, Patricia A.   "The Function of Political
        Graffiti as Artistic Creativity," NYFQ (Sept,
        1971), 27: 280-296.   California graffiti reveal
        political rebelliousness.   Many examples given.

3461.   Meine, Franklin J.   The Crockett Almanacs, Nash-
        ville Series (Chicago: Caxton Club, 1955), xxxvii,
        150pp.   Modern ed. with old illustrations of a
        famous series.

3462.   Millard, Eugenia L.   "Children's Charms and Ora-
        cles," NYFQ (W, 1951, Spr, 1952), 7: 253-268;
        8: 46-57.   Material chiefly from Albany, annotated
        and compared.

3463.   Miller, Linda.   "Playin' the Dozens Among Black
        High School Students," JOFS (Apr, 1973), n.s.,
        2: 20-29.   Insults and taunts exchanged by two
        friends.

3464. Monteiro, George. "Parodies of Scripture, Prayer,
       and Hymn," JAF (Jan-Mr, 1964), 77: 45-52.

3465. _____. "Religious Parodies," NYFQ (Mr, 1969),
       25: 59-76. Parodies of prayers, songs, and
       scripture, with many examples. Extensive ref-
       erences.

3466. Mook, Maurice A. "The Quaker and the Cuspidor,"
       MF (S, 1962), 12: 75-80. A familiar rural joke
       is not necessarily of Quaker origin.

3467. _____. "Quaker Knowledge of Quaker Folklore,"
       KFQ (Spr and S, 1959), 4: 101-5. Certain
       Quaker songs may not be true Quaker folklore.

3468. Musick, Ruth Ann and Vance Randolph. "Children's
       Rhymes from Missouri," JAF (Oct-Dec, 1950),
       63: 425-37. Various items given without com-
       parisons.

3469. Opie, Iona and Peter Opie. The Lore and Language
       of School Children (Oxford: Clarendon P., 1959),
       417pp. Seventeen categories of children's lore
       collected mostly in the British Isles. The authors
       are fully aware of American studies of children's
       lore.

3470. _____. The Oxford Dictionary of Nursery Rhymes
       (London: Oxford, 1951), xxvii, 467pp. Over 500
       rhymes, songs, etc., arranged alphabetically.
       Seventy plates and illustrations. No melodies.

3471. Patterson, Paul. "Cowboy Comedians and Horseback
       Humorists," in The Golden Log, ed. Mody C.
       Boatright et al., pp. 99-107. Local anecdotes
       from Upton Co., Texas.

3472. Peck, Thomas. "Dirty Jokes at the Academy and
       Angela Morrison," KFQ (S, 1970), 15: 93-105.
       Examples collected from private male and female
       secondary schools.

3473. Phillips, Anne. "Folkways & Mores at the University
       of Texas in the 1930's," in Tire Shrinker to Drag-
       ster, ed. Wilson M. Hudson, pp. 203-8. Mis-
       cellaneous student recollections.

3474. Pipes, William H. Say Amen, Brother (New York: William Frederick P., 1951), 210pp. Accurately recorded Negro folk sermons, eight in all.

3475. Pope, Harold Clay. "Texas Rope-Jumping Rhymes," WF (Jan, 1956), 15: 46-48. Fourteen items.

3476. Porter, Kenneth W. "Circular Jingles and Repetitious Rhymes," WF (Apr, 1958), 17: 107-111. Comments on items like "My name is Yon Yonson...."

3477. _____. "Racism in Children's Rhymes and Sayings, Central Kansas, 1910-1928," WF (Jl, 1965), 24: 191-96. Conventional versus pejorative uses.

3478. _____. "Some Examples of 'The Cante Fable in Decay'," SFQ (Je, 1957), 21: 100-3. Quoted examples plus a recollected anecdote from Kansas.

3479. Preston, Michael J. "Xerox Lore," KF (Spr, 1974), 19: 11-26. Xerox can produce visual jokes and parodies of instructions and manuals.

3480. Randolph, Vance. "Counting-Out Rhymes in Arkansas," SFQ (Dec, 1953), 17: 244-48. Thirty rhymes collected since 1928 from various Arkansas localities. Vague sources.

3481. _____. Hot Springs and Hell and Other Folk Jests and Anecdotes from the Ozarks (Hatboro, Pa.: Folklore Assoc., 1965), xxviii, 297pp. Four hundred sixty examples plus notes and bibliography.

3482. _____. "Jump Rope Rhymes from Arkansas," MF (S, 1953), 3: 77-84.

3483. Reisner, Robert George. Graffiti, Two Thousand Years of Wall Writing (New York: Cowles Book Co., 1971), xiii, 204pp.

3484. _____ and Lorraine Wechsler. An Encyclopedia of Graffiti (New York: Macmillan, 1974), 401pp.

3485. Reynolds, Anthony M. "Urban Negro Toasts: a Hustler's Views from L.A.," WF (Oct, 1974), 33: 267-300. The toast is defined as a genre of narrative poetry popular among urban Negroes. Many examples cited, some with literary sources.

3486. Rezwin, Max. Sick Jokes, Grim Cartoons and Bloody
       Marys (New York: Citadel P., 1958). A pamph-
       let with two sequels.

3487. Rhoads, Ellen. "Little Orphan Annie and Lévi-
       Strauss, the Myth and the Method," JAF (Oct-
       Dec, 1973), 86: 345-357. Analysis of the familiar
       Harold Gray comic strip, now considered a form
       of folklore. A Lévi-Strauss theory about myth
       is used.

3488. Rhone, George E. "The Giwoggle," KFQ (Spr, 1963),
       8: 44-48. A figure which terrifies before it is
       disposed of is supposedly created by witchcraft
       in Clinton Co., Penn.

3489. Rogers, E. G. "An East Tennessee Collection of
       Friendship Verses," TSFB (Mr, 1957), 23: 13-
       25. Miscellaneous group of verses from auto-
       graph albums, fly leaves, etc.

3490. Rosenberg, Bernard and Gilbert Shapiro. "Margin-
       ality and Jewish Humor," Midstream (Spr, 1958),
       4: 70-80. Jewish jokelore studied by two soci-
       ologists.

3491. Rosenberg, Bruce A. "The Aesthetics of the Folk
       Sermon," GR (W, 1971), 25: 424-438. Discus-
       sion of the rhythm, context, interaction with the
       congregation of southern folk preachers.

3492. _____. The Art of the American Folk Preacher
       (New York: Oxford, 1970), 265pp. Excellent ac-
       count of southern black preaching, with discussion
       of sermon themes, imagery, formulaic content,
       and chanting. Examples given.

3493. _____. "The Formulaic Quality of Spontaneous
       Sermons," JAF (Jan-Mr, 1970), 83: 3-20. Pre-
       view of book listed above.

3494. _____. "The Genre of the Folk Sermon," Genre
       (Je, 1971), 4: 189-211. History and tradition of
       the folk sermon with some textual examples.

3495. Rubin, Ruth. "From a Collector's Notebook: Yid-
       dish Anecdotes, Jokes, and Sayings," NYFQ

(Dec, 1964), 20: 289-295.   European and American humorous anecdotes.

3496.   Sackett, Marjorie.   "Folk Recipes in Kansas," MF
(S, 1962), 12: 81-86.   Comparison of folk recipes
from many cultures.

3497.   Sackett, S. J.   "Flemish Folklore in Kansas," WF
(Jl, 1961), 20: 175-178.   Brief listing of recipes,
cures, and customs from Belgian immigrants.

3498.   Sagendorph, Robb.   America and Her Almanacs: Wit,
Wisdom, & Weather 1639-1970 (Dublin, N.H.:
Yankee, Inc., 1970), 318pp.   History of American
almanacs.

3499.   _____.   "The Old Farmer's Almanac," AtL (Nov,
1956), 198: 87-90.   Brief comments on the most
famous American almanac by its editor.

3500.   _____.   The Old Farmer's Almanac Sampler (New
York: Ives Washburn, 1957), viii, 306pp.   Selections by the editor from the most famous American almanac.

3501.   Schiller, Riva.   "Jump Rope Songs and Games,"
NYFQ (F, 1956), 12: 200-6.   Material collected
in Buffalo.

3502.   Schillinger, Alvin W.   "Hell's Bells and Panther
Tracks: Lore of Western Sullivan County,"
NYFQ (Spr, 1953), 9: 28-39.   Anecdotes, say-
ings, epitaphs.

3503.   Schmaier, Maurice D.   "The Doll Joke Pattern in
Contemporary American Oral Humor," MF (W,
1963-64), 13: 205-16.   Seventy-three jokes about
imaginary wind-up dolls (representing entertainers,
politicians, writers, athletes, preachers, etc.)
analyzed.

3504.   Schwartz, Alvin.   Witcracks: Jokes and Jests from
American Folklore (Philadelphia: Lippincott,
1973), 62pp.   Jokes collected from folklore books
and journals and intended for a younger audience.
Brief accounts of joke genres.

3505.   Sechrest, L. and K. Olson. "Graffiti in Four Types
        of Institutions of Higher Education," JSR (1971),
        7: 62-71.

3506.   Sederberg, Nancy B. "Antebellum Southern Humor in
        the Camden Journal: 1826-1840," MissQ (W,
        1973-74), 27: 41-74. Folk anecdotes in a South
        Carolina journal.

3507.   Sellers, Kelly H. "An Ethnic Joke from the Mid-
        South," MSF (W, 1973), 1: 103-5. Ethnic jokes
        about a half-literate Negro applying for employ-
        ment.

3508.   Smith, Hope. "A Description of a Black Party,"
        JOFS (Apr, 1973), n.s., 2: 30-37. Behavior
        at a Negro weekend party: drinking, dancing,
        sexual play.

3509.   Smith, Victor J. "Tales of the Kansas City, Mexico,
        and Orient Railroad," in Mesquite and Willow, ed.
        Mody C. Boatright et al., pp. 162-70. Railroad
        anecdotes.

3510.   Spears, James E. "Playing the Dozens," MFR (W,
        1969), 3: 127-129. Brief account of famous
        Negro insult game.

3511.   Stephens, Alva Ray. "Anecdotes of Two Frontier
        Preachers," in Singers and Storytellers, ed. Mody
        C. Boatright et al., pp. 185-93. The preachers
        are Andrew Jackson Potter and Lorenzo Dow.

3512.   Stocker, Terrance L., Linda W. Dutcher, Stephen
        M. Hargrove, and Edwin A. Cook. "Social
        Analysis of Graffiti," JAF (Oct-Dec, 1972), 85:
        356-66. Graffiti collected from universities in
        Ill., Ky., and Mo., and tabulated and analyzed.

3513.   Story, M. L. "The Folklore of Adolescence: Auto-
        graph Books," SFQ (Sept, 1953), 17: 207-12.
        Familiar autograph rhymes popular in junior high
        school books in the South. Examples given but
        no sources.

3514.   _____. "The Old Family Almanac," SFQ (Dec,
        1959), 23: 233-238. Comments on a number of

family almanacs with stress on their weather lore,
cures, astrology, proverbs.

3515.   Sugg, Redding S., Jr.   "Heaven Bound," SFQ (Dec,
        1963), 27: 249-266.   Text of musical religious
        pageant given frequently since 1930 by Big Bethel
        African M.E. Church of Atlanta, Georgia.

3516.   Sullenberger, Tom E.   "Ajax Meets the Jolly Green
        Giant: Some Observations on the Use of Folklore
        and Myth in American Mass Marketing," JAF
        (Jan-Mr, 1974), 87: 53-65.   Comments on "folk-
        lure," the exploitation of folklore or myth by
        business.

3517.   Sutton-Smith, Brian.   The Folkgames of Children
        (Austin: U. of Texas P., 1972), xvi, 559pp.   A
        collection of previously published papers, most
        dealing with motor activities of New Zealand and
        American children psychological approaches to the
        study of games.

3518.   _____.   "'Shut Up and Keep Diggin': the Cruel
        Joke Series," MF (Spr, 1960), 10: 11-22.   Twelve
        categories of miscellaneous cruel jokes.

3519.   Swetnam, George.   "The Church Hymn as a Folklore
        Form," KFQ (W, 1964), 9: 144-153.   Folklore in
        church hymnody has been neglected.   Many brief
        quotations from hymnals suggest the richness of
        the field.

3520.   Tallman, Richard S.   "A Generic Approach to the
        Practical Joke," SFQ (Dec, 1974), 38: 259-274.
        A suggested classification system for practical
        jokes.

3521.   Tamony, Peter.   "The Teddy Bear: Continuum in a
        Security Blanket," WF (Jl, 1974), 33: 231-238.
        The Teddy Bear as fad, toy, chemise, and adver-
        tising symbol.

3522.   Taylor, Archer.   "The Anecdote: a Neglected
        Genre," in Medieval Literature and Folklore
        Studies, ed. Jerome Mandel and Bruce A. Rosen-
        berg, pp. 223-228.

3523. _____. "The Shanghai Gesture," FFC, no. 166
(Helsinki: Suomalainen Tiedeakatemia, 1956),
65: 3-76. Extensive account of a celebrated
gesture, as revealed in poetry, drama, and fiction.

3524. Utley, Francis Lee and Dudley Flamm. "The Urban
and the Rural Jest," JPC (Spr, 1969), 2: 563-
577.

3525. Varisco, Raymond. "Campaign Jokes--Goldwater
and Johnson," TFSB (Dec, 1965), 31: 108-12.

3526. Vickers, Ovid S. "Of Folk Verse and Friendship
Books," MFR (S, 1971), 5: 34-38. Miscellaneous
examples from books preserved by women.

3527. Wallace, William J. "The Role of Humor in the Hupa Indian Tribe," JAF (Apr-Je, 1953), 66: 135-
41. Verbal jokes, practical jokes, and droll
incidents among a Canadian Indian tribe.

3528. Wallis, Charles L. Stories on Stone: A Book of
American Epitaphs (New York: Oxford, 1954),
xv, 272pp. Only peripherally folklore.

3529. Walser, Richard G. Tar Heel Laughter (Chapel
Hill: U. of No. Car. P., 1974), 309pp. Anecdotal humor.

3530. Watkins, Floyd C. "De Dry Bones in de Valley,"
SFQ (Je, 1956), 20: 136-49. Negro preacher
Robert Parker Rumley was famous in No. Car.
for his folk sermons taking off from Ezekiel
(37: 1-10). Reprint of pamphlet dated 1896.

3531. Welsch, Roger L. "American Numskull Tales: The
Polack Joke," WF (Jl, 1967), 26: 183-86.

3532. _____. "Bigger'n Life: the Tall-Tale Postcard,"
SFQ (Dec, 1974), 38: 311-323. The vogue of
tall-tale postcards in the plains states is seen
as a complement to oral tall tales.

3533. _____. "Nebraska Finger Games," WF (Jl, 1966),
25: 173-194. With diagrams.

3534. Wepman, Dennis, Ronald B. Newman, and Murray B.
Binderman. "Toasts, the Black Urban Folk Poetry," JAF (Jl-Sept, 1974), 87: 208-224. Material collected in New York state prisons.
Toasts defined as folk recitation poems.

3535. Wilgus, D. K. and Bruce A. Rosenberg. "A Modern
Medieval Story: 'The Soldier's Deck of Cards,'"
in Medieval Literature and Folklore Studies, ed.
Jerome Mandel and Bruce A. Rosenberg, pp. 291-
303. Some American examples cited.

3536. Winkler, Louis and Carol Winkler. "Thousands of
Years of Halloween," NYFQ (Sept, 1970), 26:
204-215. Superficial account of an ancient cele-
bration.

3537. Winner, Julia Hull. "Rhymed Advertisements,"
NYFQ (Spr, 1957), 13: 32-39. Humorous ads
from merchants, tailors, and barbers in early
New York state newspapers.

3538. Wood, Ray. Fun in American Folk Rhymes (Philadelphia: Lippincott, 1952), xviii, 109pp. Tongue
twisters, rhymes, riddles, etc.

3539. Woodward, F. G. "An Early Tennessee Almanac
and Its Maker: Hill's Almanac, 1825-1862,"
TFSB (Mr, 1952), 18: 9-14. An almanac published in Fayetteville.

3540. Worstell, Emma Vietor. Jump the Rope Jingles
(New York: Macmillan, 1961), 55pp.

3541. Zeitlin, Steven J. "As Sweet As You Are: the
Structural Element in the Signed High School
Yearbook," NYFQ (Je, 1974), 30: 83-100. High
school yearbooks as folk forms.

16.   OBITUARIES

(A selective list of obituaries of prominent folklorists)

3542.   "Marius Barbeau (1883-1969)," by Edith Fowke,
        JAF (Jl-Sept, 1969), 82: 264-266.

3543.   _____ by Israel J. Katz, Ethnomusicology (Jan,
        1970), 14: 129-142.

3544.   "George Carpenter Barker (1912-1958)," by Frances
        Gillmor, WF (Jan, 1959), 18: 31-32.

3545.   "Martha Beckwith (1871-1959)," by Katherine Luo-
        mala, JAF (Oct-Dec, 1962), 75: 341-353.   A
        Beckwith bibliography included.

3546.   "Mody C. Boatright (1896-1970)," by Wilson M. Hud-
        son, JAF (Apr-Je, 1971), 84: 242-243.

3547.   "Frank C. Brown (1870-1943)," by W. Amos Abrams,
        NCarF (Jl, 1964), 12: 22-26.

3548.   "Charles Faulkner Bryan (1911-1955)," by Louis
        Nicholas, TFSB (Sept, 1955), 21: 79-80.

3549.   "Peter Henry Buck (1880-1951)," by Edwin G. Bur-
        rows, JAF (Apr-Je, 1952), 65: 148.

3550.   "Josiah H. Combs (1886-1960)," by Ed Kahn, KFR
        (Oct-Dec, 1960), 6: 101-103.

3551.   _____ by D. K. Wilgus, JAF (Oct-Dec, 1962), 75:
        354-355.

3552.   "Tom Peete Cross (1879-1951)," by Archer Taylor,
        JAF (Apr-Je, 1952), 65: 138.

3553.   "Levette J. Davidson (1894-1957)," by Arthur L.
        Campa, JAF (Apr-Je, 1958), 71: 150-151.

3554.   _____ by Louise Pound, WF (Jan, 1958), 17: 1-2.

3555.   _____ by E. C. Smith, Onoma (1956-1957), 7: ii,
        360-362.

3556.   "Arthur Kyle Davis, Jr. (1897-1972)," by Fred F.
        Knobloch, SFQ (Je, 1973), 37: 127-129.

3557.   "J. Frank Dobie (1888-1964)," by Mody C. Boat-
        right, WF (Jl, 1965), 24: 153-154.

3558.   _____ by Stith Thompson, JAF (Jan-Mr, 1965),
        78: 62-63.

3559.   "Fannie Hardy Eckstorm (1865-1946)," by Priscilla
        E. Bissell, "The Writings of Fannie Hardy Eck-
        storm: a Bibliographical Essay," in A Handful
        of Spice, ed. Richard S. Sprague (Orono: U. of
        Maine P., 1968), pp. 15-34.

3560.   "John Edwards (1932-1960)," by John Greenway, WF
        (Apr, 1961), 20: 109-111.

3561.   "Aurelio Macedonio Espinosa, Sr. (1880-1958)," by
        Austin E. Fife, WF (Apr, 1960), 19: 98.

3562.   _____ by Juan B. Rael, JAF (Oct-Dec, 1959), 72:
        347-348.

3563.   "Robert Winslow Gordon (1888-1961)," KFQ (S, 1961),
        6: 31-32.

3564.   "Isaac Garfield Greer (1881-1967)," by Arthur Pal-
        mer Hudson, JAF (Jl-Sept, 1968), 81: 258-259;
        NCarF (May, 1968), 16: 63-64; SFQ (Sept, 1968),
        32: 265-267.

3565.   "Erwin G. Gudde (1889-1969)," Names (Dec, 1969),
        17: 293.

3566.   "Woodrow Wilson Guthrie (1912-1967)," by John
        Greenway, JAF (Jan-Mr, 1968), 81: 62-64.

3567.   "Eleanor Hague (1875-1954)," by Elisabeth Waldo,
        WF (Oct, 1955), 14: 279-280.

3568. "Mildred Haun (1911-1966)," by Herschel Gower,
       TSFB (Sept, 1967), 33: 60-63.

3569. "Melville J. Herskovitz (1895-1963)," by Richard
       M. Dorson, JAF (Jl-Sept, 1963), 76: 249-250.

3570. "Sigurd Bernhard Hustvedt (1882-1954)," by Archer
       Taylor, WF (Jan, 1955), 14: 1-2.

3571. _____ by Stith Thompson, JAF (Apr-Je, 1955),
       68: 200.

3572. "George Pullen Jackson (1874-1953)," by Donald
       Davidson, "The Master of the Sacred Harp,"
       TFSB (Mr, 1954), 20: 1-8.

3573. _____ by Alton Morris, JAF (Oct-Dec, 1963), 66:
       302.

3574. "R. D. Jameson (1895-1959)," by John Greenway,
       WF (Jl, 1960), 19: 153-154.

3575. "Richard Jente (1888-1952)," by Joseph D. Clark,
       NCarF (Nov, 1971), 19: 191-193.

3576. _____ by Archer Taylor, JAF (Jl-Sept, 1953),
       66: 200.

3577. "Marjorie M. Kimmerle (1906-1963)," by Ben Gray
       Lumpkin, WF (Jl, 1963), 23: 191.

3578. "Edwin C. Kirkland (1902-1972)," by Richard M.
       Dorson, SFQ (Je, 1973), 37: 123-125.

3579. "George Korson (1899-1967)," by B. A. Botkin,
       NYFQ (Sept, 1967), 23: 237-239.

3580. _____ by Archie Green, KFQ (S, 1971), 16: 53-63.

3581. _____ by John Greenway, JAF (Oct-Dec, 1967),
       80: 343-344.

3582. _____ by Waylund D. Hand, KFQ (S, 1971), 16:
       65-67.

3583. "Ray M. Lawless (1896-1968)," by Arthur N. Wilkins,
       JAF (Oct-Dec, 1968), 81: 348-349.

3584. "MacEdward Leach (1896-1967)," by Horace Beck,
       KFQ (F, 1967), 12: 193-198.

3585. _____ by John Greenway et al., JAF (Apr-Je,
       1968), 81: 97-120. Various brief tributes to
       Leach.

3586. _____ by Wayland D. Hand, WF (Jan, 1968), 27:
       43-44.

3587. "Charles Godfrey Leland (1824-1903)," by Moritz
       Jagendorf, "Charles Godfrey Leland, Neglected
       Folklorist," NYFQ (Sept, 1963), 19: 211-219.

3588. "Ralph Linton (1893-1953)," by George Peter Mur-
       dock, JAF (Jl-Sept, 1954), 67: 309-311.

3589. "Charles Grant Loomis (1901-1963)," by M. S.
       Beeler, WF (Oct, 1963), 22: 229-230.

3590. _____ by Erwin G. Gudde, Names (Dec, 1963),
       11: 291.

3591. _____ by Francis Lee Utley, JAF (Apr-Je, 1964),
       77: 160-161.

3592. "Robert Harry Lowie (1883-1957)," by Erminie
       Wheeler-Voegelin, JAF (Apr-Je, 1958), 71: 149-
       150.

3593. "Charles F. Lummis (1859-1928)," by Dudley C.
       Gordon, "Charles F. Lummis: Pioneer American
       Folklorist," WF (Jl, 1969), 28: 175-181.

3594. "Bascom Lamar Lunsford (1882-1973)," by William
       Hugh Jansen, JAF (Apr-Je, 1974), 87: 155.

3595. "W. L. McAtee (1883-1962)," AS (Dec, 1962), 37:
       274.

3596. "John Alden Mason (1885-1967)," by Mary Butler,
       JAF (Jl-Sept, 1969), 82: 266-267.

3597. _____ by Maurice Mook, KFQ (W, 1967), 12: 281-
       285.

3598. "Vincente T. Mendoza (1894-1964)," by Américo
       Paredes, JAF (Apr-Je, 1965), 78: 154-155.

3599. "Mamie J. Meredith (1888-1966)," by B. A. Botkin,
       NYFQ (Dec, 1966), 22: 298-300.

3600. _____ by Margaret M. Bryant, AS (Oct, 1966), 41:
       216.

3601. _____ by G. Thomas Fairclough, Names (Je,
       1967), 15: 150-151.

3602. "Joan Patricia O'Bryant (1923-1964)," by Bill
       [William] Koch, WF (Apr, 1964), 25: 109-110.

3603. "Elsie Clews Parsons (1875-1941)," by Keith S.
       Chambers, "The Indefatigable Elsie Clews Par-
       sons," WF (Jl, 1973), 32: 180-198.

3604. "Louise Pound (1872-1958)," by B. A. Botkin, WF
       (Jl, 1959), 18: 201-202.

3605. _____ by B. A. Botkin, "Pound Sterling," PS
       (Spr, 1959), 33: 20-31.

3606. _____ by a committee, PADS (Apr, 1959), 31:
       31-33.

3607. _____ by Mamie J. Meredith, SFQ (Je, 1959), 23:
       132-133.

3608. _____ by Mamie J. Meredith, et al., Names (Mr,
       1959), 7: 60-62.

3609. "Frank Noah Proffitt (1913-1965)," by Frank and
       Anne Warner, JAF (Jl-Sept, 1968), 81: 259-260.

3610. _____ by Cratis Williams, MLW (Spr, 1966), 42:
       i, 6-7.

3611. "Vladimir Ja. Propp (1895-1970)," by Felix Oinas,
       JAF (Jl-Sept, 1971), 84: 338-340.

3612. "Newbell Niles Puckett (1898-1967)," by Wayland D.
       Hand, JAF (Oct-Dec, 1967), 80: 341-342.

3613. _____ by George Kummer, JOFS (Spr, 1967), 2:
       42-44.

3614. _____ by Francis Lee Utley, Names (Mr, 1968),
       16: 68-69.

3615.   "Paul Radin (1883-1959)," by J. David Sapir, <u>JAF</u>
        (Jan-Mr, 1961), 74: 65-67.

3616.   "Eloise Ramsay (1886-1964)," by Thelma G. James,
        <u>JAF</u> (Apr-Je, 1965), 78: 155.

3617.   "Robert Lee Ramsay (1880-1953)," by E. H. Cris-
        well, <u>Names</u> (Mr, 1954), 2: 70-72.

3618.   "Gladys Amanda Reichard (1893-1955)," by Esther
        S. Goldfrank, <u>JAF</u> (Jan-Mr, 69: 53-54.

3619.   "Franz Rickaby (1889-1925)," by Daniel W. Greene,
        "Fiddle and I," <u>JAF</u> (Oct-Dec, 1968), 81: 316-
        336.

3620.   "Henry W. Shoemaker (1882-1958)," by Frank A.
        Hoffman, <u>JAF</u> (Oct-Dec, 1859), 72: 345-346.

3621.   "Grace Partridge Smith (1869-1959)," by MacEdward
        Leach, <u>JAF</u> (Apr-Je, 1960), 73: 154.

3622.   "Frank G. Speck (1881-1950)," by Horace P. Beck,
        <u>JAF</u> (Oct-Dec, 1951), 64: 415-418.

3623.   "Marshall Winslow Stearns (1908-1966)," by John F.
        Szwed, <u>JAF</u> (Jl-Sept, 1967), 80: 300.

3624.   _____ by W[illiam] G. T[yrrell], <u>NYFQ</u> (Mr, 1967),
        23: 65.

3625.   "Archer Taylor (1890-1973)," by Robert J. Adams
        et <u>al</u>., <u>FF</u> (Oct, 1973), 6: no pagination.

3626.   _____ by Alan Dundes, <u>AFN</u> (Spr, 1974), 3: 3.

3627.   _____ by Wayland D. Hand, <u>JAF</u> (Jan-Mr, 1974),
        87: 3-9.

3628.   _____ by Matti Kuusi, <u>Proverbium</u> (1973), 22:
        817-818.

3629.   _____ by Hector H. Lee, <u>WF</u> (Oct, 1973), 32:
        262-264.

3630.   _____ by Donald J. Ward, <u>Fabula</u> (1974), 15:
        1/2, 124-127.

3631. "Harold William Thompson (1891-1964)," by H[elen]
       A. F[raser], NYFQ (Mr, 1964), 20: 2.

3632. _____ by Moritz Jagendorf, JAF (Oct-Dec, 1964),
       77: 346-347.

3633. "Harold W. Thompson," NYFQ (F, 1958), 14: 161-
       262. Entire issue devoted to Thompson,
       reminiscent, biographical essays by associates,
       colleagues, and students.

3634. "Francis Lee Utley (1907-1974)," by Daniel Barnes,
       AFN (F, 1974), 3: 2.

3635. _____ by Patrick B. Mullen, KF (S-F, 1974), 19:
       129-142. Includes bibliography.

3636. _____ by D. K. Wilgus, WF (Jl, 1974), 33: 202-
       204.

3637. "Richard Allen Waterman (1914-1971)," by Alan P.
       Merriam, Ethnomusicology (Jan, 1973), 17: 72-
       89.

3638. "Gordon Wilson Sr. (1888-1970)," by Kenneth Clarke
       and Mary Clarke, eds. Memorial Issue, KFR
       (Jl-Sept, 1970), 16: 68.

3639. _____ by Kenneth Clarke, TFSB (Je, 1970), 36:
       29-30.

AUTHOR INDEX

Aarne, Antti 230
Abernethy, Francis Edward 36, 37, 38, 451, 1679, 1756
Abrahams, Roger D. 255-258, 452-456, 1018, 1090, 1251-1255, 1757, 2121, 2407-2409, 2821-2827, 3345-3352
Abrams, W. Amos 1019, 1020, 1256, 2569, 3447
Ackerman, Louise M. 2984
Adams, Charles C. 2985
Adams, James N. 2986
Adams, John F. 2987
Adams, Ramon F. 46, 47, 2410, 2988, 2989
Adams, Robert G. 259
Adams, Robert J. 3625
Adams, Samuel Hopkins 2411
Adamson, J. H. 1465
Adler, Alfred 2412
Adler, Thomas 1257
Agar, Michael H. 3353
Agogino, George A. 1466
Agonito, Rosemary 1467
Aiken, Riley 1468, 1469, 1758
Ainsworth, Catherine Harris 457, 1470, 1862, 2122, 2828, 3354
Albright, R. L. H. 1021, 1022
Alderson, William L. 2990
Alexander, Gerard L. 3141
Alexander, Hartley Burr 1986
Alford, Violet 260
Allen, Harold B. 2991
Allen, Helen E. 1471
Allen, John W. 458
Allen, Lee 2123
Allen, Philip F. 2992
Allen, Ward 2994
Allison, Lelah 2124, 2125

Almeida, Renato 261
Alpers, Anthony 1987
Alvey, R. Gerald 1258
Amann, W. F. 1259
Amburgey, Don Carlos 788
Ames, Karl 262
Ames, Russell 1260, 1260a
Anderson, David D. 789
Anderson, E. H., Jr. 2995
Anderson, George K. 1759
Anderson, Henry E. 459
Anderson, John Q. 460, 1023-1025, 1472-1474, 1680, 1863, 2126-2130, 2413, 2570-2575, 2996, 2997, 3355, 3356
Anderson, Marja L. 2995
Angulo, Jaime de 1681
Arlt, Gustave O. 14
Armistead, Samuel G. 1261
Armstrong, R. P. 1760
Arner, Robert D. 2576, 2829
Arnold, Byron 790
Arora, Shirley L. 2830-2833
Arpad, Joseph J. 1761, 2577, 2578
Arrendondo, Art 1475
Asch, Moses 791, 792
Ashabranner, Brent 2414
Ashton, John W. 2834
Astrov, Margot 461, 462
Atkinson, Robert M. 3357
Atteberry, Louie 2131
Atwood, E. Bagby 2998, 2999, 3007
Auser, Cortland P. 463, 3000
Ayoub, Millicent R. 3358
Ayres, Lucille 3001

Babcock, C. Merton 2579-2582, 2835, 2836, 3002-3006
Babington, Mima 3007

385

Index